Pittsylvania County, Virginia
Register of Free Negroes
and Related Documentation

Transcribed, Extracted
and Compiled by
Alva H. Griffith

HERITAGE BOOKS
2007

HERITAGE BOOKS
AN IMPRINT OF HERITAGE BOOKS, INC.

Books, CDs, and more—Worldwide

For our listing of thousands of titles see our website
at
www.HeritageBooks.com

Published 2007 by
HERITAGE BOOKS, INC.
Publishing Division
65 East Main Street
Westminster, Maryland 21157-5026

Copyright © 2001 Alva H. Griffith

All rights reserved. No part of this book may be reproduced or transmitted in any form or by any means, electronic or mechanical, including photocopying, recording or by any information storage and retrieval system without written permission from the author, except for the inclusion of brief quotations in a review.

International Standard Book Number: 978-0-7884-1780-1

Table of Contents

Acknowledgements	v
Introduction	vii
Historical Perspective	ix
How to Use This Book	xv
Explanation of Terms	xvi
Bibliography	xvii
Register of Free Negroes	1
Related Wills and Deeds	224
1820 - 1840 Census Extractions	247
Appendix A - Slaves of John Ward	267
Appendix B - Sample Court Orders	271
Appendix C - Registrations by Year	275
Appendix D - Negroes from Elsewhere	276
Appendix E - Renewed Registrations	279
Index	283

ACKNOWLEDGEMENTS

Genealogists and historians owe a debt of gratitude to Mary Leigh Boisseau of Danville, Virginia, for sharing her discovery of the Pittsylvania Register; I owe her my gratitude for her generosity in allowing me to transcribe it. My transcriptions were made from a photocopy of the original Register made for my use by Boisseau.

Sincere appreciation is due Mr. H.F. Haymore, Clerk of the Circuit Court of Pittsylvania County, who very graciously gave me permission to publish the Register in book form. He and his staff have rendered countless services to the genealogical community on numerous occasions.

Warm and deep thanks are offered to Robert Vernon of Charlottesville, Virginia, who had the courage to recommend that an unknown researcher be given the opportunity to transcribe this valuable document. His patience and encouragement throughout the duration of this project will never be forgotten.

My non-genealogist husband, Everton L. Griffith, created several early databases I needed, tolerated my mental lapses, adjusted to living with a sometimes-housewife, allowed me to turn his computer into mine and assisted with proofreading. Our daughter, Jean E. Griffith-Thompson, arranged time in her already busy schedule for editing. Our son, Matthew R. Griffith, deserves a special thank you for knowing when to loan me his strength, energy and enthusiasm.

Thanks go also to the founders of AfriGeneas.com and the Golden Gates African-American Genealogy Team at AOL, particularly Valencia King Nelson, Angela Walton-Raji and Anita Willis, as well as to several special members of the California African American Genealogical Society (CAAGS), who were always supportive when the chips, as they often seemed to be, were down.

INTRODUCTION

The <u>Register of Free Negroes - Pittsylvania County, Virginia</u> was discovered in 1994, on a high window ledge at the County Courthouse in Chatham, Virginia, by Mary Leigh Boisseau, a well-respected Virginia genealogist, transcriber and author. The existence of the Register was unknown until her discovery. The original Register remains at the Pittsylvania County Courthouse in Chatham, in the custody of the Clerk. A copy has been donated by Boisseau to the Archives of the Library of Virginia.

This Register consists of a handwritten ledger which names, numbers and describes those free African-Americans, and perhaps other non-whites, who registered or re-registered as free persons between 16 March 1807 and 16 January 1864. It also gives the circumstances of their freedom, and contains an incomplete index. Boisseau's article about the Register was published in the May 1995 issue of <u>Piedmont Lineages</u>, the quarterly bulletin of the VA/NC Piedmont Genealogical Society of Danville, Virginia, for which she produced an accurate and complete index.

Several Acts of the Virginia Assembly had required the registration of Free Negroes (1793, 1801, and 1803), but as yet, no independent book has been located which covers the period between 1 January 1794, when registrations were to have begun, and 16 March 1807, when the first person in this Register was recorded. It is possible, as has been discovered in other Virginia counties, that registrations or freedom certificates may have been kept on loose papers, or at the back of another book holding entirely different kinds of records. Thorough research in the Court documents of Pittsylvania County for the period not covered may result in a re-creation of earlier registrations, but was not undertaken by this author.

Three Court Clerks were involved in entering the names and numbers of the Free Negroes registered in the extant volume. William Tunstall, Jr., who most often signed as Will: Tunstall, was elected Clerk of the County Court in 1790. He succeeded his father, William Tunstall, who had been Clerk since the founding of Pittsylvania County in 1767. In 1833, William H. Tunstall, who usually signed as Wm H Tunstall, followed in his father's and grandfather's footsteps as Clerk of the County Court.

When a new constitution provided for separate Clerks for the County and Circuit Courts in 1850, William H. Tunstall became Circuit Court Clerk, and Langhorne Scruggs was elected County Court Clerk. It appears that their jobs may have occasionally overlapped for a brief period of time, since both men made entries into the Register between 1850 and 1852.

The majority of people numbered in this Register were born free, primarily in Pittsylvania County. For those registrants who had moved to Pittsylvania County, earlier registrations from other counties were copied into and made a part of the Pittsylvania Register. While no active research in this regard was performed by this author, data concerning a few such registrations were located and have been included in this volume.

The Register contains the names of 637 Free Negroes who were registered in Pittsylvania County. Although registrations were to have been renewed every three years, comparatively few in Pittsylvania County were renewed. It also appears, when one compares the census data to the registrations, that many Free Negroes never bothered to register at all. This suggests that a large number of white Pittsylvanians apparently had comfortable feelings toward the free African-Americans whom they personally knew. While no research was undertaken by this author in County Court documents to ascertain how often punishment may have been levied for not having renewed one's registration, one example seen in a brief perusal of the Court Orders has been transcribed in this volume at Appendix B.

In many Virginia counties, it was customary to register Black women under their maiden names, and to add their married names as an alias; only a few examples of this practice were found in Pittsylvania County. Most of the married women who registered there did so under their married names, and were identified as the wife of [husband's name]. A number of family groups were also registered, with children identified as the child of [parent's name]. Occasionally, when a mother registered, a list of the names and ages or birthdates of her small children was included under her registration number.

There are few instances in Pittsylvania county where free African-American families were enumerated on the census as living on the same premises as slaves, without a white person being listed as the head of household. While Free Negroes in some areas of Virginia purchased their own relatives as slaves in response to the Act of 1806, this does not often seem to be the case in Pittsylvania.

Much confusion appears in the Register beginning in March 1864. Quite possibly this may reflect the stress and distraction caused by the Civil War. There had previously been only an occasional lapse in the entries of the Register, but as of that time the numbers seem hurriedly assigned. Almost all of the final registrants have been given numbers that already belong to another person.

It has been noted in the past that some Native Americans and Caucasians of darker complexions were registered as Free Negroes in Virginia. No attempt has been made by this author to determine or analyze which, if any, of the registrants in Pittsylvania County may have been other than African-American.

It is my hope that this volume will provide assistance to African-American researchers with roots in Pittsylvania County, and to all students of Virginia history in gaining insight into some of the interactions between white families and Free Negroes.

HISTORICAL PERSPECTIVE

For many years, the first recorded arrival of Africans in Virginia was believed to have taken place when 20 Africans landed in Jamestown in August 1619. Then, in 1995, William Thorndale's article in the Magazine of Virginia Genealogy, discussed a census showing 32 free African servants already enumerated in March-May 1619. While we know little of their lives, these early Africans appear to have lived and worked in the colony primarily as indentured servants, much the same as white indentured servants of that time. As other free Africans arrived and served out their terms of indenture, the total number of Free Negroes gradually increased. By 1649, colonial officers reported "...three hundred good [Negro] servants..." among fifteen thousand Englishmen. This number was small enough that white Virginians in many localities rarely saw a free African.

Even in the early years of the 17th Century, the laws of Virginia, as they pertained to free African-Americans, involved a great deal of control over their lives. Laws became increasingly more harsh as the numbers of freedmen increased. Persons who were both free and non-white were often viewed with suspicion, and many whites began to consider the Free Negro as a threat, not only in a personal sense, but also to their way of life.

Considering the penalties imposed upon them for infractions of laws of that time, it is debatable whether all of these African servants were truly "servants" by our current definition of the word. Some Virginia masters were already attempting to hold their indentured servants of all races past the end of their terms of service. By 1659, chattel slavery was also flourishing well enough for the Assembly to reduce the import taxes paid by merchants who were bringing African slaves into the colony. By 1670, a law was passed which provided that "...all servants, *not Christian*, imported into the colony *by ships*..." were slaves for life. The majority of such "servants" came from Africa or the West Indies.

White indentured servants, both male and female, lived and worked alongside free and enslaved Africans, often in deplorable circumstances. By 1641, the branding of runaway Black *and white* servants had been authorized. As a result of sharing so many daily deprivations, it should not be a surprise that close relationships often developed between them, or that children might be born. White masters also sometimes fathered children by both free and enslaved African and African-American women. As a result, an Act which was passed in 1662 became the prevailing law of the land, lasting beyond the era of slavery, and determining the legal status of African and mixed-race children:

"...Whereas some doubts have arrisen whether children got by any Englishman upon a negro woman should be slave or ffree, Be it therefore enacted and declared by this present grand assembly, thatt all children borne in this country shalbe held bond or free only according to the condition of the mother...".

A few researchers have suggested that some white masters may have been tempted to encourage liaisons between their white servant women and African-American men, since this would have provided an inexpensive additional labor force. By 1691, legislation provided that any children born of such a union would be bound to serve the master for 30 years. The white mothers of these children were also subjected to additional terms of service if they were unable to pay a hefty fine.

Legitimizing interracial relationships through marriage created an understandable problem. White female servants immigrated to the colony in far fewer numbers than white males; white men could ill afford to have the few available white women then choose African-American mates. Prior to 1662, whipping and fines for anyone guilty of fornication had been the norm, regardless of the race of the guilty parties. After 1662, however, the fines were doubled for fornication committed by "...any *christian*..." with a Negro man or woman. This suggests that such acts may have been on the rise.

A further provision of a 1691 Act stated that any white person who married a Negro or Mulatto was to be banished and removed from the colony, and fined any minister who performed such a marriage. Fifteen years later, new legislation imposed a jail term of six months on whites who intermarried with Blacks, and made clear that all Mulatto children were to be servants until they were 31 years of age. Apparently neither fines nor banishment had worked as well as expected.

Manumissions seem to have occurred in surges. It appears that by 1691, the Free Negro class had increased in size to the point that some amount of discomfort was felt by many whites. An Act of that year stated that no Negro was to be set free unless the owner was willing to pay for the expense of the ex-slave's transportation "out of the countrye" within six months after manumission. Any African-American who could prove his birth as a free person to the satisfaction of the Court, however, would be given a Certificate of Freedom.

Many early free African immigrants were baptized before their arrival in Virginia and were already Christians. As such, once their indentures ended, they were allowed the rights of other Christian freemen. Starting in 1662, however, it appears from the wording of the Virginia laws, that the term "Christian" was being modified to mean "white", or perhaps even to mean "English." During this period Irishmen, Dutchmen and other whites who were not English, often received harsher penalties than those given to Englishmen for having committed similar crimes. By 1667, new legislation provided that baptism did not "...alter the condition of the person as to his bondage or freedom...." This must have come as a relief to some slave owners, who could then baptize their slaves (and save their souls) without fear of the slaves becoming *Christian* in the fullest sense of the word.

A new law enacted in 1670 served to begin classifying Native Americans as similar to if not the same as Blacks, with regard to Christianity. This Act provided that Negroes and Indians "...though baptised and enjoyned their owne freedome..." would no longer be allowed to purchase *other Christians* as slaves, except someone "...of their owne nation...." An Act of 1682 declared that *non-Christian* servants who were imported by sea *or land* would be slaves "...whether Negroes, Moors, Mollattoes or Indians...". Africans generally arrived by ship, while Indian slaves were more often transported by land.

Virginia law became even more restrictive toward those who were considered not truly Christian by 1723. At that time, it was decided that Negro and Indian slaves could only be freed for meritorious public service, and then only at the Governor's discretion. Further, this law included a written reminder to white Virginians that Negroes, Mulattos and Indians were not Christians.

During the latter half of the 1700s, many white colonists struggled with conflicting feelings about their concepts of equality and their ideals of liberty and justice in a land where slave labor was felt to be necessary. Late in the Revolutionary War, African-Americans who could prove that they were free were allowed to enlist in the Army and Navy. Some slaves also served as substitutes for their masters or other free persons. By 1778, the African slave trade was abolished. A few historians have suggested that this may have occurred in part to financially punish England, which was the supplier of the slaves.

By 1782, the manumission of slaves was again allowed without legislative approval, so long as the former owner (or his estate) made financial provisions for old and very young slaves to prevent their becoming a public burden. Several religious groups encouraged the emancipation of slaves, and the abolitionist movement became active. Within a year, certain slaves who had served as substitutes in the Revolutionary War began to be legally freed. As other individuals began emancipating their slaves in increasing numbers, a new surge was experienced in the growth of the size of the Free Negro class.

This gave many African-Americans the ability to move from place to place in search of a better, or at least a different life; some, perhaps, had also gained a sense of their entitlement to certain rights. The sudden appearance and disappearance of unfamiliar Black faces claiming to be free in areas where whites were not used to seeing them, or certainly not seeing very many, must have been unnerving to a degree beyond our comprehension.

In 1792, Virginians learned of the Haitian Revolution (St. Domingue), and experienced an influx of new Black and brown faces from the West Indies. Some of these were slaves, some were self-liberated former slaves, and a few had probably been members of a free colored elite accustomed to enjoying the rights of freemen in Haiti. There had already been the occasional slave uprising in America. The arrival of these dark immigrants created an intense fear of new insurrections here, fomented by foreign-born Blacks, with the possibility of aid from the African-American freedmen, especially in the cities where they seemed to congregate.

By December 1793, two new Virginia laws were enacted which severely restricted the mobility of Free Negroes. The first of these was "...an Act to prevent the migration of free negroes and mulattoes into this Commonwealth, as well as any slave brought in from Africa or the West Indies islands...". This law provided for the removal of such Blacks if they should come, and fined anyone who brought them. Travelers through Virginia with free African-American servants, and masters of vessels who employed Free Negroes or Mulattos were excluded, provided these servants or employees left Virginia when their masters did.

A second Act resulted in the control of those free African-Americans already living in Virginia, regulating "...the police of towns...[to]...restrain the practice of negroes going at large...". Free Negroes and Mulattoes were to be registered and described in a book kept by the Court Clerk, including the circumstances of their claim to freedom. The Clerk was now to be paid 25 cents for a copy of a certificate, which was necessary for employment, and which was to be shown upon demand of any white person. Any Free Negro who moved to a new locality was to present his certificate to the Clerk in that area, and re-register there.

The Act of 1806, providing for the possible re-enslavement of freedmen after twelve months in the Commonwealth set off a flurry of registrations in Virginia. It made proof of the freedom of one's family prior to 1806 a priority in the lives of many African-Americans whose families had long been free. It probably also imparted a sense of security to any whites who may have felt a need for more control over their own lives or discomfort due to the presence of so many Free Negroes.

Former owners attempted to resettle their emancipated slaves, and met with varying degrees of success. Often freedmen were sent to North Carolina, Ohio, Michigan or Pennsylvania. In some areas where this was attempted, local residents were, or became, hostile to the idea. By 1820, these problems had resulted in the institution and funding of a project to colonize Liberia, Africa. It is generally believed that Liberia was colonized with African-Americans who wished to go there, but many such "colonists" were actually newly freed slaves whose former owners were resettling them.

Free Negroes in Virginia, and in the rest of the South, struggled through the middle decades of the 19th Century, as laws became more restrictive against them. When the Civil War began in 1861, more than 200,000 U.S. Colored Troops fought for the Union Army. While many of these were Free Negroes, many were also run-away slaves. Pensions were received by numerous African-Americans who fought for the Union, and their pension papers often contain genealogical information of great value.

A number of slaves accompanied their Confederate owners to war as body servants; others were sent as laborers and other menial employees, teamsters, hostlers, blacksmiths, grave diggers, cooks, and musicians. Small numbers of Free Negroes joined the Confederate Army, and others were impressed. There is no doubt that these men fought for survival when necessary. Much of what we know about them is from scattered memoirs, letters, newspaper articles, lists and other documents. Some did become eligible for Confederate pensions, but a comprehensive list of the names of Black Confederate *soldiers* is yet to be discovered, or compiled.

African-Americans had long been accepted and active as sailors. Advised by experts at the Naval Historical Center, the National Archives and the Smithsonian Institute, research was begun in 1993 at Howard University in Washington D.C. to extract data from Navy Department records on approximately 19,000 Blacks who served in the U.S. Navy during the Civil War. Research continues into pension files, ships's logs and other documents, and a database of these men has been incorporated into the National Park Service website for Civil War veterans.

The Emancipation Proclamation was signed by Abraham Lincoln in 1862, declaring the slaves who lived in the rebellious southern states to be free, but freedom was not forthcoming until the end of the Civil War. On 5 May 1865, the 13th Amendment to the U.S. Constitution was ratified, making slavery illegal. From that time forward, all Negroes would be Free.

HOW TO USE THIS BOOK

This book contains verbatim transcriptions of the Register of Free Negroes - Pittsylvania County, Virginia. Misspellings, abbreviations and punctuation (or the lack thereof) have been preserved, with the following exceptions: (1) superscripted letters, such as in the use of Rich^d for Richard, have been made normal size; (2) the use of "ffs" so common in colonial handwriting has been dispensed with in favor of "ss"; and (3) the names of all Free Negroes who registered have been capitalized.

Page numbers in the original Register are not always found on a page, and there are occasional discrepancies in page numbering, although no text has been omitted. This author has indicated the page numbers of the original Register in brackets, such as [p 135], whenever a new page of the original book begins.

There are occasional lapses in the original Register in the numbering of the registrations, such as skipped numbers or numbers used more than once. It will also be seen, particularly during the early years of the Register, that persons who renewed their registration were often given a new number. Later, however, registrants were more often renewed under their original number. Discrepancies in numbering are indicated and an explanation given when possible.

A space left blank by the writer of the document has been noted as [left blank]. In those few instances where the writer has himself used a series of periods as a blank space [as in ......] , the original designation has been used. Illegible words and phrases are designated as [illegible], and an explanation given when possible.

All editorial comment appears in brackets. All italicized words and all opinions expressed are those of the author.

Names are indexed at their first occurrence for each person, and may appear on the actual page more than once. The names of Free Negroes have been capitalized and made bold at their first appearance in the text, and the surname is capitalized in the Index; names of white individuals appear in lower case and are not bold. When the surname of any individual was not given but could be inferred, the surname will be found in its proper position in the Index in brackets. When no surname could be inferred for a Free Negro, the surname is designated as "NEGRO" in the Index.

The names of cities, counties, countries and continents are indexed under "Localities".

EXPLANATION OF TERMS

The term "African" is generally intended to describe those members of this ethnic group who came very early to the Virginia colony from Africa, whether as indentured servants or as slaves. In this volume, the terms "African-American", "Black", and "Negro", have been used interchangeably as a contemporary description of American-born members of the group.

The term "freedman" refers to an emancipated person, while the term "freeman" designates a freeborn person of any race.

A "Free Negro" is a member of a class of Negroes who are not slaves, and may have been born free or become free through emancipation. The abbreviation "FN" will sometimes replace the term "Free Negro".

The term "Mulatto" may have several definitions depending on the time period and sentiment of the society using the term. In the South, it appears to have been originally used to describe an African-American who was half white, or who at least had some recent, provable infusion of white ancestry. In some localities, a "Mulatto" was considered to be an African-American who was half Indian. The term was also used to differentiate between persons of Native-American ancestry and those who were of more obvious African ancestry, as if the word "Mulatto" were simply a color designation. In fact, a Mulatto often had lighter skin color and straighter hair texture than a full-blood African-American; white colonists may simply have considered it too difficult and time consuming to try to decipher race from the various shades of brown. There are numerous hues noted in the descriptions of the many Mulattos in the Pittsylvania Register.

When one considers that early laws often classified the two races together, "Mulatto" may have become a designation of choice used for persons of Native-American ancestry. It is possible that this confusion of terms served to deprive some Native-Americans of that part of their cultural heritage which remained once the Period of Contact with white settlers was well established. Other terms which appear to have been interchangeable with "Mulatto" were "free persons of colour", "mixed-blood" and "coloured".

BIBLIOGRAPHY

Ailsworth, Timothy S., Ann P. Keller, Lura B. Nichols, Barbara R. Walker. Charlotte County: Rich Indeed (The Charlotte County Board of Supervisors) 1979.

Bennett, Lerone, Jr. Before the Mayflower: A History of Black America Sixth Revised Edition (New York: Penguin Books) 1993.

-------------------- The Shaping of Black America: The Struggles and Triumphs of African Americans, 1619 to the 1990s (New York: Penguin Books) 1993.

Berlin, Ira. Slaves Without Masters: The Free Negro in the Antebellum South (Oxford University Press) 1974.

Boisseau, Mary Leigh. "Pittsylvania County Register of Free Negroes". Piedmont Lineages May 1995, Vol XVII, No. 2, p. 56-69.

Clement, Maude. The History of Pittsylvania County (Baltimore: Regional Publishing Company) Reprinted 1987.

Genovese, Eugene D. Roll, Jordan, Roll: The World the Slaves Made (New York: Vintage Books) 1976.

Gutman, Herbert G. The Black Family in Slavery and Freedom 1750-1925 (New York: Vintage Books) 1976.

Higginbotham, A. Leon. In the Matter of Color: Race and the American Legal Process: The Colonial Period (Oxford University Press) 1978.

Jacobs, Wilbur R. Dispossessing the American Indian (University of Oklahoma Press) 1985.

Jennings, Francis. The Invasion of America: Indians, Colonialism and the Cant of Conquest (New York: Norton) 1975.

Jordan, Ervin L. Black Confederates and Afro-Yankees in Civil War Virginia (Charlottesville: University Press of Virginia) 1995.

Morgan, Edmund S. American Slavery, American Freedom: The Ordeal of Colonial Virginia (New York: Norton) 1975.

National Park Service. Civil War, Soldiers & Sailors System; Black Sailors, The Howard University Research Project, online at <http://www.itd.nps.gov/cwss/sailors_index.html>

Russell, John H. The Free Negro in Virginia 1619-1865 (New York: Greenwood) Reprinted 1969.

Smith, Steven D. and Zeidler, James A. A Historic Context for the African American Military Experience, Chapter 3, (Champaign IL: U.S. Army Corps of Engineers) 1998.

Stewart, Roma Jones. Liberia Genealogical Research (Chicago: Homeland Publications) 1991.

Thorndale, William. "The Virginia Census of 1619." Magazine of Virginia Genealogy Summer 1995, Vol. 33, No. 3, p. 155-170.

Works Project Administration, Workers of the Writers' Program. The Negro In Virginia (Winston Salem, North Carolina: Blair) 1994.

Wright, Donald R. African Americans in the Colonial Era: From African Origins Through the American Revolution (Arlington Heights IL: Harlan Davidson) 1990.

Wynne, Frances Holloway. Register of Free Negroes and also of Dower Slaves, Brunswick County, Virginia 1803-1850 (Fairfax, Virginia) 1983

REGISTER OF FREE NEGROES
PITTSYLVANIA COUNTY, VA.

[p 1] Molly- No 1- Pittsylvania County Clerks Office March 16th 1807- Register of a Negro Woman named **MOLLY** Emancipated by James Richardson sen. Decd by his will of Record in Pittsylvania Court The said Negro Woman MOLLY is five feet eight inches and three quarters high of a Yellowish complexion, Slim made and about thirty five years of age- Teste Will. Tunstall CPC.

D. Dodson- No 2- Description of **DOTIA DODSON** a free negro woman registered in the Clerks Office of Pittsylvania County the 18th day of May 1810. The said DOTIA DODSON is a black woman about four feet eleven inches high, about twenty five years old, no apparent mark or scar except the loss of one of her front under teeth- Will. Tunstall CPC- renewed 16th March 1819

Peggy- No 3- Pittsylvania County Sct- Registered with the Clerk of the Court for the County aforesaid this the twenty first day of May in the year of our Lord 1810, **PEGGY** a Negro Woman of a dark complexion no marks perceivable except a small scar over the right eye, about five feet three inches high and about twenty one years of age- which said Peggy was emancipated by the last Will and Testament of James Richardson duly recorded in my office- Teste Will. Tunstall Ck

Geo Rivers- No 4- Pittsylvania County Sct: **GEORGE RIVERS** a Negro Man of light complexion about two and twenty years of age and about five feet six inches high has a very flat nose and no scar perceivable, this day produced at the Clerks office of the said County a certificate in these words "I do hereby certify that GEORGE RIVERS an apprentice bound to me has served his time and is entitled to his freedom- this is therefore to authorise you to grant to the said GEORGE RIVERS a pass as the law directs The clk: of Pittsylva Wm Smith 19th Decr 1810. The said GEORGE RIVERS is therefore registered in my office as the law directs- Certified this 20th day of December in the year of our Lord 1810- Teste Will: Tunstall Ck:

[p 2] Geo: Rivers- No 5- Pittsylvania Clerks Office 20th January 1812- **GEORGE RIVERS** a Negro man of light complexion about twenty three years old and about five foot six inches high, has a very flat nose and no scars perceiveable, this day produced at this Office a certificate in these words, "I do hereby certify that GEORGE RIVERS an apprentice bound to me has served his time and is entitled to his freedom. This is therefore to authorise you to grant to the said Rivers a pass as the law directs- Wm Smith The Clerk of Pittsylvania 19th Decr 1810. The said GEORGE RIVERS is therefore registered in my office as the law directs- Certified the day and year first above mentioned. Teste   Wm Tunstall Clk
[Appears to be the same person as No. 4]

Nancy Day- No 6- Pittsylvania Clerks Office 17th November 1812- **NANCY DAY** a light Mulatto Woman about twenty eight years old and about five feet five inches high, no scars perceivable said to have been born free but held in slavery by Moses Hodges this day produced at this Office a certificate in these words "I hereby release all right, title, interest and claim whatsoever to NANCY DAY a Mulatto Woman and her children. As witness my hand and seal this sixteenth day of November 1812-Moses Hodges (Sen) Witness Saml M. Lovell, Edward Carter, Jesse Leftwich" The said NANCY DAY is therefore registered in my office as the law directs- Certified the day and year first above mentioned-Will: Tunstall Ck:

[p 3]   Lue- No 7- Pittsylvania Clerks Office **LUE** a free Negro of Yellow complexion aged about twenty eight years about five feet Nine & one half inches high with a Scar over his right eye also one on the left arm or wrist & one under each elbow, & one on the third finger of the left hand with uncommon ankles- this day produced in my office a copy of the Will of William Ansley Decd which appears from the Certificate thereon endorsed was duly recorded in the Court of Loudon County [sic], a clause of which is in these words to wit "And a Negro LUE to be free at the age of twenty five", And also the affidavit of Jacob Fadely, William Woody & Geo: Hammat in these words "Virginia, Loudon County Sct July 2nd 1813- Then came Jacob Fadely, William Woody and George Hammat before me one of the Justices for the County aforesaid and made oath that Negro LUE aged about 28 years old, 5 feet 9 1/2 inches high with a scar over his right eye, also one on the left arm or wrist and one

near each elbow & one on the 3rd finger of the left hand with an uncommon set of ankles this day shown by Alexr Murvey is the same person mentioned in the last Will of Wm Ansley Decd of which the foregoing is a copy & that the said LUE is well known to the deponents- John McComick" The said Lue is therefore registered in my Office as the law directs. Given under my hand as Clerk of the Court of said County of Pittsylvania this 23rd day of July 1813- Will: Tunstall Ck:

[p 4] W. Rivers- No 8- **WYAT RIVERS** a free negro Man who served his time with William Smith is this [sic] registered in the Clerks Office of Pittsylvania County- The said WYAT RIVERS is a black Man with bushy hair about twenty four years of age, about five feet nine inches- has thick lips, a little impediment in his speech and a down look- Given under my hand this 19th day of June 1815- Will: Tunstall Clerk of Pittsylvania County, Virginia

D. Wiley- No 9- Description of **DEBORAH WILEY** a free Girl registered by the Clerk of Pittsylvania County the 18th of March 1816. The said Deborah Wiley is a Mulatto Girl between 18 and 19 years of age about five feet four or five inches high, has black bushy hair, acqueline [sic] nose, effeminate voice and rather pleasing countenance- Will. Tunstall CPC

A. Flood   - Virginia, Pittsylvania County   -   No 10   - **ALEXANDER FLOOD** a dark Mulatto Man, five feet eight inches high about fifty one years of age, one of his upper fore teeth out, has a small scar under his left eye & one on the first joint of his fore-finger of the left hand and who produced a certificate of his being born free in the County of Amelia, was registered in the Clerks Office of the County aforesaid the 21st day of October 1816. Will: Tunstall Ck:

C. Flood- Virginia, Pittsylvania County- No 11- **COLEMAN FLOOD** a dark Mulatto Man a free born son of ALEXANDER FLOOD & LEVINA his wife about twenty years of age has a Scar just below his under lip, and one under left jaw, about four feet nine or ten inches high was registered in the Clerks Office of the County aforesaid the 21st day of October 1816- Will: Tunstall CPC [p 5]   L. Flood- No 12- Virginia, Pittsylvania County **LEVINA FLOOD** wife of ALEXANDER FLOOD a Mulatto Woman about forty eight years of age five feet seven inches high has two moles on her right cheek, has long bushy hair, said to have been born free in the County of Brunswick was registered in the Clerks Office of the County aforesaid the 23rd day of October 1816- Will: Tunstall

S.& P. Flood- No 13- Virginia, Pittsylvania County- **SITHE FLOOD & PHURA FLOOD** dark Mulatto Girls, twin daughters of ALEXANDER FLOOD and LEVINA [FLOOD] his wife eight years old the 23rd of March last; SITHE has a mole under her chin & PHURA a small black speck on the upper lip; have short curled hair, were registered in the Clerks Office of the County aforesaid the 23rd of October 1816 Will:Tunstall Ck **[Note two children on the same Register.]**

C. Flood- No 14- Virginia, Pittsylvania County- **CHARITY FLOOD** a Mulatto Girl daughter of ALEXANDER FLOOD & LEVINA his wife about thirteen years old has fine bushy hair, about four feet eleven inches high, has rather thick lips, a smooth skin and pleasing countenance was registered in the Clerks Office of the County aforesaid the 23rd day of October 1816- Will: Tunstall CP

[p 6] A. Roe- No 15- Pittsylvania County Sct: **ABRAM ROE** a free born dark Mulatto Man who was bound to and served an apprenticeship with Jesee Walton Sen. of the said County is twenty two years old the 25th of Decemr 1816. about five feet 3 or four inches high has short wooly hair, no particular mark or Scar, has thick lips and big nostrils, was registered in the Clerks Office of Pittsylvania County this 30th day of December 1816-   Will: Tunstall Clerk of Pittsylvania

B.Laurence- Pittsylvania County Va- No 16. **BERRY LAURENCE** a black man about five feet seven inches high, about fifty years of age, has a Scar on the left cheek and very grey hair, one of his upper fore teeth out, produced a certificate from the Clerk of the County Court of Charlotte of his being free born & Registered in the Clerks Office of said County Court of Charlotte the 21st Octo 1799, was this [left blank] registered in the Clerks Office of the

County of Pittsylvania aforesaid 17th March 1817- Teste Will:Tunstall

H. Laurence- Pittsylvania County Virginia- No 17- **HANNAH LAURENCE** a free born dark Mulatto Woman wife of BERRY LAURENCE about thirty five years of age very fleshy with long black hair about four feet 10 inches high was registered in the Clerks Office of Pittsylvania County the 17th March 1817- Will: Tunstall

S.A. Laurence- Pittsylvania County Va- No 18- **SALLY ANN LAURENCE** a free born dark Mulatto Girl daughter of BERRY LAURENCE & HANNAH his wife nineteen years old the 14th May next with long bushy hair about five feet high was registered in the Clerks Office the 17th March 1817- Will: Tunstall

[p 7] L. & M.A. Laurence- Pittsylvania County Va- No 19 & 20- **LOUISA [LAURENCE]** and **MARY ANN LAURENCE** two small free born Mulatto Girls, children of BERRY LAURENCE & HANNAH his wife, LOUISA about 5 years old the 14th May next & MARY ANN 4 years old the 16th of Jany: next, each having long bushy hair, was registered in the Clerks Office the 17th March 1817- Will: Tunstall **[Note two Register Nos. for two children]**

E. Gray- No 21- State of Virginia Pittsylvania County to wit Pursuant to the act of Assembly passed the 25th day of January 1803 intitled [sic] "an act more effectually to restrain the practice of Negroes going at large" **ELIZABETH GRAY** was on the 20th day of October 1817 duly registered in the County Court of Pittsylvania: The said ELIZABETH GRAY is a Mulatto Woman about forty nine years of age four feet eleven inches high, has a Scar on the left side of her chin occasioned by a burn, and another on the left side of her neck, and was born free - Given under my hand as Clerk of the said Court this 20th day of October 1817. Teste Will: Tunstall

B. Davis- No 22- State of Virginia Pittsylvania County to wit Pursuant to the act of assembly passed the 25th day of January 1803 entitled an act more effectually to restrain the practice of Negroes going about at large. **BECKY DAVIS** was duly registered in the County of Pittsylvania the 18th day of November 1817, the said BECKY DAVIS is a Mulatto Woman eighteen years of age the 29th day of July last past, about five feet five inches high has thick short hair and big nostrils and was born free Given under my hand as Clerk of the said County Court the 18th day of November 1817- Will: Tunstall

[p 8]   James- No 23- Pittsylvania County Clerks Office **JAMES [WORSHAM]** a black Man emancipated by the Will of John Worsham late of the County of Pittsylvania about 65 years of age, about five feet eight inches high and all his front teeth out except three below, his little toe on the right foot crooked the end inclining outward- registered 18th August 1818- Teste   Will: Tunstall CPC

Phillis- No 24- Pittsylvania County clerks Office **PHILLIS [WORSHAM]** a dark Mulatto Woman about 55 years old about 5 feet six inches high has a wart on the forefinger of the right hand emancipated by the Will of John Worsham Decd - registered the 18th August 1818 - Teste   Will:Tunstall CPC

Jenny- Pittsylvania County Clerks Office- No 25-   **JENNY [WORSHAM]** a dark Mulatto Woman about 50 years of age about five feet four inches high, has a Scar on the top of the forefinger of the right hand between the first two joints, emancipated by the Will of John Worsham- registered the 18th August 1818.   Teste Will: Tunstall

W. Rivers- No 26- Pittsylvania Clerks Office to wit - **WYAT RIVERS** a free man of colour who served his time with William Smith of said County was this day registered in my said Office The said WYATT RIVERS is a black Man with bushy hair has thick lips, a Small impediment in his speech & a down look- Given under my hand this 19th day of October 1818.   Will: Tunstall CPC **[Renewal]**

[p 9]   A. Chavers- Virginia Pittsylvania County to wit No 27- Pursuant to the act of assembly passed the 2d day of March 1819 entitled " an act reducing into one the Several acts concerning Slaves, free Negroes and Mulattos" **ALEXANDER CHAVERS** is on this day registered in the Clerks Office of the County aforesaid:

the said **ALEXANDER CHAVERS** is a black man about thirty seven years of age five feet seven inches high, has a Small Scar on his forehead and Several on his left hand occasioned by the fire when working at the blacksmiths trade, to learn which, he served an apprenticeship with Robert Johns as appears by Johns certificate of his discharge dated the 17th of November 1804- Will:Tunstall Clerk of Pittsylvania County Court

J. Reynolds- No 28- Virginia Pittsylvania County to wit Pursuant to the Act of Assembly in that case made and provided **JUBIA REYNOLDS** a free man of colour this 17th day of August 1819 registered in the Clerks Office of the Said County Court the said JUBIA REYNOLDS is a Mulatto Man about five feet ten or eleven inches high, about twenty nine years of age, no apparent mark or Scar except a Small Scar on the right temple- Teste Will: Tunstall

Jas Davis- No 29- **JAMES DAVIS** a free born Mulatto boy who served his time with Jonathon B. Dawson is this day registered in the Clerks Office of Pittsylvania County according to law- The said JAMES DAVIS is a bright Mulatto twenty two years of age last Septemr about six feet high, has short bushy hair without any apparent mark or scar- Given under my hand this 17th day of November 1819- Will: Tunstall CPC

W. Owen- No 30- **WILLIAM OWEN** a dark brown five feet & half an inch high about 38 years of age this day produced in my Office a certificate from under the hand of J. Grammer [p 10] Clerk of the Hustings Court of the Town of Petersburg of his being free born & raised in the County of Sussex. The said WILLIAM OWEN has a scar on the upper part of the left side of his forehead and on the ball of his great toe of the right foot and also on his left hand and near the first joint of the thumb by trade a Carpenter & Shoemaker- The said WILLIAM OWEN is this 22nd day of February 1820 registered in the Clerks Office of Pittsylvania County- Teste Will:Tunstall

A. Chavers- No 31- Virginia Pittsylvania County to wit Pursuant to the act of Assembly passed the 2d day of March 1819, entitled "an act reducing into one the Several acts concerning Slaves, free negroes and Mulattos" - **ALEXANDER CHAVERS** is on this 20th day of June 1820 registered in the Clerks Office of the County aforesaid. The said ALEXANDER CHAVERS is a black Man, about thirty seven years of age, five feet seven inches high has a Small Scar on his forehead and Several on his left hand occasioned by fire when working at the Blacksmiths trade, to learn which he served an apprenticeship with Robert Johns who by his certificate discharged him the 17th day of November 1804- Given under my hand and seal of Office this 20th day of June 1820- Will: Tunstall Clerk of Pittsylvania County Court **[Renewal]**

M. Wooten- No 32- Virginia Pittsylvania County to wit Pursuant to the act of assembly passed the 2d day of March 1819 entitled an act reducing into the Several acts concerning Slaves free Negroes and Mulattos - **MILLY WOOTEN** is on this 17th day of July 1820 registered in the Clerks Office of the County aforesaid: the said MILLY [p 11] WOOTEN is bright Mulatto Woman about thirty years of age five feet 3 3/4 Inches high, has long straight hair intermixed with white hairs has no apparent marks or Scar, served her time with Moses Echols of this County to whom she was bound by an overseer of the poor, having been free born- Given under my hand this day and date above written. Will:Tunstall CPC

M. Chavis- No 33- Virginia Pittsylvania Clerks Office to wit- Pursuant to the provisions of the act of Assembly passed the 2d day of March 1819 <u>intitled</u> "an act concerning Slaves, free Negroes and Mulattos" - **MILLY CHAVIS** was on the 20th day of June 1822 registered in my said Office: the said MILLY CHAVIS is a bright Mulatto woman about 54 years of age about five feet five inches high has black bushy hair and has no aparant [sic] marks or scar. She was formerly held in slavery by James Arthur who obtained her by gift from William Bennett, but has lately recovered her freedom by a suit in the County Court of Pittsylvania as being a decendant of a free woman- Given under my hand the day and date above mentd. Will: Tunstall CPC

W. Rivers- Pittsylvania Clerks Office to wit **WYATT RIVERS** a free man of colour who served his time with William Smith of Said County was this day registered in my Office the said WYATT RIVERS is a black man with bushy hair about thirty years of age, about five feet nine inches high, has thick lips, a Small impediment in his speech and a down look - Given under my hand this 18th day of June 1821- Will: Tunstall CPC   [Renewal]

[p 12]   D. Dobson- Virginia Pittsylvania County to wit- (See No. 2) Pursuant to the act of Assembly in that case made and provided the register of **DOTIA DOBSON** a free Woman of colour made the 18th May 1810 is this 16th day of March 1819 renewed in the Clerks Office of the said County Court - the said DOTIA DOBSON is a black Woman about four feet eleven inches high about thirty four or thirty five years of age, no apparent mark or scar except the loss of one of her front under teeth - Teste   Will:Tunstall CPC **[Renewal, and correction of surname; letter b is underlined in surname; note by Clerk to see Registration No. 2.]**

J. Denson- No 34- Virginia Pittsylvania Clerks Office to wit- Pursuant to the provisions of the Act of Assembly passed the 2d day of March 1819 entitled "an act to reduce into One the Several acts concerning Slaves free Negroes and Mulattos"- **JAMES [DENSON]** otherwise called **JIM DENSON** who by the Copy of a former register made by the Clerk of Southampton Court appeared to have been born free was this day registered at my office aforesaid- The said JAMES (otherwise called JIM DENSON) is a black man about thirty nine years of age about five feet eight and a half inches high, has a Small nob or Scar on his right wrist which he says was occasioned by the cut of axe and no other mark or scar apparent- Given under my hand this 11th day of September 1822 Will: Tunstall CPC

Ro: Byrd- No 35- Virginia Pittsylvania Clerks Office to wit- Pursuant to the provisions of the act of Assembly passed the 2d day of March 1819 entitled "an act to reduce into one the Several acts concerning Slaves, free Negroes and Mulattos"- **ROBERT BYRD** is a bright Mulatto Man about sixty three years of age about five feet three [p 13] inches high, he has black hair nearly straight somewhat mixed with grey hairs, a scar about the centre of his forehead, one on his under lip and another on his right hand made by a cut that occasions the forefinger to be stiff- Given under my hand this 11th day of September 1822- Will: Tunstall CPC

T. Mason- No 36- Virginia Pittsylvania Clerks Office to wit- Pursuant to the provisions of the act of Assembly passed the 2d day of March 1819 intitailed [sic] "an act to reduce into One the Several acts concerning Slaves, free Negroes and Mulattos"- **TED MASON** who was born free as appears by a certificate of Ira Ellis with whom he served for a limited time, was this day registered in my office- The said TED MASON is a black man about twenty one years old, about five feet three inches high with short nappy hair, has a large Scar on the left wrist, which appears to have been occasioned by a burn and a Small Scar on the left side of the forehead and no other mark or scar apparent- Given under my hand this 16th day of December 1822- Will: Tunstall CP

S. Hendrick- No 37- Virginia Pittsylvania County to wit- Pursuant to the provisions of the act of Assembly passed the 2d day of March 1819 entituled [sic] "an act to reduce into one the Several acts Concerning Slaves, free Negroes and Mulattos"- **SAMUEL HENDRICK** who was born free as appears by the affidavit of William Beal and Samuel Hunt made before the County Court of Pittsylvania the 21st day of January 1823 was this day registered in [p 14] my office-The Said SAMUEL HENDRICK is a dark Mulatto Man about twenty one years of age, five feet six and a half inches high with short wooly hair- he has no scar or mark apparent- Given under my hand this 17th day of February 1823- Will: Tunstall CPC

J. Booker- No 38- Virginia Pittsylvania Clerks Office to wit- Pursuant to the provisions of the act of Assembly passed the 2d day of March 1819 entituled [sic] "an act to reduce into one the Several acts Concerning Slaves, free Negroes and Mulattos"- **JESSE BOOKER** who was emancipated by the last will and Testament of Caleb Ellis Deceased of record in the Sussex Court, as appeared by a certificate of Ira Ellis Exor: of the said Caleb Ellis Decd was this day registered in my office- The Said JESSE BOOKER is a dark Mulatto Man about twenty five years of age, five feet four and a half inches high has short wooly hair, has a large mouth and shows his teeth very much when he smiles- he has no mark or Scar apparent- Given under my hand this 17th day of May 1824- Teste Will: Tunstall CP renewed in 1837 certd at August Court of that year, but a copy not retained-

Jas Davis- No 39- Pittsylvania Clerks Office to wit **JAMES DAVIS** a free born Mulatto man who served his time with Jonathon B. Dawson is this day registered in the clerks office of Pittsylvania County according to law- The said JAMES DAVIS is a bright Mulatto twenty seven years of age next September about six feet high has bushy hair with a Scar on the left side of his mouth, also one on each hand [p 15] Given under my hand this 5th day of June 1824- Will: Tunstall CPC   **[Renewal of No 29]**

J. Davis- No 40- Pittsylvania Clerks Office to wit Pursuant to an act of Assembly passed the 2d day of March 1819 entituled [sic] "an act reducing into one the several acts Concerning Slaves, free Negroes and Mulattos"- **JEFFREY DAVIS** was this day duly registered in the Clerks Office of the County Court of Pittsylvania- The Said JEFFREY DAVIS is a Mulatto Man about twenty nine years of age last November, about five feet eight inches high has a full black beard and black eye brows and was born free- Given under my hand as clerk of the said Court this 5th day of June 1824- Will: Tunstall

P. Davis- No 41- Pittsylvania Clerks Office to wit **PATTY DAVIS** a free born Mulatto woman who served her time with Jonathon B. Dawson is this day registered in my said office according to law- The said PATTY DAVIS is a bright Mulatto twenty three years old the 8th day of May last five feet two and 1/4th inches high, has long bushy hair with a Scar on the back of the right hand occasioned by a burn Given under my hand this 7th day of June 1824- Will: Tunstall

M. Davis- No 42- Pittsylvania Clerks Office to wit **MILLY DAVIS** a free born Mulatto woman who served her [p 16] time with Jonathon B. Dawson is this day registered in my said office according to law- The said MILLY DAVIS is a bright Mulatto twenty three years old the 8th day of May last five feet two and 1/4th inches high, has long bushy hair & she has no mark or Scar apparent- Given under my hand this 7th day of June 1824- Will: Tunstall CP

L. Hendrick- No 43- Pittsylvania Clerks Office to wit **LETITIA HENDRICK** a free born Mulatto woman was this day registered in my aforesaid office according to law- The said **LETITIA HENDRICK** is a bright Mulatto woman about forty three years of age, about five foot and one half inch high, has long bushy hair with a Small Scar on the left side of her forehead & another on the right arm near the elbow - Given under my hand this 8th day of June 1824 Will:Tunstall CP   Renewed 18 June 1827 & certified Renewed in 1832 & certified (June court 1832) **[Renewal data written later.]**

W. Rivers- ___ Virginia, Pittsylvania Clerks Office to wit- **WYATT RIVERS** a free man of colour who served his time with William Smith of said County was this day registered in my office- the said WYATT RIVERS is a black man with bushy hair about thirty three years of age about five feet nine inches high has thick lips, a small impediment in his speech & a downe [sic] look- Given under my hand this 21st day of June 1824 Will: Tunstall CPC **[No number is given, and space is left blank; Renewal of No. 8]**

[P 17] Geo. Rivers- No 44- Pittsylvania County Court Clerks Office 21st (See No 4) June 1824 **GEORGE RIVERS** a free born man of colour who served his time with William Smith of said County was this day registered in my said office The said GEORGE RIVERS is of light complexion about thirty five years of age with bushy hair about five feet six inches high, has a flat nose and no mark or scar perceivable- Given under my hand this day and date above written- Will: Tunstall CP **[Renewal of No. 4]**

S. Davis- No 45- Virginia, Pittsylvania Clerks Office to wit Pursuant to the act of Assembly passed the 2d day of March 1819 entitled "an act reducing into one the several acts Concerning Slaves, free Negroes and Mulattos" - **SUSANNAH DAVIS** a free born woman of colour was this day duly registered in the Clerks Office of Pittsylvania County Court- The Said SUSANNAH DAVIS is a bright Mulatto Woman twenty one years of age the 4th day of last March about five feet two and three fourths inches high, has no apparent mark or scars- Given under my hand as clerk of the said Court this 21st day of June 1824- Will: Tunstall CPC

C. Hendrick- No 46- Pittsylvania Clerks Office to wit **CREACY HENDRICK** a free born woman of colour was this day duly registered in my said office- the said CREACY HENDRICK is of dark complexion with black wooly hair about twenty six years of age four feet, eleven & one [p 18] half inches high has a scar on the left wrist- Given under my hand this 22nd day of June 1824- Will: Tunstall CPC

S. Hendrick- No 47- Pittsylvania Clerks Office to wit **SUSANNAH HENDRICK** a free born woman of colour was this day duly registered in my said office- the said SUSANNAH HENDRICK is of dark complexion about twenty five years of age five feet two inches high & has long bushy hair- Given under my hand this 22nd day of June 1824- Will: Tunstall CPC

John Going- No 48- Pittsylvania Clerks Office to wit According to the act of Assembly in that case made and provided **JOHN GOING** was this day registered in my said Office according to law- The said JOHN GOING is a dark Mulatto Man about forty eight years old five feet.....eight inches high, has a high forehead and is rather inclined to be bald with short nappy hair-he now has a wound on the third finger of the left hand which will probably leave a Scar on the inside of that finger, and is said to have been born free- Given under my hand this 15th day of November 1824- Will: Tunstall CPC

[p 19] James Going- No 49- Virginia Pittsylvania County Clerks Office Viz: Pursuant to the act of Assembly passed the 2nd day of March 1819 entitled "an act reducing into one the several acts Concerning Slaves, free Negroes and Mulattos"- **JAMES GOING** a free born man of colour as was proven to the satisfaction of the Court of sd County on Yesterday was this day duly registered in the Clerks Office of Pittsylvania County Court- The said JAMES GOING is a bright Mulatto man twenty six years of age about five feet eight & half inches high, has straight coarse hair and grey eyes, has no apparent scar or mark except two large scars on the front part of his right ankle the upper occasioned by the cut of a scythe blade and the lower by the cut of an axe- Given under my hand as clerk of the said County Court this 16th day of November 1824 Will: Tunstall   Renewed 17 Decr 1827 & Nord 211 (No copy kept)

John Going- No 50- Virginia Pittsylvania County to wit Pursuant to the act of Assembly passed the 2nd day of March 1819 entitled "an act reducing into one the several acts Concerning Slaves, free Negroes and Mulattos"- **JOHN GOING** a free born man of colour as satisfactorily proven to the Court of said County on the 15th Inst: was this day duly registered in the Clerks Office of the said County according to law. The said JOHN GOING is a dark Mulatto twenty one years of age in April next five feet seven and one quarter inches high has short black nappy hair, dark hazel eyes, has no apparent scar or mark- Given under my hand as clerk of the said County Court this 16th day of November 1824- Will: Tunstall

[p 20]   P. Going- No 51- Virginia, Pittsylvania County to wit Pursuant to the act of Assembly entitled "an act reducing into one the several acts Concerning Slaves, free Negroes and Mulattos"- **POLLY GOING** a free born woman of colour as was satisfactorily proven to the Court of said County on the 15 Instant was this day duly registered in the Clerks Office of the said County according to law- The said POLLY GOING is a dark Mulatto woman about twenty four years of age, has short black hair and black eyes, five feet five and a quarter inches high, has a Scar on her forehead about the edge of her hair about the size of a dollar occasioned by a burn Given under my hand as clerk of the said Court this 16th day of November 1824- Will: Tunstall   Copd again & certfd the 17th Decr 1827

B. Going- No 52- Virginia Pittsylvania County to wit- Pursuant to the act of Assembly passed the 2d day of March 1819 entitled "an act reducing into one the several acts Concerning Slaves, free Negroes and Mulattos"- **BURWELL GOING** a free born Man of Colour as was proven to the satisfaction of the Court of said County on Yesterday was this day duly registered in the Clerks Office of the said County Court- The said BURWELL GOING is a Mulatto man six feet one inch high twenty two years of age the 12th of April last past, has black curled hair, has no apparent scar or mark, his eyes are of a dark grey or hazel colour- Given under my hand as clerk of said County Court this 16th day of November 1824- Will: Tunstall [p 21]   B. Going- No 53- Virginia Pittsylvania County to wit- Pursuant to the act of Assembly passed on the 2d day of March 1819 entitled "an act reducing into one the several acts Concerning Slaves, free Negroes and Mulattos" **BETSY GOING** a free woman of Colour as was satisfactorily proven to the Court of said County on the 15th Instant was this day duly registered in the Clerks Office of the said Court- The said BETSY GOING is a Mulatto woman about twenty eight years of age about five feet two & half inches high has long black hair and very black eyes, has a large neck of a wen like appearance and no apparent scar or mark- Given under my hand this 16th day of November 1824- Will: Tunstall CPC Copd again & certfd the 17th Decr 1827

D. Scott- No 54- Virginia Pittsylvania County to wit- Pursuant to the act of Assembly passed the 2d day of March 1819 entitled "an act reducing into one the several acts Concerning Slaves, free Negroes and Mulattos"- **DANIEL SCOTT** is this day duly registered in the Clerks Office of the County aforesaid- The said DANIEL SCOTT is a bright Mulatto man about thirty seven years of age the 20th day of June 1824 five feet five & an half inches high has thick bushy hair is a thick well made man has no apparent mark or Scar, except two scars on the instep of the left foot about one inch apart and was born free as appears by the Oath of William L. Fentross made in the Court of said County- Given under my hand as clerk of the sd Court.... this 16th day of April 1825- Will: Tunstall

C. Young- No 55- Virginia Pittsylvania County to wit- Pursuant to the provisions of the act of Assembly [p 22] passed the 2d (2nd day) of March 1819 entitled "an act reducing into one the Several acts Concerning Slaves, free Negroes and Mulattoes"- **CHESLEY YOUNG** a free born man of colour was this day duly registered in the Clerks Office of the County aforesaid: The said CHESLEY YOUNG is a bright Mulatto man about six feet high, twenty three years old the 30th day of December next has thick bushy hair has no apparent mark or scar except a small scar on the nose & a scar on the left leg: the said CHESLEY YOUNG is son of ANTHONY YOUNG and MARY [YOUNG] his wife as appears from the register of the Clerk of the County Court of Charlotte- Given under my hand as clerk of the said Court....this 16th day of May 1825- Will: Tunstall

Jim Harroway- No 56- Pittsylvania County Clerks Office to wit- **JIM [HARROWAY]** a bright Mulatto Man about 44 years of age with a Scar on the middle finger of his left hand 5 feet 9 inches high who was emancipated by the last will and Testament of George Harraway Decd this day produced a certificate of his having been registered in the County Court of Charlotte in these words to wit, "Virginia. At a Court held for Charlotte County the 6 day of March 1821 on the motion of William & Charles McKinney executors of George Harraway Decd the Court doth order that the following Negro man who was emancipated by the will of the sd George Harraway be registered as a free person according to the law to wit, JIM aged about 41 years of light complexion, has a Scar on the middle finger of his left hand 5 feet 9 inches high- The above named JIM was registered as a free person this 6 day of March 1821 according to law- I Winslow Robinson Clerk of the County Court of Charlotte do hereby certify that the foregoing entries are truly copied from the records of my office- In [p 23] testimony whereof I have hereunto set my hand and affixed the seal of the said County at my office (Seal) this 19th day of March 1821- Winslow Robinson C. Whereupon the said JIM is registered in my said office as the law directs- Given under my hand this 20th day of June 1825- Will: Tunstall

Molly- No 57- Pittsylvania County Clerks Office to wit **MOLLEY [HARROWAY]** a woman of light complexion about thirty seven years old last March has a Scar on her right arm & a small scar on her breast, five feet 3 1/4 inches high emancipated by the last Will and Testament of George Harraway Decd this day produced a certificate of her having been registered in the County Court of Charlotte in these words to wit, "At a Court held for Charlotte County the 6 day of March 1821 on the Motion of William & Charles McKinney executors of George Harraway Decd the Court doth order that the following Negro woman who was emancipated by the will of the said George Harraway be registered as a free person according to the law to wit, MOLLY aged about thirty three years of light complexion, has a scar on her right arm & a small scar on her breast, 5 feet 3 1/4 inches high. The above named

MOLLY was registered in the Clerks Office of the County Court of Charlotte as a free person this 1st day of March 1821 according to law- Whereupon the said certificate is registered in my office as the law directs- Given under my hand this 20th day of June 1825- Will: Tunstall CPC

U. Chavis- No 58- Virginia Pittsylvania Clerks Office to wit- Pursuant to the provisions of the act of Assembly passed the 2d (2nd day) of March 1819 entitled "an act reducing into one the Several acts Concerning Slaves, free Negroes and Mulattoes" **UNA CHAVIS** was on the 12th day of August 1825 registered in my said Office. The [p 24] said UNA CHAVIS is a dark Mulatto Woman about 24 years of age, five feet 3 1/2 inches high has black bushy hair and a Scar on the inside of her right arm near the elbow. She was formerly held in Slavery by John Arthur who obtained her by gifts from William Bennett, but has lately recovered her freedom by a suit in the County court of Pittsylvania as being a descendant of a free Woman- Will:Tunstall CPC

J. Denson- No 59- Pittsylvania County Clerks Office to wit- Pursuant to the provisions of the act of Assembly passed the 2d day of March 1819 entitled "an act to reduce into one the several acts concerning Slaves free Negroes and Mulattoes" **JAMES [DENSON]** otherwise called **JIM DENSON** who (by copy of a former register made by the clerk of Southampton County Court) appears to have been born free was this day registered in my office aforesaid The said JAMES (otherwise called JIM DENSON) is a black man about forty two years of age, about five feet eight and a half inches high, has a Small not [sic] or scar on his right wrist which he says was occasioned by the cut of an axe, and no other mark or scar apparent- Given under my hand this 19th day of September 1825 Will: Tunstall CPC   (renewed 17 Nov 1828 & no copy) **[Renewal of No. 34]**

Ro: Fowler- No 60- Virginia Pittsylvania Clerks Office to wit- Pursuant to the provisions of the act of Assembly passed the 2d (2nd day) of March 1819 entitled "an act reducing into one the several acts Concerning Slaves, free Negroes and Mulattoes" **ROBERT FOWLER** was on this day [p 25] duly registered in my office aforesaid. The said ROBERT FOWLER is a bright Mulatto

Man about six feet one and three fourth inches high, stout made has short wooly hair & has no apparent mark or scar. The said ROBERT FOWLER was emancipated by Deed from the heirs of Joseph Fowler Decd and permitted to remain in this State by an order of the Court of said County- Given under my hand this 19th day of September 1825 - Will: Tunstall CPC

B. Chavers- No 61- Virginia Pittsylvania Clerks Office SC- Pursuant to the provisions of the act of Assembly passed the 2d (2nd day) of March 1819 entitled "an act to reduce into one the several acts Concerning Slaves, free Negroes and Mulattoes" **BENJAMIN CHAVERS** (who by the copy of a register made by the Clerk of Franklin County Court the 1st day of May 1809) appears to have been born free was this day registered & No. in the Clerks Office aforesaid. The said BENJAMIN CHAVERS is a black man about fifty years of age, about five feet seven inches high, stammers a little in his speech, has no apparent scar or mark has short coarse hair & has lost his upper teeth- Given under my hand this 20th day of February 1826 Will: Tunstall CPC

Malinda- No 62- Pittsylvania County Clerks Office April 17 1826- **MALINDA** a Mulatto woman emancipated by the will of Sarah Herndon Deceased was this day registered in the Clerks office aforesaid according to law. The said MALINDA is a bright Mulatto five feet six inches high, has a smooth skin with long straight black hair, has a small Scar on her chin one over the wrist of the right [p 26] arm occasioned by a burn and two other small ones on the same arm between the wrist and the elbow - Given under my hand this 17th day of April 1826- Will: Tunstall CPC

C. Stephens- No 63- Virginia to wit **CATHARINE STEPHENS** a woman of colour emancipated by John Terry by deed of record in the County Court of Pittsylvania was this day registered in the Clerks office of the said County Court according to law- The said CATHARINE STEPHENS is a black woman about forty five years of age, five feet two and an half inches high, has short wooly hair, with a small Scar between her eyes occasioned as she says by the Chicken Pox- Given under my hand this 20th day of June 1826- Will: Tunstall CPC

L. Stephens- No 64- Virginia to wit **LUCRETIA STEPHENS** a woman of colour who was emancipated by deed from John Terry of record in Pittsylvania Court was this day registered in the Clerks office of the County Court according to the provisions of the act of Assembly in that case made and provided- The said LUCRETIA STEPHENS is a black woman about twenty eight years of age, about four feet nine inches and three quarters high, has short wooly hair and a small Scar on the left side of the face opposite the cheek- Given under my hand this 20th day of June 1826- Will: Tunstall CC

[p 27]   W. Stephens- No 65- Virginia to wit- **WILMOTH STEPHENS** a free born woman of colour daughter of CATHARINE STEPHENS who was emancipated by John Terry by deed of record in the Clerks Office of Pittsylvania County was this day registered in my office of the County Court according to law- The said WILMOTH STEPHENS is a black woman about twenty five years of age, about four feet eleven and a fourth inches high and has no apparent mark or Scar- Given under my hand this 20th day of June 1826- Will:Tunstall CC

P. Stephens- No 66- Virginia to wit- **PHILLIS STEPHENS** a woman of colour and Daughter of CATHARINE STEPHENS who was emancipated by deed from John Terry of record in Pittsylvania County Court was this day registered in the Clerks office of the said County Court according to law The said PHILLIS STEPHENS is a black woman about twenty two years of age, five feet three & a half inches high has short wooly hair has a scar on the right cheek about 2 inches long occasioned by the cut of a knife and one on the right arm occasioned by a burn- Given under my hand this 20th day of June 1826- Will: Tunstall CPC

A. Stephens- No 67- Virginia to wit- **AGGY STEPHENS** a woman of colour and Daughter of [p 28] CATHARINE STEPHENS who was emancipated by John Terry by deed of record in the County Court of Pittsylvania was this day registered in the Clerks office of the said County of Pittsylvania according to law- The said AGGY STEPHENS is a black woman about eighteen or Nineteen years of age, five feet three & half inches high has short wooly hair without any apparent mark or scar- Given under my hand this 20th day of June 1826- Will: Tunstall CPC

G. Davis- No 68- Pittsylvania Clerks Office to wit- **GILES DAVIS** a free born Mulatto man who served his time with Jonathon B. Dawson is this day registered in the Clerks office of the said County according to law- The said GILES DAVIS is a bright Mulatto twenty one years of age the 5th day of May last about five feet ten inches high has bushy hair without any apparent mark or scar- Given under my hand this 17th day of July 1826- Will: Tunstall CC

B. Hendrick- No 69- Virginia Pittsylvania County Clerks Office to wit- Pursuant to the provisions of the act of Assembly passed the 2d (2nd day) of March 1819 entitled "an act to reduce into one the several acts Concerning Slaves, free Negroes and Mulattoes" **BOOKER HENDRICK** a free born man of colour who was bound by an order of the Court of said County to Obadiah Ham with whom he served apprenticeship until his arrival to the age of twenty one years was this day registered in the Clerks Office aforesaid. [p 29] The said BOOKER HENDRICK is a black man five feet two & half inches high, has short bushy hair a small scar on his forehead over the left eye near the edge of his hair & has a considerable gap between his under front teeth- Given under my hand this 18th day of September 1826- Will: Tunstall CPC

[Registers No 70 - No 170, all of which involve the former slaves of John Ward, Senior, were certified to be correct at the January Court 1827. On Registers No 171 and No 172, the month of certification at court has been left blank.]

Richd Lynch- Virginia Pittsylvania County to wit- No 70- At the instance of John Ward and Lynch Dillard Executors of the last Will and Testament of John Ward Senior Deceased duly proven and recorded in the Court of said County **RICHARD LYNCH** a man of colour emancipated by the said Will was this day Numbered and registered in the Clerks Office of the said Court, pursuant to the provisions of the act of Assembly in that case made & provided. The said RICHARD LYNCH is a dark Mulatto man 24 years of age five feet eight and one fourth inches high has a scar on the back of his left hand occasioned by a cut- Given under my hand as Clerk of the said Court this 5th day of January 1827- Will: Tunstall CC

Dorcas- Virginia Pittsylvania County to wit- No. 71- At the instance of John Ward and Lynch Dillard Executors of the last Will and Testament of John Ward Senior Deceased duly proven and recorded in the Court of said County **DORCAS [LYNCH]** (wife of RICHARD LYNCH) a woman of colour emancipated by the said Will was this day numbered and registered in the Clerks Office of the said Court, pursuant to the provisions of the act of Assembly in that case made & provided- The said DORCAS is of bright complexion about twenty two years of age five feet 1 1/4 inches high, has a scar on the first joint of the fore finger of [p 30] the left hand Given under my hand as Clerk of the said Court this 5th day of January 1827- Will: Tunstall

Rhoda Lynch- Virginia Pittsylvania County to wit- No 72- At the instance of John Ward and Lynch Dillard Executors of the last Will and Testament of John Ward Senior Deceased duly proven and recorded in the Court of said County **RHODA LYNCH** a child of RICHARD & DORCAS LYNCH, of colour emancipated by the said Will was this day numbered and registered in the Clerks Office of the said Court pursuant to the provisions of the act of Assembly in that case made & provided- The said RHODA is about three months old- Given under my hand as Clerk of the said Court this 5th day of January 1827- Will: Tunstall

B. Roberts- Virginia Pittsylvania County to wit- No 73- At the instance of John Ward and Lynch Dillard Executors of the last Will and Testament of John Ward Senior Decd duly proven and recorded in the Court of said County **BETSY ROBERTS** a girl of colour emancipated by the said Will was this day numbered and registered in the Clerks Office of the said Court, pursuant to the provisions of the act of Assembly in that case made & provided- The said BETSY ROBERTS is a child of PLEASANT & HANAH & is of rather light complexion said to be seventeen years old five feet four & a fourth inches high, has a small scar under the left jaw occasioned by a burn, her fore finger on the right hand crooked at the last or nail joint Given under my hand as Clerk of the said Court this 5th day of January 1827- Will: Tunstall [p 31] **[no name given in margin]**- Virginia Pittsylvania County to wit, No 74- At the instance of John Ward and Lynch Dillard Executors of the last Will and Testament of John Ward Senior Deceased duly proven and recorded in the Court of said County **ELVY ROBERTS** a girl of colour emancipated by the said Will was this day numbered and registered in the Clerks Office of the said Court, pursuant to the provisions of the act of Assembly in that case made & provided- The said ELVY ROBERTS is a child of PLEASANT & HANNAH [ROBERTS] & is of a light complexion said to be about sixteen years old five feet 3 1/4 inches high, has a small scar under the left corner of the right eye and a long scar on the top of her head occasioned by a cut- Given under my hand as Clerk of the said Court this 5th day of January 1827- Will: Tunstall

P. Roberts- Virginia Pittsylvania County to wit- No 75- At the instance of John Ward and Lynch Dillard Executors of the last Will and Testament of John Ward Senr deceased duly proven and recorded in the Court of said County **PAULINA ROBERTS** a girl of colour emancipated by the said Will was this day numbered and registered in the Clerks Office of the said Court, pursuant to the provisions of the act of Assembly in that case made & provided- The said PAULINA ROBERTS is a child of PLEASANT & HANNAH & is of light complexion about 14 years old five feet high, has a long scar over the left eye and a scar on the back of the right hand- Given under my hand as Clerk of the said Court this 5th day of January 1827- Will: Tunstall

L. Roberts- Virginia Pittsylvania County to wit- No 76- At the instance of John Ward and Lynch Dillard Executors of the last Will and Testament of John Ward Senior deceased duly proven and recorded in the Court of said County **LAURA ROBERTS** a girl of colour [p 32] emancipated by the said Will was this day numbered and registered in the Clerks Office of the said Court, pursuant to the provisions of the act of Assembly in that case made & provided- The [sic] LAURA ROBERTS is a child of PLEASANT & HANNAH ROBERTS & is of bright complexion about thirteen years old four feet ten & a half inches high the left ear missing said to be natural- Given under my hand as Clerk of the said Court this 5th day of January 1827- Will: Tunstall

P. Roberts- Virginia Pittsylvania County to wit- No 77- At the instance of John Ward and Lynch Dillard Executors of the last Will and Testament of John Ward Senior Decd. duly proven and recorded in the said County **PENELOPE ROBERTS** a Girl of colour emancipated by the said Will was this day numbered and Registered in the Clerks Office of the said Court, pursuant to the provisions of the act of Assembly in that case made & provided- The said PENELOPE ROBERTS is a child of PLEASANT & HANNAH ROBERTS & is of light complexion about ten years old four feet six and quarter inches high, no mark or scar apparent- Given under my hand as Clerk of the said Court this 5th day of January 1827- Will: Tunstall

C. Roberts- Virginia Pittsylvania County to wit- No 78- At the instance of John Ward and Lynch Dillard Executors of the last Will and Testament of John Ward Senior Deceased duly proven and recorded in the Court of said County **CHARLES ROBERTS** a boy of colour emancipated by the said Will was this day numbered and registered in the Clerks Office of the said Court, pursuant to the provisions of the act of Assembly in that case made & provided- The said CHARLES ROBERTS is a child of PLEASANT & [p 33] HANNAH ROBERTS & is of bright complexion eight years old four feet one and quarter inch high, no apparent mark or scar- Given under my hand as Clerk of the said Court this 5th day of January 1827- Will:Tunstall

J. Roberts- Virginia Pittsylvania County to wit- No 79- At the instance of John Ward and Lynch Dillard Executors of the last Will and Testament of John Ward Senior Deceased duly proven and recorded in the Court of said County **JOHN ROBERTS** a boy of colour emancipated by the said Will was this day numbered and registered in the Clerks Office of the said Court, pursuant to the provisions of the act of assembly in that case made & provided- The said JOHN ROBERTS is a child of PLEASANT and HANNAH ROBERTS & is of light complexion three years old next June two feet ten inches high, no mark or scar apparent- Given under my hand as Clerk of the said Court this 5th day of January 1827- Will: Tunstall

P. Roberts- Virginia Pittsylvania County to wit- No 80- At the instance of John Ward and Lynch Dillard Executors of the last Will and Testament of John Ward Senior Deceased duly proven and recorded in the Court of said County **PLEASANT ROBERTS** a man of colour emancipated by the said Will was this day numbered & registered in the Clerks Office of the said Court, pursuant to the provisions of the act of assembly in that case made & provided- The said PLEASANT ROBERTS is of bright complexion thirty eight years old the 25th of last month five feet Eleven and a half inches high, has a scar over the left eye one on the nose between the eyes and one on the end of the forefinger of the left hand said to be occasioned by a whitlow or fellon- Given under my hand as Clerk of the said Court this 5th day of January 1827- Will: Tunstall

[p 34] H. Roberts - Virginia Pittsylvania County to wit- No 81- At the instance of John Ward and Lynch Dillard Executors of the last Will and Testament of John Ward Senior Deceased duly proven and recorded in the Court of said County **HANNAH ROBERTS** a woman of colour emancipated by the said Will was this day numbered & registered in the Clerks Office of the said Court, pursuant to the provisions of the act of assembly in that case made & provided The said HANNAH is the wife of PLEASANT ROBERTS & is of light complexion thirty three years old five feet two inches high, no mark or scar apparent- Given under my hand as Clerk of the said Court this 5th day of January 1827- Will: Tunstall

P. Lynch- Virginia Pittsylvania County to wit- No 82- At the instance of John Ward and Lynch Dillard Executors of the last Will and Testament of John Ward Senior Deceased duly proven and recorded in the Court of said County **PETER LYNCH** a man of colour emancipated by the said Will was this day numbered & registered in the Clerks Office of the said Court, pursuant to the provisions of the act of assembly in that case made & provided- The said PETER LYNCH is of rather light complexion twenty three years old five feet eleven and a half inches high, has a very small scar on the side of the jaw & on the end of the jaw & on the back of the neck about the edge of the hair- Given under my hand as Clerk of the said Court this 5th day of January 1827- Will: Tunstall [p 35] D Ward- Virginia Pittsylvania County to wit- No 83- At the instance of John Ward and Lynch Dillard Executors of the last Will and Testament of John Ward Senior Deceased duly proven and recorded in the Court of said County **DANIEL WARD** a Man of colour emancipated by the said Will was this day numbered & registered in the Clerks Office of the said Court, pursuant to the provisions of the act of assembly in that case made & provided- The said DANIEL WARD is a black man 21 years old five feet eight inches high has a scar on the right hand just below the first joint of the thumb- Given under my hand as Clerk of the said Court this 5th day of January 1827- Will: Tunstall

B Johnson- Virginia Pittsylvania County to wit- No 84- At the instance of John Ward and Lynch Dillard Executors of the last Will and Testament of John Ward Senr Deceased duly proven and recorded in the Court of said County **BENJAMIN JOHNSON** a man of colour emancipated by the said Will was this day numbered & registered in the Clerks Office of the said Court, pursuant to the provisions of the act of assembly in that case made & provided- The said BENJAMIN JOHNSON is a black man fifty eight years old five feet five inches high has a scar in the middle of his forehead- Given under my hand as Clerk of the said Court this 5th day of January 1827- Will: Tunstall

[Numbers out of sequence; Registration No 85 skipped here, but added in later.]

[p 36] J Johnson- Virginia Pittsylvania County to wit- No 86- At the instance of John Ward and Lynch Dillard Executors of the last Will and Testament of John Ward Senior Decd duly proven and recorded in the Court of said County **JERRY JOHNSON** a man of colour emancipated by the said Will was this day numbered & registered in the Clerks Office of the said Court, pursuant to the provisions of the act of assembly in that case made & provided- The said JERRY JOHNSON is a son of BENJAMIN JOHNSON & is a black man 18 years old five feet seven and three fourth inches high, has a small scar on the back of the left hand Given under my hand as Clerk of the said Court this 5th day of January 1827-   Will: Tunstall

H Ward- Virginia Pittsylvania County to wit- No 87- At the instance of John Ward and Lynch Dillard Executors of the last Will and Testament of John Ward Senr Deceased duly proven and recorded in the Court of said County **HARRY WARD** a man of colour emancipated by the said Will was this day numbered & registered in the Clerks Office of the said Court, pursuant to the provisions of the act of assembly in that case made & provided- The said **HARRY WARD** is a black man who says he is between 30 and 40 years old five feet six and a half inches high has two small scars between the eyebrows, a small one on the left eyebrow & a long one on the first joint of the forefinger of the left hand- Given under my hand as Clerk of the said Court this 5th day of January 1827- Will: Tunstall

[p 37] B Johnson- Virginia Pittsylvania County to wit- No 85 - At the instance of John Ward and Lynch Dillard Executors of the last Will and Testament of John Ward Senr deceased duly proven and recorded in the Court of said County **BENJAMIN JOHNSON [JR]** a man of colour emancipated by the said Will was this day numbered & registered in the Clerks Office of the said Court, pursuant to the provisions of the act of assembly in that case made & provided- The said **BENJAMIN JOHNSON** is a son of **BENJAMIN JOHNSON** & is a black man twenty five years old five feet seven and a half inches has two small scars on the forehead one of his shoulders rather lower than the other said to be occasioned by extracting the shoulder blade- Given under my hand as Clerk of the said Court this 5th day of January 1827- Will:Tunstall **[Numbers out of sequence; Registration No 85 added in here.]**

L Ward- Virginia Pittsylvania County to wit- No 88- At the instance of John Ward and Lynch Dillard Executors of the last Will and Testament of John Ward Senior Deceased duly proven and recorded in the Court of said County **LYDIA WARD** a woman of colour emancipated by the said Will was this day numbered & registered in the Clerks Office of the said Court, pursuant to the provisions of the act of Assembly in that case made & provided- The said **LYDIA WARD** is the wife of **HARRY WARD** and is about 45 years old of rather light complexion five feet four and a half inches high, has no apparent mark or scar Given under my hand as Clerk of the said Court this 5th day of January 1827- Will: Tunstall

Sarah Ward- Virginia Pittsylvania County to wit- No 89- At the instance of John Ward and Lynch [p 38] Dillard Executors of the last Will and Testament of John Ward Senr Deceased duly proven and recorded in the Court of said County **SARY WARD** a Girl of colour emancipated by the said Will was this day numbered & registered in the Clerks Office of the said Court, pursuant to the provisions of the Act of Assembly in that case made & provided- The said SARY WARD is the child of HARRY and LYDIA WARD & is of light complexion, twelve years old four feet eight and a quarter inches high, has a very small scar on the forehead in the edge of the hair Given under my hand as Clerk of the said Court this 5th day of January 1827- Will: Tunstall

B Ward- Virginia Pittsylvania County to wit- No 90- At the instance of John Ward and Lynch Dillard Executors of the last Will and Testament of John Ward Senr Decd duly proven and recorded in the Court of said County **BOB WARD** a boy of colour emancipated by the said Will was this day numbered & registered in the Clerks Office of the said Court, pursuant to the provisions of the act of Assembly in that case made & provided. The said BOB WARD is the child of HARRY and LYDIA WARD & is black, nine years old three feet seven and a quarter inches high, no mark or scar apparent- Given under my hand as Clerk of the said Court this 5th day of January 1827- Will: Tunstall

A Ward- Virginia Pittsylvania County to wit- No 91- At the instance of John Ward and Lynch Dillard Executors of the last Will and Testament of John [p 39] Ward Senior Deceased duly proven and recorded in the Court of said County **ANDERSON WARD** a boy of colour emancipated by the said Will was this day numbered & registered in the Clerks Office of the said Court, pursuant to the provisions of the Act of Assembly in that case made & provided. The said ANDERSON WARD is a child of HARRY and LYDIA WARD & is black, seven years old three feet seven and a quarter inches high, no mark or scar apparent- Given under my hand as Clerk of the said Court this 5th day of January 1827- Will: Tunstall

J Ward- Virginia Pittsylvania County to wit- No 92- At the instance of John Ward and Lynch Dillard Executors of the last Will and Testament of John Ward Senr Deceased duly proven and recorded in the Court of said County **JUDITH WARD** a Girl of colour emancipated by the said Will was this day numbered & registered in the Clerks Office of the said Court, pursuant to the provisions of the act of Assembly in that case made & provided- The said JUDITH WARD is a child of HARRY and LYDIA WARD & is of rather light complexion going on three years old two feet nine and three fourths inches high, has a burn on the back of the left hand which will probably leave a scar- Given under my hand as Clerk of the said Court this 5th day of January 1827- Will: Tunstall

L Craddock- Virginia Pittsylvania County to wit- No 93- At the instance of John Ward and Lynch Dillard Executors of the last Will and Testament of John Ward Senior Deceased duly proven and recorded in the Court of said County **LEWIS CRADDOCK** a man of colour [p 42] emancipated by the said Will was this day numbered & registered in the Clerks Office of the said Court, pursuant to the provisions of the act of assembly in that case made & provided- The said LEWIS CRADDOCK is a black man seventy five years old, five feet eight inches high has a scar on his left cheek, the joint of the right wrist much longer than that of the left Given under my hand as Clerk of the said Court this 5th day of January 1827- Will: Tunstall **[Pages are misnumbered. Page numbers 40 and 41 are omitted, but no entries are missing.]**

W Craddock- Virginia Pittsylvania County to wit- No 94- At the instance of John Ward and Lynch Dillard Executors of the last Will and Testament of John Ward Senior Deceased duly proven and recorded in the Court of said County **WINNEY CRADDOCK** a woman of colour emancipated by the said Will was this day numbered & registered in the Clerks Office of the said Court, pursuant to the provisions of the Act of Assembly in that case made & provided- The said WINNEY CRADDOCK is the wife of LEWIS CRADDOCK and is of bright complexion forty-five years old, four feet eleven and three fourth inches high, the middle finger of her right hand stiff and is near sighted Given under my hand as Clerk of the said Court this 5th day of January 1827- Will: Tunstall

J Craddock- Virginia Pittsylvania County to wit- No 95- At the instance of John Ward and Lynch Dillard Executors of the last Will and Testament of John Ward Senior Deceased duly proven and recorded in the [p 43] Court of said County **JEFFERSON CRADDOCK** a man of colour emancipated by the said Will was this day numbered & registered in the Clerks Office of the said Court, pursuant to the provisions of the act of Assembly in that case made & provided- The said JEFFERSON CRADDOCK is a son of LEWIS and WINNEY CRADDOCK and is of bright complexion five feet three and three fourth inches high no mark or scar apparent- Given under my hand as Clerk of the said Court this 5th day of January 1827-   Will: Tunstall

Lucy Craddock- Virginia Pittsylvania County to wit- No 96- At the instance of John Ward and Lynch Dillard Executors of the last Will and Testament of John Ward Senior Deceased duly proven and recorded in the Court of said County **LUCY CRADDOCK** a Girl of colour Emancipated by the said Will was this day numbered & registered in the Clerks Office of the said Court, pursuant to the provisions of the Act of Assembly in that case made & provided- The said LUCY CRADDOCK is a child of LEWIS and WINNEY CRADDOCK and is of rather light complexion, sixteen years old, five feet three inches high, has a small scar on the left forefinger and a long one on the top of the right hand Given under my hand as Clerk of the said Court this 5th day of January 1827-   Will: Tunstall

M Craddock- Virginia Pittsylvania County to wit- No 97- At the instance of John Ward and Lynch Dillard Executors of the last Will and Testament of John Ward Senior Deceased duly proven and recorded in the [p 44] Court of said County **MARTHA CRADDOCK** a Girl of colour Emancipated by the said Will was this day numbered & Registered in the Clerks Office of the said Court, pursuant to the provisions of the act of Assembly in that case made and provided- The said MARTHA CRADDOCK is a child of LEWIS & WINNEY CRADDOCK and is of light complexion, ten years old, four feet three inches high, has a small scar on the forehead near the edge of the hair- Given under my hand as Clerk of the said Court this 5th day of January 1827-   Will: Tunstall

J Craddock- Virginia Pittsylvania County to wit- No 98- At the instance of John Ward and Lynch Dillard Executors of the last Will and Testament of John Ward Senior Deceased duly proven and recorded in the Court of said County **JOHN CRADDOCK** a boy of colour Emancipated by the said Will was this day numbered & registered in the Clerks Office of the said Court, pursuant to the provisions of the act of Assembly in that case made and provided- The said JOHN CRADDOCK is a child of LEWIS & WINNEY CRADDOCK and is of rather light complexion, twelve years old, four feet three and a half inches high, no mark or scar apparent- Given under my hand as Clerk of the said Court this 5th day of January 1827-   Will: Tunstall

CA Craddock- Virginia Pittsylvania County to wit- No 99- At the instance of John Ward and Lynch Dillard Executors of the last Will and Testament of John Ward Senior Deceased duly proven and recorded in the [p 45] Court of said County **CORY ANN CRADDOCK** a Girl of colour Emancipated by the said Will was this day numbered & registered in the Clerks Office of the said Court, pursuant to the provisions of the Act of Assembly in that case made and provided- The said CORY ANN CRADDOCK is a child of LEWIS & WINNEY CRADDOCK and is of light complexion, eight years old, three feet eleven inches high, has a scar on her forehead over her left eye- Given under my hand as Clerk of the said Court this 5th day of January 1827- Will: Tunstall

P Craddock- Virginia Pittsylvania County to wit- No 100- At the instance of John Ward and Lynch Dillard Executors of the last Will and Testament of John Ward Senior Decd duly proven and recorded in the Court of said County **PERMELIA CRADDOCK** a Girl of colour Emancipated by the said Will was this day numbered & registered in the Clerks Office of the said Court, pursuant to the provisions of the act of Assembly in that case made and provided- The said PERMELIA CRADDOCK is a child of LEWIS & WINNEY CRADDOCK and is of bright complexion, five years old, three feet six and a half inches high, has a scar of a white appearance on the back of her right hand occasioned by a burn- Given under my hand as Clerk of the said Court this 5th day of January 1827-   Will: Tunstall

M Craddock- Virginia Pittsylvania County to wit- No 101- At the instance of John Ward and Lynch Dillard Executors of the last Will and Testament of John [p 46] Ward Senior Decd duly proven and recorded in the Court of said County **MOURNING CRADDOCK** a Girl of colour Emancipated by the said Will was this day numbered & Registered in the Clerks Office of the said Court, pursuant to the provisions of the act of Assembly in that case made and provided- The said MOURNING CRADDOCK is a child of LEWIS & WINNEY CRADDOCK of light complexion, three years old, three feet high, no mark or scar apparent- Given under my hand as Clerk of the said Court this 5th day of January 1827- Will: Tunstall

Mary Craddock- Virginia Pittsylvania County to wit- No 102 At the instance of John Ward and Lynch Dillard Executors of the last Will and Testament of John Ward Senior Decd duly proven and recorded in the Court of said County **MARY CRADDOCK** a Girl of colour Emancipated by the said Will was this day numbered & Registered in the Clerks Office of the said Court, pursuant to the provisions of the Act of Assembly in that case made and provided. The said MARY CRADDOCK is a child of LEWIS & WINNEY CRADDOCK about three months old, of light complexion, no mark or scar apparent- Given under my hand as Clerk of the said Court this 5th day of January 1827-Will: Tunstall

J Greenhill- Virginia Pittsylvania County to wit- No 103- At the instance of John Ward and Lynch [p 47] Dillard Executors of the last Will and Testament of John Ward Senior Deceased duly proven and recorded in the Court of said County **JOHN GREENHILL** a man of colour Emancipated by the said Will was this day numbered & registered in the Clerks Office of the said Court, pursuant to the provisions of the act of Assembly in that case made & provided- The said JOHN GREENHILL is black seventy five years old, five feet two an eighth inches high has a small scar on the left side of his nose, the left thumb nail split by a cut & is bald- Given under my hand as Clerk of the said Court this 9th day of January 1827- Will: Tunstall

S Greenhill- Virginia Pittsylvania County to wit- No 104- At the instance of John Ward and Lynch Dillard Executors of the last Will and Testament of John Ward Senr Deceased duly proven and recorded in the Court of said County **SYLVA GREENHILL** a Woman of colour Emancipated by the said Will was this day numbered & registered in the Clerks Office of the said Court, pursuant to the provisions of the Act of Assembly in that case made and provided. The said SYLVA GREENHILL a black woman wife of JOHN GREENHILL sixty years old five feet two and three fourth inches high has a Scar on the chin rather on the right side- Given under my hand as Clerk of the said Court this 9th day of January 1827- Will: Tunstall

G Randolph- Virginia Pittsylvania County to wit- No 105- At the instance of John Ward and Lynch Dillard Executors of the last Will and Testament of John Ward Senr Deceased duly proven and recorded in the Court of said County **GILBERT RANDOLPH** a Man of colour Emancipated by the said Will was this day numbered [p 48] & registered in the Clerks Office of the said Court, pursuant to the provisions of the act of Assembly in that case made and provided. The said GILBERT RANDOLPH is a black man fifty five years old five feet one and a half inch high has a Scar on the left cheek occasioned by a burn, somewhat bald Given under my hand as Clerk of the said Court this 9th day of January 1827- Will: Tunstall

B Randolph- Virginia Pittsylvania County to wit- No 106- At the instance of John Ward and Lynch Dillard Executors of the last Will and Testament of John Ward Senior Deceased duly proven and recorded in the Court of said County **BIDDY RANDOLPH** a woman of colour emancipated by the said Will was this day numbered & registered in the Clerks Office of the said Court, pursuant to the provisions of the act of Assembly in that case made and provided. The said BIDDY RANDOLPH is a wife of GILBERT RANDOLPH, is a black woman sixty five or seventy years old five feet two and a half inches high her right thumb stubbed occasioned by a felon and her right forefinger nail split or broken occasioned by a whitlow- Given under my hand as Clerk of the said Court this 9th day of January 1827- Will: Tunstall

C Tolbert- Virginia Pittsylvania County to wit- No 107- At the instance of John Ward and Lynch Dillard Executors of the last Will and Testament of John Ward Senior Deceased duly proven and recorded in the Court of said County **CHRISTOPHER TOLBERT** a Man of colour emancipated by the said Will was this day numbered [p 49] & registered in the Clerks Office of the said Court, pursuant to the provisions of the act of assembly in that case made and provided. The said CHRISTOPHER TOLBERT is a black man sixty five years old five feet six inches and three quarters high has a long scar on the right side of the head and is bald- Given under my hand as Clerk of the said Court this 9th day of January 1827- Will: Tunstall

J Farmer- Virginia Pittsylvania County to wit- No 108- At the instance of John Ward and Lynch Dillard Executors of the last Will and Testament of John Ward Senior Deceased duly proven and recorded in the Court of said County **JAMES FARMER** a Man of colour Emancipated by the said Will was this day numbered & registered in the Clerks Office of the said Court, pursuant to the provisions of the act of Assembly in that case made and provided. The said JAMES FARMER is a black man about forty years old five feet six and a half inches high his little finger of the right hand crooked- Given under my hand as Clerk of the said Court this 9th day of January 1827 - Will: Tunstall

H Brooks- Virginia Pittsylvania County to wit- No 109- At the instance of John Ward and Lynch Dillard Executors of the last Will and Testament of John Ward Senior Decd duly proven and recorded in the Court of said County **HOLLIDAY BROOKS** a man of colour Emancipated by the said Will was this day numbered & registered in the Clerks Office of the said Court, [p 50] pursuant to the provisions of the act of Assembly in that case made and provided- The said HOLLIDAY BROOKS is a black man forty years old five feet seven and a quarter inches high has a very small scar in the forehead over the right eye- Given under my hand as Clerk of the said Court this 9th day of January 1827- Will: Tunstall

J Williams- Virginia Pittsylvania County to wit- No 110- At the instance of John Ward and Lynch Dillard Executors of the last Will and Testament of John Ward Senior Deceased duly proven and recorded in the Court of said County **JACKSON WILLIAMS** a Man of colour Emancipated by the said Will was this day Numbered & Registered in the Clerks Office of the said Court, pursuant to the provisions of the act of Assembly in that case made and provided. The said JACKSON WILLIAMS is a black man forty years old five feet five and a half inches high has a scar near the right ear one on the left cheek and a hole on the right cheek occasioned as he says by the tooth ach [sic]. Given under my hand as Clerk of the said Court this 9th day of January 1827- Will: Tunstall

W Tantarobogus- Virginia Pittsylvania County to wit- No 111- At the instance of John Ward and Lynch Dillard Executors of the last Will and Testament of John Ward Senior Deceased duly proven and recorded in the Court of said County **WILLIAM TANTAROBOGUS** of colour Emancipated by the said Will was this day numbered & [p 51] registered in the Clerks Office of the said Court, pursuant to the provisions of the act of Assembly in that case made and provided. The said WILLIAM TANTAROBOGUS is a black man supposed to be fifty five years old five feet one and a quarter inch high has a scar on the left eye brow and on the left side of the head the little finger on the left hand stiff- Given under my hand as Clerk of the said Court this 9th day of January 1827- Will: Tunstall

S Ward- Virginia Pittsylvania County to wit- No 112- At the instance of John Ward and Lynch Dillard Executors of the last Will and Testament of John Ward Senr Deceased duly proven and recorded in the Court of said County **SAMUEL WARD** a Man of colour Emancipated by the said Will was this day numbered & registered in the Clerks Office of the said Court, pursuant to the provisions of the act of Assembly in that case made and provided. The said SAMUEL WARD is adjudged to be sixty years of age five feet five and a half inches high his colour between that of a black and Mulatto, no apparent mark or scar, has a gap between his two upper front teeth- Given under my hand as Clerk of the said Court this 10th day of January 1827- Will: Tunstall

L Ward- Virginia Pittsylvania County to wit- No 113- At the instance of John Ward and Lynch Dillard Executors of the last Will and Testament of John Ward Senior Deceased duly proven and recorded in the Court of said County **LUCY WARD** a woman of colour [p 52] emancipated by the said Will was this day numbered and registered in the Clerks Office of the said Court, pursuant to the provisions of the act of Assembly in that case made and provided- The said LUCY WARD is the wife of SAMUEL WARD, & is a black woman fifty six years of age five feet four and a quarter inches high has thick bushy Gray hair and an uneven set of teeth- Given under my hand as Clerk of the said Court this 10th day of January 1827- Will: Tunstall

A Ward- Virginia Pittsylvania County to wit- No 114- At the instance of John Ward and Lynch Dillard Executors of the last Will and Testament of John Ward Senior Deceased duly proven and recorded in the Court of said County **AARON WARD** a Man of colour Emancipated by the said Will was this day numbered and registered in the Clerks Office of the said Court, pursuant to the provisions of the act of Assembly in that case made and provided- The said AARON WARD is a black man son of SAMUEL [WARD] & LUCY WARD, thirty four years of age five feet seven inches high, no apparent mark or scar- Given under my hand as Clerk of the said Court this 10th day of January 1827- Will: Tunstall

H Ward- Virginia Pittsylvania County to wit- No 115- At the instance of John Ward and Lynch Dillard Executors of the last Will and Testament of John Ward Senior Deceased duly proven and recorded in [p 53] the Court of said County **HANDY WARD** a Man of colour Emancipated by the said Will was this day numbered and registered in the Clerks Office of the said Court, pursuant to the provisions of the act of Assembly in that case made and provided- The said HANDY WARD son of SAMUEL WARD is a man of light complexion twenty years old, five feet eight and a half inches high, has a small scar on the left side of the forehead near the hair- Given under my hand as Clerk of the said Court this 10th day of January 1827- Will: Tunstall

C Ward- Virginia Pittsylvania County to wit- No 116- At the instance of John Ward and Lynch Dillard Executors of the last Will and Testament of John Ward Senior Deceased duly proven and recorded in the Court of said County **CHARLES WARD** a boy of colour Emancipated by the said will was this day numbered and registered in the Clerks Office of the said Court, pursuant to the provisions of the Act of Assembly in that case made and provided-

The said CHARLES WARD son of SAMUEL WARD is a boy of light complexion four feet eleven and a quarter inches high twelve years next July, has a small scar over the right eye near the hair and a small one in a cross direction of the right temple- Given under my hand as Clerk of the said Court this 10th day of January 1827- Will: Tunstall

M Ward- Virginia Pittsylvania County to wit- No 117- At the instance of John Ward and Lynch Dillard Executors of the last Will and Testament of [p 54] John Ward Senior Deceased duly proven and recorded in the Court of said County **MARY WARD** a Woman of colour emancipated by the said Will was this day numbered and registered in the Clerks Office of the said Court, pursuant to the provisions of the act of Assembly in that case made and provided- The said MARY WARD daughter of SAMUEL WARD is a Mulatto Woman twenty two years old five feet six and three fourth inches high short curled hair no apparent mark or scar, except a black Mole on the side of the jaw near the Ear- Given under my hand as Clerk of the said Court this 10th day of January 1827- Will: Tunstall

R Ward- Virginia Pittsylvania County to wit- No 118- At the instance of John Ward and Lynch Dillard Executors of the last Will and Testament of John Ward Senior Deceased duly proven and recorded in the Court of said County **RACHEL WARD** a woman of colour emancipated by the said Will was this day numbered and registered in the Clerks Office of the said Court, pursuant to the provisions of the act of Assembly in that case made and provided- The said RACHEL WARD daughter of SAMUEL [WARD] & LUCY [WARD] is a black woman seventeen years old five feet five and a half inches high has a small scar over the right eye about the size and length of a pin & has short hair- Given under my hand as Clerk of the said Court this 10th day of January 1827- Will: Tunstall

P Ward- Virginia Pittsylvania County to wit- No 119- At the instance of John Ward and Lynch Dillard Executors of the last Will and Testament of John Ward Senior Deceased duly proven and recorded in [p 55] the Court of said County **PATSY WARD** a Girl of colour Emancipated by the said Will was this day numbered and registered in the Clerks Office of the said Court, pursuant to the provisions of the act of Assembly in that case made and provided- The said PATSY WARD a daughter of SAMUEL [WARD] & LUCY [WARD] is a Girl of light complexion ten years old four feet nine and a quarter inches high, no apparent mark or scar, has short hair- Given under my hand as Clerk of the said Court this 10th day of January 1827- Will: Tunstall

H Ward- Virginia Pittsylvania County to wit- No 120- At the instance of John Ward and Lynch Dillard Executors of the last Will and Testament of John Ward Senior Deceased duly proven and recorded in the Court of said County **HANNAH WARD** a woman of colour emancipated by the said Will was this day numbered and registered in the Clerks Office of the said Court, pursuant to the provisions of the act of Assembly in that case made and provided- The said HANNAH WARD daughter of SAMUEL [WARD] & LUCY [WARD] is a black woman twenty six years old five feet five and a quarter inches high has a scar on the back of the neck occasioned by a burn, her little finger of the left hand much crooked, has lost two of her upper front teeth- Given under my hand as Clerk of the said Court this 10th day of January 1827- Will: Tunstall

Charles- Virginia Pittsylvania County to wit- No 121- At the instance of John Ward and Lynch [p 55] Dillard Executors of the last Will and Testament of John Ward Senior Deceased duly proven and recorded in the Court of said County **CHARLES [WARD]** a boy of colour Emancipated by the said will was this day numbered and Registered in the Clerks Office of the said Court, pursuant to the provisions of the Act of Assembly in that case made and provided- The said CHARLES is a child of HANNAH WARD, about twelve months old of light complexion- Given under my hand as Clerk of the said Court this 10th day of January 1827- Will: Tunstall

Jno: Ward- Virginia Pittsylvania County to wit- No 122- At the instance of John Ward and Lynch Dillard Executors of the last Will and Testament of John Ward Senior Deceased duly proven and recorded in the.....Court of said County **JOHN WARD** a boy of colour Emancipated by the said will was this day numbered and

Registered in the Clerks Office of the said Court, pursuant to the provisions of the Act of Assembly in that case made and provided- The said JOHN WARD son of HANNAH WARD, is a black boy in his eleventh year four feet eight and three fourth inches high no apparent mark or scar- Given under my hand as Clerk of the said Court this 10th day of January 1827- Will: Tunstall

H Ward- Virginia Pittsylvania County to wit- No 123- At the instance of John Ward and Lynch Dillard Executors of the last Will and Testament of [p 57] John Ward Senior Deceased duly proven and recorded in the Court of said County **HARRISON WARD** a boy of colour emancipated by the said will was this day numbered and Registered in the Clerks Office of the said Court, pursuant to the provisions of the Act of Assembly in that case made and provided- The said HARRISON WARD son of HANNAH WARD, is a black boy in his eighth year four feet three inches and three quarters high has no apparent mark or scar- Given under my hand as Clerk of the said Court this 10th day of January 1827-Will: Tunstall

L Ward- Virginia Pittsylvania County to wit- No 124- At the instance of John Ward and Lynch Dillard Executors of the last Will and Testament of John Ward Senior Deceased duly proven and recorded in the Court of said County **LINDY WARD** a boy [sic] of colour emancipated by the said will was this day numbered and Registered in the Clerks Office of the said Court, pursuant to the provisions of the Act of Assembly in that case made and provided- The said LINDEY WARD daughter of HANNAH WARD, is of light complexion eight years old and twin sister of HARRISON WARD, four feet & half inch high, has a scar over the joint of the wrist of the right hand about the size of a marble- Given under my hand as Clerk of the said Court this 10 day of January 1827- Will: Tunstall

S Ward- Virginia Pittsylvania County to wit- No 125- At the instance of John Ward and Lynch Dillard Executors of the last Will and Testament of [p 58] John Ward Senr Deceased duly proven and recorded in the Court of said County **SIMON WARD** a boy of colour emancipated by the said will was this day numbered and Registered in the Clerks Office of the said Court, pursuant to the provisions of the Act of Assembly in that case made and provided-

The said SIMON WARD is a son of HANNAH WARD, is a black boy four years old three feet four inches and a quarter high, no apparent mark or scar- Given under my hand as Clerk of the said Court this 10th day of January 1827- Will: Tunstall

J Ward- Virginia Pittsylvania County to wit- No 126- At the instance of John Ward and Lynch Dillard Executors of the last Will and Testament of John Ward Senr Deceased duly proven and recorded in the Court of said County **JACK WARD** a Man of colour Emancipated by the said will was this day numbered and registered in the Clerks Office of the said Court, pursuant to the provisions of the Act of Assembly in that case made and provided- The said JACK WARD son of SAMUEL WARD is of light complexion five feet nine and a quarter inches high about thirty years old, strong and stout made, no apparent mark or Scar- Given under my hand as Clerk of the said Court this 10th day of January 1827- Will: Tunstall

Christian- Virginia Pittsylvania County to wit- No 127- At the instance of John Ward and Lynch Dillard Executors of the last Will and Testament of John Ward Senior Deceased duly proven and recorded in [p 59] the Court of said County **CHRISTIAN [WARD]** a woman of colour emancipated by the said will was this day numbered and registered in the Clerks Office of the said Court, pursuant to the provisions of the act of Assembly in that case made and provided- The said CHRISTIAN [WARD] wife of JACK WARD is of light complexion, about twenty years old has thick bushy hair five feet seven and a quarter inches high, a Scar on the right side of the chin about the size & length of a pin- Given under my hand as Clerk of the said Court this 10th day of January 1827- Will: Tunstall

L Ward- Virginia Pittsylvania County to wit- No. 128- At the instance of John Ward and Lynch Dillard Executors of the last Will and Testament of John Ward Senior Deceased duly proven and recorded in the Court of said County **LYNCH WARD** a boy of colour Emancipated by the said will was this day numbered and Registered in the Clerks Office of the said Court, pursuant to the provisions of the act of Assembly in that case made and provided- The said LYNCH WARD is a son of JACK WARD, is two years old two feet ten inches high of light complexion, no apparent mark or scar- Given under my hand as Clerk of the said Court this 10th day of January 1827- Will: Tunstall

Jas Ward- Virginia Pittsylvania County to wit- No 129- At the instance of John Ward and Lynch Dillard Executors of the last Will and Testament of John Ward Senior Deceased duly proven and recorded in the Court of said County **JAMES WARD** a man of colour [p 60] Emancipated by the said will was this day numbered and registered in the Clerks Office of the said Court, pursuant to the provisions of the act of Assembly in that case made and provided- The said JAMES WARD a son of SAMUEL WARD, is of light complexion twenty five years old five feet nine inches high stout made has a scar on the side of his forefinger of the left hand opposite the first joint- Given under my hand as Clerk of the said Court this 10th day of January 1827- Will: Tunstall

J Callaway- Virginia Pittsylvania County to wit- No. 130- At the instance of John Ward and Lynch Dillard Executors of the last Will and Testament of John Ward Senior Deceased duly proven and recorded in the Court of said County **JACK CALLAWAY** a man of colour Emancipated by the said will was this day numbered and Registered in the Clerks Office of the said Court, pursuant to the provisions of the act of Assembly in that case made and provided- The said JACK CALLAWAY is a black man about forty eight years of age, five feet six and a half inches high, of light complexion, has a small scar across the forehead Given under my hand as Clerk of the said Court this 10th day of January 1827- Will: Tunstall

Letty- Virginia Pittsylvania County to wit- No 131- At the instance of John Ward and Lynch Dillard Executors of the last Will and Testament of John Ward Senior Deceased duly proven and recorded in the Court of said County **LETTY [CALLAWAY]** a woman of colour emancipated by the said will was this day numbered [p 61] and registered in the Clerks Office of the said Court, pursuant to the provisions of the Act of Assembly in that case made and provided- The said LETTY wife of JACK CALLAWAY is black, five feet high, appears to be about forty five years old, has a Scar on the brow of the left eye, and has lost some of her teeth- Given under my hand as Clerk of the said Court this 10th day of January 1827- Will: Tunstall

P Callaway- Virginia Pittsylvania County to wit- No 132- At the instance of John Ward and Lynch Dillard Executors of the last Will and Testament of John Ward Senior Deceased duly proven and recorded in the Court of said County **POLLY CALLAWAY** a Girl of colour Emancipated by the said will was this day numbered and registered in the Clerks Office of the said Court, pursuant to the provisions of the act of Assembly in that case made and provided- The said POLLY CALLAWAY daughter of JACK CALLAWAY, is nine years old, of light complexion, four feet four and three quarters inches high, no apparent mark or scar Given under my hand as Clerk of the said Court this 10th day of January 1827- Will: Tunstall

C Allen- Virginia Pittsylvania County to wit- No 133- At the instance of John Ward and Lynch Dillard Executors of the last Will and Testament of John Ward Senior Deceased duly proven and recorded in the Court of said County **CAEZAR ALLEN** a man of colour Emancipated by the said will was this day numbered and Registered in the Clerks Office of the said Court, [p 62] pursuant to the provisions of the act of Assembly in that case made and provided- The said CAEZAR ALLEN is a black man about thirty seven years old has a small Scar between his eyes and on the back of the left hand, has lost all his toes from the effects of frost- Given under my hand as Clerk of the said Court this 11th day of January 1827 - Will: Tunstall

D Ward- Virginia Pittsylvania County to wit- No 134- At the instance of John Ward and Lynch Dillard Executors of the last Will and Testament of John Ward Senior Deceased duly proven and recorded in the Court of said County **DAVID WARD** a man of colour Emancipated by the said will was this day numbered and Registered in the Clerks Office of the said Court, pursuant to the provisions of the act of Assembly in that case made and provided- The said DAVID WARD is a stout Mulatto Man five feet ten inches high thirty years of age 25th of last Month Decemr, has a small scar about the middle of his forehead about the length and size of a pin and one on the back of his right hand about an inch and a half long occasioned by a cut- Given under my hand as Clerk of the said Court this 11th day of January 1827- Will: Tunstall

Nancy Ward- Virginia Pittsylvania County to wit- No 135- At the instance of John Ward and Lynch Dillard Executors of the last Will and Testament of John Ward Senior Deceased duly proven and recorded in [p 63] the Court of said County **NANCY WARD** a Woman of colour Emancipated by the said will was this day numbered and Registered in the Clerks Office of the said Court, pursuant to the provisions of the act of Assembly in that case made and provided- The said NANCY WARD is a Mulatto Woman about twenty eight years of age five feet four inches high long black hair has no apparent mark or scar but has the appearance of a Wen on the right side of the throat, her two upper front teeth decayed- Given under my hand as Clerk of the said Court this 11th day of January 1827- Will: Tunstall

G Ward- Virginia Pittsylvania County to wit- No 136- At the instance of John Ward and Lynch Dillard Executors of the last Will and Testament of John Ward Senior Deceased duly proven and recorded in the Court of said County **GEORGE WARD** a boy of colour Emancipated by the said Will was this day numbered and Registered in the Clerks Office of the said Court, pursuant to the provisions of the act of Assembly in that case made and provided- The said GEORGE WARD is a son of NANCY, is a very bright Mulatto sixteen years old five feet nine inches high has black bushy hair, and a scar on the right side of his nose Given under my hand as Clerk of the said Court this 11th day of January 1827- Will: Tunstall

J Ward- Virginia Pittsylvania County to wit- No 137- At the instance of John Ward and Lynch Dillard Executors of the last Will and Testament of John Ward Senior Deceased duly proven and recorded in [p 64] the Court of sd County **JOSEPH WARD** a boy of colour Emancipated by the said Will was this day numbered and Registered in the Clerks Office of the said Court, pursuant to the provisions of the act of Assembly in that case made and provided- The said JOSEPH WARD is a son of NANCY [WARD], is a Mulatto boy twelve years old five feet high has a scar on the left side of the forehead one on the right side near the hair and one on the thumb of the left hand between the joints- Given under my hand as Clerk of the said Court this 11th day of January 1827- Will: Tunstall

M Ward- Virginia Pittsylvania County to wit- No 138- At the instance of John Ward and Lynch Dillard Executors of the last Will and Testament of John Ward Senior Deceased duly proven and recorded in the Court of said County **MOLLEY WARD** a Woman of colour Emancipated by the said will was this day numbered and Registered in the Clerks Office of the said Court, pursuant to the provisions of the act of Assembly in that case made and provided- The said MOLLY WARD is a black woman about sixty years old five feet one inch high, has a Scar through the brow of the left eye in a cross direction- Given under my hand as Clerk of the said Court this 11th day of January 1827- Will: Tunstall

A Ward- Virginia Pittsylvania County to wit- No 139- At the instance of John Ward and Lynch Dillard Executors of the last Will and Testament of John Ward Senior Deceased duly proven and recorded in [p 65] the Court of said County **AMANDA WARD** a Girl of colour emancipated by the said will was this day numbered and Registered in the Clerks Office of the said Court, pursuant to the provisions of the act of Assembly in that case made and provided- The said AMANDA WARD is a small bright Mulatto Girl in her fourth year, long straight hair, about three feet high, has several large Scars on the left side of the face occasioned by the Kings Evil- Given under my hand as Clerk of the said Court this 11th day of January 1827- Will: Tunstall

P Lynch- Virginia Pittsylvania County to wit No 140- At the instance of John Ward and Lynch Dillard Executors of the last Will and Testament of John Ward Senior Deceased duly proven and recorded in the Court of said County **PHIL LYNCH** a boy of colour Emancipated by the said will was this day numbered and Registered in the Clerks Office of the said Court, pursuant to the provisions of the act of Assembly in that case made and provided The said PHIL LYNCH is a boy of light complexion about fifteen years old four feet ten and three fourth inches high, has a Scar under the right eye and a small dark coloured mark on the left cheek. Given under my hand as Clerk of the said Court this 11th day of January 1827- Will: Tunstall

C Lynch- Virginia Pittsylvania County to wit- No 141- At the instance of John Ward and Lynch Dillard Executors of the last Will and Testament of John Ward Senior Deceased duly proven and recorded in the Court of said County **CHANY LYNCH** a Girl of colour [p 66] Emancipated by the said will was this day numbered and Registered in the Clerks Office of the said Court, pursuant to the provisions of the act of Assembly in that case made and provided- The said CHANEY LYNCH is a Girl of light complexion about twelve years old five feet and a half inch high, no apparent mark or Scar- Given under my hand as Clerk of the said Court this 11th day of January 1827- Will: Tunstall

Jos Mundal- Virginia Pittsylvania County to wit- No 142- At the instance of John Ward and Lynch Dillard Executors of the last Will and Testament of John Ward Senior Deceased duly proven and recorded in the Court of said County **JOSEPH MUNDAL** a Man of colour emancipated by the said will was this day numbered and Registered in the Clerks Office of the said Court, pursuant to the provisions of the act of Assembly in that case made and provided. The said JOSEPH MUNDAL is a black Man forty five years old five feet three and three fourths inches high has a scar on the back of the right hand and also on the wrist joint, the little finger of the left hand stiff in the last joint- Given under my hand as Clerk of the said Court this 12th day of January 1827- Will: Tunstall

C Mundal- Virginia Pittsylvania County to wit- No 143- At the instance of John Ward and Lynch Dillard Executors of the last Will and Testament of John Ward Senior Deceased duly proven and recorded in [p 67] the Court of said County **CRITTY MUNDAL** a Woman of colour emancipated by the said will was this day numbered and Registered in the Clerks Office of the said Court, pursuant to the provisions of the act of Assembly in that case made and provided- The said CRITTY MUNDAL is a black woman about thirty five years old five feet six and a half inches high has a scar on the back of the right hand and two small ones over the right eye- Given under my hand as Clerk of the said Court this 12th day of January 1827- Will: Tunstall

Peter- Virginia Pittsylvania County to wit- No 144- At the instance of John Ward and Lynch Dillard Executors of the last Will and Testament of John Ward Senior Deceased duly proven and recorded in the Court of said County **PETER [MUNDAL]** a boy of colour Emancipated by the said Will was this day numbered and Registered in the Clerks Office of the said Court, pursuant to the provisions of the act of Assembly in that case made and provided- The said PETER is a child of CRITTY MUNDAL & is black, four months old- Given under my hand as Clerk of the said Court this 12th day of January 1827- Will: Tunstall

E Mundal- Virginia Pittsylvania County to wit- No 145- At the instance of John Ward and Lynch Dillard Executors of the last Will and Testament of John Ward Senior Deceased duly proven and recorded in the Court of said County **ELIZA MUNDAL** a Girl of colour emancipated by the said Will was this day numbered and Registered in the Clerks Office of the said Court, [p 68] pursuant to the provisions of the act of Assembly in that case made and provided- The said ELIZA MUNDAL daughter of CRITTY MUNDAL is a black girl four foot two inches and a half high, twelve years old has no apparent mark or scar- Given under my hand as Clerk of the said Court this 12th day of January 1827- Will: Tunstall

Tho: Mundal- Virginia Pittsylvania County to wit- No 146- At the instance of John Ward and Lynch Dillard Executors of the last Will and Testament of John Ward Senior Deceased duly proven and recorded in the Court of said County **THOMAS MUNDAL** a boy of colour emancipated by the said Will was this day numbered and registered in the Clerks Office of the said Court, pursuant to the provisions of the act of Assembly in that case made and provided- The said THOMAS MUNDAL is a black boy son of CRITTY MUNDAL four feet three inches high, nine years old, no mark or scar apparent- Given under my hand as Clerk of the said Court this 12th day of January 1827- Will: Tunstall

B Mundal- Virginia Pittsylvania County to wit- No 147- At the instance of John Ward and Lynch Dillard Executors of the last Will and Testament of John Ward Senior Deceased duly proven and recorded in the Court of said County **BETSY MUNDAL** a Girl of colour Emancipated by the said Will was this day numbered and [p 69] registered in the Clerks Office of the said Court, pursuant to the provisions of the act of Assembly in that case made and provided- The said BETSY MUNDAL is of light complexion, daughter of CRITTY MUNDAL six years old, four feet & half an inch high, has a scar from the elbow to the wrist of the left arm occasioned by a burn- Given under my hand as Clerk of the said Court this 12th day of January 1827- Will: Tunstall

L Mundal- Virginia Pittsylvania County to wit- No 148- At the instance of John Ward and Lynch Dillard Executors of the last Will and Testament of John Ward Senior Deceased duly proven and recorded in the Court of said County **LAURENZO MUNDAL** a boy of colour Emancipated by the said Will was this day numbered and registered in the Clerks Office of the said Court, pursuant to the provisions of the act of Assembly in that case made and provided- The said LAURENZO MUNDAL is a black boy son of CRITTY MUNDAL five years old three feet eleven inches high has no mark or scar apparent- Given under my hand as Clerk of the said Court this 12th day of January 1827- Will: Tunstall

W Mundal- Virginia Pittsylvania County to wit- No 149- At the instance of John Ward and Lynch Dillard Executors of the last Will and Testament of John Ward Senior Deceased duly proven and recorded in the Court of said County **WOODSON MUNDAL** a boy of colour [p 70] Emancipated by the said Will was this day numbered and registered in the Clerks Office of the said Court, pursuant to the provisions of the act of Assembly in that case made and provided- The said WOODSON MUNDAL is a black boy son of CRITTY MUNDAL three feet five inches high, four years old, has a scar on the left tempile [sic] and on the left wrist and a burn on the right wrist which will probably leave a considerable Scar- Given under my hand as Clerk of the said Court this 12th day of January 1827- Will: Tunstall

Wm Mundal- Virginia Pittsylvania County to wit- No 150- At the instance of John Ward and Lynch Dillard Executors of the last Will and Testament of John Ward Senior Deceased duly proven and recorded in the Court of said County **WILLIAM MUNDAL** a boy of colour Emancipated by the said Will was this day numbered and registered in the Clerks Office of the said Court, pursuant to the provisions of the act of assembly in that case made and provided- The said WILLIAM MUNDAL is a black boy son of CRITTY MUNDAL, three feet one and three fourth inches high, three years old has a scar on the forehead over the left eye- Given under my hand as Clerk of the said Court this 12th day of January 1827- Will: Tunstall

D Mundal- Virginia Pittsylvania County to wit- No 151- At the instance of John Ward and Lynch Dillard Executors of the last Will and Testament of John Ward Senior Deceased duly proven and recorded in [p 71] the Court of said County **DOCTOR MUNDAL** a boy of colour Emancipated by the said Will was this day numbered and registered in the Clerks Office of the said Court, pursuant to the provisions of the act of assembly in that case made and provided- The said DOCTOR MUNDAL is a black boy son of CRITTY MUNDAL two years old about two feet eight inches high, no scar or mark apparent- Given under my hand as Clerk of the said Court this 12th day of January 1827- Will: Tunstall

Jos Mundal- Virginia Pittsylvania County to wit- No 152- At the instance of John Ward and Lynch Dillard Executors of the last Will and Testament of John Ward Senior Deceased duly proven and recorded in the Court of said County **JOSEPH MUNDAL** a boy of colour Emancipated by the said Will was this day numbered and registered in the Clerks Office of the said Court, pursuant to the provisions of the act of Assembly in that case made and provided- The said JOSEPH MUNDAL is a black boy son of CRITTY MUNDAL about eighteen months old, two feet seven inches high, has a black spot (mark) on the right cheek- Given under my hand as Clerk of the said Court this 12th day of January 1827- Will: Tunstall

R West- Virginia Pittsylvania County to wit- No 153- At the instance of John Ward and Lynch Dillard Executors of the last Will and Testament of John Ward Senior Deceased duly proven and recorded in [p 72] the Court of said County **ROWLAND WEST** a Man of colour emancipated by the said will was this day numbered and Registered in the Clerks Office of the said Court, pursuant to the provisions of the act of Assembly in that case made and provided- The said ROWLAND WEST is a black Man twenty five years old five feet seven inches high, has a scar under the left eye Given under my hand as Clerk of the said Court this 12th day of January 1827- Will: Tunstall

Clary West- Virginia Pittsylvania County to wit- No 154- At the instance of John Ward and Lynch Dillard Executors of the last Will and Testament of John Ward Senior Deceased duly proven and recorded in the Court of said County **CLARY WEST** a Woman of colour emancipated by the said will was this day numbered and Registered in the Clerks Office of the said Court, pursuant to the provisions of the act of Assembly in that case made and provided- The said CLARY WEST wife of ROWLAND WEST is a black woman twenty three years old five feet two inches high has a very small scar on the upper lip occasioned by a cut- Given under my hand as Clerk of the said Court this 12th day of January 1827- Will: Tunstall

Otey- Virginia Pittsylvania County to wit- No 155- At the instance of John Ward and Lynch Dillard Executors of the last Will and Testament of John Ward Senior Deceased duly proven and recorded in [p 73] the Court of said County **OTEY [WEST]** a boy of colour Emancipated by the said Will was this day numbered and registered in the Clerks Office of the said Court, pursuant to the provisions of the Act of Assembly in that case made and provided- The said OTEY is a child of CLARY WEST, of light complexion about five months old- Given under my hand as Clerk of the said Court this 12th day of January 1827   Will: Tunstall

N West- Virginia Pittsylvania County to wit- No 156- At the instance of John Ward and Lynch Dillard Executors of the last Will and Testament of John Ward Senior Deceased duly proven and recorded in the Court of said County **NANCY WEST** a Girl of colour Emancipated by the said Will was this day numbered and registered in the Clerks Office of the said Court, pursuant to the provisions of the Act of Assembly in that case made and provided- The said NANCY WEST is a black Girl daughter of CLARY WEST, seven years old three feet eleven and three fourths inches high, no mark or scar apparent- Given under my hand as Clerk of the said Court this 12th day of January 1827-   Will: Tunstall

W West- Virginia Pittsylvania County to wit- No 157- At the instance of John Ward and Lynch Dillard Executors of the last Will and Testament of John Ward Senior Deceased duly proven and recorded in the Court of said County **WALKER WEST** a Girl [sic] of colour [p 74] Emancipated by the said Will was this day numbered and registered in the Clerks Office of the said Court, pursuant to the provisions of the Act of Assembly in that case made and provided- The said WALKER WEST is a dark Mulatto boy son of CLARY WEST, five years old next March, three feet four inches high, no mark or scar- Given under my hand as Clerk of the said Court this 12th day of January 1827- Will: Tunstall

Jincey West- Virginia Pittsylvania County to wit- No 158- At the instance of John Ward and Lynch Dillard Executors of the last Will and Testament of John Ward Senior Deceased duly proven and recorded in the Court of said County **JINCEY WEST** a Girl of colour emancipated by the said Will was this day numbered and registered in the Clerks Office of the said Court, pursuant to the provisions of the act of Assembly in that case made and provided- The said JINCEY WEST is a black Girl daughter of CLARY WEST, two years old, two feet nine inches high, no mark or scar apparent- Given under my hand as Clerk of the said Court this 12th day of January 1827- Will: Tunstall

R Johnson- Virginia Pittsylvania County to wit- No 159- At the instance of John Ward and Lynch Dillard Executors of the last Will and Testament of John Ward Senior Deceased duly proven and recorded in the Court of said County **RACHEL JOHNSON** a Woman of colour [p 75] Emancipated by the said will was this day numbered and Registered in the Clerks Office of the said Court, pursuant to the provisions of the act of Assembly in that case made and provided- The said RACHEL JOHNSON is a black woman about twenty six years old five feet four and a half inches high has scars on both hands occasioned by burns and a long scar on the right little finger from cutting off a fifth finger Given under my hand as Clerk of the said Court this 12th day of January 1827- Will: Tunstall

Sophia- Virginia Pittsylvania County to wit- No 160- At the instance of John Ward and Lynch Dillard Executors of the last Will and Testament of John Ward Senior Deceased duly proven and recorded in the Court of said County **SOPHIA [JOHNSON]** a Girl of colour emancipated by the said Will was this day numbered and registered in the Clerks Office of the said Court, pursuant to the provisions of the Act of Assembly in that case made and provided- The said SOPHIA is a mulatto child of RACHEL JOHNSON, about eighteen months old- Given under my hand as Clerk of the said Court this 12th day of January 1827- Will: Tunstall

Geo Johnson- Virginia Pittsylvania County to wit- No 161- At the instance of John Ward and Lynch Dillard Executors of the last Will and Testament of John Ward Senior Deceased duly proven and recorded in the Court of said County **GEORGE JOHNSON** a man [sic] of colour Emancipated by the said Will was this day numbered [p 76] and registered in the Clerks Office of the said Court, pursuant to the provisions of the act of Assembly in that case made and provided- The said GEORGE JOHNSON is a black boy ten years old four feet eight and three fourth inches high, has a scar under the left temple- Given under my hand as Clerk of the said Court this 12th day of January 1827- Will: Tunstall

A Johnson- Virginia Pittsylvania County to wit- No 162- At the instance of John Ward and Lynch Dillard Executors of the last Will and Testament of John Ward Senior Deceased duly proven and recorded in the Court of said County **ANNACA JOHNSON** a Girl of colour emancipated by the said Will was this day numbered and registered in the Clerks Office of the said Court, pursuant to the provisions of the act of Assembly in that case made and provided- The said ANNACA JOHNSON is a black Girl eight years old four feet two and a half inches high has a scar on the forehead near the hair and one near the corner of the left eye Given under my hand as Clerk of the said Court this 12th day of January 1827- Will: Tunstall

I Ward- Virginia Pittsylvania County to wit- No 163- At the instance of John Ward and Lynch Dillard Executors of the last Will and Testament of John Ward Senior Deceased duly proven and recorded in the Court of said County **ISBEL WARD** a Woman of colour emancipated by the said will was this day numbered and [p 77] Registered in the Clerks Office of the said Court, pursuant to the provisions of the act of Assembly in that case made and provided The said ISBEL WARD is a black woman forty five years

old five feet three inches high has a large Scar on the right arm just above the wrist and one on the left cheek- Given under my hand as Clerk of the said Court this 12th day of January 1827-
Will: Tunstall

P Ward- Virginia Pittsylvania County to wit- No 164- At the instance of John Ward and Lynch Dillard Executors of the last Will and testament of John Ward Senior Deceased duly proven and recorded in the Court of said County **PEGGY WARD** a Girl of colour emancipated by the said will was this day numbered and Registered in the Clerks Office of the said Court, pursuant to the provisions of the act of Assembly in that case made and provided The said PEGGY WARD is a black girl daughter of ISBEL WARD twenty one years old five feet four and a quarter inches high has a scar on the right side of the face and on the neck under the left jaw and has very large eyes- Given under my hand as Clerk of the said Court this 12th day of January 1827-   Will: Tunstall

V Ward- Virginia Pittsylvania County to wit- No 165- At the instance of John Ward and Lynch Dillard Executors of the last Will and Testament of John Ward Senior Deceased duly proven and recorded in the Court of said County **VINEY WARD** a Girl of colour emancipated by the said will was this day numbered and Registered in the Clerks Office of the said Court, [p 78] pursuant to the provisions of the act of Assembly in that case made and provided- The said VINEY WARD is a black girl daughter of ISBEL WARD twelve years old five feet high no scar or mark apparent- Given under my hand as Clerk of the said Court this 12th day of January 1827-   Will: Tunstall

P Ward- Virginia Pittsylvania County to wit- No 166- At the instance of John Ward and Lynch Dillard Executors of the last Will and testament of John Ward Senior Deceased duly proven and recorded in the Court of said County **PETER WARD** a Man [sic] of colour emancipated by the said will was this day numbered and Registered in the Clerks Office of the said Court, pursuant to the provisions of the act of Assembly in that case made and provided- The said PETER WARD is a son of ISBEL WARD of rather light complexion four feet one quarter of an inch high, Eight years old has a very small scar on the forehead- Given under my hand as

Clerk of the said Court this 12th day of January 1827- Will: Tunstall

P Henry- Virginia Pittsylvania County to wit- No 167- At the instance of John Ward and Lynch Dillard Executors of the last Will and Testament of John Ward Senior Deceased duly proven and recorded in the Court of said County **PATSEY HENRY** a Woman of colour Emancipated by the said will was this day numbered and Registered in the Clerks Office of the said Court, pursuant to the provisions of the act of Assembly in that [p 79] case made and provided- The said PATSEY HENRY is a black woman seventy five years old five feet one and a half inch high has a Scar on the right jaw near the corner of the mouth also a long one on the left wrist- Given under my hand as Clerk of the said Court this 12th day of January 1827- Will: Tunstall

C Johnson- Virginia Pittsylvania County to wit- No 168- At the instance of John Ward and Lynch Dillard Executors of the last Will and Testament of John Ward Senior Deceased duly proven and recorded in the Court of said County **CHARLES JOHNSON** a Man of colour emancipated by the said will was this day numbered and Registered in the Clerks Office of the said Court, pursuant to the provisions of the act of Assembly in that case made and provided. The said CHARLES JOHNSON is a black man five feet five & three fourth inches high, twenty eight years old last April, has a scar between the eyes and one on the upper part of the left hand- Given under my hand as Clerk of the said Court this 12th day of January 1827. Will: Tunstall

S Ward- Virginia Pittsylvania County to wit- No 169- At the instance of John Ward and Lynch Dillard Executors of the last Will and Testament of John Ward Senior Deceased duly proven and recorded in the Court of said County **SIMON WARD** a Man of colour Emancipated by the said will was this day numbered and Registered in the Clerks Office of the said Court, pursuant to the provisions of the act of Assembly in that case made and provided- The said SIMON WARD is a man of light complexion twenty six years old five feet nine and [p 80] a half inches high has a small scar on his chin and a small wen on the back of the wrist of the left hand and is squint eyed- Given under my hand as Clerk of the said Court this 15th day of January 1827- Will: Tunstall

Saml Ward- Virginia Pittsylvania County to wit- No 170- At the instance of John Ward and Lynch Dillard Executors of the last Will and Testament of John Ward Senior Deceased duly proven and recorded in the Court of said County **SAMUEL WARD JUNIOR** a man of colour Emancipated by the said will was this day numbered and Registered in the Clerks Office of the said Court, pursuant to the provisions of the Act of Assembly in that case made and provided- The said SAMUEL WARD JR is a black man twenty three years old five feet eleven and a half inches high has a very small scar on his nose and one on the thick part of the right hand, several small ones on the left hand and one on the last joint of the little finger of the left hand- Given under my hand as Clerk of the said Court this 15th day of January 1827- Will: Tunstall

H Dudley- Virginia Pittsylvania County to wit- No 171- At the instance of John Ward and Lynch Dillard Executors of the last Will and Testament of John Ward Senior Deceased duly proven and recorded in the Court of said County **HENRY DUDLEY** a Man of colour Emancipated by the said Will was this day numbered and Registered in the Clerks Office of the said Court, pursuant to the provisions of the Act of Assembly in that [p 81] case made and provided- The said HENRY DUDLEY is a man of light complexion between thirty five and forty years of age five feet seven inches and a quarter high has a scar on his forehead over the left eye and one on the inside of his left little finger occasioned by a cut- Given under my hand as Clerk of the said Court this 31st day of January 1827- Will: Tunstall

D Adams- Virginia Pittsylvania County to wit- No 172- At the instance of John Ward and Lynch Dillard Executors of the last Will and Testament of John Ward Senior Deceased duly proven and recorded in the Court of said County **DAVID ADAMS** a Man of colour Emancipated by the said Will was this day numbered and Registered in the Clerks Office of the said Court, pursuant to the provisions of the Act of Assembly in that case made and provided The said DAVID ADAMS is a dark Mulatto Man about fifty years of age six feet high has a small scar on the left cheek, a small one on the left side of his chin and the end of his little finger of the left hand has been split by a cut, has lost several of his under front teeth & is a little bald- Given under my hand as Clerk of the said Court this 31st day of January 1827- Will: Tunstall

[For Registers No 173 - No 194, which also involve former slaves of John Ward, Senior, the registrations were certified correct at the February Court 1827.]

S Dudley- Virginia Pittsylvania County to wit- No 173- At the instance of John Ward and Lynch Dillard Executors of the last Will and Testament of John Ward Senior Deceased duly proven and recorded in the Court of said County **SALLY DUDLEY** a woman of colour Emancipated by the said Will was this day numbered and Registered in the Clerks Office of the said Court, [p 82] pursuant to the provisions of the act of Assembly in that case made and provided The said SALLY DUDLEY (wife of HENRY DUDLEY) a woman of light complexion, about thirty three years of age, five feet four and a half inches high has a mole or black spot on the back of the left hand Given under my hand as Clerk of the said Court this 15th day of February 1827- Will: Tunstall

M Adams- Virginia Pittsylvania County to wit- No 174- At the instance of John Ward and Lynch Dillard Executors of the last Will and Testament of John Ward Senior Deceased duly proven and recorded in the Court of said County **MILLY ADAMS** a woman of colour Emancipated by the said Will was this day numbered and Registered in the Clerks Office of the said Court, pursuant to the provisions of the Act of Assembly in that case made and provided The said MILLY ADAMS wife of DAVID ADAMS is about forty eight years of age five feet six inches high, a very black woman, has a scar over her right eye, no other apparent mark or scar- Given under my hand as Clerk of the said Court this 17th day of February 1827- Will: Tunstall

James- Virginia Pittsylvania County to wit- No 175- At the instance of John Ward and Lynch Dillard Executors of the last Will and Testament of John Ward Senior Deceased duly proven and recorded in the Court of said County **JAMES [ADAMS]** a boy of colour Emancipated by the said Will was this day numbered and registered in the Clerks Office of the said Court, pursuant to the provisions of the act of Assembly in that case made and provided- The said JAMES son of DAVID [p 83] [ADAMS] & MILLY ADAMS is ten years old 25th December last, about four feet six inches high- a black boy and has no apparent mark or scar- Given under my hand as Clerk of the said Court this 17th day of February 1827- Will: Tunstall

M Adams- Virginia Pittsylvania County to wit- No 176- At the instance of John Ward and Lynch Dillard Executors of the last Will and Testament of John Ward Senior Deceased duly proven and recorded in the Court of said County **MARY ADAMS** a Girl of colour Emancipated by the said Will was this day numbered and Registered in the Clerks Office of the said Court, pursuant to the provisions of the act of Assembly in that case made and provided. The said MARY ADAMS is a Daughter of DAVID & MILLY ADAMS is about six years old three feet eleven inches high of rather bright complexion, has no apparent mark or scar- Given under my hand as Clerk of the said Court this 17th day of February 1827- Will: Tunstall

Milley Adams- Virginia Pittsylvania County to wit- No 177- At the instance of John Ward and Lynch Dillard Executors of the last Will and Testament of John Ward Senior Deceased duly proven and recorded in the Court of said County **MILLEY ADAMS** a Girl of colour emancipated by the said Will was this day numbered and registered in the Clerks Office of the said Court, pursuant to the provisions of the act of Assembly in that case made and provided- The said MILLEY ADAMS is a Daughter of DAVID & MILLY ADAMS is four years old last January, three feet [p 84] five inches high has thick bushy hair of bright complexion, no apparent mark or scar- Given under my hand as Clerk of the said Court this 17th day of February 1827- Will: Tunstall

S Adams- Virginia Pittsylvania County to wit- No 178- At the instance of John Ward and Lynch Dillard Executors of the last Will and Testament of John Ward Senr Deceased duly proven and recorded in the Court of said County **SALLY ADAMS** a Girl of colour Emancipated by the said Will was this day numbered and registered in the Clerks Office of the said Court, pursuant to the provisions of the act of Assembly in that case made and provided- The said SALLY ADAMS is a Daughter of DAVID & MILLY ADAMS about two feet ten inches high two years old the 1st of Nov last, of bright complexion, no apparent mark or scar- Given under my hand as Clerk of the said Court this 17th day of February 1827- Will: Tunstall

Tho Jordan- Virginia Pittsylvania County to wit- No 179- At the instance of John Ward and Lynch Dillard Executors of the last Will and Testament of John Ward Senr Deceased duly proven and recorded in the Court of said County **THOMAS JORDAN** a boy of colour emancipated by the said Will was this day numbered and registered in the Clerks Office of the said Court, pursuant to the provisions of the act of Assembly in that case made and provided- The said THOMAS JORDAN is five feet high twelve years old October last, of bright complexion has the [p 85] Kings Evil on the right jaw and several scars occasioned thereby, a small scar on the left hand & over each eye- Given under my hand as Clerk of the said Court this 17th day of February 1827-   Will: Tunstall

A Dudley- Virginia Pittsylvania County to wit- No 180- At the instance of John Ward and Lynch Dillard Executors of the last Will and Testament of John Ward Senior Deceased duly proven and recorded in the Court of said County **ANNICA DUDLEY** a Woman of colour emancipated by the said Will was this day numbered and registered in the Clerks Office of the said Court, pursuant to the provisions of the act of Assembly in that case made and provided- The said ANNICA DUDLEY is a daughter of HENRY & SALLY DUDLEY five feet five inches & a quarter high about nineteen years old of very bright complexion has two small scars, the one on the left hand and the other on the wrist- Given under my hand as Clerk of the said Court this 17th day of February 1827-   Will: Tunstall

L Dudley- Virginia Pittsylvania County to wit- No 181- At the instance of John Ward and Lynch Dillard Executors of the last Will and Testament of John Ward Senior Deceased duly proven and recorded in the Court of said County **LUSEY DUDLEY** a Girl of colour emancipated by the said Will was this day numbered and registered in the Clerks Office of the said Court, pursuant to the provisions of the act of Assembly in that case made and provided- The said LUSEY DUDLEY is a daughter of HENRY & SALLY DUDLEY five feet five & a quarter inches high about seventeen years old of light complexion, has [p 86] thick bushy hair has a scar on the left hand has a black streak running up the left thumb nail Given under my hand as Clerk of the said Court this 17th day of February 1827- Will: Tunstall

Aaron Dudley- Virginia Pittsylvania County to wit- No 182- At the instance of John Ward and Lynch Dillard Executors of the last Will and Testament of John Ward Senior Deceased duly proven and recorded in the Court of said County **AARON DUDLEY** a boy of colour emancipated by the said Will was this day numbered and registered in the Clerks Office of the said Court, pursuant to the provisions of the act of Assembly in that case made and provided- The said AARON DUDLEY is a son of HENRY & SALLY DUDLEY five feet 2 inches high, going on sixteen years old of bright complexion (very) has a scar on his forehead about 1/2 inch long- no other apparently- Given under my hand as Clerk of the said Court this 17th day of February 1827-   Will: Tunstall

G Dudley- Virginia Pittsylvania County to wit- No 183- At the instance of John Ward and Lynch Dillard Executors of the last Will and Testament of John Ward Senior Deceased duly proven and recorded in the Court of said County **GEORGE DUDLEY** a boy of colour emancipated by the said Will was this day numbered and registered in the Clerks Office of the said Court, pursuant to the provisions of the act of Assembly in that case made and provided- The said GEORGE DUDLEY son of HENRY & SALLY [p 87] DUDLEY five feet one and a quarter inches high, about thirteen years old and dark complexion has no apparent mark or scar Given under my hand as Clerk of the said Court this 17th day of February 1827- Will: Tunstall

M Dudley- Virginia Pittsylvania County to wit- No 184- At the instance of John Ward and Lynch Dillard Executors of the last Will and Testament of John Ward Senior Deceased duly proven and recorded in the Court of said County **MARY DUDLEY** a Woman [sic] of colour emancipated by the said Will was this day numbered and registered in the Clerks Office of the said Court, pursuant to the provisions of the act of Assembly in that case made and provided The said MARY DUDLEY is a daughter of HENRY & SALLY DUDLEY four feet eight and a quarter inches high, about ten years old of bright complexion- two small scars one over each eye- Given under my hand as Clerk of the said Court this 17th day of February 1827- Will: Tunstall

Sam: Dudley- Virginia Pittsylvania County to wit- No 185- At the instance of John Ward and Lynch Dillard Executors of the last Will and Testament of John Ward Senior Deceased duly proven and recorded in the Court of said County **SAM DUDLEY** a boy of colour Emancipated by the said Will was this day numbered and registered in the Clerks Office of the said Court, pursuant to the provisions of the act of Assembly in that case made and provided- The said SAM DUDLEY is a son of HENRY & SALLY DUDLEY four feet two and three fourth inches high, about eight years old of bright complexion, has a scar on his forehead over the left eye- [p 88] Given under my hand as Clerk of the said Court this 17th day of February 1827- Will: Tunstall

John Dudley- Virginia Pittsylvania County to wit- No 186- At the instance of John Ward and Lynch Dillard Executors of the last Will and Testament of John Ward Senior Deceased duly proven and recorded in the Court of said County **JOHN DUDLEY** a boy of colour emancipated by the said Will was this day numbered and registered in the Clerks Office of the said Court, pursuant to the provisions of the act of Assembly in that case made and provided The said JOHN DUDLEY is a son of HENRY & SALLY DUDLEY three feet nine and a half inches high, about six years old of bright complexion, has a long scar over the left eyebrow- Given under my hand as Clerk of the said Court this 17th day of February 1827- Will: Tunstall

H Dudley- Virginia Pittsylvania County to wit- No 187- At the instance of John Ward and Lynch Dillard Executors of the last Will and Testament of John Ward Senior Deceased duly proven and recorded in the Court of said County **HUNDLEY DUDLEY** a boy of colour emancipated by the said Will was this day numbered and registered in the Clerks Office of the said Court, pursuant to the provisions of the act of Assembly in that case made and provided-

The said HUNDLEY DUDLEY is a son of HENRY & SALLY DUDLEY three feet four inches high, about four years old, bright complexion, has no apparent mark or scar- Given under my hand as Clerk of the said Court this [p 89] 17th day of February 1827- Will: Tunstall

H Dudley- Virginia Pittsylvania County to wit- No 188- At the instance of John Ward and Lynch Dillard Executors of the last Will and Testament of John Ward Senior Deceased duly proven and recorded in the Court of said County **HENRY DUDLEY** a boy of colour emancipated by the said Will was this day numbered and registered in the Clerks Office of the said Court, pursuant to the provisions of the act of Assembly in that case made and provided- The said HENRY DUDLEY is a son of HENRY & SALLY DUDLEY two feet nine inches high, 2 years old, of the white Negro appearance, yellow eyes, no apparent mark or scar- Given under my hand as Clerk of the said Court this 17th day of February 1827- Will: Tunstall

WG Dudley- Virginia Pittsylvania County to wit- No 189- At the instance of John Ward and Lynch Dillard Executors of the last Will and Testament of John Ward Senior Deceased duly proven and recorded in the Court of said County **WM GREEN DUDLEY** a boy of colour emancipated by the said Will was this day numbered and registered in the Clerks Office of the said Court, pursuant to the provisions of the act of Assembly in that case made and provided- The said WILLIAM GREEN DUDLEY son of LUCY DUDLEY is about two years old, a bright Mulatto, no apparent mark or scar Given under my hand as Clerk of the said Court this 17th day of February 1827-   Will: Tunstall

[p 90] Wm Powell- Virginia Pittsylvania County to wit- No 190- At the instance of John Ward and Lynch Dillard Executors of the last Will and Testament of John Ward Senior Deceased duly proven and recorded in the Court of said County **WILLIAM POWELL** a man of colour emancipated by the said Will was this day numbered and registered in the Clerks Office of the said Court, pursuant to the provisions of the act of the Assembly in that case made and provided- The said WILLIAM POWELL is about seventy years old four feet eight and a half inches high, a black man- a large scar on

the left side of his head occasioned by a burn- no other apparent scar or mark- Given under my hand as Clerk of the said Court this 19th day of February 1827- Will: Tunstall

N Hodges- Virginia Pittsylvania County to wit- No 191- At the instance of John Ward and Lynch Dillard Executors of the last Will and Testament of John Ward Senior Deceased duly proven and recorded in the Court of said County **NED HODGES** a man of colour emancipated by the said Will was this day numbered and registered in the Clerks Office of the said Court, pursuant to the provisions of the act of Assembly in that case made and provided The said NED HODGES is about seventy years old five feet seven and three fourth inches high of light complexion, a Scar on the back of the neck occasioned by a burn & a Small wen upon the back of the wrist of the left hand, no other apparent mark or scar- Given under my hand as Clerk of the said Court this 19th day of February 1827- Will: Tunstall

[p 91] S Ward- Virginia Pittsylvania County to wit- No 192 At the instance of John Ward and Lynch Dillard Executors of the last Will and Testament of John Ward Senior Deceased duly proven and recorded in the Court of said County **SAUL WARD** a man of colour emancipated by the said Will was this day numbered and registered in the Clerks Office of the said Court, pursuant to the provisions of the act of Assembly in that case made and provided- The said SAUL WARD is about twenty five years old [?] five feet seven and three fourth inches high of light complexion a Scar on the back of the neck occasioned by a burn & a Small wen upon the back of the wrist of the left hand, no other apparent mark or scar- Given under my hand as Clerk of the said Court this 19th day of February 1827- Will: Tunstall **[The author questions that the physical description of this man and the one just ahead of him are exactly alike except for their ages. A mistake may have been made by the Clerk while copying into the original ledger book.]**

G Bobbitt- Virginia Pittsylvania County to wit- No 193- At the instance of John Ward and Lynch Dillard Executors of the last Will and Testament of John Ward Senior Deceased duly proven and recorded in the Court of said County **GEORGE BOBBITT** a man of colour emancipated by the said Will was this day numbered and registered in the Clerks Office of the said Court, pursuant to the provisions of the act of assembly in that case made and provided- The said GEORGE BOBBITT is a man of bright complexion about forty years of age, five feet five inches high has a scar between the eyes, a Small nitch [sic] in the rim of the left ear and a scar on the last joint of his little finger of the left hand- Given under my hand as Clerk of the said Court this 19th day of February 1827- Will: Tunstall

[p 92] B Shelton- Virginia Pittsylvania County to wit- No 194- At the instance of John Ward and Lynch Dillard Executors of the last Will and Testament of John Ward Senior Deceased duly proven and recorded in the Court of said County **BUCK SHELTON** a man of colour emancipated by the said Will was this day numbered and registered in the Clerks Office of the said Court, pursuant to the provisions of the act of assembly in that case made and provided The said BUCK SHELTON is a black man about thirty years old five feet seven and a half inches high his little finger of the right hand crooked- no apparent mark- Given under my hand as Clerk of the said Court this 19th day of February 1827- Will: Tunstall

[Registers No 195-202, for the former slaves of John Ward, Senior, were certified correct as of the March Court 1827.]

M Johnson- Virginia Pittsylvania County to wit- No 195- At the instance of John Ward and Lynch Dillard Executors of the last Will and Testament of John Ward Senior Deceased duly proven and recorded in the Court of said County **MATILDA JOHNSON** a Woman of Colour emancipated by the said Will was this day numbered and registered in the Clerks Office of the said Court, pursuant to the provisions of the act of assembly in that case made and provided- The said MATILDA JOHNSON wife of BENJAMIN JOHNSON a woman of light complexion thirty one years old five feet three and one quarter inches high has a scar on the first joint of the right thumb, one on the first joint of the left forefinger, one on the inside & one on the outside of the left wrist, also over the right eye- Given under my hand as Clerk of the said Court this 12th day of March 1827- Will: Tunstall [p 93] Nancy- Virginia Pittsylvania County to wit- No 196 At the instance of John Ward and Lynch Dillard Executors of the last Will and Testament of John Ward Senior Deceased duly proven and recorded in the Court of said County **NANCY [JOHNSON]** a Girl of colour Emancipated by the said Will was this day numbered and registered in the Clerks Office of the said Court, pursuant to the provisions of the act of the assembly in that case made and provided- The said NANCY is a child of BEN & MATILDA JOHNSON about six weeks old and of light complexion- Given under my hand as Clerk of the said Court this 12th day of March 1827- Will: Tunstall

Charlotte Johnson- Virginia Pittsylvania County to wit- No 197- At the instance of John Ward and Lynch Dillard Executors of the last Will and Testament of John Ward Senior Deceased duly proven and recorded in the Court of said County **CHARLOTTE JOHNSON** a Girl of colour Emancipated by the said Will was this day numbered and registered in the Clerks Office of the said Court, pursuant to the provisions of the act of Assembly in that case made and provided- The said CHARLOTTE JOHNSON is a reputed Daughter of BEN & MATILDA JOHNSON- sixteen years old last September, four feet eleven and a quarter inches high, has a Scar on the back of the left hand, and on the right jaw, one on the left cheek and one on the left eye brow- of rather light complexion- Given under my hand as Clerk of the said Court this 12th day of March 1827- Will: Tunstall

Dorcas Johnson- Virginia Pittsylvania County to wit- No 198- At the instance of John Ward and Lynch [p 94] Dillard Executors of the last Will and Testament of John Ward Senior Deceased duly proven and recorded in the Court of said County **DORCAS JOHNSON** a Girl of colour emancipated by the said Will was this day numbered and registered in the Clerks Office of the said Court, pursuant to the provisions of the act of the Assembly in that case made and provided The said DORCAS JOHNSON is the reputed Daughter of BEN & MATILDA JOHNSON- fourteen years old in September last, four feet seven inches high, has a round Scar over the left corner of the left eye & is of light complexion- Given under my hand as Clerk of the said Court this 12th day of March 1827- Will: Tunstall

Moses Johnson- Virginia Pittsylvania County to wit- No 199 At the instance of John Ward and Lynch Dillard Executors of the last Will and Testament of John Ward Senior Deceased duly proven and recorded in the Court of said County **MOSES JOHNSON** a boy of colour emancipated by the said Will was this day numbered and registered in the Clerks Office of the said Court, pursuant to the provisions of the act of Assembly in that case made and provided- The said MOSES JOHNSON is a reputed son of BEN & MATILDA JOHNSON, is ten years old the 2d day of November last, four feet three and a half inches high, has a Scar immediately between the eyes & one over the right eye & is of light complexion- Given under my hand as Clerk of the said Court this 12th day of March 1827- Will: Tunstall

Sucky Johnson- Virginia Pittsylvania County to wit- No 200 At the instance of John Ward and Lynch [p 95] Dillard Executors of the last Will and Testament of John Ward Senior Deceased duly proven and recorded in the Court of said County **SUCKY JOHNSON** a Girl of colour emancipated by the said Will was this day numbered and registered in the Clerks Office of the said Court, pursuant to the provisions of the act of the Assembly in that case made and provided- The said SUCKY JOHNSON is a reputed daughter of BEN & MATILDA JOHNSON, of light complexion, six years old in June next, three feet four inches high, has two long scars on the right side of the neck in a cross direction Given under my hand as Clerk of the said Court this 12th day of March 1827- Will: Tunstall

Gib Johnson- Virginia Pittsylvania County to wit- No 201 - At the instance of John Ward and Lynch Dillard Executors of the last Will and Testament of John Ward Senior Deceased duly proven and recorded in the Court of said County **GIB JOHNSON** a boy of colour emancipated by the said Will was this day numbered and registered in the Clerks Office of the said Court, pursuant to the provisions of the act of Assembly in that case made and provided- The said GIB JOHNSON is a reputed son of BEN & MATILDA JOHNSON, two years old in November last, about two feet eight inches high, has a new or fresh Scar on the forehead, of rather light complexion- Given under my hand as Clerk of the said Court this 12th day of March 1827-   Will: Tunstall

M Roberts- Virginia Pittsylvania County to wit- No 202- At the instance of John Ward and Lynch Dillard Executors of the last Will and Testament of John Ward Senior Deceased duly proven and recorded in the Court of said County **MOLLY ROBERTS** a woman of Colour emancipated by the said Will was this day numbered and registered in the Clerks Office of the said Court, pursuant to the provisions of the act of Assembly in that case made and provided- The said MOLLEY ROBERTS is a black woman five feet four inches and a quarter high, about seventy or seventy five years old, has a Scar under each eye and a small one at the corner of the right eye- Given under my hand as Clerk of the said Court this 19th day of March 1827-   Will: Tunstall

[Register No 203 for a former slave of John Ward Senior was not certified as correct until the June Court 1827.]

Milly Tucker- Virginia Pittsylvania County to wit- No 203- At the instance of John Ward and Lynch Dillard Executors of the last Will and Testament of John Ward Senior Deceased duly proven and recorded in the Court of said County **MILLY TUCKER** a Woman of Colour emancipated by the said Will was this day numbered and registered in the Clerks Office of the said Court, pursuant to the provisions of the act of the Assembly in that case made and provided- The said MILLY TUCKER is a woman of bright complexion five feet two inches high, about fifty five years old, has a small scar on the right wrist occasioned by a burn and another between the thumb and forefinger of the right hand on a cross direction about the size and length of a pin- Given under my hand as Clerk of the said Court this 20th day of April 1827-
Will: Tunstall

C Dabney- Virginia Pittsylvania County to wit- No 204- At the instance of John Ward and Lynch Dillard Executors of the last Will and Testament of John Ward Senior Deceased duly proven and recorded in the Court of said County **CATO DABNEY** a free man of Colour [p 97] who produced to the Court a certificate from John Williams of this County of his being free born and of his having served his time with him, was this day numbered and registered in the Clerks Office of the County Court of Pittsylvania according to law- The said CATO DABNEY is of Black complexion about 21 years of age, five feet six and one quarter inches high, has a scar just above the left wrist about one and an half inches long occasioned by the cut of a knife- Given under my hand as Clerk of the said Court this 18th day of June 1827- Will: Tunstall **[The author questions whether this register may have been a mistake on the part of the Clerk, who began writing it as if for a freed slave of John Ward Senior, then gave information that the registrant was born free.]**

Tho: Going- Pittsylvania County July 16th, 1827- No 205- **THOMAS GOING** a man of Colour son of JOHN GOING of the sd County who served part of his time with Francis Callaway as appears by his certificate was this day Numbered and registered in the Clerks Office of said County according to law- The said THOMAS GOING is of light complexion, 21 years of age in June last five feet ten inches & 1/4 high, has a scar on the back of his left hand, some small ones on the fingers of that hand, the nail of the little finger of the same hand has a considerable ridge on it occasioned by a hurt- Given under my hand as Clerk of the said Court the date above- Will:Tunstall   Certified at July Court 1827 to be correct

D Stephens- Pittsylvania Clerks Office Sct- No 206- **DISSE STEPHENS** a free born woman of Colour who served her time with William Hall as appears by his certificate was this day registered in the Clerks Office of said County according to law- The said DICE STEPHENS is a black Woman twenty five years old the 15th day of March last five feet one and a [p 98] half inches high has a small Scar just above the point of the right elbow- Given under my hand this 17th day of September 1827- Will:Tunstall- Certified at September Court 1827 to be correct

H Reynolds- Virginia Pittsylvania County to wit- No 207- Pursuant to the provisions of the act of Assembly in that case made and provided, **HENRY REYNOLDS** was this day numbered and registered in the Clerks Office of said County- The said HENRY REYNOLDS is a free born Mulatto man twenty one years of age last month, about six feet two & a half inches high and has a scar over the left eye- Given under my hand as Clerk of the Court of said County this 26th day of October 1827- Will: Tunstall- Certified at July Court 1827 to be correct

P Going - No 208 - Certd 17th Decr 1827 but no copy kept **[This appears to be a renewal for POLLY GOING, earlier registered as No 51.]**

B Going- Virginia Pittsylvania County to wit- No 209- Pursuant to the act of Assembly entitled "an act reducing into one the several acts concerning Slaves free Negroes and Mulattos" **BURWELL GOING** a free born Man of Colour as was satisfactorily proven to the Court of the said County on the 17th Instant was numbered and registered in the Clerks Office of Pittsylvania according to law- The said BURWELL GOING is a Mulatto man six feet one inch high, twenty five years of age the 12th of April last has black curled hair, his eyes of a dark gray or hazle [sic] colour, has no apparent mark or scar- Given under my hand as Clerk of the said County this 17th day of December 1827- Will: Tunstall **[Renewal No. 52]**

[p 99] **[Register No. 210 has been skipped.]**

M Mason- Pittsylvania County Sct- No 211- **MARY MASON** alias **MARY ROSS** a Woman of Colour Emancipated by John Mason of Greensville County by Deed of record in the County Court of Greensville as appears by a copy of said deed and by a Certificate of the Revd Ira Ellis was this day Numbered and registered in the Clerks Office of Pittsylvania County according to law- The said MARY alias MARY ROSS is a black Woman about forty one years of age, five feet high has no apparent mark or scar except a Small mole under the left eyelid- Given under my hand as Clerk of the County Court of said County the 21st Jany: 1828- Will: Tunstall- Certified at January Court 1828 to be correct

S Mason- Pittsylvania County Sct- No 212- **SILVIA MASON** a free born Woman of Colour as appears by a Certificate of the Revd Ira Ellis with whom she served an apprenticeship part of time is this day numbered and registered in the Clerks Office of Pittsylvania County according to law- The said SILVIA MASON is a black Woman about twenty two years of age, five feet three and three fourth inches high has no apparent mark or scar is the daughter of

MARY alias MARY ROSS this day registered- Given under my hand as Clerk of the County Court of said County this 21st day of January 1828- Will: Tunstall- Certified at January Court 1828 to be correct

H Mason- Pittsylvania County Sct- No 213- **HARRY MASON** son of MARY MASON alias MARY ROSS a free born boy of Colour as appears by the Certificate of Revd Ira Ellis was this day numbered and registered in the Clerks Office of Pittsylvania County according to law- The said HARRY MASON is a black boy [p 100] about ten years old four feet two and three fourth inches high has no apparent mark or scar- Given under my hand as Clerk of the County Court of said County this 21st day of January 1828- Will: Tunstall Certified at January Court 1828 to be correct

P Mason- Pittsylvania County Sct- No 214- **POLLY MASON** daughter of MARY MASON a free born Girl of Colour was this day numbered and registered in the Clerks Office of Pittsylvania County according to law- The said POLLY MASON is a black Girl about seven or eight years old three feet nine inches and a half high has no apparent mark or scar- Given under my hand as Clerk of the County Court of said County this 21st day of January 1828- Will: Tunstall Certified at January Court 1828 to be correct

F Mason- Pittsylvania County Sct- No 215- **FANNY MASON** a free born Girl of Colour & daughter of MARY MASON alias MARY ROSS was this day numbered and registered in the Clerks Office of Pittsylvania County according to law- The said FANNY MASON is a black girl about five or six years old three feet ten inches high, no apparent mark or scar- Given under my hand as Clerk of the Court of said County this 21st day of January 1828 - Will:Tunstall- Certified at Jany: Court 1828 to be correct

[p 101] Wm Mason- Pittsylvania County Sct- No 216- **WILLIAM MASON** a free born boy of Colour & son of MARY MASON alias MARY ROSS was this day numbered and registered in the Clerks Office of Pittsylvania County according to law- The said WILLIAM MASON is a black boy between two and three years old two feet nine inches high, no apparent mark or scar- Given under my hand

as Clerk of the Court of said County this 21st day of January 1828- Will: Tunstall- Certified at January Court 1828 to be correct

S Mason- Pittsylvania County Sct- No 217- **STEPHEN MASON** a free born boy of Colour & child of SILVIA MASON was this day Numbered and registered in the Clerks Office of Pittsylvania County according to law- The said STEPHEN MASON is a boy of light complexion about fifteen months old, no apparent mark or scar- Given under my hand as Clerk of the Court of said County this 21st day of January 1828 - Will: Tunstall- Certified at January Court 1828 to be correct

G Mason- Pittsylvania County Sct- No 218- **GEORGE MASON** a free born boy of Colour was this day Numbered and registered in the Clerks Office of Pittsylvania County according to law- The said GEORGE MASON is a son of SILVIA MASON- black boy about two months old, no apparent mark or scar Given under my hand as Clerk of the Court of said County this 21st day of January 1828- Will: Tunstall- Certified at January Court 1828 to be correct

[p 102] L Reynolds- Virginia Pittsylvania County to wit- No 219- Pursuant to the provisions of the act of Assembly in that case made and provided, **LEWIS REYNOLDS** was this day numbered and registered in the Clerks Office of said County- The said LEWIS REYNOLDS is a free born black man twenty one years of age the 20th day of December last, about five feet four inches and a half high has a dark spot on his left cheek and a dark mark under the right eye about an inch long- Given under my hand as Clerk of the Court of said County this 18th day of February 1828-Will: Tunstall- Certified at Feby: Court 1828 to be correct

W Reynolds- Pittsylvania County to wit- No 220- Pursuant to the provisions of the act of the Assembly in that case made and provided, **WINIFRED REYNOLDS** was this day registered in the Clerks Office of said County- The said WINIFRED REYNOLDS is a free born Woman of rather a light complexion about twenty three years of age, five feet four and three quarter inches high has large eyes, but no apparent mark or scar- Given under my hand as Clerk of the Court of said County this 10th day of March 1828- Will: Tunstall- Certified at March Court 1828 to be correct

E Reynolds - Va Pittsylvania County to wit - No 221- Pursuant to the provisions of the act of Assembly in that case made and provided, **ESTHER REYNOLDS** was this day registered in the Clerks Office of said County- The said ESTHER REYNOLDS is a free born black Woman twenty six years old in April next, five feet four inches and a half high has a scar on her upper lip from the left corner of her mouth to her nose and a small one on the first joint of the forefinger of the left hand- Given under my hand this 15th day of March 1828 - Will: Tunstall

[p 103] Jim Denson- Pursuant to the provisions of the act of Assembly in that case made & provided, the Register of JIM alias **JIM DENSON** who was registered in the Clerks Office of Pittsylvania County on the 19th day of September 1825 was this day renewed in the said Office- The said JIM alias JIM DENSON who it appears from a former register made by the Clerk of Southampton County Court was born free, is a black man about forty five years of age, about five feet eight inches high, has a Small knot or Scar on his right wrist, occasioned or as he says by the cut of an axe & no other apparent mark or scar- Given under my hand at Office this 17th day of November 1828- Will: Tunstall Clk- Certified at November Court 1828 to be correct **[Renewal No. 34]**

R Rumley- Pittsylvania County Clerks Office Jany: 19th 1829- No 222 - **RHODY RUMLEY** a free born Woman of Colour as appears by a certificate from under the hand of James Dyer with whom she served an apprenticeship is this day Nd and Registered in the Clerks Office aforesaid according to law The said RHODY RUMLEY is a dark Mulatto woman Eighteen years old the 4th day of March 1829, five feet one and three fourth inches high has long bushy hair and no apparent mark or scar - Given under my hand this 19th day of January 1829 - Will: Tunstall CPC- Certd at January Court 1829 to be correct

L Gee- Virginia Pittsylvania County to wit- No 223 - Pursuant to the act of Assembly in such cases made and provided, **LUCINDA GEE** a Woman of colour who is said to have been born free is this day registered in the Clerks Office of said County The said LUCINDA GEE is a dark Mulatto woman about two and twenty years of age, five feet one quarter of an inch high, and has a Small scar at the outer corner of the left eye, without any other apparent mark or scar- Given under my hand as Clerk of the Court of said County this 10th day of February 1829- Will: Tunstall- Certified at May Court 1829 to be correct

[p 104] R Redmon- Virginia Pittsylvania County to wit No 224- Pursuant to the act of Assembly in such case made and provided, **RICHARD REDMON** a man of colour who it appears agreeably to a Register made by the Clerk of the County Court of Halifax was born of a white Woman is this day registered in the Clerks Office of the County of Pittsylvania The said RICHARD REDMON is a Mulatto man about two and forty years of age, five feet eight and three fourth inches high, has a scar in each Eyebrow, one in the right corner of the forehead about an inch long and one at the end of the little finger of the left hand without any other apparent mark or scar- Given under my hand as Clerk of the Court of said County this 20th day of July 1829- Will: Tunstall   Certified

AC Reynolds- Pittsylvania County Clerks Office May 18th 1830- No 225- **ANN CAROLINE REYNOLDS** a free Woman of Colour who served part of her time with Mrs Lattice Johnson [?] late of this County and the balance of her time with Wm R Chaplin Esqr is this day numbered & registered in the Clerks Office aforesaid according to law- The said ANN CAROLINE is a dark Mulatto Girl 19 years of age this Month, 5 feet one inch high, has long bushy hair, has a scar on the right side of the forehead near the hair, about an inch long occasioned by a cut- Given under my hand as Clerk of the Court of said County the day above- Will: Tunstall- Certified at May Court 1830 to be correct

S Reynolds- Pittsylvania County Clerks Office May 18th 1830- No 226- **SOPHIA REYNOLDS** a free born Woman of Colour who served her time with Benja Sadler late of said County as appears by her indenture of Apprenticeshp in sd Office is this day registered in said Office according to law- The said SOPHIA REYNOLDS is a very bright Mulatto [p 105] five feet three inches high, in the 25th year of her age has very straight light coloured hair has a Small Scar on the last joint of the forefinger of the left hand and a large black mole near the left eye- Given under my hand as Clerk of the Court of said County the day above- Will: Tunstall- Certified at May Court 1830 to be correct

Wm Going- Virginia to wit- Pursuant to the act of Assembly in such case made and provided, **WILLIAM GOIN** a free born man of colour and son of JOHN GOIN was this day registered in the Clerks Office of the County of Pittsylvania The said WM GOIN is a dark Mulatto man twenty one years of age the 15th day of October last, about five feet ten and a quarter inches high, has a Small Scar on the second joint of the left thumb and one on the out corner of the left eye, has only one toe on the right foot, no other apparent mark or scar Given under my hand as Clerk of the County Court of Pittsylvania the 21st day of June 1830- Will: Tunstall- Certified at June Court 1830 to be correct **[No Registration Number given.]**

BO Crane- Virginia Pittsylvania County to wit No 227- Pursuant to the act of Assembly in such case made and provided, **BENJAMIN O. CRANE** a man of colour who it appears by the oath of Dance Pearman was born free, was this day numbered and registered in the Clerks Office of the County Court of said County- The said BENJAMIN O. CRANE is a bright Mulatto man about forty one years of age, five feet seven inches high, has a defect in his loins said to be occasioned by cold which renders him somewhat a cripple, has no apparent mark or scar- Given under my hand this 19th day of July 1830- Will: Tunstall- Certified at July Court 1830 to be correct

[p. 106] Jas Burnett- Virginia Pittsylvania County to wit No 228- Pursuant to the act of Assembly in such case made and provided **JAMES BURNETT** a free born man of colour was this day numbered and registered in the Clerks Office of the County Court of sd County- The said JAMES BURNETT is of rather light complexion, one and twenty years of age the 16th day of January last- about five foot seven inches high- has a scar between the left ear and temple about an inch long and a small one on the back of the left hand- Given under my hand as clerk of the County court aforesaid this 16th day of November 1830- Will:Tunstall

A. Going- Virginia Pittsylvania County to wit- No 209-Pursuant to the act of Assembly entitled "an act reducing into one the several acts concerning slaves free Negroes and Mulattoes" **BURWELL GOING** a free born man of colour as was satisfactorily proven to the court of the said County on the 17th day of December 1827 was this day reregistered in the Clerk's office of the County Court of said county- The said BURWELL GOING is a mulatto man six feet one inch and three quarters high twenty eight years of age the 12th of April last his eyes of a dark gray or hazle [sic] colour has no apparent mark or scar. Given under my hand as clerk of the said Court the 20th day of December 1830. Will:Tunstall CP- Certified at December Court 1830 to be correct **[Renewal of No. 52]**

A. Day- Virginia Pittsylvania County to wit No 229- Pursuant to the act of Assembly in such case made and provided **ANDERSON DAY** a free born man of colour who served an apprenticeship with Nathan Hutcherson of this County is this day numbered and registered in the clerks office of the County Court [p. 107] of said County- The said ANDERSON DAY is a dark Mulatto man five foot nine inches and one fourth of an inch high between twenty four and twenty five years of age has a scar on the base of the forefinger of his right hand another on the back of his right hand near the first joint of the little finger and another small scar a little below his left cheek- no other apparent mark or scar- given under my hand as clerk of the said Court this 16th day of May 1831- Will Tunstall- Certified at May Court 1831 to be correct

P. Pounds- Virginia Pittsylvania Clerks Office to wit- No 230- **PRISCILLA POUNDS** a free born woman of colour is this day numbered and registered in the said office according to law- The said PRISCILLA POUNDS is a bright Mulatto woman four feet eleven inches and a half high about thirty five years of age has a scar on the outside of the right wrist, also two small ones on the upper part of the right arm near the elbow, said to be occasioned by a burn and a very small one on the forehead over the left eye- has no other apparent mark or scar- Given under my hand as clerk of the Court aforesaid this 23rd day of May 1831- Will: Tunstall- Certified at February Court 1832 to be correct

R. Cole- Virginia Pittsylvania County to wit- No 230- Pursuant to the act of Assembly in such case made & provided **RITTER COLE** a free born woman of colour is this day numbered and registered in the clerks office of the County Court of said County- The said RITTER COLE is of rather light complexion five feet four and a half inches high, three and twenty years of age without any apparent mark or scar- Given under my hand as clerk of the County Court of said County [p.108] the 26th day of May 1831- Will: Tunstall- certified at June Court 1831 to be correct **[Duplicate number; used for the registration just prior.]**

Robin Cole- Virginia Pittsylvania county to wit- No 231- Pursuant to the act of Assembly in such case made & provided **ROBIN COLE** a free born man of colour is this day numbered and registered in the clerks office of the county Court of said County- The said ROBIN COLE is of dark complexion five foot seven and a quarter inches high about two and twenty years of age has a small scar between the third and little finger of the left hand and two small ones on the right cheek without any other apparent mark or scar- Given under my hand as clerk of the County Court of said County this 26th day of May 1831- Will: Tunstall- Certified at June Court 1831 to be correct

Pleas Cole- Virginia Pittsylvania County to wit- No 232- Pursuant to the act of Assembly in such case made and provided **PLEASANT COLE** a free born Man of colour is this day numbered and registered in the Clerks office of the County Court of said County- The said PLEASANT COLE is of dark complexion, five feet nine and a half inches high about two and twenty years of age, has a scar on the nose between the eyes without any other apparent mark or scar- Given under my hand as Clerk of the County Court of said County this 26th day of May 1831- Will: Tunstall- Certified at June Court 1831 to be correct

[p 109] N. Cole -Virginia Pittsylvania County to wit- No 233- Pursuant to the act of Assembly in such case made and provided **NANCY COLE** a free born Woman of colour is this day numbered and registered in the Clerks office of the County Court of said County- The said NANCY COLE is a black woman five feet ten inches high, thirty one or two years of age has a small scar on the back of the right hand and one rather long on the left eyebrow without any other apparent mark or scar- Given under my hand as

Clerk of the County Court of said County this 26th day of May 1831- Will: Tunstall- Certified at June Court 1831 to be correct

E. Cole- Virginia Pittsylvania County to wit- No 234- Pursuant to the act of Assembly in such case made and provided **ELENDER COLE** a free born Woman of colour is this day numbered and registered in the Clerks office of the County Court of said County- The said ELENDER COLE is a Bright Mulatto five feet ten and three fourth inches high, nineteen years of age has a small scar on the back of the middle joint of the right forefinger without any other apparent mark or scar- Given under my hand as Clerk of the County Court of said County this 26th day of May 1831- Will: Tunstall- Certified at June Court 1831 to be correct

P. Cole- Virginia Pittsylvania County to wit- No 235- Pursuant to the act of Assembly in such case made and provided **PANTHEA COLE** a free born Woman of colour is this day numbered and registered in the Clerks office of the County Court of said [p 110] County- The said PANTHEA COLE is a Bright Mulatto Girl five feet high, fourteen years old in April last has a small scar on the left arm occasioned by a burn and a small one on the right side of the forehead, without any other apparent mark or scar- Given under my hand as Clerk of the County Court of said County this 26th day of May 1831- Will: Tunstall- Certified at June Court 1831 to be correct

Mary Reynolds- Virginia Pittsylvania County to wit- No 236- Pursuant to the act of Assembly in such case made and provided **MARY REYNOLDS** a free born Woman of colour is this day numbered and registered in the Clerks office of the County Court of said County- The said MARY REYNOLDS is a black woman five feet eleven and three quarters inches high, two and thirty years of age in Mch: last, has a very small scar on the forehead, no other apparent mark or scar- Given under my hand as Clerk of the County Court of said County this 26th day of May 1831- Will: Tunstall- Certified at June Court 1831 to be correct

L. Cole- Virginia Pittsylvania County to wit- No 237- Pursuant to the act of Assembly in such case made and provided **LUCY COLE** a free born Woman of colour is this day numbered and registered in the Clerks office of the County Court of said County- The said LUCY COLE is a Mulatto about forty years of age, five feet nine a quarter inches high and has a considerable scar on the under part of the right arm from a burn - no other apparent mark or scar - [p 111] Given under my hand as Clerk of the County Court of said County this 26th day of May 1831- Will:Tunstall - Certified at June Court 1831 to be correct

J. Cole- Virginia Pittsylvania County to wit- No 238- Pursuant to the act of Assembly in such case made and provided **JINCEY COLE** a free born Woman of colour is this day numbered and registered in the Clerks office of the County Court of said County- The said JINCEY COLE is of dark complexion, five feet five and a quarter inches high, 26 years old the 15th day of January last, has a very small scar on the back of the right hand- no other apparent mark or scar- Given under my hand as Clerk of the County Court of said County this 26th day of May 1831- Will: Tunstall- Certified at June Court 1831 to be correct

E.A. Valentine- Virginia Pittsylvania County to wit- No 239- Pursuant to the act of Assembly in such case made and provided **ELIZA ANN VALENTINE** a free born Woman of colour is this day numbered and registered in the Clerks office of the County Court of said County- The said ELIZA ANN VALENTINE is of dark complexion five feet six and seven eighths inches high one and twenty years of age the 10th day of August next, has a scar on the forehead in the edge of the hair- no other apparent mark or scar- Given under my hand as Clerk of the County Court of said County this 26th day of May 1831- Will: Tunstall- Certified at June Court 1831 to be correct

[p 112] P. Valentine- Virginia Pittsylvania County to wit- No 240- Pursuant to the act of Assembly in such case made and provided **POLLY VALENTINE** a free born Woman of colour is this day numbered and registered in the Clerks office of the County Court of said County- The said POLLY VALENTINE is of dark complexion five feet six inches high and twenty years of age the 16th day of December next, & has a scar on the inside of the left hand near the 1st joint of the thumb- Given under my hand as Clerk of the

County Court of said County this 26th day of May 1831- Will: Tunstall- Certified at June Court 1831 to be correct

A. Valentine - Virginia Pittsylvania County to wit - No 241 Pursuant to the act of Assembly in such case made and provided **AMY VALENTINE** a free born Woman of colour is this day numbered and registered in the Clerks office of the County Court of said County- The said AMY VALENTINE is of dark complexion four feet eleven and three fourth inches high about fifty five years of age, has a scar on the upper part of the right wrist about an inch long, also a very small one on the outer corner of the right eye, and the third finger of the left hand rather dubbed- Given under my hand as Clerk of the County Court of said County this 30th day of May 1831- Will:Tunstall- Certified at June Court 1831 to be correct

P. Valentine- Virginia Pittsylvania County to wit- No 242- Pursuant to the act of Assembly in such case made and provided **POLLY VALENTINE** a free born Woman of colour is this day numbered and registered in the Clerks office of the County Court of said County- The said POLLY VALENTINE is of dark [p 113] complexion five feet and three fourths of an inch high about 26 years of age has a small scar on the upper part of the right hand and one on the right wrist, said to be occasioned by a burn- no other apparent mark or scar- Given under my hand as Clerk of the County Court of said County this 30th day of May 1831- Will: Tunstall- Certified at June Court 1831 to be correct

S. Valentine- Virginia Pittsylvania County to wit- No 243- Pursuant to the act of Assembly in such case made and provided **SAMUEL VALENTINE** a free born Man of colour is this day numbered and registered in the Clerks office of the County Court of said County- The said SAMUEL VALENTINE is of dark complexion five feet two and a half inches high about six and twenty years of age has a large scar on the forehead rather over the left eye and a small one near the middle of the forehead, no other apparent mark or scar- Given under my hand as Clerk of the County Court of said County this 30th day of May 1831- Will: Tunstall- Certified at June Court 1831 to be correct

L. Valentine- Virginia Pittsylvania County to wit- No 244- Pursuant to the act of Assembly in such case made and provided **LUCY VALENTINE** a free born woman of colour is this day numbered and registered in the Clerks office of the County Court of said County- The said LUCY VALENTINE is a bright Mulatto five feet two inches high about three and twenty years of age has a small scar about an inch long on the inside of the left wrist, also a small one on the upper part of the right hand near the wrist and a small one in the forehead- no other apparent mark or scar- [p 114] Given under my hand as Clerk of the County Court of said County this 30th day of May 1831- Will: Tunstall- Certified at June Court 1831 to be correct

M. Valentine- Virginia Pittsylvania County to wit- No 245- Pursuant to the act of Assembly in such case made and provided **MANUEL VALENTINE** a free born Man of colour is this day numbered and registered in the Clerks office of the County Court of said County- The said MANUEL VALENTINE is black, five feet nine and an half inches high, thirty two years of age, has two large scars on his right arm about the elbow and no other apparent mark or scar- Given under my hand as Clerk of the County Court of said County this 30th day of May 1831- Will: Tunstall- Certified at June Court 1831 to be correct

R. Valentine- Virginia Pittsylvania County to wit- No 246- Pursuant to the act of Assembly in such case made and provided **ROYAL VALENTINE** a free born Man of colour is this day numbered and registered in the Clerks office of the County Court of said County- The said ROYAL VALENTINE is black, five feet three inches high, about six and thirty years of age, has a scar on the brow of the right eye & a small one below it, no other apparent mark or scar- Given under my hand as Clerk of the County Court of said County this 30th day of May 1831- Will: Tunstall- Certified at [left blank] Court 183[left blank] to be correct

[p 115] S. Hendricks- Pittsylvania County clerks Office May 30th 1831- No 37- **SAMUEL HENDRICKS** a free born Man of colour who was registered in this office the 23rd day of February 1823 returned his register for renewal- The said SAMUEL HENDRICKS is a dark Mulatto man about twenty nine years of age. Five feet six

and an half inches high [illegible words crossed out] and has no apparent mark or scar- Given under my hand as Clerk of the County Court of said County the day above- Will: Tunstall- Certified at [left blank] Court 183[left blank] to be correct **[Renewal]**

N. Valentine- Virginia to wit- No [left blank] - Pursuant to the act of Assembly in such case made and provided **NANCY VALENTINE** a free born woman of colour as appears by a register from under the hand of the Clerk of the County of Lunenburg is this day numbered and registered in the Clerks office of the County Court of Pittsylvania according to law- The said NANCY VALENTINE is a woman of dark brown complexion five feet nine inches high fifty four years of age & has a scar over the right eye- Given under my hand as Clerk of the County Court of said County this [left blank] day of [left blank] 1831- Will:Tunstall - Certified at [left blank] Court 183[left blank] to be correct **[Noted in margin as (Not numbered).]**

B. Redmond- Virginia Pittsylvania County to wit- No 247- Pursuant to the act of Assembly in such case made and provided **BETSY REDMOND** a free born woman of colour is this day numbered and registered in the Clerks office of the County Court of said County- The said BETSY REDMOND is a dark Mulatto or of light complexion [p 116] three and forty years of age five feet four inches high has a small scar in the left eyebrow without any other apparent mark or scar- Given under my hand as Clerk of the County Court of said County this 18th day of June 1831- Will: Tunstall- Certified at August Court 1831 to be correct-

M. Cousins- Virginia Pittsylvania County to wit- No 248- Pursuant to the act of Assembly in such case made and provided **MILLEY COUSINS** a free born woman of colour is this day numbered and registered in the Clerks office of the County Court of said County- The said MILLEY COUSINS is a bright Mulatto, crosseyed, one and twenty years of age, five feet two inches and a half high has a small scar on the middle joint of the left thumb without any other apparent mark or scar- Given under my hand as Clerk of the County Court of said County this 18th day of June 1831- Will: Tunstall- Certified at August Court 1831 to be correct-

Jas Smith- Virginia Pittsylvania County to wit- No 249- Pursuant to the act of Assembly in such case made and provided **JAMES SMITH** a free born Man of colour is this day numbered and registered in the Clerks office of the County Court of said County- The said JAMES SMITH is of dark complexion nearly black, five feet eight inches and a quarter high, about forty one years of age, has a scar on the upper part of the left hand nearly two inches long, also one on the large joint of the forefinger of the left hand a considerable one covering nearly the whole of the right wrist said to be occasioned by a scall [sic], one near the upper corner or part of the left ear, a small one near the corner of the left eye, one on [p 117] the right cheek, one extending from the right ear nearly to the corner of the eye, one in the right eyebrow, and a considerable one extending from the left under jaw bone round under the throat to the hair under the right ear- Given under my hand as Clerk of the County Court of said County this 21st day of June 1831- Will: Tunstall- Certified at June Court 1831 to be correct

J Fishneck- Virginia Pittsylvania County to wit- No 250- Pursuant to the act of Assembly in such case made and provided **JONAH FISHNECK** a man of colour emancipated by Charles Kennon of the County of Halifax in the State aforesaid as appears by a copy of the deed of emancipation duly recorded in the said county of Halifax is this day numbered and registered in the Clerks office of the County Court of said County- The said JONAH FISHNECK is black, five feet five and three quarters inches high, fifty two years of age the 1st day of April last, has two small scars on the back of the left hand, and one about an inch long between the eyebrows- Given under my hand as Clerk of the County Court of said County this 21st day of June 1831- Will: Tunstall- Certified at June Court 1831 to be correct

E. Dodson- Pittsylvania County Clerks Office June 22 1831- No 251- Pursuant to the act of Assembly in such case made and provided **ELIZA DODSON** a free woman of colour as appears by a certificate of John Walters is this day numbered and registered in the Clerks office of the County Court of said County- The said ELIZA DODSON is a black woman about twenty one years of age, four feet ten inches and a half high has no apparent mark or scar in her face, but has two scars across the right arm just above the wrist- Given under my hand as Clerk of the County Court of said County this 22nd [p 118] day of June 1831- Will: Tunstall- Certified at August Court 1831 to be correct-

R. Roe- Virginia Pittsylvania County to wit- No 252- Pursuant to the act of Assembly in such case made and provided **RHODA ROE** a free born woman of colour is this day numbered and registered in the Clerks office of the County Court of said County- The said RHODA ROE is a black woman five feet two inches high about one and thirty years of age has a scar about an inch and a half long on the right wrist, a small one on the end of the right forefinger also a small one on the Middle joint of the left thumb somewhat resembling the letter A. also one on the same thumb near the large joint- Given under my hand this 18th day of July 1831- Will: Tunstall- Certified at July Court 1831 to be correct-

R. Mason- Virginia Pittsylvania County to wit- No 253- Pursuant to the act of Assembly in such case made and provided **ROBERT MASON** a free born Man of colour was this day numbered and registered in the Clerks office of the County Court of said County- The said ROBERT MASON is of dark complexion about twenty one years of age five feet seven inches high, has a small scar on the right wrist & has a scar on the left arm about five or six inches long- Given under my hand as Clerk of the County Court aforesaid this 1st day of October 1831- Will: Tunstall- Certified at March Court 1833 to be correct-

Jas Stewart- Virginia Pittsylvania County to wit- No 254- Pursuant to the act of Assembly in such case made and provided **JAMES STEWART** a free man of colour is this day numbered and registered in the Clerks office of the County Court of said County- [p 119] The said JAMES STEWART is a man of dark complexion one and twenty years of age, five feet eleven inches high without any apparent mark or scar- Given under my hand as clerk of said County this 7th day of October 1831- Will: Tunstall- Certified

J. Going- Virginia Pittsylvania County to wit- No 255- Pursuant to the act of Assembly in such case made and provided **JESSE GOING** a free man of colour is this day numbered and registered in the clerks office of the County Court of said County- The said

JESSE GOING is of dark complexion about twenty one years of age, five feet eleven inches high without any apparent mark or scar- Given under my hand as clerk of the County Court of said County this 21st day of November 1831- Will: Tunstall- Certified at Novemr Court 1831 to be correct-

P. Wilson- Pittsylvania Clerks Office 19 November 1831- No 256- **PETER WILSON** a free man of colour is this day numbered and registered in the said office- The said PETER WILSON is a bright Mulatto man twenty one years of age the 16th day of February last, five feet eight inches high, has a small long scar on the right forefinger and one on the right cheek or under the outer corner of the right eye and no other apparent mark or scar- Will: Tunstall Ck- Certified at Novemr Court 1831 to be correct-

R. Shelton- Pittsylvania Clrks Office 23rd of Nov 1831- No 257- **RANDAL SHELTON** a free man of colour is this day numbered and registered in the said office- The said RANDAL SHELTON is a black man five feet five inches [p 120] high has a small scar on the lower part of his forehead nearly between his eyes without any other apparent mark or scar & 22 years old the 4th of July next- Will: Tunstall Ck- Certified at Novemr Court 1831 to be correct-

F. Robinson- Virginia Pittsylvania County Sct- No 258- **FAITHY ROBINSON** a woman of colour emancipated by the Will of Caleb Ellis Deceased late of the of the County of Sussex as appears by the certificate of Ira Ellis was this day numbered and registered in the Clerks office of the said County Court according to law- The said FAITHY ROBINSON is a black woman about fifty years of age five feet three and three fourth inches high has no apparent mark or scar- Given under my hand as Clerk of the County Court of said County this 19th day of December 1831- Will: Tunstall CPC- Certified at Decr Court 1831 to be correct-

S Friend- Virginia Pittsylvania County to wit- No 259- Pursuant to the act of Assembly in such case made and provided **SARAH FRIEND** a free woman of colour is this day numbered and registered in the clerks office of the County Court of said County- The said SARAH FRIEND is a black woman one and twenty years of age about Christmas last, five feet two inches high and has a small scar in her forehead without any other apparent mark or scar- Given under my hand as clerk of the County Court of said County this 6th day of February 1832 - Will: Tunstall CPC- Certified at February Court 1832 to be correct-

Saml Short- Virginia Pittsylvania County Clerks Office to wit- No 260- **SAML. SHORT** a free man of colour who was emancipated by [p 121] the last Will and Testament of Benjamin Webber Deceased as appears by a register taken by the Clerk of the County Court of Cumberland is this day numbered and registered in the Clerks office aforesaid- The said SAMUEL SHORT is a man of black complexion about thirty four years of age the 24th day of this month (February) five feet four and a quarter inches high, without any apparent mark or scar- Given under my hand as Clerk of the County Court of Pittsylvania this 21st February 1832- Will: Tunstall CPC- Memo.- This register was made out but not having been received by the Court the within mentd Saml. Short was again registered the 19th day of October 1835 as No 290 which vacates the No 260- see page [left blank]

M.A. Reynolds- Virginia Pittsylvania Clerks Office- No 261- **MARY ANN REYNOLDS** a free born Girl of colour is this day numbered and registered in the said office according to law- The said MARY ANN REYNOLDS is a very bright mulatto Girl eighteen years old the second day of September 1831 five feet six inches high has two small scars on the left thumb and one rather under the left jaw- She also has a small mole under the left eye- Given under my hand as clerk of the County Court of said County this 12th day of March 1832- Will: Tunstall- Certified at March Court 1832 to be correct-

Jno Richardson- Virginia Pittsylvania Clerks Office Sct- No 262- **JOHN RICHARDSON** a free man of colour is this day numbered and registered in the said office according to law- The said JOHN RICHARDSON is a black man five and twenty years of age in June next five feet four and a half inches high without any apparent mark or scar- Given under my hand as clerk of the County Court of said County this 16th day of April 1832- Will: Tunstall- [p 122] Certified at May Court 1832 to be correct-

Wm Cole- Virginia Pittsylvania Clerks Office Sct- No 263- **WILLIAM COLE** a free man of colour is this day numbered and registered in the said Office according to law- The said WILLIAM COLE is a black man thirty years of age the 6th day of March last, five feet six inches and a half high, has a scar on the forefinger of the left hand, also a small one on the nose and a small [sic] on the forehead rather over the left eye- Given under my hand as clerk of the County Court of said County this 18th day of June 1832- Will: Tunstall- Certified at June Court 1832 to be correct-

B. Richardson- Virginia Pittsylvania Clerks Office Sct- No 264- **BETSY RICHARDSON** a free woman of colour is this day numbered and registered in the said office according to law- The said BETSY RICHARDSON is a black woman two and twenty years of age four feet ten inches high without any apparent mark or scar- Given under my hand as clerk of the County Court of said County this 18th day of June 1832 - Will: Tunstall - Certified at August Court 1832 to be correct-

J. Reynolds- Virginia Pittsylvania Clerks Office Sct- No 265- **JINNEY REYNOLDS** a free Woman of colour is this day numbered and registered in the said office according to law- The said JINNEY REYNOLDS is a black woman five feet five inches high [left blank] years of age, has a small scar on the back of the left hand also one near the right wrist and a mole on the left side of the upper lip- Given under my hand as clerk of the County Court of said [p 123] County this 29th day of August 1832- Will: Tunstall- Certified at March Court 1833 to be correct-

M. Reynolds- Virginia Pittsylvania Clerks Office Sct- No 266- **MARTHA REYNOLDS** a free woman of colour is this day numbered and registered in the said office according to law- The said MARTHA REYNOLDS is a black woman Eighteen years of age Christmas next five feet two and three quarters inches high has a scar on the back of the left hand, a small one on the first joint of the left thumb and a very small one on her forehead- Given under my hand as clerk of the County Court of said County this 29th day of August 1832- Will: Tunstall- Certified at [left blank] Court 1832 to be correct

H. Roberts- Virginia Pittsylvania Clerks Office to wit- No 266- **HENRY ROBERTS** a man of colour who hath been duly registered in the clerks office of the County Court of Middlesex as appears by a register from the said County Court of Middlesex is this day registered [sic] the clerks office of Pittsylvania aforesaid- The said HENRY ROBERTS is a man of dark complexion about t[illegible]ty five or six years of age, five feet seven inches and a half high, has a small scar on his left wrist, a large wart on the inside of the left hand & a scar under the left eye- Given under my hand as clerk of the County Court of said County this 17th day of December 1832- Will: Tunstall- Certified at Decr Court 1832 to be correct **[Duplicate number; used for the registration just prior.]**

Tho: Going- Virginia Pittsylvania Clerks Office Sct- No 205- **THOMAS GOING** a man of colour heretofore numbered and registered in the said office this day returned his said registration for renewal- [p 124] The said THOMAS GOING is of light complexion twenty six years old in June last five feet ten inches and a half high, has a scar on the back of his left hand, the nail of the little finger of the same hand has a considerable ridge on it occasioned by a hurt- Given under my hand as clerk of the County Court of said County this 1st day of December 1832- Will: Tunstall- Certified at Decr Court 1832 to be correct **[Renewal]**

J. Denson- Pittsylvania Clerks Office to wit- No 34- JIM alias **JIM DENSON** a man of colour heretofore numbered and registered in the said office this day returned his said registration for renewal- The said JIM alias JIM DENSON is a black man who it appears from a former register made by the Clerk of Southampton County Court was born free is about forty nine years of age about five feet eight inches high has a small knot or scar on his right wrist occasioned as he says by the cut of an axe, without any other apparent mark or scar- Given under my hand as clerk of the County Court of Pittsylvania this 7th day of December 1832- Will: Tunstall- Certified at Decr Court 1832 to be correct **[Renewal]**

R Reynolds- Virginia Pittsylvania Clerks Office Sct- No 268- **REBECCA REYNOLDS** a free born woman of colour is this day numbered and registered in the said office according to law- The said REBECCA REYNOLDS is a bright Mulatto woman eight and twenty years of age the tenth day of June next, five feet one and a half inches high, has a small long scar on the back of the right thumb and a small one on the side of the right forefinger- Given under my hand as clerk of the County Court of said County this 15th day of March 1833- Will: Tunstall- Certified at March Court 1833 to be correct

[p 125] J Reynolds- Virginia Pittsylvania Clerks Office Sct- No 269- **JOEL REYNOLDS** a free born man of colour is this day numbered & registered in the said office according to law- The said JOEL REYNOLDS is a bright Mulatto Man about eight and twenty years of age, five feet nine and three fourths inches high, has a small scar on the first joint of the left forefinger, some small scars on the second joint of the left thumb said to be occasioned by sawing- Given under my hand as clerk of the said Court this 18th day of March 1833- Will: Tunstall- Certified at March Court 1833 to be correct

S Smith- Virginia Pittsylvania Clerks Office Sct- No 270- **SILVA SMITH** a free woman of colour is this day numbered & registered in the said office according to law- The said SILVA SMITH is a woman of dark complexion about three and twenty years of age five feet one inch high, has a scar on the corner of the right eye and a small one on the right wrist- Given under my hand as clerk of the County Court of said County this 18th day of March 1833- Will: Tunstall- Certified at March Court 1833 to be correct-

M Smith- Virginia Pittsylvania Clerks Office Sct- No 271- **MARIA SMITH** a free woman of colour is this day numbered & registered in the said office according to law- The said MARIA SMITH is a woman of dark complexion about nineteen years of age, five feet two and a half inches high has a small scar on the left eye and also on the back of the right hand- Given under my hand as clerk of the County Court of said County this 18th day of March 1833- Will: Tunstall- Certified at March Court 1833 to be correct-

[p 126] J. Reynolds- Virginia Pittsylvania Clerks Office Sct- No 272- **JOANNA REYNOLDS** a free woman of colour is this day numbered & registered in the said Office according to law- The said

JOANNA REYNOLDS is a Mulatto woman nineteen years of age next August, five feet three and a quarter inches high has a small mole on the right side of her face- Given under my hand as clerk of the County Court of said County this 18th day of March 1833- Will: Tunstall- Certified at March Court 1833 to be correct-

J. Cousins- Virginia Pittsylvania Clerks Office Sct- No 273- **JACOB COUSINS** a free man of colour is this day numbered & registered in the said office according to law- The said JACOB COUSINS is a man of dark complexion about two and thirty years of age, five feet five and a half inches high has a scar over the right eye and a small one over the left eye, also one under the chin, a cut on the inside of the right hand and has a stiff knee which causes him to limp- Given under my hand as clerk of the County Court of said County this 18th day of March 1833- Will: Tunstall- Certified at March Court 1833 to be correct-

D. Reynolds- Virginia Pittsylvania Clerks Office Sct- No 274- **DOCTOR REYNOLDS** a free born man of colour is this day numbered & registered in the said office according to law- The said DOCTOR REYNOLDS is a bright Mulatto man two and twenty years of age in October last, five feet eleven inches high, has a large scar on the left wrist, also one on the back of his right hand and his little finger on [left blank] hand crooked and stiff- Given under my hand as clerk of the County Court of said County this 18th day of March 1833- Will: Tunstall- Certified at March Court 1833 to be correct-

[p 127] J. Mason- Virginia Pittsylvania Clerks Office Sct- No 275- **JEFFERSON MASON** a free man of colour is this day numbered & registered in the said office according to law- The said JEFFERSON MASON is a black man two and twenty years of age, five feet three and a half inches high, has two small scars on the back of his right hand, one on the right wrist, and a small one on his forehead- Given under my hand as clerk of the County Court of said County this 18th day of March 1833- Will: Tunstall- Certified at March Court 1833 to be correct-

R Reynolds- Virginia Pittsylvania Clerks Office Sct- No 276- **RICHARD REYNOLDS** a free man of colour is this day numbered and registered in the said office according to law- The said RICHARD REYNOLDS is a bright Mulatto Man about five and twenty years of age five feet eleven inches high and has a scar near his left ear- Given under my hand as clerk of the County Court of said County this 18th day of March 1833- Will: Tunstall

S. Durham- Virginia Pittsylvania Clerks Office Sct- No 277- **SAMUEL DURHAM** a free man of colour is this day numbered and registered in the said office according to law- The said SAMUEL DURHAM is a bright Mulatto Man two & twenty years of age the 7th day of this month (March) six feet one inch and a quarter high, has a scar on the back of his right hand and a small one between the joints of the right thumb- Given under my hand as clerk of the County Court of said County this 18th day of March 1833- Will: Tunstall- Certified at March Court 1833 to be correct-

[p 128] L Smith- Virginia Pittsylvania Clerks Office Sct- No 278- **LETHE SMITH** alias **LETHE FLAGG** a free born Woman of colour is this day numbered and registered in the said office according to law- The said LETHE SMITH alias FLAGG is a bright Mulatto woman about five and thirty years of age, five feet two inches high, has a small mole on the right side of her chin and a small one under her left jaw- Given under my hand as clerk of the County Court of said County this 19th day of March 1833- Will: Tunstall- Certified at March Court 1833 to be correct-

F Smith- Virginia Pittsylvania Clerks Office Sct- No 279- **FANNY SMITH** a free woman of colour is this day numbered and registered in the said office according to law- The said FANNY SMITH is a black woman six and twenty years of age the 12th day of this month (March) five feet one a quarter [sic] inches high has a scar on the left wrist and the nail of the right forefinger disfigured as she says by a cancer [sic]- Given under my hand as clerk of the County Court of said County this 19th day of March 1833- Will: Tunstall- Certified at March Court 1833 to be correct-

L Richardson- Virginia Pittsylvania Clerks Office Sct- No 280- **LIZA RICHARDSON** a free woman of colour is this day numbered & registered in the said office according to law- The said LIZA RICHARDSON is a woman of rather light complexion nineteen years of age in February last five feet six and a half inches high & has a small scar under the left eye- Given under my hand as clerk of the County Court of said County this 19th day of March 1833- Will: Tunstall- Certified at March Court 1833 to be correct

[p 129] SB Jackson- Virginia Pittsylvania Clerks Office to wit- No 281- **SAMUEL B. JACKSON** a free man of colour who has been duly registered in the Clerks Office of the County Court of Charlotte as appears by a register in his possession is this day numbered and registered in the Clerks Office of Pittsylvania County Court- The said SAMUEL B. JACKSON is a black Man five feet five inches high about twenty three years of age has some scars on his left wrist, has a small scar on third [sic] joint of the right forefinger, a small one on the second joint of the same finger and a small scar on his forehead. Given under my hand as Clerk of said County of Pittsylvania this 16th day of July 1833- Will: Tunstall- Certified at July Court 1833 to be correct-

B Burnett- Virginia Pittsylvania Clerks Office to wit- No 282- **BOLING BURNETT** a free man of colour who has regularly served his apprenticeship with Wm Payne of this County as appears by a certificate of the said Payne now in his possession is this day numbered & registered in the Clerks Office of the said County Court- The said BOLING BURNETT is of dark complexion five feet two inches and a half in height, has a scar on the first joint of the thumb of the left hand & a small one on the back of the same hand, has a scar on the upper lip and a small scar on the forehead- Given under my hand as clerk of the County Court of said County this 20th day of August 1833- Will: Tunstall- Certified at August Court 1833 to be correct-

B.Going- Virginia Pittsylvania County to wit- No 209- **BURWELL GOING** a free born man of colour who hath been heretofore registered in the Office of the said County this day returned his register for renewal- The said BURWELL GOING is a Mulatto Man six feet one inch high, thirty one years of age the 12th of April last, his eyes of a dark gray or hazle colour [p 130] has no apparent mark or scar- Given under my hand this 20th day of January 1834- Will: Tunstall- Certified at January Court 1834 to be correct-
[Renewal]

Jas Going- Virginia Pittsylvania County to wit- No 211- **JAMES GOING** a free man of colour as appeared to the satisfaction of the Court in 1830 and who hath been heretofore registered in the Clerks Office of the said County this day returned his register for renewal- The said JAMES GOING is a bright Mulatto Man about thirty five years of age in May next, five feet eight inches and a half high, has eyes rather gray and no apparent mark or scar- Given under my hand as Clerk of the said Court this 20th day of January 1834- Will: Tunstall- Certified at January Court 1834 to be correct- **[This is an incorrect number, belonging to MARY MASON alias MARY ROSS. This renewal is actually for No. 49.]**

Wm Chavis- Virginia Pittsylvania Clerks Office Sct- No 283- **WILLIAM CHAVIS** a free born man of colour is this day numbered and registered in the said office according to law- The said WILLIAM CHAVIS is a Mulatto Man five feet seven inches and a quarter in height twenty two years of age the 1st day of May next has a scar on the wrist of about an inch in length & a small one on the back of the left thumb- Given under my hand as clerk of the County Court of said County this 14th day of February 1834- Will: Tunstall- Certified at February Court 1833 to be correct-

T Burnett- Virginia Pittsylvania Clerks Office Sct- No 284- **THENY BURNETT** a free born woman of colour who hath served an apprenticeship with James [May] and George May, as appears as [p 131] well by the Indenture of said apprenticeship as from the certificate of said George May filed is this day numbered and registered in said office according to law- The said THENY BURNETT is of light complexion, thirty years of age in July next, five feet two and an half [sic] inches high, the right little finger is somewhat crooked & has a small scar on the second joint of the left forefinger which is a little dubbed- Given under my hand as clerk of the County Court of said County this 19th day of May 1834- Will: Tunstall- Certified at May Court 1834 to be correct-

Wm Goin- Virginia to wit- No 285- **WILLIAM GOIN** a free born man & son of JOHN GOIN who hath been heretofore registered in the Clerks Office of the County Court of Pittsylvania this day returned his said register for renewal- The said WILLIAM GOIN is a dark Mulatto Man twenty six years of age the 15th day of this month (Octo) five feet ten inches and three quarters high, has a small scar on the second joint of the left thumb and one on the outer corner of the left eye, has only one toe on the right foot, no other apparent mark or scar- Given under my hand as Clerk of the County Court of Pittsylvania this 20th day of October 1834- Will: Tunstall- Certified at April Court 1835 to be correct- **[No number was given to him when he first registered on 21 June 1830.]**

R Burnett- Virginia Pittsylvania Clerks Office to wit- No 287- **REAMY BURNETT** a free born Man of colour is this day registered in the said office according to law- The said REAMY BURNETT is of rather light complexion one and twenty years of age the 20th day of September last, five feet two and a half inches high has a small long scar on the right cheek, also a small one on the upper part of the right hand and has unusually thick lips, particularly the upper one- No other apparent mark [p 132] or scar- Given under my hand as clerk of the County Court of Pittsylvania this 19th day of January 1835- Will: Tunstall- Certified at January Court 1835 to be correct- **[Number is out of sequence; see the next registration.]**

P Star- Virginia Pittsylvania Clerks Office to wit- No 286- **PATRICK STAR** a free born Man of colour who hath duly served his apprenticeship with Washington Shelton as appears by a certificate of that fact from the said Shelton now on file is this day numbered and registered in said Office- The said PATRICK STAR is of bright complexion five feet four and one quarter inches high has a small scar on the finger next to the little one on the right hand and a small one on the upper lip running from the left side of the nose and is about 21 years of age- Given under my hand as clerk of the County Court of said County this 19th day of January 1835- Will: Tunstall- Certified at January Court 1835 to be correct- **[Number is out of sequence; see registration just prior.]**

H Reynolds- Virginia Pittsylvania Clerks Office to wit- No 288- **HANNAH REYNOLDS** a free woman of colour is this day numbered and registered in my office according to law- The said HANNAH is a bright Woman aged fifty six years or thereabouts, five feet three inches and a quarter in height, a small mole on the left nose and one on the left ear, long straight hair and has several teeth out- No other visible mark or scar- Given under my hand as clerk of the County Court this 20th day of July 1835- Will: Tunstall- Certified at [left blank] Court 183[left blank] to be correct-

[p 133] C Reynolds- Virginia Pittsylvania Clerks Office to wit- No 289- **CINDA REYNOLDS** a free Girl of colour is this day numbered and registered in my office according to law- The said CINDA is very bright, aged fifteen years the 15th day of June last, five feet seven inches high, has a scar about an inch in length on the back of the neck & has long straight hair without other apparent mark or scars- Given under my hand as clerk of the County Court this 20th day of July 1835- Will: Tunstall- Certified at August Court 1835 to be correct-

J Denson- Pittsylvania Clerks Office- No 34- JIM alias **JIM DENSON** a man of colour who has been heretofore registered and numbered in the said Office this day returned his said register for renewal- The said JIM alias JIM DENSON is a black man who it appears from a former register made by the Clerk of Southampton County Court was born free, is about fifty two years of age, five feet eight inches high, has a small knot or scar on his right wrist, occasioned as he says by the cut of an axe, but has no other apparent mark or scar- Given under my hand as Clerk of the County Court of said County of Pittsylvania this 15th day of August 1835- Will: Tunstall- Certified at August Court 1835 to be correct- **[Renewal]**

Saml Short- Virginia Pittsylvania Clerks Office to wit- No 290- **SAMUEL SHORT** a free man of color who it appears was emancipated by the last Will and Testament of Benjamin Webber Decd late of the County of Cumberland is this day numbered and registered in this office according to law- The said SAMUEL SHORT is a man of black complexion about thirty seven years of age five feet four and a half inches high & has a small scar on the forehead immediately in the edge of the hair- [p 134] without any other apparent mark or scar- Given under my hand as clerk of the County Court of said County this 19th day of October 1835- Will: Tunstall- Certified at October Court 1835 to be correct- **[Renewal]**

H Roberts- Virginia Pittsylvania Clerks Office Sct- No 266- **HENRY ROBERTS** a man of colour who hath been heretofore registered in the Clerks Offices of the County Court of Middlesex and Pittsylvania this day returned his register for renewal- The said HENRY ROBERTS is a man of dark complexion about thirty eight or nine years of age, five feet seven inches and a half high has a small scar on his left wrist, a small scar in the left hand occasioned by a wart and a scar under the left eye- Given under my hand as clerk of the County Court of said County of Pittsylvania this 15th day of November 1835- Will: Tunstall- Certified at [left blank] Court 1835 to be correct- **[Renewal]**

[Here there is a stamped or drawn hand in the margin with finger pointing toward the right to the following notation.]

The following Registers were inadvertently omitted to be entered in their proper places-

L Hendrick- Virginia Pittsylvania Clerks Office June 18th 1827- **LETITIA HENDRICK** a free born Woman of Colour heretofore No: & Registered in this office this day delivered up the certificate of her register and was again registered according to law- The said LETITIA HENDRICK is a bright Mulatto Woman, about forty six years old about five feet one inch high has long bushy hair, with a small scar on the left side of her forehead and another on the right arm near the elbow- [No signature of Clerk]- Certified at [left blank] Court to be correct- **[No number given; Appears to be the Renewal of Register No. 43]**

[p 135] Jas Going- Virginia Pittsylvania County Court- No 211- Pursuant to the provisions of the act of assembly passed the 2nd day of March 1819 entitled "an act reducing into one the several acts concerning Slaves, free Negroes and Mulattos" **JAMES GOING** a free born man of colour as appears to the satisfaction of the Court was this day duly numbered and registered in the Clerks office of the County Court of said County- the said JAMES GOING is a bright Mulatto Man about thirty two years of age in May next five feet nine inches high his eyes rather grey and no apparent mark or scar- Given under my hand as Clerk of the said Court this 20th day of December 1830- Will: Tunstall- Certified at Decr Court

1830 to be correct- [A notation in the margin with a drawing of a hand states: See page 130. However, No 211 on page 130 is an incorrect number for this person; this renews No 49.]

S Hendrick- Virginia Pittsylvania County to wit- No 47- Pursuant to the provisions of the act of Assembly passed the 2nd day of March 1819 entitled "an act reducing into one the several acts concerning Slaves, free Negroes and Mulattos" **SUSANNA HENDRICK** a free born woman of colour who was registered in the Clerks office of the County Court of said County the 22nd day of June 1824 this day returned her register for renewal- the said SUSANNA HENDRICK is of dark complexion about two and thirty years of age five feet and an inch and a half high without any apparent mark or scar- Given under my hand as Clerk of the County Court of said County this 21st day of June 1831- Will: Tunstall- Certified at [left blank] Court 183[left blank] to be correct- **[Renewal]**

Jesse Booker- Virginia Pittsylvania County to wit- No 38- Pursuant to the act of Assembly in such case made and provided **JESSE BOOKER** a free man of colour heretofore numbered & registered in the Clerks office of the County Court of said [p 136] County this day returned his said register for renewal- The said JESSE BOOKER is of light complexion about thirty two years of age, five feet four inches and a half high has a large mouth and shows his teeth very much when he smiles and has a small scar near the right wrist just over the thumb joint- Given under my hand as Clerk of the County Court of said County this 25th day of June 1831- Will: Tunstall- Certified at August Court 1831 to be correct- **[Renewal]**

P Davis- Virginia Pittsylvania County to wit- Pursuant to the act of Assembly in such case made and provided **PATTY DAVIS** a free born woman of colour who was registered in the Clerks Office of the County Court of said County the 7th day of June 1824 this day returned her register for renewal- The said POLLY DAVIS is a bright Mulatto, thirty years of age the 8th day of May last five feet three and a half inches high and has a scar on the back of the right hand said to have been occasioned by a burn without any other apparent mark or scar- Given under my hand as Clerk of the

County Court of said County this 21st day of June 1831- Will: Tunstall- Certified at [left blank] Court 183[left blank] to be correct- **[Renewal of No 41.]**

Geo Rivers- Pittsylvania Clerks Office- 22nd November 1831- No 4- **GEORGE RIVERS** a free Man of Colour heretofore numbered & registered in the said office this day returned his said register for renewal- The said GEORGE RIVERS is of light complexion about 42 years of age five feet 2 3/4 inches high no apparent mark or scar- Will: Tunstall- Certified at Novr Court 1831 to be correct- **[Renewal]**

[p 137] John Going- Virginia Pittsylvania County to wit- No 50- **JOHN GOING** a free born Man of Colour heretofore registered in the Clerks Office of the County Court of said County this day returned his register for renewal- The said JOHN GOING is a dark Mulatto Man seven and twenty years of age in April last five feet seven and a quarter inches high has dark hazle eyes & without any apparent mark or scar- Given under my hand as Clerk of the County Court aforesaid this 21st day of November 1831- Will: Tunstall- Certified at Novr Court 1831 to be correct- **[Renewal]**

L Hendrick- Virginia Pittsylvania County Clerks Office Sct- No 43- **LETITIA HENDRICK** a free born woman of colour heretofore numbered and registered in this office this day returned the certificate of her register for renewal- The said LETITIA HENDRICK is a bright Mulatto Woman about fifty two years of age, five feet one inch high has a small scar on the left side of her forehead and another on the right arm near the elbow- Given under my hand as Clerk of the County Court of said County this 18th day of June 1832- Will: Tunstall- Certified at June Court 1832 to be correct- **[Renewal]**

W Stephens- Virginia Pittsylvania Clerks Office to wit- No 65- **WILMOTH STEPHENS** a free born Woman of colour, Daughter of CATHERINE STEPHENS who was emancipated by John Terry by deed of record in the Clerks Office of Pittsylvania County Court, this day returned her said register for renewal- The said WILMOTH STEPHENS is a black woman about thirty three years of age, four feet eleven and a half inches high with no [p 138] apparent mark or scar- Given under my hand as Clerk of the County Court of said County this 13th day of March 1834- Will: Tunstall- Certified at [left blank] Court 183[left blank] to be correct- **[Renewal]**

Thos Going- Virginia Pittsylvania Clerks Office Sct- No 205- **THOMAS GOING** a free man of colour and who has been heretofore numbered and registered in the said Office this day returned his said register for renewal- The said THOMAS GOING is of light complexion thirty years of age in June last, five feet ten inches and a half high has a scar on the back of his left hand and the nail of the little finger of the same hand has a considerable ridge on it occasioned by a hurt- Given under my hand as Clerk of the County Court of said County this 19th day of September 1836- Wm H Tunstall- Certified at September Court 1836- **[Renewal]**

Elisha Reynolds- Virginia Pittsylvania Clerks Office Sct- No 291- **ELISHA REYNOLDS [Sr.]** a free born man of colour is this day numbered and registered in the said Office according to law- The said ELISHA REYNOLDS is Mulatto Man five feet nine and a quarter inches high, thirty seven years of age the 21st of August last according to a register of the same in his possession- has a small slit in the left ear and no other mark or scar- Given under my hand as Clerk of the County Court of said County this 19th day of November 1836- Wm H Tunstall **[The name of the county in which he originally registered is not given.]**

[p 139] Mariah Reynolds- Virginia Pittsylvania Clerks Office Sct- No 292- **MARIAH REYNOLDS** a free born woman of colour is this day numbered and registered in the said Office according to law- The said MARIAH REYNOLDS is Mulatto Woman about thirty three years of age according to a Memorandum of the same in her possession, is four feet four and a half inches high, has a scar on the second joint of the right thumb and a small one on the left wrist- Given under my hand as Clerk of the County Court of said County this 19th day of November 1836- Wm H Tunstall

Mary Reynolds- Virginia Pittsylvania Clerks Office Sct- No 293- **MARY REYNOLDS** a free born girl of colour is this day numbered and registered in the said Office according to law- The said MARY

REYNOLDS is a bright Mulatto Girl sixteen years old the 11th of February last five feet and a half inch high, with no apparent mark or scar- Given under my hand as Clerk of the County Court of said County this 19th day of November 1836- Wm H Tunstall

Milly Reynolds- Virginia Pittsylvania Clerks Office Sct- No 294- **MILLY REYNOLDS** a free born Girl of colour is this day numbered and registered in the said Office according to law- The said MILLY REYNOLDS is a Mulatto Girl fourteen years old the 14th of July last five feet two and an half inches high, and has a small scar on the right hand just above the thumb- Given under my hand as Clerk of the County Court of sd County this 19th day of November 1836- Wm H Tunstall

[p 140] Antho Reynolds- Virginia Pittsylvania Clerks Office Sct- No 295- **ANTHONY REYNOLDS** a free born boy of colour is this day numbered and registered in the said Office according to law- The said ANTHONY REYNOLDS is a Mulatto boy ten years old the 22nd of August last four feet nine inches high, has two small scars in the forehead with no other apparent mark or scar- Given under my hand as Clerk of the County Court of said County this 19th day of November 1836- Wm H Tunstall

Elisha Reynolds- Virginia Pittsylvania Clerks Office Sct- No 296- **ELISHA REYNOLDS [Jr.]** a free born boy of colour is this day numbered and registered in the said Office according to law- The said ELISHA REYNOLDS is a Mulatto boy seven years old the 15th day of January last, four feet two inches high, with no apparent mark or scar- Given under my hand as Clerk of the County Court of said County this 19th day of November 1836 - Wm H Tunstall

America Reynolds- Virginia Pittsylvania Clerks Office Sct- No 297- **AMERICA REYNOLDS** a free born Girl of colour is this day numbered and registered in the said Office according to law- The said AMERICA REYNOLDS is a Mulatto Girl five years old the 18th of June last three feet ten inches high, with no apparent mark or scar- Given under my hand as Clerk of the County Court of said County this 19th day of November 1836- Wm H Tunstall

Hannah Reynolds- Virginia Pittsylvania Clerks Office Sct- No 298- **HANNAH REYNOLDS** a free born Girl of colour is this day numbered and registered in the said Office according to law- The said HANNAH REYNOLDS is a Mulatto Girl three years of age the 7th of April last three feet two inches high with no apparent mark or scar- Given under my hand as Clerk of the County Court of said County this 19th day of November 1836- Wm H Tunstall

Peggy Day- Virginia Pittsylvania Clerks Office Sct- No 299- **PEGGY DAY** a free born woman of colour is this day numbered and registered in the said Office according to law- The said PEGGY DAY is about forty two years of age, five feet two & a half inches high, of rather light complexion has a small round scar on her forehead, a mole over the left eye, without other apparent mark or scar- Given under my hand as Clerk of the County Court of said County this 16th day of January 1837- Wm H Tunstall

[p 142] Polly Cole- Pittsylvania Clerks Office Sct - No 300- **POLLY COLE** a free Woman of Colour is this day numbered and registered in the said Office according to law- The said POLLY COLE is a bright Mulatto Woman about nineteen years of age about five feet six and a quarter inches high has a scar on the forefinger of the left hand said to be occasioned by a Cut and another near the left wrist rather on the thumb and a mole on the upper lip without any other apparent mark or scar- Given under my hand as Clerk of the County Court of said County this 17th day of April 1837- Wm H Tunstall

William Hendrick- Pittsylvania Clerks Office Sct- No 301- **WILLIAM HENDRICK** a free man of Colour is this day numbered and registered in the said Office according to law- The said WILLIAM HENDRICK is a man of dark Complexion about twenty two years of age about five feet five and a quarter inches high & has a scar on each joint of the left thumb without any other apparent mark or scar- Given under my hand as Clerk of the County Court of said County this 19th day of June 1837- Wm H Tunstall

John Hendrick- Pittsylvania Clerks Office Sct - No 302- **JOHN HENDRICK** a free man of Colour is this day numbered and registered in the said Office according to law- The said JOHN HENDRICK is a man of rather dark Complexion about twenty six years of age about five feet five inches high & has a scar on the back of the left hand and one on the joint of the thumb of the right hand, without any other apparent mark or scar- Given under my hand as Clerk of the County Court of said County this 19th day of June 1837- Wm H Tunstall

Temperance Hendrick - Pittsylvania Clerks Office Sct - No 303- **TEMPERANCE HENDRICK** a free Woman of Colour is this day numbered [p 143] and registered in the said Office according to law- The said TEMPERANCE HENDRICK is a woman of rather light Complexion about twenty years of age five feet two inches high & has a scar on her right arm just above the wrist without any other apparent mark or scar- Given under my hand as Clerk of the County Court of said County this 19th day of June 1837- Wm H Tunstall

Caty Star- Pittsylvania Clerks Office Sct- No 304- **CATY STAR** a free Woman of Colour is this day numbered and registered in the said Office according to law- The said CATY STAR is a Woman of rather light Complexion about twenty one years of age four feet ten inches high and has a scar on the joint of the forefinger of the left hand and one just above the joint of the same finger and one on the back of the right hand rather on the joint of the finger without any other apparent mark or scar- Given under my hand as Clerk of the County Court of said County this 21st day of June 1837- Wm H Tunstall

Winny Star - Pittsylvania Clerks Office Sct - No 305- **WINNY STAR** a free Woman of Colour is this day numbered & registered in the said Office according to law- The said WINNY STAR is a woman of rather light Complexion five feet one inch high nearly blind in the left eye and has a very small scar Just above the joint of the thumb of the right hand without any other apparent mark or scar- Given under my hand as Clerk of the County Court of said County this 19th day of June 1837- Wm H Tunstall

Lucy Ann Dobson- Pittsylvania Clerks Office Sct- No 306- **LUCY ANN DOBSON** a free Woman of Colour is this day numbered &

registered in the said Office according to law- The said LUCY ANN DOBSON is a Woman of dark Complexion about 30 years of age 5 feet 1 inch high & has a scar on the left cheek supposed to be occasioned by a burn a scar over the left eye and one in the forehead occasioned by cuts one near the joint of the [p 144] thumb of the left hand several on the left wrist and two on the right wrist without any other apparent mark or scar- Given under my hand as Clerk of the County Court of said County this 22nd day of August 1837- Wm H Tunstall

Jane Davis- Va Pittsylvania County to wit- No 307- **JANE DAVIS** a free Woman of Colour is this day numbered & registered in the said Office according to law- The said JANE DAVIS is a mulatto Woman about twenty one years of age five feet four and an half inches high & has a scar on the Wrist of the right hand without any other apparent Mark or Scar- Given under my hand as Clerk of the said Court this 18th day of September 1837- Wm H Tunstall

Letitia Johnson- Pittsylvania Clerks Office Sct- No 308- **LETITIA JOHNSON** a free Woman of Colour is this day numbered [p 143] and registered in the said Office according to law- The said LETITIA JOHNSON is about 5 feet 2 inches high of a rather light Complexion twenty four years of age the 1st day of March next has a scar on the inside of the left arm just above the wrist said to be occasioned by a burn without any other apparent mark or scar- Given under my hand as Clerk of the County Court of said County this 18th day of September 1837- Wm H Tunstall

Joseph Bybee- Pittsylvania County to wit- No 309- **JOSEPH BYBEE** a free man of Colour is this day numbered & registered in the Clerks office of the County Court of sd County according to Law- The said JOSEPH BYBEE is a mulatto Man about twenty seven years of age five feet three and a half inches high with the left arm considerably smaller than the other and has a scar on the forehead occasioned by a burn without any other apparent mark or scar- Given under my hand as Clerk of the County Court aforesaid this 16th day of Octr 1837- Wm H Tunstall

[p 145] Julia Ann Reynolds- Pittsylvania Clerks Office Sct- No 310- **JULIA ANN REYNOLDS** a free Woman of Colour is this day

numbered and registered in the Clerks office of the County Court aforesaid according to Law- The said JULIA ANN REYNOLDS is a bright Mulatto Woman fifty six years of age the 4th of February next five feet three and a fourth inches high has small scars on the back of the left hand also a small one in the forehead and a very large one on the right arm- Given under my hand as Clerk of the County Court aforesaid this 21st day of Novem 1837- Wm H Tunstall

Sarah Winn Reynolds- Pittsylvania County to wit- No 311- **SARAH WINN REYNOLDS** a free Woman of Colour is this day numbered and registered in the Clerks office of the County Court aforesaid according to Law- The said SARAH WINN REYNOLDS is a dark Mulatto Woman twenty years of age the 9th of this month five feet one and a fourth inches high has a small scar on the last joint of the right middle finger and another on the last joint of the little finger without &ct- Given under my hand as Clerk of the County Court aforesaid this 21st day of Novr 1837- Wm H Tunstall

Jane Harriett Reynolds- Pittsylvania County to wit- No 312- **JANE HARRIETT REYNOLDS** a free Woman of Colour is this day numbered and registered in the Clerks office of the County Court aforesaid according to Law - The said JANE HARRIETT REYNOLDS is a dark Mulatto Woman nineteen years of age five feet one and a half inches high and has a small Mark on the right Cheek and a small scar on the first joint of the right thumb without any other apparent Mark or scar- Given under my hand as Clerk of the County Court aforesaid this 21st day of Novem 1837- Wm H Tunstall

[p 146] Royal Bolling- Virginia Pittsylvania County Clerks Office Sct- No 313- **ROYAL BOLLING** a free born man of Colour is this day numbered and registered in the said Office according to Law- The said ROYAL BOLLING is a dark Mulatto man five feet four and a half inches high about seven and twenty years of age has a small scar on the outer corner of the left eye brow and a long one on the inside of the third finger of the left hand without any other apparent mark or scar- Given under my hand as Clerk of the County Court aforesaid this 18th day of June 1838- Wm H Tunstall- Certified at June Court 1838-

Eliza Bowling- Virginia Pittsylvania County Clerks Office Sct- No 314- **ELIZA BOLLING** a free woman of Colour is this day numbered and registered in the said Office according to Law- The said ELIZA BOLLING is a red Mullatto [sic] about four feet Eight and three quarter inches high about seven and twenty years of age has a Very Small Scar over the right Corner of the mouth Shows her teeth very plainly- without any other apparent Mark or Scar- Given under my hand as Clerk of the County Court aforesaid this 18th day of June 1838- Wm H Tunstall- Certified at June Court 1838-

Henry Reynolds- Virginia Pittsylvania County Clerks Office Sct- No 315- **HENRY REYNOLDS** a free born man of Colour is this day numbered and registered in the said Office according to Law- The said HENRY REYNOLDS is a mullatto [sic] man about thirty years of age Six feet high (in boots) has a Small Scar over the left eye his left Thumb disfigured about the nail without any other apparent mark or scar- Given under my hand as Clerk of the County Court aforesaid this 18th day of June 1838- Wm H Tunstall- Certified at June Court 1838-

[p 147] Patsey Reynolds- Virginia Pittsylvania County Clerks Office Sct- No 316- **PATSEY REYNOLDS** wife of HENRY REYNOLDS a free born Woman of Colour is this day numbered and registered in the said Office according to Law- The said PATSEY REYNOLDS is a Woman of Very dark Complexion five feet three and a half inches high has a Small long Scar on her left jaw without any other apparent Mark or Scar- Given under my hand as Clerk of the said Court this 18th day of June one thousand eight hundred and thirty Eight- Wm H Tunstall- Certified at June Court 1838-

Bryant Soyars- Virginia Pittsylvania County Clerks Office Sct- No 317- **BRYANT SOYARS** a free born man of Colour is this day numbered and registered in the said Office according to Law- The said BRYANT SOYARS is of dark complexion five feet nine and three fourth inches high about two and twenty years of age has a small scar near the right Temple a small one in the right eye brow one on the lower part of the left hand and another on the inside of the left forefinger without any other apparent mark or scar- Given under my hand as Clerk of the said Court this 18th day of June 1838- Wm H Tunstall- Certified at June Court 1838-

Narcissa A Cole- Virginia Pittsylvania County Clerks Office Sct- No 318- **NARCISSA ADALINE COLE** a free woman of Colour is this day numbered and registered in the said Office according to Law- The said NARCISSA is a very bright mullatto [sic] Girl six feet half an inch high seventeen years of age this month without any apparent mark or scar- Given under my hand as Clerk of the said Court this 18th day of June 1838- Wm H Tunstall- Certified at June Court 1838-

[p 148] Susan Gaines- Virginia Pittsylvania County Clerks Office Sct- No 319- **SUSAN GAINES** a free woman of Colour is this day numbered and registered in the said Office according to law- The said SUSAN GAINES is of rather light complexion five feet five inches high about nine and twenty years of age has a very small round scar on the back of the right hand without any other apparent mark or scar- Given under my hand as Clerk of the said Court this 18th day of June 1838- Wm H Tunstall- Certified at June Court 1838-

Polly Davis- Virginia Pittsylvania County Clerks Office Sct- No 320- **POLLY DAVIS** a free woman of Colour is this day numbered and registered in the said Office according to Law- The said POLLY DAVIS is a bright Mullatto [sic] Woman five feet two and a half inches high three and twenty years of age in July next has a large Scar on the inside of the left wrist without any apparent Mark or Scar- Given under my hand as Clerk of the said Court this 18th day of June 1838- Wm H Tunstall- Certified at June Court 1838-

Nancy Jones- Virginia Pittsylvania County Clerks Office Sct- No 321- **NANCY JONES** a free woman of Colour is this day numbered and registered in the said Office according to Law- The said NANCY JONES is a bright mullatto [sic] five feet three and three fourth inches high about forty two years of age her nose rather low between the eyes without any apparent mark or scar- Given under my hand as Clerk of the said Court this 18th day of June 1838- Wm H Tunstall- Certified at June Court 1838-

[p 149] William Slone- Virginia Pittsylvania County Clerks Office Sct- No 322- **WILLIAM SLONE** a free born man of Colour is this day numbered and registered in the said Office according to Law- The said WM SLONE is a mullatto [sic] man about twenty six years of age five feet ten and a quarter inches high has a long Scar on the left arm without any apparent mark or scar- Given under my hand as Clerk of the County Court aforesaid this 18th day of June 1838- Wm H Tunstall- Certified at June Court 1838-

David Ellis-Virginia Pittsylvania County Clerks Office Sct- No 323- **DAVID ELLIS** a free born man of Colour is this day numbered and registered in the said Office according to Law- The said DAVID ELLIS is of very dark Complexion five feet 3 inches high twenty seven years of age has a small scar on his under lip one on the left Wrist and a mark running from near the Thumb to the same wrist joint without any other apparent mark or scar- Given under my hand as Clerk of the County Court aforesaid this 18th day of June 1838- Wm H Tunstall- Certified at June Court 1838-

John Whitticer-Virginia Pittsylvania County Clerks Office Sct- No 324- **JOHN WHITTICER** a free man of Colour is this day numbered and registered in the said Office according to Law- The said JOHN WHITTICER is of light Complexion twenty seven years of age five feet seven and a half inches high has a Small Scar just above the left corner of the left eye brow one on the left forefinger & another between the forefinger and the middle one both long ones without any other apparent mark or scar- Given under my hand as Clerk of the said Court this 18th day of June 1838- Wm H Tunstall- Certified at June Court 1838-

[p 150] Panthea Cole- Virginia Pittsylvania County Court Clerks Office Sct- No 235- **PANTHEA COLE** a free woman of Colour heretofore registered in the said Office according to Law is this day Re-registered according to law- The said PANTHEA is a bright mullatto [sic] five feet nine inches high one and twenty years of age in April last has a Small Scar on the left arm and a very Small one on the right side of the forehead and another very small one nearly between the left little finger & the one next thereto without any other apparent mark or scar- Given under my hand as Clerk of the

said Court this 18th day of June 1838- Wm H Tunstall- Certified at June Court 1838- **[Renewal]**

David Lewis-Virginia Pittsylvania County Court Clerks Office Sct- No 325- **DAVID LEWIS** a free man of Colour is this day numbered and registered in the said Office according to Law. The said DAVID LEWIS is of rather light complexion seven and thirty years of age in February last five feet nine and a quarter inches high (in pumps) has a Small Mole on the left side of the nose & a Small Scar on the right wrist without any other apparent mark or scar- Given under my hand as clerk of the said Court this 18th day of June 1838- Wm H Tunstall-Certified at June Court 1838.

Alexander Flag-Virginia Pittsylvania County Court Clerks Office Sct- No 326- **ALEXANDER FLAG** a free born man of Colour is this day numbered and registered in the said Office according to Law. The said ALEXANDER FLAG is of rather light complexion about seven and twenty years of age in February last five feet five and a half inches high (in shoes) has a scar on the right wrist one on the left corner of the forehead and a very small long one on the last joint of the left forefinger without any other apparent mark or scar- Given under my hand this 18th day of June 1838- Wm H Tunstall-Certified at June Court 1838.

[p 151] Jarvis Watts-Virginia Pittsylvania County Court Clerks Office Sct- No 327- **JARVIS WATTS** a free born man of Colour is this day numbered and registered in the said Office according to Law- The said JARVIS WATTS is of dark complexion four and twenty years of age five feet seven inches high (in boots) has several scars on his forehead one of them between the eye brows without any other apparent mark or Scar- Given under my hand as clerk of the said Court this 18th day of June 1838- Wm H Tunstall- Certified at June Court 1838.

James Fells-Virginia Pittsylvania County Court Clerks Office Sct- No 328- **JAMES FELLS** a free man of Colour is this day numbered and registered in the said Office according to Law- The said JAMES FELLS is of a rather light complexion seven and thirty years of age in February last five feet eight and a half inches high (in boots) has a Small Scar near the left eye two small ones on the left thumb a small one on the left wrist and another Small one on the neck near the throat without any other apparent mark or Scar- Given under my hand as clerk of the said Court this 18th day of June 1838- Wm H Tunstall-Certified at June Court 1838.

David Reynolds-Virginia Pittsylvania County Court Clerks Office Sct- No 329- **DAVID REYNOLDS** a free man of Colour is this day numbered and registered in the said Office according to Law- The said DAVID REYNOLDS is a bright mullato [sic] about five feet nine and three quarter inches high (in boots) twenty six years of age has a Scar on the lower part of the left thumb & another just below the last joint of the left forefinger and a very small one on the right nostril- Given under my hand as clerk of the County aforesaid this 19th day of June 1838- Wm H Tunstall- Certified at June Court 1838.

[p 152] Sally Reynolds-Virginia Pittsylvania County Court Clerks Office Sct- No 330- **SALLY REYNOLDS** a free woman of Colour & wife of DAVID REYNOLDS is this day numbered and registered in the said Office according to Law. The said SALLY REYNOLDS is of light complexion five feet four and a quarter inches high nine and twenty years of age has a Scar in the middle of her forehead one on the right arm 2 Small ones on the left forefinger & another on the left Thumb- without any other apparent mark or Scar- Given under my hand as clerk of the County aforesaid this 19th day of June 1838- Wm H Tunstall- Certified at June Court 1838.

Coleman Reynolds-Virginia Pittsylvania County Court Clerks Office Sct- No 331- **COLEMAN REYNOLDS** a free woman of Colour is this day numbered and registered in the said Office according to Law. The said COLEMAN REYNOLDS is of rather light complexion five feet seven inches high has several small scars on each hand twenty three years of age in March last- without any other apparent mark or Scar- Given under my hand as clerk of the County aforesaid this 19th day of June 1838- Wm H Tunstall- Certified at June Court 1838.

Doctor Reynolds-Virginia Pittsylvania County Court Clerks Office Sct- No 332- **DOCTOR REYNOLDS** a free born man of Colour is this day numbered and registered in the said Office according to

Law. The said DOCTOR REYNOLDS is a mullato [sic] man five feet ten and three quarters inches high seven and twenty years of age has a Scar on the under part of the left wrist the left little finger stiff without any other apparent mark or Scar- Given under my hand as clerk of the County aforesaid this 19th day of June 1838- Wm H Tunstall- Certified at June Court 1838. **[Renewal of No. 274]**

[p 153] Richard Jumper-Virginia Pittsylvania County Court Clerks Office Sct- No 333- **RICHARD JUMPER** a free born Man of Colour is this day numbered and registered in the said Office according to law. The said RICHARD JUMPER is about five feet ten and a half inches high and 20 years of age has two Scars on the back of the right hand one on the right forefinger one on the middle joint of the left forefinger and has on each hand what is commonly called a sixth finger without any other apparent mark or Scar- Given under my hand as clerk of the County aforesaid this 19th day of June 1838- Wm H Tunstall- Certified at June Court 1838.

James Jenkins-Virginia Pittsylvania County Clerks Office Sct- No 334- **JAMES JENKINS** a free born man of Colour is this day numbered and registered in the said Office according to law. The said JAMES JENKINS is of dark complexion about fifty years of age five feet six & a half inches high has a Scar on the left cheek one above the right eye and a large one on the right side of the neck near the throat- Given under my hand as clerk of the said Court this 19th day of June 1838- Wm H Tunstall- Certified at June Court 1838.

Susan Jenkins-Virginia Pittsylvania County Court Clerks Office Sct- No 335- **SUSAN JENKINS** a free born woman of Colour is this day numbered and registered in the said Office according to Law. The said SUSAN JENKINS is of a rather light complexion five feet two & a half inches high eight and thirty years of age the thirtieth December next has two small specks above the right eye one on the back of the right hand & two on the back of the left hand and a small Scar on the upper part of the left wrist without any other apparent mark or Scar- Given under my hand as clerk of the said County aforesaid this 19th day of June 1838- Wm H Tunstall- Certified at June Court 1838.

[p 154] Winny Reynolds-Virginia Pittsylvania County Court Clerks Office Sct- No 336- **WINNY REYNOLDS** a free born woman of Colour is this day registered in the said Office according to Law. The said WINNY REYNOLDS is of rather light complexion five feet four & three fourths inches high about three and thirty years of age has large eyes but no apparent Mark or Scar- Given under my hand as clerk of the said Court this 19th day of June 1838- Wm H Tunstall- Certified at June Court 1838. **[Renewal of No. 220]**

Susan Kirks-Virginia Pittsylvania County Court Clerks Office Sct- No 337- **SUSAN KIRKS** a free born woman of Colour is this day numbered and registered in the said Office according to Law. The said SUSAN KIRKS is of rather a yellow Complexion about five and twenty years of age five feet one inch and a quarter high has three long marks across the back of the right hand said to be occasioned by Scratch of a Cat without any other apparent Mark or Scar- Given under my hand as clerk of the County aforesaid this 19th day of June 1838- Wm H Tunstall- Certified June Court 1838.

Vervain Jackson-Virginia Pittsylvania County Court Clerks Office Sct- No 338- **VERVAIN JACKSON** a free born man of Colour is this day numbered and registered in the said Office according to Law. The said VERVAIN JACKSON is of light Complexion two and twenty years of age in March last five feet six & a half inches high has a Scar on the forehead has a small scar on the upper part of the right hand a small one on the back of the left hand and one on the left arm near the wrist without any other apparent Mark or Scar- Given under my hand as clerk of the County aforesaid this 19th day of June 1838- Wm H Tunstall- Certified at June Court 1838.

[p 155] Mary Ann Copage-Virginia Pittsylvania County Court Clerks Office Sct- No 339- **MARY ANN COPAGE** a free born woman of Colour is this day numbered and registered in the said Office according to Law. The said MARY ANN COPAGE is a red Mullatto [sic] one and twenty years of age five feet five and one fourth inches high has a very Small Scar on the left little finger and one on the left side of the neck without any other apparent Mark or Scar- Given under my hand as clerk of the said Court this 19th day of June 1838- Wm H Tunstall- Certified at June Court 1838.

Milton Reynolds-Virginia Pittsylvania County Court Clerks Office Sct- No 340- **MILTON REYNOLDS** a free born man of Colour is this day numbered and registered in the said Office according to Law. The said MILTON REYNOLDS is a very bright Mulatto five feet seven and a half inches high about two and twenty years of age in June last has a Scar over the right corner of the left eyebrow another on the lower part of the back of the right hand another on or near the middle joint of the left forefinger and another on the back of the left middle finger between the 2nd & third joints and one on the right arm without any other apparent Mark or Scar- Given under my hand as clerk of the County Court aforesaid this 16th day of July 1838- Wm H Tunstall- Certified at July Court to be correct.

Randol Johnson-Virginia Pittsylvania County Court Clerks Office Sct- No 341- **RANDOL JOHNSON** a free born man of Colour is this day numbered and registered in the said Office according to Law. The said RANDOL JOHNSON is a bright Mulatto five feet six and a quarter inches high one & twenty years of age the 10th day of March last has a long Scar over the left eye, a small one on the large part of the thumb near the wrist one on the throat and a large one on the inside of the right wrist without any other apparent Mark or Scar- Given under my hand as clerk of the County Court aforesaid this 16th day of July 1838- Wm H Tunstall- Certified at July Court 1838 to be correct.

[p 158] William Reynolds-Virginia Pittsylvania County Court Clerks Office Sct- No 342- **WILLIAM REYNOLDS** a free born man of Colour is this day numbered and registered in the said Office according to Law. The said WILLIAM REYNOLDS is of rather light Complexion five feet seven and three quarter inches high three and twenty years of age in June last & has a tolerbly [sic] high forehead without any other apparent Mark or Scar- Given under my hand as clerk of the County Court aforesaid this 16th day of July 1838- Wm H Tunstall- Certified at July Court 1838 **[Page is incorrectly numbered; should be p 156.]**

Polly Ross- Virginia Pittsylvania County Court Clerks Office Sct- No 343- **POLLY ROSS** a free born woman of Colour is this day numbered and registered in the said Office according to law. The said POLLY ROSS is of rather brown or light Complexion about nineteen years of age five feet high without any apparent Mark or Scar- Given under my hand as clerk of the County Court aforesaid this 16th day of July 1838- Wm H Tunstall- Certified at July Court 1838 to be correct [This may be a Renewal of No. 215, a child of Mary MASON alias ROSS.]

Lucinda Valentine- Virginia Pittsylvania County Court Clerks Office Sct- No 224- **LUCINDA VALENTINE** alias **LUCINDA MASON** (wife of ROBERT MASON) a free born woman of Colour is this day re-registered in the said Office according to law. The said LUCINDA is a bright mulatto five feet half an inch high about thirty years of age has a small scar about an inch long on the inside of the left wrist, one on the upper part of the right hand near the wrist a small one on the forehead & another on the left side of the throat without any apparent Mark or Scar- Given under my hand as clerk of the County Court aforesaid this 16th day of July 1838- Wm H Tunstall- Certified at July Court 1838   **[Renewal; Incorrectly numbered as 224, but should be 244; married after her original registration as LUCY VALENTINE.]**

[p 157] Robert Mason- Virginia Pittsylvania County Court Clerks Office Sct- No 253- **ROBERT MASON** a free born man of Colour is this day re-registered in the said Office according to law. The said ROBERT MASON is of dark complexion about eight and twenty years of age five feet seven and a quarter inches high has a small Scar on the right wrist one on the left arm about five or six inches long and a very small one over the left eye without any other apparent mark or Scar- Given under my hand as clerk of the County Court aforesaid this 16th day of July 1838- Wm H Tunstall- Certified at July Court 1838   **[Renewal]**

Martha Reynolds- Virginia Pittsylvania County Court Clerks Office Sct- No 266- **MARTHA REYNOLDS** a free born woman of Colour heretofore Registered in the said Office is this day again Re-registered according to law. The said MARTHA REYNOLDS is of a rather light Complexion twenty three years of age last Christmas five feet three and a half inches high has a small Scar on the back of the left hand another on the 1st Joint of the left thumb another on the forehead and one near the outer Corner of the left eye without any other apparent mark or Scar- Given under my hand the 21st day of June one thousand eight hundred and thirty eight- Wm H Tunstall- Certified at June Court 1838 **[Renewal; The word 'again' in Line 3 has been struck over.]**

Robert Cousins- Virginia Pittsylvania County Court Clerks Office Sct- No 344- **ROBERT COUSINS** a free born man of Colour is this day numbered and registered in the said Office according to Law. The said ROBERT COUSINS is a bright Mallatto [sic] five feet six and a quarter inches high about forty three years of age has a Scar across the left wrist and is very bald without any other apparent Mark or Scar- Given under my hand as clerk of the County Court aforesaid this 21st day of August 1838- William H Tunstall- Certified at August Court 1838

[Beginning here, the registrants' names are no longer consistently written in the margin of the Register.]

[p 158] Virginia Pittsylvania County Court Clerks Office Sct- No 345- **PETER VALENTINE** a free born man of Colour is this day numbered and registered in the said Office according to law. The said PETER VALENTINE is of black complexion five feet two and a half inches high about twenty six years of age has a Scar on the forehead over the left eye & another on the left jaw & a small one on the right side of the nose & another not very plain in the forehead without any other apparent Mark or Scar- Given under my hand as clerk of the County Court aforesaid this 22nd day of August 1838- William H Tunstall- Certified at August Court 1838

Virginia Pittsylvania County Court Clerks Office Sct- No 246- **ROYAL VALENTINE** a free born man of Colour is this day re-registered in the said Office according to law. The said ROYAL VALENTINE is a black man five feet two inches and three quarters high has several small Scars over his eyes and a large scar on the right jaw without any other apparent mark or Scar- Given under my hand as clerk of the County Court aforesaid this 22nd day of August 1838- William H Tunstall- Certified at August Co 38 **[Renewal]**

Virginia Pittsylvania County Court Clerks Office Sct- No 346- **ELIZA REYNOLDS** a free born woman of Colour is this day numbered and registered in the said Office according to law- The said ELIZA REYNOLDS is a very bright mullatto [sic] in the 21st year of her age five feet one inch and a quarter high, has a very small Scar on the inside and another on the outside of the left wrist, has two moles under the left eye forehead, has tolerably straight, light hair, and both little fingers have the appearance of being crooked, without any other apparent Mark or Scar- Given under my hand as clerk of the County Court aforesaid this 22nd day of August 1838- William H Tunstall- Certified at August Court 1838.

[p 159] Virginia Pittsylvania County Court Clerks Office Sct- No 243- **SAMUEL VALENTINE** a free born man of Colour is this day re-registered in the said Office according to law. The said SAMUEL VALENTINE is of dark complexion five feet two and a half inches high about three and thirty years of age has a large scar on the forehead rather over the left eye and a small one near the middle of the forehead without any other apparent mark or Scar- Given under my hand as clerk of the County Court aforesaid this 22nd day of August 1838- William H Tunstall- Certified at August Co 38 **[Renewal]**

Virginia Pittsylvania County Court Clerks Office Sct- No 241- **POLLY VALENTINE** a free born woman of Colour is this day re-registered in the said Office according to law. The said POLLY VALENTINE is of dark complexion five feet six inches high about thirty four years of age the 16th day of December next has a small scar on the large joint of the left forefinger & one on the right wrist and another on the upper part of the back of the left hand without any other apparent mark or Scar- Given under my hand as clerk of the County Court aforesaid this 22nd day of August 1838- William H Tunstall- Certified at August Co 38 **[Renewal; however, there has been a mix-up, as this number belongs to AMY VALENTINE. POLLY's number was originally 242.]**

Virginia Pittsylvania County Court Clerks Office Sct- No 347- **JUDY VALENTINE** a free born woman of Colour is this day numbered and registered in the said Office according to Law- The said JUDY VALENTINE is of black complexion about twenty four years of age this month five feet two inches and a quarter high, has a small long Scar on the back of the left hand one in the left cheek one on the forehead another over the left eye & another in or near the right eyebrow without any other apparent Mark or Scar- Given under my hand as clerk of the County Court aforesaid this 22nd day of August 1838- William H Tunstall- Certified at August Court 1838.

[p 160] Virginia Pittsylvania County Court Clerks Office Sct- No 348- **CLEM HARRAWAY** a man of Colour Emancipated by the Will of George Harraway Decd as appears by a register from the County Court of Charlotte County is this day registered in the said Office according to law- The said CLEM HARRAWAY is a very bright Mullatto [sic] five feet nine inches and a half high thirty one years of age the 18th day of August last, has a small mole over his right eye and one on the left side of his neck without any other apparent Mark or Scar- Given under my hand as clerk of the County Court aforesaid this 17th day of September 1838- William H Tunstall- Certified at Septemr Co 38.

Virginia Pittsylvania County Court Clerks Office Sct- No 349- **JANE HARRAWAY** a free born woman of Colour as appears from a copy of her register certified by the Clerk of the County Court of Campbell [County] is this day numbered and registered in the said Office according to law- The said JANE HARRAWAY is a bright Mullatto [sic] woman twenty nine years of age the 17th day of November next five feet five inches high, has a small black mole on the right cheek and another rather under the left corner of the mouth without any other apparent Mark or Scar- Given under my hand as clerk of the County Court aforesaid this 17th day of September 1838- William H Tunstall- Certified at Septemr Co 38.

Virginia Pittsylvania County Court Clerks Office Sct- No 350- **MARTHA MARSHALL** a free born woman of Colour is this day numbered and registered in the said Office according to law- The said MARTHA MARSHALL is a very bright Mullatto [sic] five feet six inches high, about nineteen years of age the 18th day of August last and has a Scar on the right middle finger and one on [p 161] the left little finger without any other apparent Mark or Scar-

Given under my hand as clerk of the County Court aforesaid this 17th day of September 1838- William H Tunstall- Certified at Septemr Co 38.

Virginia Pittsylvania County Court Clerks Office Sct- No 351- **BURTON REYNOLDS** a free born man of Colour is this day numbered and registered in the said Office according to law- The said BURTON REYNOLDS is a bright mullatto [sic] man five feet seven inches and a half high, Eight and thirty years of age the 28th day of October next has a Scar on the upper part of the left hand near the wrist & one on the left wrist without any other apparent mark or Scar- Given under my hand as clerk of the County Court aforesaid this 17th day of September 1838- Wm H Tunstall- Certified at September Co 38.

Virginia Pittsylvania County Court Clerks Office Sct- No 352- **POLLY REYNOLDS** (Wife of BURTON REYNOLDS) a free born Woman of Colour is this day numbered and registered in the said Office according to law- The said POLLY REYNOLDS is a bright Mullatto [sic] Woman five feet seven and a quarter inches high, thirty years old last March has two warts on the right middle finger directly on her middle joint and a very small Scar on the back of the left hand without any other apparent mark or Scar- Given under my hand as clerk of the County Court aforesaid this 17th day of September 1838- Wm H Tunstall- Certified at September Co 38.

Virginia Pittsylvania County Court Clerks Office Sct- No 353- **MARTHA REYNOLDS** a free born Girl of Colour and daughter of BURTON & POLLY REYNOLDS is this day numbered [p 162] and registered in the said Office according to law- The said MARTHA REYNOLDS is a bright Mullatto [sic] Girl five feet three inches high, twelve years old the 23rd day of July last, has a Scar on the inside of the left wrist and a small one on the left forefinger without any other apparent mark or Scar- Given under my hand as clerk of the County Court aforesaid this 17th day of September 1838- Wm H Tunstall- Certified at September Court 1838.

Mary Young- Virginia Pittsylvania County Court Clerks Office Sct- No 354- **MARY YOUNG** a free born woman of Colour is this day numbered & registered in the said Office according to Law- The said MARY YOUNG is of light complexion five feet high, twenty three years of age the thirtieth day of August last, has a very small Scar on the back of the left hand over the joint of the third fingger [sic] a small mole near the outer Corner of the left eye and another near the large Joint of the right middle finger Without any other apparent mark or Scar- Given under my hand this 15th day of October 1838- William H Tunstall Clk- Certified at Octo Court 1838.

Anthony Young- Virginia Pittsylvania County Court Clerks Office Sct- No 355- **ANTHONY YOUNG** a free born man of Colour is this day numbered & registered in the said Office according to Law- The said ANTHONY YOUNG is a mulato [sic] man five feet eight and a half inches high, twenty one years of age the Twenty ninth March last, has a long Scar over the left eye brow, one between the nose and the left corner of the mouth and another on the upper part of the left thumb- also four others on the upper part of the left forefinger without any other apparent mark or Scar- Given under my hand this 15th day of October 1838- William H Tunstall Cl- Certified at Octo Court 1838.

[p 163] Parthenia Young- Virginia Pittsylvania County Court Clerks Office Sct- No 356- **PARTHENIA YOUNG** a free born woman of Colour is this day numbered & registered in the said Office according to Law- The said PARTHENIA YOUNG is a mulato [sic] woman five feet six inches high, nineteen years of age the first day of September last, has a small Scar near the outer corner of the Left eye a small one next the right nostril and another on the upper part of the left thumb without any other apparent mark or Scar- Given under my hand as clerk of the County Court aforesaid this 15th day of October 1838- William H Tunstall Cl- Certified at Octo Court 1838.

Martha Young- Virginia Pittsylvania County Court Clerks Office Sct- No 357- **MARTHA YOUNG** a free born woman of Colour is this day numbered & registered in the said Office according to Law- The said MARTHA YOUNG is a mulato [sic] Girl five feet two and a half inches high, Sixteen years of age the 4th Instant, has a Scar rather between the nose and the left eye brow Without any other apparent mark or Scar- Given under my hand this 15th day of October 1838- William H Tunstall Cl- Certified at Octo Court 1838.

Sally Ann Young- Virginia Pittsylvania County Court Clerks Office Sct- No 358- **SALLY ANN YOUNG** a free born woman of Colour is this day numbered & registered in the said Office according to Law- The said SALLY ANN YOUNG is a girl of a very light complexion four feet eleven and a half inches high, Fourteen years of age the sixth day of November next, has a very small Scar on the forehead rather near the left eye & another on the throat without any other apparent mark or Scar- Given under my hand this 15th day of October 1838- William H Tunstall Cl- Certified at Octo Court 1838.

[p 164] Nancy Phillips- Virginia Pittsylvania County Court Clerks Office Sct- No 359- **NANCY PHILLIPS** a free born woman of Colour is this day numbered & Registered in the said Office according to Law- The said NANCY PHILLIPS is of rather light complexion five feet five and a half inches high, said to be eight and forty years of age this Month, has a few very small Scars not very distinct on the outer side of each arm, a small one on the inner side of the left arm just above the wrist, and a very small one immediately between the eyes without any other apparent mark or Scar- Given under my hand as clerk of said County this 18th day of March 1839- Wm H Tunstall- Certified at March Court 1839.

James Mann- Virginia Pittsylvania County Court Clerks Office Sct- No 360- **JAMES MANN** a free born man of Colour is this day numbered & Registered in the said Office according to Law- The said JAMES MANN is a bright mulatto five feet four inches and a half high, two and twenty years of age the 25th day of December last, has a Small Scar rather between the nail and Joint of the right thumb, a small one on the second joint of the left little finger, a small one on the first joint of the next finger, and a large one on the breast without any other apparent mark or Scar- Given under my hand as clerk of the County Court aforesaid this 20th day of May 1839- Wm H Tunstall [p 165] Virginia Pittsylvania County Court Clerks Office Sct- No 359- **ROBERT SMITH** a free born man of Colour as appears from a Copy of his register in the County Court of Chesterfield is this day Numbered & Registered in the said Office according to Law- The said ROBERT SMITH is a black man five feet eight and a half inches high with shoes, nineteen years of age, has a Small Scar on the left thumb a mark on the back of the right hand a small scar or nick on the under lid of the left eye and another on the left side of the forehead in the edge of the hair, without any other apparent mark or Scar- Given under my hand as clerk of the County Court aforesaid this 20th day of August 1839- Wm H Tunstall- Certified at August Co 1839- **[This registration number is a duplicate, and was given just above to NANCY PHILLIPS.]**

Virginia Pittsylvania County Court Clerks Office Sct- No 360- **THOMAS SMITH** a free born man of Colour as appears from a Copy of his register in the County Court of Chesterfield is this day Numbered & Registered in the said Office according to Law- The said THOMAS SMITH is a man of light complexion five feet ten & a half inches high with shoes, Twenty four years of age, has two Small Scars on the right wrist, another very small one on the under part of the left wrist and another on the upper part of the left thumb, without any other apparent mark or Scar- Given under my hand as clerk of the County Court of said County this 20th day of August 1839- Wm H Tunstall- Certified at August Co 1839- **[This registration number is a duplicate, and was given just above to JAMES MANN.]**

Virginia Pittsylvania County Court Clerks Office Sct- No 361- **LINDSEY WASHINGTON WILLIAMS** a free born man of Colour as appears from a Copy of his register from the County of Henrico is this day numbered & registered in the said Office according to Law- The said LINDSEY WASHINGTON WILLIAMS is a man of rather light complexion about five and twenty years of age, five feet six & [p 166] a half inches high in shoes, has a Scar on the left arm between the elbow and shoulder without any other apparent Mark or Scar- Given under My hand as clerk of the County Court of said County this 20th day of August 1839- Wm H Tunstall- Certified at Aug Co 1839-

Virginia Pittsylvania County Court Clerks Office Sct- No 362- **THOMAS ROBERTSON** a free born man of Colour is this day numbered & registered in the said Office according to Law- The said THOMAS ROBERTSON is a black man six feet one inch high in shoes, has lost one of his upper front teeth without any other apparent Mark or Scar- Given under my hand as clerk of the County Court aforesaid this 16th day of September 1839- Wm H Tunstall- Certified Sept Co 1839-

Virginia Pittsylvania County Court Clerks Office Sc- No 363- **ANNA CHAVIS** a free born woman of Colour is this day numbered & registered in the said office according to law- The said ANNA CHAVIS is a woman of rather light complexion five feet three & a half inches high in shoes, about fifty four years of age, has a small mole on the neck without any other apparent Mark or Scar- Given under my hand as clerk of the County Court aforesaid this 16th day of September 1839- Wm H Tunstall- Certified Sept Co 1839-

Virginia Pittsylvania County Court Clerks Office Sc- No 290- **SAMUEL SHORT** a free man of Colour who it appears was emancipated by the last will and testament of Benjamin Webber decd late of the County of Cumberland heretofore numbered and registered in this office is this day re-registered in the said office according to law- The said SAMUEL SHORT is a man of black complexion about forty years of age, five feet five inches and a quarter high, has a small scar on the forehead immediately in the edge of the [p 167] hair several small Scars between his fingers on the left hand without any other apparent Mark or Scar- Given under my hand as clerk of the County Court aforesaid this 16th day of September 1839- Wm H Tunstall- Certified Sept Co 1839- **[Renewal]**

Virginia Pittsylvania County Court Clerks Office Sc- No 273- **JACOB COUSINS** a free man of Colour is this day numbered & registered in the said office according to law- The said JACOB COUSINS is a man of dark complexion about forty years of age five feet five & a half inches high, has a scar over the right eye and a small one over the left eye, Also one under the chin, a Cut on the inside of the right hand, and has a stiff knee which causes him to limp- Given under my hand as clerk of the County Court of said

County this 10th day of June 1840- Wm H Tunstall- Certifd June Court 1840- **[Renewal]**

Virginia Pittsylvania County Court Clerks Office Sc- No 364- **MILDRED LEWIS** a free born woman of Colour is this day Numbered & registered in the said office according to law- The said MILDRED LEWIS is a mulatto woman five feet five & a half inches high in shoes, three and twenty years of age the 4th day of July last, without any other apparent mark or Scar- Given under my hand as Clerk of the County Court aforesaid this 18th day of August 1840- Wm H Tunstall- Certifd Aug Court 1840-

Virginia Pittsylvania County Court Clerks Office Sc- No 365- **REBECCA DAVIS** formerly **REBECCA MACKLIN** a free born woman of Colour as appears from a Copy of her register certified by the Clerk of the County Court of Mechlenburg is this day numbered & registered in the said office according to Law- The said REBECCA DAVIS is a woman of rather light complexion, five feet quarter of an inch high, has a small scar on the left arm just below the elbow without any other apparent Mark or Scar- Given under my hand as Clerk of the County Court aforesaid [p 168] this 24 day of September 1840- Wm H Tunstall- Certifd Sep Co 1840.

Samuel Walls Register-Virginia Pittsylvania County Court Clerks Office Sc- No 366- **SAMUEL WALLS** a free born man of Colour as appears from a Copy of his register certified by the Clerk of the County Court of Rockbridge is this day numbered & registered in the said office according to Law- The said SAMUEL WALLS is a man of light complexion, 37 years old the fifteenth day of April last, five feet six inches & a half high, has a small scar between the eyes on the upper part of the nose, has a number of small scars partly under the left side of his breast, also a scar on the inside of the right leg above the ankle without any other apparent Mark or Scar- Given under my hand as Clerk of the County Court aforesaid this 21st day of September 1840- Wm H Tunstall- Certified Sep Co 1840.

John Davis Register-Virginia Pittsylvania County Court Clerks Office Sc- No 367- **JOHN DAVIS** a free born man of Colour is this day numbered & registered in the said office according to law- The said JOHN DAVIS is a man of yellow complexion Twenty two years old the 20th day of October next, five feet eight inches high in boots, a small scar on the forefinger of the left hand, without any other apparent mark or Scar- Given under my hand this 24th day of September 1840- Wm H Tunstall- Certifd Sep Court 1840-

Virginia Pittsylvania County Court Clerks Office Sct- No 368- **ALEXANDER POUNDS** a free born man of Colour is this day numbered & registered in the said office according to Law- The said ALEXANDER POUNDS is a mulatto man one & twenty years of age the 10th day of April last, five feet four & three quarter inches high in Shoes, has a very Small Scar just above the right corner of his mouth and no other apparent mark or Scar- [p 169] Given under my hand as clerk of the said County Court This 17th day of November 1840- Wm H Tunstall

Virginia Pittsylvania County Court Clerks Office Sc- No 329- **DAVID REYNOLDS** a free born man of Colour heretofore numbered and registered in this office is this day re-registered in the said office according to law- The said DAVID REYNOLDS is a bright mulatto five feet ten inches high in boots, about Twenty nine years of age in June next, has a small Scar on the lower part of the left thumb another just below the last joint of the left forefinger and a very small one on the right nostril, without any other apparent mark or scar- Given under my hand as Clerk of the said County this 21st day of December 1840- Wm H Tunstall- Certifd at December Court 1840- **[Renewal]**

Virginia Pittsylvania County Court Clerks Office Sc- No 315- **HENRY REYNOLDS** a free born man of Colour heretofore numbered and registered in this office is this day re-registered in the said office according to law- The said HENRY REYNOLDS is a mulatto man about thirty three years of age in June next, about six feet three inches high in boots, has a small scar over the left eye, his left thumb disfigured about the nail, without any other apparent mark or scar- Given under my hand as Clerk of said County this 21st day of December 1840- Wm H Tunstall- Certifd at Decem Co 1840- **[Renewal]**

Virginia Pittsylvania County Court Clerks Office Sc- No 369- **MARY DAVIS** a free born woman of Colour is this day numbered and registered in the said office according to law- The said MARY DAVIS is a bright mulatto nineteen years old the twenty fifth day of January last, five feet three inches high, has a small scar near the large joint of the left forefinger, and another on the left jaw, without any other apparent mark or scar- Given under my hand as Clerk of said County this 20th day of September 1841- Wm H Tunstall- (Certified at Sep Co 1841)

[p 170] Virginia Pittsylvania County Court Clerks Office Sc- No 370- **WYATT JENKINS** a free born man of Colour is this day numbered and registered in the said office according to law- The said WYATT JENKINS is of tawny colour, three and twenty years old the thirteenth day of October next, five feet seven inches and a half high, has a scar on the inside of the right arm just above the wrist, and another on the upper part of the back of the left hand about two inches long- without any other apparent mark or scar- Given under my hand as Clerk of said County this 20th day of September 1841- Wm H Tunstall- Certified at Sep Co 1841

Virginia Pittsylvania County Court Clerks Office Sc- No 371- **ROBERT JENKINS** a free born man of Colour is this day numbered and registered in the said office according to law- The said ROBERT JENKINS is a man of tawny complexion, nineteen years old the fifteenth day of July last, five feet five and three quarter inches high, has a scar on the forehead in the edge of the hair, one on the right cheek, one on the upper part of the right arm just above the wrist, and another on the left arm just above the wrist without any other apparent mark or scar- Given under my hand as Clerk of said County this 20th day of September 1841- Wm H Tunstall- Certified at Sep Co 1841

Virginia Pittsylvania County Court Clerks Office Sc- No 372- **WILLIAM JENKINS** a free born man of Colour is this day numbered and registered in the said office according to law- The said WILLIAM JENKINS is of tawny complexion, one and twenty years old the eighth day of December next, five feet seven and three quarter inches high, has a long scar on the back of the left hand, one between the second and third joint of the left forefingers, the finger next to the little one on the left hand stiff or crooked with a scar on it, has another scar on the left temple without any other apparent mark or scar- Given under my hand as Clerk of said County this 20th day of September 1841- Wm H Tunstall- Certified at Sep Co 1841

[p 171] Virginia Pittsylvania County Court Clerks Office Sc- No 334- **JAMES JENKINS** a free born man of Colour is this day re-registered in the said office according to law- The said JAMES JENKINS is of rather light complexion, about fifty three years old five feet six inches and a half high, has a scar on the left cheek, one above the right eye and a large one on the right side of the neck near the throat. Given under my hand as Clerk of said County this 20th day of September 1841- Wm H Tunstall- Certified at Sep Co 1841 **[Renewal]**

Virginia Pittsylvania County Court Clerks Office Sc- No 373- **ELIJAH DAVIS** a free born man of Colour is this day numbered and registered in the said office according to law- The said ELIJAH DAVIS is a mulatto man, Twenty one years old the first day of this month (October) five feet five and a half inches high, has a small scar at the side of the left eye, without any other apparent mark or scar- Given under my hand as Clerk of said County this 19th day of October 1841- Wm H Tunstall- Certified at Octo Co 1841

Virginia Pittsylvania County Court Clerks Office Sc- No 374- **MARY JANE JENKINS** a free born woman of Colour is this day numbered and registered in the said office according to law- The said MARY JANE JENKINS is of a brown complexion, five feet three inches high, fifteen years old the eighth day of April next, has a small scar on the forehead, has another scar on the joint of the right wrist, without any other apparent mark or scar- Given under my hand as Clerk of the County Court of said County this fifteenth day of November 1841- Wm H Tunstall- Certifd at Nov Co 1841

Virginia Pittsylvania County Court Clerks Office Sc- No 375- **SALLY ANN JENKINS** a free born woman of Colour is this day numbered and registered in the said office according to law- The said SALLY ANN JENKINS is of a brown complexion, five feet two inches high, fourteen years old the twenty seventh day of January next, has a scar immediately under the left ear, has another [p 172] scar on the left hand near the wrist, without any other apparent mark or scar- Given under my hand as Clerk of the County Court of said County this fifteenth day of November 1841- Wm H Tunstall- (Certified at Nov Co 1841)

Virginia Pittsylvania County Court Clerks Office Sc- No 335- **SUSAN JENKINS** a free born woman of Colour is this day re-registered in the said office according to law- The said SUSAN JENKINS is of a rather light complexion, five feet three and a quarter inches high, forty one years of age the 30th day of December next, has two small specks above the right eye, one on the back of the right hand & two on the back of the left hand, and a small scar on the upper part of the left wrist, without any other apparent mark or scar- Given under my hand as Clerk of the County Court of said County this 15th day of November 1841- Wm H Tunstall- Certifd at Nov Co 1841   **[Renewal]**

Virginia Pittsylvania County Court Clerks Office Sc- No 376- **JOHN SOYARS** a free born man of Colour is this day numbered and registered in the said office according to Law- The said JOHN SOYARS is a man of a brown complexion, five feet six and a half inches high, twenty one years old the 25 day of March last, has a scar on the right side of the head, a small scar on his nose, has a scar on the joint of the wrist of the left hand and another small scar on his breast, without any other apparent mark or scar- Given under my hand as Clerk of the County Court of said County this 21st day of June 1842- Wm H Tunstall- (Certified June Co 1842)

[p 173] Virginia Pittsylvania County Court Clerks Office Sc- No 287- **REAMY BURNETT** a free born man of Colour is this day re-registered in the said office according to Law- The said REAMY BURNETT is of rather light complexion, twenty eight years old the 30 day of September last, five feet three inches and a half high, has a small long scar on the right cheek, also a small one on the upper part of the right hand, and has rather thick lips, without any other apparent mark or scar. Given under my hand as Clerk of the said County Court of Pittsylvania this 18th day of July 1842- Wm H Tunstall- (Certifd July Court 1842)   **[Renewal]**

Virginia Pittsylvania County Court Clerks Office Sct- No 262- **JOHN RICHARDSON** a free born man of Colour heretofore registered in the said Office this day applied for a renewal of the same- The said JOHN RICHARDSON is a black man five and thirty years of age in June last- five feet four & a half inches high, without any apparent mark or scar- Given under my hand as clerk of said County this 16th day of August 1842- Wm H Tunstall- (Certified at August Court 1842) **[Renewal]**

Virginia Pittsylvania County Court Clerks Office Sc- No 377- **JUDY STARR** a free woman of colour is this day numbered and Registered in the said office according to Law- The said JUDY STARR is a woman of tawny complexion and supposed to be from fifty to fifty five years old, four feet eleven inches and a half high, the Middle finger on the left hand is mashed at the end, without any other visible mark or scar- Given under my hand as Clerk of the County Court of said County this 15th day of August 1842- Wm H Tunstall- Certified Sep Court 1842

[p 174] Virginia Pittsylvania County Court Clerks Office Sc- No 378- **SAMUEL BURNETT** a free born man of colour is this day numbered and registered in the said office according to Law- The said SAMUEL BURNETT is of a Tawny complexion, Twenty Four years old the 13 day of next April, Five feet three and a half inches high, has a scar on the outer corner of the left eye, two small ones on his forehead, a tolerable large one on the neck & a high forehead, with no other visible mark or scar- Given under my hand as Clerk of the County Court of said County this 22nd day of November 1842- Wm H Tunstall- (Certified Nov Co 1842)

Virginia Pittsylvania County Court Clerks Office Sc- No 379- **STEPHEN ROBERTSON** a free born man of colour is this day numbered and Registered in the said office according to Law- The said STEPHEN ROBERTSON is a black man, five feet nine and a half inches high, twenty one years old the [left blank] day of [left blank] last, has a small yellow scar under the left eye, and a tolerable high forehead, with no other visible mark or scar- Given under my hand as Clerk of the County Court aforesaid this 13th day of May 1843- Wm H Tunstall- Certified May Co 1843

Virginia Pittsylvania County Court Clerks Office Sc- No 323- **DAVID ELLIS** a free born man of Colour is this day re-registered in the said office according to Law- The said DAVID ELLIS is of a very dark complexion, five feet three inches high, thirty two years old last June, has a small scar on his underlip, one on the left wrist, and a mark running from near the forefinger to the same wrist joint, has a small scar on the back of the other hand, without any other apparent mark or scar. Given under my hand as Clerk of the County Court of said County this 24th day of August 1843- Wm H Tunstall- Certified at Aug Court 1843 **[Renewal]**

[p 175] Virginia Pittsylvania County Court Clerks Office Sc- No 362- **THOMAS ROBERTSON** a free born man of Colour heretofore numbered and registered in the said office is this day re-registered according to law- The said THOMAS ROBERTSON is a black man, six feet one inch high in shoes, about 23 years old, has lost one of his upper front teeth, has a tolerable large scar across the first joint of the right little finger has a small scar on the left side of the middle finger of the left hand, without any other apparent mark or scar. Given under my hand this 15th day of September 1843- Wm H Tunstall Cl- Certified at September Co 1843 **[Renewal]**

Virginia Pittsylvania County Court Clerks Office Sc- No 380- **BETSEY HENDRICK** a free born woman of colour is this day numbered and Registered in the said office according to law- The said BETSEY HENDRICK is of black complexion, about twenty three years of age five feet and a quarter of an inch high, has a scar on the left cheek, the right forefinger cut off, and the middle finger of the same hand crooked, without any other apparent mark or scar- Given under my hand as Clerk of the County Court of said County this 15th day of October 1843- Wm H Tunstall- Certified at October Court 1843

Virginia Pittsylvania County Court Clerks Office Sc- No 381- **SALLY HENDRICK** a free born woman of colour is this day Numbered and registered in the said office according to law- The said SALLY HENDRICK is of a yellow complexion, about nineteen years old five feet four inches and a half high, has a scar on the right side of the neck caused by a burn, has only two toes on the left foot, the others having been cut off, without any other apparent mark or scar- Given under my hand this 15th day of October 1843- Wm H Tunstall Cl- Certified at October Court 1843

[p 176] No 382- **EMILY DODSON** a free born woman of colour is this day numbered and registered in the Clerks Office of the County Court of Pittsylvania according to law- The said EMILY DODSON is a woman of yellow complexion, four feet eleven inches high, eighteen years old the 22nd day of March 1843, has a Small Scar under the nose and a small Scar on the underlip, without any other apparent mark or scar- Given under my hand this 20th day of November A.D. 1843- William H Tunstall Cl- Certified Nov Co 1843

Virginia to wit- **WILMOTH STEPHENS** a free born woman of Colour daughter of CATHERINE STEPHENS who was emancipated by John Terry by deed of Record in the Clerks Office of Pittsylvania County Court, is this day re-registered in my office of the County Court of Pittsylvania according to Law- The said WILMOTH STEPHENS is a black woman, about forty three years old the 20th day of last June four feet eleven and three quarters inches high, has two small Scars on the left hand, one of which is near the wrist, another small scar on the middle joint of the first forefinger of the right hand, without any other apparent mark or scar- Given under my hand this 16th day of September 1844- Wm H Tunstall Clk- Certified Sept Co 1844 **[Renewal]**

Virginia to wit- No 383- **CHANEY STEPHENS** a free born woman of Colour is this day numbered and registered in the Clerks Office of the County Court of Pittsylvania according to Law- The said CHANEY STEPHENS is of a light complexion, about Twenty six years of age, five feet high, has several yellow marks on both cheeks & one on her chin, has a scar on the left temple caused by rising, a small scar between the first and second fingers of the right hand, has a small scar on the middle joint of the forefinger of the left hand, without any other apparent mark or scar- Given under my hand this the 16th day of September 1844- Wm H Tunstall Clk- Certified Sept Co 1844 [p 177] Virginia to wit- No 384- **MARTHA JANE STEPHENS** a free born woman of Colour is this day numbered and Registered in the Clerks Office of the County Court of Pittsylvania according to Law- The said MARTHA JANE STEPHENS is of a dark complexion, will be nineteen years old in February next, five feet three and a quarter inches high, has a scar on the inside of the left wrist, one on the back of the left hand, and one on the thumb of the same hand, without any other apparent mark or scar- Given under my hand this the 16th day of September 1844- Wm H Tunstall Clk- Certified Sept Co 1844

Virginia to wit- No 385- **MARY ANN STEPHENS** a free born woman of Colour is this day numbered and registered in the Clerks Office of the County Court of Pittsylvania according to Law- The said MARY ANN STEPHENS is of a dark complexion, Ninteen [sic] years old in February next, five feet two and a half inches high, has a scar on the side of the left wrist near the joint, without any other apparent mark or scar- Given under my hand this the 16th day of September 1844- Wm H Tunstall Clk- Certified Sept Co 1844

Virginia to wit- No 386- **SILVA STEPHENS** a free born woman of Colour is this day Numbered and registered in the Clerks Office of the County Court of Pittsylvania according to Law- The said SILVA STEPHENS is of a yellow complexion, about thirty five years old, five feet one and three quarters of an inch high, has a small scar on the side of the right wrist, another scar on the inside of the left wrist, another on the right side of the neck, without any other apparent mark or scar- Given under my hand this the 16th day of September 1844- Wm H Tunstall Clk- Certified Sept Co 1844

Virginia to wit- No 387- **HENRY STEPHENS** a free born man of Colour is this day Numbered and registered in the Clerks Office of the County Court of Pittsylvania according to Law- The said HENRY STEPHENS is of a dark complexion, Twenty four years [p 178] old the 21st day of Last June, five feet six & a quarter inches high, has several scars on the right hand near each other about the first joints of the fingers, several scars on the left hand near the first joints of the fingers, one on the chin & a large scar on the head, without any other apparent mark or scar- Given under my hand this the 16th day of September 1844- Wm H Tunstall Clk- Certified Sept Co 1844

Virginia to wit- No 387- **CHARITY STEPHENS** a free born woman of Colour is this day Numbered and registered in the Clerks Office of the County Court aforesaid according to Law- The said CHARITY STEPHENS is a woman of brown complexion, five feet four and three quarters high, thirty nine years of age the 10th day of January last, has a small black mole on the inside of the forefinger of the right hand, has a scar on the inside of the forefinger of the left hand, another on the corner of the right temple and has small ones on the forehead, without any other apparent mark or scar- Given under my hand this the 16th day of September 1844- Wm H Tunstall- Certified Sept Co 1844 **[Duplicate number; number was given just above to HENRY STEPHENS.]**

Virginia Pittsylvania County Court Clerks Office SC- No 66- **PHILLIS STEPHENS** a free born woman of Colour and daughter of CATHERINE STEPHENS who was emancipated by John Terry of record in Pittsylvania County Court, is this day re-registered in the said clerks office according to Law- The said PHILLIS STEPHENS is a woman of brown complexion, about forty one years of age, five feet four and a quarter inches high, has a Scar on the right Cheek about two inches long, has a swelling in the middle finger of the right hand near the hand, without any other apparent mark or scar- Given under my hand as Clerk of the County Court aforesaid this 17th day of February 1845- Wm H Tunstall- Certified at Feby Court 1845 **[Renewal]**

Virginia Pittsylvania County Court Clerks Office SC- No 67- **AGGA STEPHENS** a free born woman of Colour and daughter of CATHERINE [p 179] STEPHENS who was emancipated by deed from John Terry of record in Pittsylvania County Court, was this day re-registered in the said clerks office according to Law- The said AGGA STEPHENS is a woman of brown Complexion, five feet three and a half inches high, about thirty eight years of age, has a very Small Scar on the upper lip near the middle without any other apparent mark or scar- Given under my hand as Clerk of the

County Court aforesaid this 17th day of February 1845- Wm H Tunstall- Certified at Feby Court 1845 **[Renewal]**

Virginia Pittsylvania County Court Clerks Office SC- No 388- **SALLY STEPHENS** a woman of Colour and daughter of CATHERINE STEPHENS who was emancipated by Deed from John Terry of record in Pittsylvania County Court, was this day numbered and Registered in the said clerks office according to Law-The said SALLY STEPHENS is a woman of dark Complexion, five feet two and three quarters inches high, about twenty four or five years of age, has a very small scar on the right side of the forehead, without any other apparent mark or scar- Given under my hand as Clerk of the County Court aforesaid this 17th day of February 1845- Wm H Tunstall- Certified at Feby Court 1845

Virginia Pittsylvania County Court Clerks Office SC- No 389- **WM STEPHENS** a man of Colour and son of CATHERINE STEPHENS who was emancipated by Deed from John Terry of record in Pittsylvania County Court, was this day Numbered and Registered in the said clerks office according to Law- The said WM STEPHENS is a man of dark Complexion, about twenty seven years of age, five feet five and a quarter inches high has a small scar on the left side of the left hand near the wrist, without any other apparent mark or scar- Given under my hand as Clerk of the County Court aforesaid this 17th day of February 1845- Wm H Tunstall- Certified at Feby Court 1845

[p 180] Virginia Pittsylvania County to Wit- No 390- **MILLY DAVIS** a free born Woman of Colour is this day numbered and registered in the clerks office of the county court of Pittsylvania in the state aforesaid according to law- The said MILLY is a bright mulatto thirty years old the 27th of this month, five feet and a quarter of an inch high has a scar on the left side of her face near the ear, without any other apparent mark or scar- Given under my hand as Clerk of said Court aforesaid this 18th day of October 1845- Wm H Tunstall- Certified at October Court 1845

Virginia Pittsylvania County to Wit- No 391- **CATHERIN DAVIS** a free born woman of Colour is this day numbered and registered in the Clerks Office of the County Court of Pittsylvania in the State aforesaid according to Law- The said CATHERINE is a bright mulatto nineteen years old the 1st day of July last five feet one and a quarter inches high, without any other apparent mark or scar- Given under my hand as Clerk of said Court this 18th day of October 1845- Wm H Tunstall- Certified at October Court 1845

Virginia Pittsylvania County Sc- No 392- **LUCINDA DAVIS** a free born woman of Colour is this day numbered and registered in the Clerks Office of the County Court of Pittsylvania in the State aforesaid according to law- The said LUCINDA is a bright mulatto twenty three years old the 18th day of December next, five feet four inches high, has a mole between the eyes, another on the left side of the face near the mouth, without any other apparent mark or scar- Given under my hand as Clerk of said Court this 18th day of October 1845- Wm H Tunstall- Certified at October Court 1845

Virginia Pittsylvania County Sc- No 393- **NANCY DAVIS** a free born woman of Colour is this day numbered and registered in the Clerks Office of the County Court of Pittsylvania [p 181] in the State aforesaid according to law- The said NANCY is a bright mulatto twenty eight years old the 27th of this month, five feet three & a half inches high, has a small scar on the back of the right hand, without any other apparent mark or scar- Given under my hand as Clerk of said Court this 18th day of October 1845- Wm H Tunstall- Certified at October Court 1845

Virginia Pittsylvania County Sc- No 394- **FANNY ROSS** a free born woman of colour is this day numbered and registered in the Clerks Office of the County Court of Pittsylvania in the State aforesaid according to law- The said FANNY is of a tawny complexion about twenty two years of age, five feet six inches high, has a small mole over the left eye, a small scar on her chin, has another scar on the back of the left arm, without any other apparent mark or scar- Given under my hand as Clerk of said Court this 18th day of October 1845- Wm H Tunstall- Certified at October Court 1845 **[This may be a Renewal of No. 214, a child of Mary MASON alias ROSS.]**

Virginia Pittsylvania County Sc- No 395- **WILLIAM DAVIS** a free born man of colour is this day numbered and registered in the

Clerks Office of the County Court of Pittsylvania in the state aforesaid according to law- The said WILLIAM DAVIS is a man of yellow complexion about twenty six years of age, five feet five and a half inches high, has a small scar on the right side of the face about an inch or thereabouts from the corner of the mouth, another small scar on the side of the left arm near the wrist, without any other apparent mark or scar- Given under my hand as Clerk of said Court this 20th day of October 1845- Wm H Tunstall- Certified at October Court 1845

Virginia Pittsylvania County Sc- No 396- **ELIZA DAVIS** a free born woman of colour is this day numbered and registered in the Clerks Office of the County Court of Pittsylvania in the state aforesaid according to law- [p 182] The said ELIZA is a mulatto woman about thirty two years of age, five feet five and a half inches high, has a scar on the back of the left hand, another on the knuckol [sic] of the middle finger of the left hand, without any other apparent mark or scar- Given under my hand as Clerk of said Court this 20th day of October 1845- Wm H Tunstall Clk- Certified at October Court 1845

Virginia Pittsylvania County Sc- No 397- **ALBERT DAVIS** a free born man of colour is this day numbered and registered in the Clerks Office of the County Court of Pittsylvania according to law- The said ALBERT is a man of rather yellow complexion will be twenty two years old the twenty fifth day of next March, five feet eleven and a half inches high, has a small scar under the nose & another on the neck without any other apparent mark or scar- Given under my hand as clerk of the said Court this 20th day of October 1845- Wm H Tunstall Clk- Certified at October Court 1845

Virginia Pittsylvania County Sc- No 398- **ALFRED DAVIS** a free born man of colour is this day numbered and registered in the Clerks Office of the County Court of Pittsylvania according to law- The said ALFRED DAVIS is a man of rather yellow complexion will be twenty two years old the 20th day of March next, five feet eleven inches and a quarter high, has a small scar on the side of the right arm near the wrist, without any other apparent mark or scar- Given under my hand as clerk of the said Court this 20th day of October 1845- Wm H Tunstall Clk- Certified at October Court 1845

Virginia Pittsylvania County Sc- No 399- **HENDERSON COLE** a free born man of colour is this day numbered and registered in the Clerks Office of the County Court of Pittsylvania in the State [p 183] according to Law- The said HENDERSON is a man of bright complexion about twenty four years old the nineteenth day of December next, five feet three and a half inches high, has a scar on the right side of his neck another on his forehead, and another about an inch in length on the first Joint of the thumb of the left hand, without any other apparent mark or scar- Given under my hand as clerk of said Court this sixth day of November 1845- Wm H Tunstall Clk- Certified at November Court 1845

Virginia Pittsylvania County Sc- No 400- **NANCY COLE,** wife of HENDERSON COLE, a free born woman of colour is this day numbered and registered in the Clerks Office of the County Court of Pittsylvania in the State aforesaid according to law- The said NANCY is a yellow woman twenty two years old the 10th day of June next, five feet three inches and a half high, has a scar on the left arm near the wrist, without any other apparent mark or scar- Given under my hand as clerk of said Court this sixth day of November 1845- Wm H Tunstall Clk- Certified at November Court 1845

Virginia Pittsylvania County Sc- No 401- **POLLY STAR,** a free born woman of colour is this day numbered and registered in the Clerks Office of the County Court of said County according to law- The said POLLY STAR is a mulatto woman eighteen years of age five feet half an inch high with Shoes, has a scar on the back of the right hand and one on the upper part of the left wrist without any other apparent mark or scar- Given under my hand as clerk of said Court this 18th day of November 1845- Wm H Tunstall Clk- Certified at Novemr Court 1845

[p 184] No 402- **WILLIAM ROBERTSON,** a free born man of Colour is this day numbered and Registered in the Clerks Office of the County Court of Pittsylvania according to law- The said WILLIAM ROBERTSON is of a rather light complexion, Smooth skin, one and twenty years of age Sometime since July last, five feet ten inches high in Shoes, has a very Small Scar between the first & second joint of the left little finger Scarcely perceptable [sic]

and another of the same character near the middle joint of the left forefinger without any other apparent mark or Scar- Given under my hand as clerk of said Court this 10th day of December 1845- Wm H Tunstall- Certified Decr Court 1845

No 403- **GREEN HARRIS,** a free born man of Colour is this day numbered and Registered in the Clerks Office of the County Court of Pittsylvania according to law- The said GREEN HARRIS is of a bright mulattoe [sic] twenty one years of age in September last, five feet five & a half inches high in thick Sole Shoes, has a very Small Scar on the forehead over the right eye, also one rather long over the Corner of the same eye, the two being about an inch or little more apart, without any other apparent mark or Scar- Given under my hand as clerk of said Court this 16th day of January 1846- Wm H Tunstall Clk- Certified February Court 1846

Virginia Pittsylvania County Sc- No 404- **ISAAC STARR,** a free born boy [sic] of Colour is this day numbered and registered in the Clerks Office of the County Court of Pittsylvania according to law- The said ISAAC STARR is a man of bright complexion, twenty one years old the 3rd day of June last, five feet eight inches high, has a scar over the brow of the left eye, has another on the first joint of the forefinger of the left hand, another on the second joint of the little finger of the same hand, another on the second joint of the third finger of the same hand, has another scar on the back of the right hand about an inch from the thumb, has another small scar just over the second joint of the third finger of the same hand [p 185] without any other apparent mark or Scar- Given under my hand as clerk of said Court this 20th day of July 1846- Wm H Tunstall- Certified July Court 1846

Virginia Pittsylvania County Court Clerks Office Sc- No 405- **JOSIAH DAY,** a free man [the word "boy" stricken out and "man" written above the line] of Colour is this day numbered and registered in the said office according to law- The said JOSIAH is a man of Brown Complexion, twenty three years old the 4th day of July last, five feet six inches high in boots, has a scar on the left hand opposite the little finger on said hand, without any other apparent mark or Scar- Given under my hand as clerk of said

Court the 17th day of December 1846- Wm H Tunstall- Certified December Court 1846

Virginia Pittsylvania County Court Clerks Office Sc- No 406- **WOODY WILEY,** a free born man of Colour is this day numbered and registered in the said office according to law- The said WOODY WILEY is a yellow man, twenty eight years old the 4th day of October last, five feet nine inches high, has a very small burn on the left hand nearly opposite the thumb, without any other apparent mark or Scar- Given under my hand as clerk of said Court the 16th day of January 1847- Wm H Tunstall Cl- Certified January Co 1847

[p 186] Virginia Pittsylvania County Court Clerks Office Sc- No 407- **GEORGE WILEY,** a free born man of Colour is this day numbered and registered in the said office according to law- The said GEORGE WILEY is a yellow man, twenty six years old the 3rd day of this month, six feet high, has a Scar on the forehead nearly opposite the left eye, has another Scar on the first joint of the thumb of the left hand, another Scar on the back of the left hand, another Scar on the middle finger of the left hand between the first and second joints & has two teeth broken out in front on the upper Jaw, without any other apparent mark or Scar- Given under my hand as clerk of said Court the 16th day of January 1847- Wm H Tunstall Cl- Certified January Co 1847

Pittsylvania County Sct- Number 408- **REUBEN STEPHENS,** a free born man of Colour is this day numbered and registered in the Clerks office of the County Court aforesaid in the State of Virginia according to law- The said REUBEN STEPHENS is a black man, twenty two years old the 3rd day of June last, five feet four inches and a quarter high in shoes, has a small scar near the right corner of the right eye, another on the first finger of the left hand between the first and second joints, another on the left arm near the inside of the said arm not very far from the wrist, has also two scars on the second finger of the right hand, one between the first and second and the other between the second and third joints of the same finger, has another scar on the third finger of the said right hand between the first and second joint, and has two other scars on the right joint of the wrist of the said right hand, has another small scar on the second finger of the left hand and has several small scars on the back of the left hand, without any other apparent mark or Scar- Given under my hand as clerk of said Court the 10th day of August 1847- Wm H Tunstall- Certified Aug Court 1847 [in margin]

[p 187] No 409- **POLLY THOMPSON,** a free born woman of Colour is this day Numbered and registered in the Clerks Office of the County Court of Pittsylvania in the State of Virginia according to law- The said POLLY THOMPSON is a woman of yellow complexion five feet six and three quarter inches high, about thirty two years of age, has a Scar on the left arm near the elbow occasioned by a Scald and extending nearly around the arm, without any other apparent mark or Scar- The said POLLY THOMPSON has with her three children, two daughters and a son, the oldest daughter named **ELIZA JANE [THOMPSON]** eight years old the 29th day of last March, the second daughter named **MARY ELIZABETH [THOMPSON]** five years old the 7th day of June last, and a third a boy named **DANIEL THOMAS [THOMPSON]** three years old 29th day of March last- Given under my hand this 18th day of October 1847- Wm H Tunstall Clk- Certified Oct Court 1847   **[Note 3 children's names on the same register number with mother.]**

No 410- **DANIEL FREEMAN,** a free born man of Colour as appeared by his Register made by the Clerk of the County Court of Halifax County Virginia is this day Numbered and registered in the Clerks Office of the County Court of Pittsylvania in the State aforesaid according to law- The said DANIEL FREEMAN is a man of yellow complexion thirty five years old last September five feet four inches and a quarter high in Shoes, has lost all his toes except the big toe on his left foot, has a large Scar on the right side of his breast, has a Scar on the upper edge of his forehead near the hair of his head, without any other apparent mark or scar- Given under my hand as Clerk of Said Court this 16th day of October 1847- Wm H Tunstall- Certified October Court 1847

[p 188] No 411- **MARTHA JENKINS,** a free born woman of Colour is this day numbered and registered in the Clerks Office of the County Court of Pittsylvania according to law- The said MARTHA

JENKINS is a yellow woman eighteen years old the ninth day of August last five feet two inches & a half high, has a small scar on her forehead, another near the left eye, and left temple of the head, another small scar on her neck in front, has a small mole on the upper part of her breast without any other apparent mark or scar- Given under my hand as Clerk of said Court this 20th day of December 1847- Wm H Tunstall- Certified December Court 1847

No 412- **CLEMENT JENKINS,** a free born boy of colour is this day Numbered and registered in the Clerks Office of the County Court of Pittsylvania according to law- The said CLEMENT JENKINS is of yellow complexion seventeen years old the eighth day of May last, five feet three inches high, has a large Scar on the right side of the neck, another near the left side of the wrist of the left hand, another on or near the first joint of the thumb of the said hand, another on the middle finger of the said left hand near the first joint, without any other apparent mark or scar- Given under my hand as Clerk of said Court this 20th day of December 1847- Wm H Tunstall- Certified December Court 1847

No 413- **ELIZABETH JENKINS,** a free born girl of colour is this day Numbered and registered in the Clerks Office of the County Court of Pittsylvania according to law- The said ELIZABETH JENKINS is of yellow complexion fourteen years old the tenth day of June last, five feet three inches and three quarters high, has a Gautre [sic] [p 189] (supposed to be) on the right side of the neck, without any other apparent mark or Scar- Given under my hand as Clerk of the said Court this 20th day of December 1847- Wm H Tunstall- Certified December Court 1847

No 414- **NANCY JENKINS,** a free born girl of colour is this day numbered and Registered in the Clerks Office of the County Court of Pittsylvania according to law- The said NANCY JENKINS is of yellow complexion twelve years old the 15th day of October last, four feet nine and a quarter inches high, has a small scar under the right ear, without any other apparent mark or scar- Given under my hand as Clerk of the said Court this 20th day of December 1847- Wm H Tunstall- Certified December Court 1847

No 415- **WM RICHARDSON,** a free born man of colour is this day numbered and registered in the Clerks Office of the County Court of Pittsylvania in the State of Virginia according to law- The said WILLLIAM RICHARDSON is of brown complexion about twenty three years old in February last, five feet seven inches and a quarter high in boots, without any apparent mark or Scar- Given under my hand as Clerk of said Court this 21st day of March 1848- Wm H Tunstall- Certified March Court 1848

No 22- **REBECCA DAVIS,** a free born woman of colour is this day re-registered in the Clerks Office of the County Court of Pittsylvania in the State of Virginia according to law- The said REBECCA DAVIS is a mulatto woman five feet three inches and a half high in shoes, forty nine years old the 29th day of July next, has thick short hair & a small scar on the side of the left wrist, without any other apparent mark or Scar- Given under my hand as Clerk of the said Court this 17th day of April 1848- Wm H Tunstall- Certified Apr Court 1848 [in margin] **[Renewal]**

[p 190] Pittsylvania County- No 394- **FANNY ROSS,** a free born woman of Colour who was heretofore numbered and registered in this office is this day re-registered in the Said Office according to law- The said FANNY ROSS is of a tawny complexion about twenty five years of age on October next, five feet six inches and a quarter high, has a Small Mole nearly over the inner Corner of the left eye, has a Small Scar on her Chin, has another Scar on the back of the left arm, another on the back of the left hand near the thumb and nearly opposite the first finger of the said hand without any other apparent mark or Scar- the said FANNY ROSS has a Small Child named **AMY [ROSS]** about two years of age in May last, without any [the word "other" crossed out] apparent mark or scar- Given under my hand as Clerk of the Said Court this 17th day of July 1848- Wm H Tunstall- Certified July Court 1848 **[Renewal is for adult, who may be a child of MARY MASON alias ROSS; Note child's name added to this registration number.]**

No 369- **MARY DAVIS,** a free born woman of Colour who has been numbered and registered in the Clerks Office of the County Court of Pittsylvania is this day again registered in the said office according to law- The said MARY DAVIS is a bright mulatto twenty six years of age the 25th day of January last, five feet three inches high, has a small scar near the large joint of the left forefinger, another on the left jaw, without any other apparent mark or scar- Given under my hand as Clerk of the Said Court this 16th day of October 1848- Wm H Tunstall- (Certified at Oct Court 1848) **[Renewal]**

No 416- **JANE DAVIS,** a free born Woman of Colour is this day numbered and registered in the Clerks Office of the County Court of Pittsylvania according to law- The said JANE DAVIS is a mulatto eighteen years old the 17th day of August last, five feet six inches and a quarter high, has a very small scar under the left [illegible] of the nose, another scar on the [illegible], also a scar on the [illegible] to the little finger of the left hand and the second joint without any other apparent [p 191] mark or Scar- Given under my hand as Clerk of the said Court this 16th day of October 1848- Wm H Tunstall- (Certified at Oct Court 1848)

No 417- **MARSHALL GOINGS,** a free born man of Colour is this day numbered and registered in the Clerks Office of the County Court of Pittsylvania according to law- The said GOINGS is a man of brown complexion five feet seven inches and one eighth of an inch high, about [left blank] years old, has a small scar on the inside of the right thumb, another scar on the inside of the first finger of the right hand near the first joint, has a small scar on the forehead, another over the left eye, and a small mole on the left side of the nose- Given under my hand as Clerk of said Court this 10th day of June 1849- Wm H Tunstall

No 418- **WASHINGTON STEPHENS,** a free born man of Colour is this day numbered and registered in the Clerks Office of the County Court of Pittsylvania according to law- The said WASHINGTON STEPHENS is a man of rather dark complexion about twenty three years old the 22nd day of February last, five feet eight inches high in shoes, has a large scar on the right cheek, a small scar on the side of the joint of the first finger of the right hand, has his right ankle sprained, without any other apparent mark or scar- Given under my hand as Clerk of the said Court this 18th day of June 1849- Wm H Tunstall

No 419- **JOHN VALENTINE**, a free born man of Colour, is this day numbered and registered in the Clerks Office of the County Court of Pittsylvania according to law- The said JOHN VALENTINE is a man of yellow complexion twenty two years old the 21st day of August next, five feet ten inches and three quarters of an inch high in shoes, has blue eyes, a small scar on the left side of the upper lip & another on the right cheek, without any other apparent mark or scar- Given under my hand as Clerk of the said Court this the 18th day of June 1849- Wm H Tunstall

No 420- **RICHARD DAVIS**, a free born man of Colour, is this day numbered and registered in the Clerks Office of the County Court of Pittsylvania according to law- The said RICHARD DAVIS is a man of yellow Complexion twenty two years old in July next, five feet ten and a half inches high in shoes, has a small scar on his forehead, another on the left side of his neck, a couple of scars on the [p 192] inside of the right wrist, a small scar near the first joint of the first hand, the first finger of said right hand between the second and last joints thereof being crooked with a small scar, another scar near the nail of the first finger of the left hand, without any other apparent mark or scar- Given under my hand as Clerk of the said Court this the 18th day of June 1849- Wm H Tunstall

No 421- **GEORGE DAVIS**, a free born man of Colour, is this day numbered and registered in the Clerks Office of the County Court of Pittsylvania according to law- The said GEORGE DAVIS is a man of yellow complexion about twenty one years old, five feet eleven inches and a quarter high in shoes, has a scar nearly two & a half inches in length on the outside of the right arm near the elbow, Another scar on the outside of the said arm near the wrist, another on the outside of the wrist of said arm, another scar on the first finger of the right hand near the first joint, without any other apparent mark or scar- Given under my hand as Clerk of the said Court this the 18th day of June 1849- Wm H Tunstall

No 422- **CLEMENT BURNETT**, a free born man of Colour, is this day numbered and registered in the Clerks Office of the County Court of Pittsylvania according to law- The said CLEMENT BURNETT is a man of yellow complexion fifty years old the 30th day of September next, five feet five inches high in shoes, has a small scar nearly over the right eye, a small mole on the right temple, another on the left side of his nose, has a small scar on the inside of the right arm near the elbow, another on the inside of the right wrist, with the finger next to the little finger on the right hand crooked, without any other apparent mark or scar- Given under my hand as Clerk of the said Court this the 18th day of June 1849- Wm H Tunstall

No 423- **POLLY REYNOLDS,** a free born woman of colour, is this day numbered and registered in the Clerks Office of the County Court of Pittsylvania according to Law- The said POLLY REYNOLDS is a woman of yellow complexion nineteen years old the 10th day of last March, four feet eleven inches high in slippers, has a small mole on the forehead, another on the neck in front, and another on the breast, without any other apparent mark or scar- Given under my hand as Clerk of the [p 193] County Court aforesaid this the 18th day of June 1849- Wm H Tunstall

No 424- **NANCY ROE,** a free born woman of Colour, is this day numbered and registered in the Clerks Office of the County Court of Pittsylvania according to law- The said NANCY ROE is a woman of dark complexion about fifty years of age, five feet two and a half inches high in shoes, has a small scar on the edge of the inside of the right wrist next to the hand, without any other apparent mark or scar- Given under my hand as Clerk of the said Court this the 18th day of June 1849- Wm H Tunstall

No 425- **JANE ROE,** a free born woman of Colour, is this day numbered and registered in the Clerks Office of the County Court of Pittsylvania according to law- The said JANE ROE is a woman of dark complexion about eighteen years of age, five feet one and a quarter inches high in slippers, has a small scar on the right breast, without any other apparent mark or scar- Given under my hand as Clerk of the said Court this the 18th day of June 1849- Wm H Tunstall

No 426- **NATHAN COLE,** a free born man of Colour, is this day numbered and registered in the Clerks Office of the County Court of Pittsylvania according to law- The said NATHAN COLE is a man of dark complexion twenty years of age the 14th of last April, five feet eight inches and a quarter high in shoes, has a small scar on the back of the middle finger of the left hand between the first and second joints of said finger, without any other apparent mark or scar- Given under my hand as Clerk of the said Court this the 18th day of June 1849- Wm H Tunstall

[p 194] No 427- **DICK MORGAN,** a black man of Colour who was emancipated by the last Will and Testament of Robert Morgan decd as appears by the Register of the said DICK made by the Clerk of the County Court of Charlotte County, is this day numbered and registered in the Clerks Office of the County Court of Pittsylvania according to law- The said DICK MORGAN is about thirty two years of age, five feet six inches high in Shoes, has a small scar over the left eye, another scar on the right Cheek, another on the outside of the Right Wrist, & another on the back of the left hand, without any other apparent mark or scar- Given under my hand as Clerk of the said Court this the 18th day of June 1849- Wm H Tunstall

No 428- **SCOTT STEPHENS,** a free born man of Colour, is this day numbered and registered in the Clerks Office of the County Court of Pittsylvania according to law- The said SCOTT STEPHENS is a black man five & twenty years of age the 14th day of July next, five feet nine inches and a quarter high without shoes, has a small scar about three fourths of an inch long rather between the left thumb & forefinger, another about an inch long near the large joint of the left forefinger, a small one on the upper part of the left wrist, a small one on the left cheek, and a very considerable one on the right knee reaching nearly half way around, without any other apparent mark or scar- Given under my hand as Clerk of the said Court this the 19th day of June 1849- Wm H Tunstall

No 69- **BOOKER HENDRICK,** a free born man of Colour who has been heretofore numbered and registered in the Clerks Office of the County Court of Pittsylvania is this day again Registered in the said office according to law- The said BOOKER HENDRICK is a man of brown complexion about thirty nine years of age, five feet two and a half inches high in shoes, has a large scar on his forehead, without any other apparent mark or scar- Given under my hand as Clerk of the Said Court this 18th day of June 1849- Wm H Tunstall- **[Renewal]**

[p 195] No 429- **WM STEPHENS,** a free born man of Colour, is this day numbered and registered in the Clerks Office of the County Court of Pittsylvania in the State of Virginia according to law- The said WM STEPHENS is a black man twenty three years of age, five feet eight inches high in boots, has a scar near the first joint of the middle finger of the right hand, another on the right hand near the first joint of the thumb, has another scar over the left eye, another on the left side of his face near the eye, another on the left side of the neck, without any other apparent mark or scar- Given under my hand as Clerk of the said Court this 17th day of September 1849- Wm H Tunstall- Certified at Sept Court 1849

No 217- **STEPHEN MASON,** a free born man of colour who has been heretofore numbered and registered in the Clerks Office of the County Court of Pittsylvania is this day again Registered in the said office according to law- The said STEPHEN MASON is a man of yellow complexion about twenty two years and two months old, five feet & ten inches high in shoes, has a small scar on his left cheek, another on the right cheek near the nose, another on the back of his right wrist, another on the inside of the same wrist, another on the back of the left hand near the wrist, another scar on the back of the first finger of the left hand on the side and near the second joint of said finger, another on the outside of the little finger of said left hand near the second joint, without any other apparent mark or scar- Given under my hand as Clerk of the Said Court this 15th day of October 1849- Wm H Tunstall- Certified at October Court 1849 **[Renewal]**

No 430- **RICHARD WILEY,** a free born man of Colour, is this day numbered and registered in the Clerks Office of the County Court of Pittsylvania according to Law- The said RICHARD WILEY is a man of yellow complexion about twenty four years old the 1st day of October last, five feet six inches high in shoes, has a round scar on the left cheek or jaw, has another on the right arm near the shoulder and has black bushy hair, without any other apparent mark or scar- Given under my hand as Clerk of said Court this

19th day of November 1849- Wm H Tunstall- Certified at November Court 1849

[p 196] No 431- **EVANS WILEY,** a free born man of Colour, is this day numbered and registered in the Clerks Office of the County Court of Pittsylvania according to Law- The said EVANS WILEY is a man of yellow complexion twenty one years old the 10th day of last February, five feet seven and three quarters inches high in shoes, has a scar on the inside of the first finger near the end and has black bushy hair, without any other apparent mark or scar- Given under my hand as Clerk of said Court this 19th day of November 1849- Wm H Tunstall- Certified November Court 1849

No 432- **JAMES HARRIS,** a free born man of Colour, is this day numbered and registered in the Clerks Office of the County Court of Pittsylvania according to Law- The said JAMES HARRIS is a man of dark complexion twenty one years old the 19th day of October last, five feet three and three quarters inches high in shoes, has two small scars on the back of the right arm, one of them on or near the joint of the wrist, has two small ones on the inside of the same arm, one small one on the inside of the finger next to the little finger of the right hand near the end, has a scar about an inch long across the back of the left arm, and one other scar on the inside of the left wrist- without any other apparent mark or scar- Given under my hand as Clerk of the said Court this 19th day of November 1849- Wm H Tunstall- Certified November Court 1849

No 331- **COLEMAN REYNOLDS,** a free born man of colour who has been heretofore numbered & registered in the Clerks Office of the County Court of Pittsylvania is this day again Registered in the said office according to law- The said COLEMAN REYNOLDS is a man of dark complexion about forty one years of age, five feet seven inches and a quarter high in shoes, has some small scars on the back of the left hand without any other apparent mark or scar- Given under [p 197] my hand as Clerk of said Court this 19th day of November 1849- Wm H Tunstall- Certified November Court 1849 **[Renewal of No 331; however, the original registration is for a female, and the age seems incorrect.]**

No 345- **PETER VALENTINE** a free born man of colour who has been heretofore numbered & registered in the Clerks Office of the County Court of Pittsylvania is this day reregistered in the said office according to Law- The said PETER VALENTINE is a man of dark complexion five feet three and a half inches high in shoes, about thirty seven years old, has a scar on the forehead over the left eye, another on the right side of the forehead just above the temple, two small ones on the back of the left hand, another small one on the side of the left wrist near the joint, another on the back of the left arm near the wrist & another on the joint of the right wrist, without any other apparent mark or scar- Given under my hand as clerk of said Court this 17th day of December 1849- Wm H Tunstall- Certified December Court 1849 **[Renewal]**

No 433- **CAROLINE STEPHENS,** a free born woman of colour, is this day numbered and registered in the Clerks Office of the County Court of Pittsylvania according to Law- The said CAROLINE STEPHENS is a woman of tawny complexion, about twenty seven years old, five feet eight and a half inches high without shoes, has a small long scar on the outer part of the left little finger- without any other apparent mark or scar- Given under my hand as Clerk of said Court this 17th day of December 1849- Wm H Tunstall

[p 198] No 434- **BERRY SMITH,** a free born man of colour, is this day numbered and registered in the Clerks Office of the County Court of Pittsylvania according to Law- The said BERRY SMITH is a man of brown complexion, twenty three years old in September next, five feet eight inches and a quarter high without Shoes, has a long mark on the back of the right arm just above the wrist, a Scar on the upper part of the Same arm below the elbow, another one on the under part of the left arm near the wrist, and one on the inside of the first joint of the thumb on the left hand near the wrist, and has bushy hair, without any other apparent mark or scar- Given under my hand as Clerk of said Court this 18th day of January 1850- Wm H Tunstall- (Certified 21st Jan 1850)

No 387- **HENRY STEPHENS** a free born man of colour who has been heretofore ["appointed" has been crossed out] numbered and registered in the Clerks Office of the County Court of Pittsylvania

Virginia is again registered in the said office according to Law- The said HENRY STEPHENS is of a dark complexion thirty years old the 21st day of June next, five feet six and a half inches high in shoes, has a small scar on the first finger of the right hand between the first and second joints, has a small scar near the first joint of the second and third fingers of the same hand produced by a burn, has a small scar on the right side of the wrist of the same hand near the joint thereof, has several small Scars near the first joints of the fingers on the left hand, has a scar on the chin, another on the forehead, & a large one on top of his head, without any other apparent mark or scar- Given under my hand as clerk of the said Court this 19th day of March 1850- Wm H Tunstall C- (Certified at March Court 1850) **[Renewal]**

No 435- **MARTHA DAVIS,** a free born man [sic] of colour, is this day numbered and registered in the Clerks Office of the County Court of Pittsylvania in the State of Virginia according to Law- The said MARTHA DAVIS is a woman of yellow complexion, twenty five years old the 10th day of January last, five feet and a quarter of an inch high in her stockings, and is without any apparent mark or scar- The said MARTHA DAVIS has three children to Wit- **PHILIP [DAVIS]** a boy Six years old the 12th day of February last, **CATHERINE [DAVIS]** aged five years old the 2nd day of August next, and **MARIAH [DAVIS]** aged two years old the 11th day of July next- Given under my hand as Clerk of the said Court this 20th day of May 1850- Wm H Tunstall- Certified at May Court 1850 **[Note 3 children are registered on the same number with mother.]**

[p 199] No 436- **JANE RICHARDSON,** a free born woman of colour, is this day numbered & registered in the Clerks Office of the County Court of Pittsylvania in the State of Virginia according to Law- The said JANE RICHARDSON is a dark mulatto woman, about forty years of age, four feet and eleven inches high in slippers, has two small scars on the forehead, without any other apparent mark or scar- Given under my hand as Clerk of said Court this 17th day of June 1850- Wm H Tunstall- (Certified June Court 1850)

Virginia, Pittsylvania County August Court 1850- It is ordered that the Clerk of this Court register **ROANN MAYO** a free woman of Colour according to Law- No 437- The said ROANN MAYO was born free in the County aforesaid, was nineteen years old the 1st day of April last, is of a tawny colour five feet three & 1/4 inches in thin soled shoes, has a long scar on the outer part of the left arm, and one about the edge of the hair rather over the left eye- without any other apparent mark or scar- Given under my hand as Clerk of the County Court of said County this 22nd day of August 1850- Wm H Tunstall

Virginia, Pittsylvania County August Court 1850- It is ordered that the Clerk of this Court register **LEANNA REYNOLDS**, wife of JUBA REYNOLDS, a free woman of Colour according to Law- No 438- The said LEANNA REYNOLDS was born free in the County aforesaid, is about forty three years of age, black complexion 5 feet, five and 3/4 inches high, has a very small scar near the outer corner of the left eye and a small wen or enlargement on the large joint of the right little finger, without any other apparent mark or scar- Given under my hand as Clerk of the County Court of said County this 22nd day of August 1850- Wm H Tunstall- (Copy furnished 2d October 1851)

[p 200] Virginia, Pittsylvania County August Court 1850- It is ordered that the Clerk of this Court register **LOUISA JANE MASON**, wife of STEPHEN MASON, a free woman of Colour according to Law- No 439- The said LOUISA JANE MASON was born free in the County aforesaid, was nineteen years of age the 17th day of July last, is of a tawny colour five feet two & 1/2 inches high in thin shoes, has a small scar between the second & third joints of the left forefinger and a mole on the back of the left hand, without any other apparent mark or scar- Given under my hand as Clerk of the County Court of said County this 22nd day of August 1850- Wm H Tunstall- (Copy furnished 10th September 1851)

Virginia, Pittsylvania County August Court 1850- It is ordered that the Clerk of this Court register **PANTHEA REYNOLDS**, a free woman of Colour according to law- No 440- The said PANTHEA REYNOLDS was born free in the County aforesaid, was sixteen years old the 17th day of April last, is of tawny colour five feet &

one inch high in thin shoes, has a small scar on the back of the right hand, another long one on the back of the right middle finger, another in the forehead and a very small one on the large joint of the left forefinger, without any other apparent mark or scar- Given under my hand as Clerk of the County Court of said County this 22nd day of August 1850- Wm H Tunstall

Virginia, Pittsylvania County August Court 1850- It is ordered that the Clerk of this Court register **TURNER ABERNATHY VALENTINE** a free man of Colour according to Law- No 441- The said TURNER ABERNATHY VALENTINE was born free in said County, was twenty one years of age the 10th day of this month, is a very bright mulatto, five feet seven inches high without shoes, has a mole on the right cheek [followed by a line that has been stricken], a very small scar on the right side of the jaw bone (below [p 201] the mole) and one on the upper part of the right hand near the wrist joint occasioned by a burn, without any other apparent mark or scar- Given under my hand as Clerk of the County Court of said County this 22nd day of August 1850- Wm H Tunstall- (Copy furnished September 27th 1850)

Virginia, Pittsylvania County November Court 1850- It is ordered that the Clerk of this Court register **ANGELINE GREEN VALENTINE** a free person of Colour according to Law- No 442- The said ANGELINE GREEN VALENTINE was born free in the County of Halifax, Virginia, was twenty five years of age the 22nd day of April last, is of a light tawny complexion, five feet five inches and a half high in shoes, a long [left blank] scar on the back of the right hand, a small round scar on the back of the same hand, a small one on the forehead near the edge of the hair & another on the upper part of the breast near the neck- without any other apparent mark or scar- Given under my hand as Clerk of the County Court of said County this 20th day of November 1850- Wm H Tunstall- (Copy furnished 12th December 1850)

Virginia, Pittsylvania County November Court 1850- It is ordered that the Clerk of this Court register **CHARLES CARRINGTON VALENTINE** a free person of Colour according to Law- No 443- The said CHARLES CARRINGTON VALENTINE was born free in the County aforesaid, will be twenty four years of age the 1st day of

December next, of a tawny complexion, five feet & five inches high without shoes, has a small scar on the end of the left forefinger, a long scar on the forehead a little below the edge of the hair, without any other apparent mark or scar- Given under my hand as Clerk of the County Court of said County this 20th day of November 1850- Wm H Tunstall- (Copy furnished 12th December 1850)

[p 202] Virginia, Pittsylvania County November Court 1850- It is ordered that the Clerk of this Court register **NANCY MARGARET VALENTINE** a free person of Colour according to Law- No 444- The said NANCY MARGARET VALENTINE was born free in the County of Pittsylvania, was twenty one years of age the 27th day of this present month (November), of a yellow complexion, five feet two inches high without shoes- has a mark on the upper part of the jaw just below the temple, a very small scar on the back of the right forefinger near the thumb- without any other apparent mark or scar- Given under my hand as Clerk of the County Court of said County this 20th day of November 1850- Wm H Tunstall- (Copy furnished 12th December 1850)

Virginia, Pittsylvania County November Court 1850- It is ordered that the Clerk of this Court register **JORDAN M. VALENTINE** a free person of Colour according to Law- No 445- The said JORDAN M. VALENTINE was born free in the County of Pittsylvania, was sixteen years old the 17th day of the last month, of a dark tawny colour five feet two & a half inches high without shoes- has a small scar on the forehead nearly over the right eye- without any other apparent mark or scar- Given under my hand as Clerk of the County Court of said County this 20th day of November 1850- Wm H Tunstall- (Copy furnished 12th December 1850)

Virginia, Pittsylvania County November Court 1850- It is ordered that the Clerk of this Court register **JAMES EDWIN VALENTINE** a free person of Colour according to Law- No 446- The said JAMES EDWIN VALENTINE was born [p 203] free in the County of Pittsylvania, was [sic] twenty three years of age the 4th day of next May, is six feet high without shoes, of a tawny complexion, has a large scar on the throat, another large one on the side of the wrist of the left arm- another small one on the back of the left hand- without any other apparent mark or scar- Given

under my hand as Clerk of the County Court of said County this
20th day of November 1850- Wm H Tunstall- (Copy furnished 12th
December 1850)

Virginia, Pittsylvania County October Court 1850- It is ordered
that the Clerk of this Court register **SALLY ELIZABETH
STEPHENS** a free person of Colour according to Law- No 447- The
said SALLY ELIZABETH STEPHENS was born free in the County
aforesaid, will be twenty one years of age in January next (Jany
1851) of a yellow complexion with straight black hair, is five feet
two inches high, has rather a protruding mouth, without any other
apparent mark or scar- Given under my hand as Clerk of the
County Court of said County this 30th day of November 1850- Wm
H Tunstall- Fee & tax pd **[Written in margin]**

Virginia, Pittsylvania County October Court 1850- It is ordered
that the Clerk of this Court register **CATHERINE ROBERTSON
JANE STEVENS** a free person of Colour according to Law- No
448- The said CATHERINE ROBERTSON JANE STEPHENS was
born free in the County of Pittsylvania, will be nineteen years of
age in February next (February 1851), is a very bright mulatto with
hair rather inclined to curl & of a sandy colour- has hazle [sic] eyes
& is five feet two and a half inches high without any apparent
mark or scar- Given under my hand as Clerk of the County Court
of said County this 30th day of November 1850- Wm H Tunstall-
Fee & tax pd **[Written in margin]**

[p 204] Virginia, Pittsylvania County October Court 1850- It is
ordered that the Clerk of this Court register **MARTHA STEVENS**
a free person of Colour according to Law- No 449- The said
MARTHA STEVENS a free born woman of colour was born free in
the County aforesaid, is about thirty years of age, is of a black
complexion is five feet & two inches high, has a scar on the
forehead over the left eye, has another small one on the largest
joint of the left forefinger, has another on the end of the right
forefinger- and one on the back of the neck, without any other
apparent mark or scar- Given under my hand as Clerk of said
Court this 30th day of November 1850- Wm H Tunstall- Fee pd
[Written in margin]

Virginia, Pittsylvania County December Court 1850- It is ordered that the Clerk of this Court register **MARIAH REYNOLDS** a free woman of colour according to Law- No 450- The said MARIAH REYNOLDS was born free in the County aforesaid, was twenty seven years of age in September last, is a very bright mulatto, is five feet three and a half inches high in thin shoes, has a small one on the left thumb and another small one on the left wrist- without any other apparent mark or scar- Given under my hand as Clerk of said Court this 18th day of December 1850- Wm H Tunstall- Copy furnished Decr 1850

Virginia, to Wit- At a Court held for the County of Pittsylvania the 20th day of January 1851 "It is ordered that the Clerk of this Court register **CHARLES DAVIS** a free man of colour of this County according to Law"- No 451- The said CHARLES DAVIS is this day numbered and registered in the Clerk's Office of the Court of the County & State aforesaid agreeable to the above order- He is about [p 205] twenty four years of age, of a Tawny complexion, is five feet, eight inches and a half high in shoes, has a long scar on the joint of the wrist, a small one on the left cheek bone, has a Small Scar just behind the right ear & said to have been born free in the County of Campbell & State aforesaid- Given under my hand as Clerk of said Court this 4th day of February 1851- Wm H Tunstall

Virginia, Pittsylvania County, to Wit- At a Court held for the County aforesaid the 21st day of April A.D. 1851- "It is ordered that the Clerk of this Court register **GEORGE DAVIS** a mulatto man who was born free according to Law"- No 452- The said GEORGE DAVIS is this day numbered and registered in the Clerk's Office of the Court of the County & State aforesaid agreeable to the above order- He will be twenty two years old in August next, a bright mulatto and is five feet seven inches high without shoes, has a mole on the lower part of the back of his neck, another on the outer part of the left arm above the elbow & has a small crooked scar on the outer part of the second joint of the left little finger, without another apparent mark or scar and was born in the County aforesaid, Given under my hand as Clerk of said Court this 24th day of April 1851- Wm H Tunstall- (Copy furnished April 26th 1851)

Virginia, Pittsylvania County, to Wit- At a Court continued & held for the County aforesaid at the Court house on Tuesday the 17th day of December 1850- "On the motion of **FRANK COUSINS** by counsel and it appearing by a copy of his register from the clerk of the Hustings Court of the Corporation of Lynchburg that he is a free man of colour it is ordered that the Clerk register the said FRANK COUSINS according to Law"- No 453- The said FRANK COUSINS is this day numbered and [p 206] registered in the Clerks office of the Court of Pittsylvania County agreeable to the above order- He is thirty nine years of age, yellow complexion, five feet, nine inches and a half high in shoes, has a small scar about an inch long across the forehead, over the left corner of the left eye, has a scar on the lower part of the left ear, has a curved scar on back of the right hand without any other apparent mark or scar- Given under my hand as Clerk of said Court at the Court house this 24th day of June 1851- Wm H Tunstall- (Copy furnished June 25th 1851)

Virginia, Pittsylvania County, to Wit- At a Court held for the County of Pittsylvania this 18th day of August 1851- "It appearing to the satisfaction of the Court that **ROBERT WASHINGTON VALENTINE** and **JAMES COLE** free persons of colour were born free in this County, it is ordered that the Clerk of the Court register the said ROBERT WASHINGTON VALENTINE and JAMES COLE according to Law"- No 454- The said ROBERT WASHINGTON VALENTINE is this day numbered and registered in the Clerks office of the Court of Pittsylvania County agreeable to the above order- He will be twenty one years of age the 22nd day of October next, bright mulatto, five feet nine inches and 1/8 high without shoes, a small scar on the back of the left wrist, has dark sandy hair, curls, has a scar on the inside of the right ankle just above the joint, without any other apparent mark or scar- Given under my hand as Clerk of said Court at the Court House this 20th day of August 1851- Wm H Tunstall- (Copy furnished 20th Aug 1851) **[Note that 2 persons have received the same number under this Court ruling, but only one person was described.]**

[p 207] Virginia, Pittsylvania County, To wit- At a Court held for the County of Pittsylvania at the Court House on Monday the 15th

day of September 1851- "It is ordered that the Clerk register **DELPHIA ROBERTSON** a free woman of colour"- No 455- The said DELPHIA ROBERTSON is this day numbered and registered in the Clerks office of the Court of Pittsylvania County agreeable to the foregoing order- She was forty five years of age the 7th day of December last, dark complexion and is five feet four and three fourth inches high in thin soled shoes, has a scar on the outer part of the joint of the right wrist and has the end cut off of the middle finger of her right hand, without any other apparent mark or scar- Given under my hand as Clerk of said Court at the Court house this 6th day of January 1852- Wm H Tunstall- (Copy furnished 26th January 1852)

Virginia, Pittsylvania County, To wit- At a Court held for the County of Pittsylvania the 16th day of February 1852- "It is ordered that the Clerk of this Court register **JAMES DAVIS** a mulatto man, who was born free in this County, according to Law"- No 456- Pursuant to the above order the said JAMES DAVIS is this day numbered & Registered in the Clerks office of said County according to Law- He is a mulatto man of a rather ginger cake colour, twenty one years of age the 30th day of August 1851, five feet eight inches high, has a slight scar on the right jaw and has lost the tooth on the left of the two front ones, without any other apparent mark or scar and was certified by said Court born free in the County of Pittsylvania- Wm H Tunstall- (Copy furnished 19th day of February 1852)

[p 208] Virginia, County of Pittsylvania, To wit- At a Court continued and held for the County of Pittsylvania at the Court House thereof the 18th day of May 1852- "It appearing to the satisfaction of the Court that **CLAIBORNE COOPER** a free boy of colour the son of LETTY COOPER was born free in the County of Lunenburg in this State, it is ordered that the Clerk of this Court register the said CLAIBORNE COOPER according to Law"- No 457- Pursuant to the above order the said CLAIBORNE COOPER is this day numbered and registered in the Clerks office of said County Court according to Law- He was fourteen years of age the 18th day of March last, is a bright mulatto four feet eleven inches & a half high without shoes, has bushy hair, a small scar on the back of the left middle finger where it joins the hand- & several

small scars of the forefinger of the left hand, without any other apparent mark or scar- Given under my hand as Clerk of said Court at the Court House this 20th day of May 1852- Wm H Tunstall- (Copied 20th May 1852)

Virginia, County of Pittsylvania, To wit- At a Court continued and held for the County of Pittsylvania at the Court House thereof the 18th day of March 1851- "It was ordered that the Clerk register **FANNY HARRIS** formerly **FANNY SMITH** a free woman of colour according to Law"- No 458- In pursuance of the foregoing order the said FANNY HARRIS is this day numbered and registered in the Clerks office of said County Court according to Law- She was forty five years of age the 29th of March last, is of black complexion and five feet two inches high in thin soled shoes, has a scar on the left wrist, has a small scar on the back of the right middle finger near the hand and has the end of her right forefinger cut off with the nail grown down over it, and said to be born free in said County- without any other apparent mark or scar- Given under my hand as Clerk of said County Court [p 209] this 7th day of July 1852- L. Scruggs- (Copy furnished 7th July 1852)
[Appears to be a renewal of No. 278.]

Virginia, to wit- At a Court held for the County of Pittsylvania at the Court House on Monday the 17th day of December 1849- "It appearing to the Court that the Register of **PHILIS STEPHENS** has been accidentally lost or destroyed it is ordered that the Clerk of this Court do renew the registration of the said PHILIS according to Law"- No 66- Pursuant to the above order the said PHILIS STEPHENS is this day numbered and reregistered in the Clerks office of the said County Court according to Law- She is about forty eight years of age, of a brown complexion, five feet four and a quarter inches high in slippers, has a lump on the back of the right middle finger, has a large scar on the back of the right arm just about the elbow, has a long scar on her right jaw, has a mole on the upper part of the breast, has a small scar on the left elbow and has scars on the back of the left arm between her elbow and wrist occasioned by a burn & born free in this County- Given under my hand as Clerk of the County Court aforesaid this 30th day of June 1852- Wm H Tunstall- (Copy furnished 30th July 1852)
[Renewal]

Virginia, to wit- At a Court continued and held for the County of Pittsylvania at the Court House thereof on Tuesday the 22nd day of June 1852- "It was ordered that the Clerk of this Court renew the Register of **WINNY REYNOLDS** a free woman of colour who was born free in this County"- No 336- Pursuant to the foregoing order of Court the said WINNY REYNOLDS is this day numbered and reregistered in the Clerks office of the said County Court according to Law- She is about forty seven years of age, dark complexion, five feet five and a half inches high in slippers, has large eyes & bushy hair without any other apparent mark or [p 210] scar and born free in the County aforesaid, Given under my hand as Clerk of the County Court this 30th day of June 1852- Wm H Tunstall- (Copy furnishd 30th June 1852) **[Renewal]**

Virginia, to wit- At a Court continued & held for the County of Pittsylvania the 22nd day of June 1852- "It is ordered that the Clerk Register **JANE GARNES** a free woman of colour according to Law, it appearing by her Register from the County Clerk of the Hustings Court of Danville that the said JANE GARNES was born free in the County of Mechlenburg in this State"- No 459- Pursuant to the foregoing order of Court the said JANE GARNES is this day numbered and registered in the Clerks office of the said County Court according to Law- She is about forty two years of age, dark complexion five feet four and a half inches high in slippers, has a small scar on the left cheek, has a mark on the inner part of the left wrist, high cheek bones, bushy hair, and has lost her right eye tooth, & free born in Mechlenburg County, Given under my hand as Clerk of said County Court this 30th day of June 1852- Wm H Tunstall- (Copy furnished 30th June 1852)

Number 460- **PARTHENA STEPHENS** a free negro born free in the County of Pittsylvania Virginia is this day numbered and registered in the Clerks Office of the County Court of said County according to law- The said PARTHENA STEPHENS is a woman of brown complexion, nineteen years old the 19th day of June last, five feet three inches and a quarter of an inch high in thin shoes, has a small scar near the second joint of the middle finger of the left hand, without any other apparent mark or scar on her face, head or hands- Given under my hand as Clerk of the said Court this 21st day of July 1852- L. Scruggs- (order at July Court 1852 & copy & furnished 21st July 1852)

Number 461- **JORDAN GREEN STEPHENS** a free Negro born free in the County of Pittsylvania Virginia is this day numbered and registered in the Clerks Office of the County Court of said County according to law- The said JORDAN GREEN STEPHENS is of a brown complexion, eighteen years old the 14th day of August next, five feet four inches high in shoes, has a small scar on the left side of his chin, without any other apparent mark [p 211] or scar on his face, head or hands- Given under my hand as Clerk of the said Court this 21st day of July 1852- L. Scruggs- (order at July Court 1852 & copy furnished 21st July 1852)

Number 462- **MADOLA MARIA STEPHENS** a free negro born free in the County of Pittsylvania Virginia is of a dark complexion, fourteen years old the 14th day of June last, five feet one and a half inches high in thin shoes, without any apparent mark or scar on her face, head or hands- Given under my hand as Clerk of the said Court this 21st day of July 1852- L. Scruggs- (order at July Court 1852 & copy & furnished 21st July 1852)

Number 463- **SUSAN ANN JONES** a free person of colour born free in the County of Pittsylvania Virginia is of a black complexion, twenty two years old, four feet eleven and an eighth inches high in slippers, has a small scar on the back of the left hand, two scars on the right arm above the elbow (one of them round form) & a long scar on the back of the neck or shoulders, without any other apparent mark or scar- Given under my hand as Clerk of the County Court for the County aforesaid this 18th day of August 1852- L. Scruggs- (order at Aug Court 1852 & copy furnished [left blank] Aug 1852)

Number 464- JAMES DAVIS a free born man of colour is this day numbered and registered in the Clerks office of the County Court of Pittsylvania County according to law. The said **JAMES W. DAVIS** was born free in said County, is of a brown complexion, twenty two years old the 25th day of December last, five feet seven inches and three quarters of an inch high in shoes, has two small scars near the first joint of the left thumb (on the outside of the thumb) has a small scar on the 3rd finger of the left hand between the first and second joints (on the outside of the finger) without any other apparent mark or scar on his face, head or hands- Given under my hand as Clerk of the County Court afsaid County this 21st day of August 1852- L. Scruggs- order at August Court 1852 & copy furnished 25 Aug 1852)

[p 212] Number 9- **DEBORAH WILEY** a free negro born free who hath been numbered and Registered in the Clerks office of the County Court of Pittsylvania County is this day again registered in the said office according to law. The said DEBORAH WILEY is a yellow woman, five feet two and a half inches high in shoes, about fifty seven years of age, has a small mole near the right corner of her mouth, several moles on & near the right side of her nose and on her left cheek, without any other apparent mark or scar on her face, head or hands- Given under my hand as Clerk of the said Court this 24th day of September 1852- L. Scruggs- (order at Sept Co 1852 & copy furnished 24th Sept 1852) **[Renewal]**

Number 465- **NATHANIEL WILEY** a free negro born free in Pittsylvania County is this day numbered and Registered in the Clerks office of said County according to law. The said NATHANIEL WILEY is of yellow complexion, twenty years old the 17th day of February next, five feet nine inches high in shoes, has a small scar near the corner of the left eye, has a small scar on the inner corner of the left hand without any other apparent mark or scar on his face, head or hands- Given under my hand as Clerk of the said Court this 24th day of September 1852- L. Scruggs- order at Sept Court 1852 & copy furnished 24 Sept 1852

Number 466- **MARTHA JANE WILEY** a free negro born free in Pittsylvania County is this day numbered and registered in the Clerks office of the County Court of said County according to law- The said MARTHA JANE WILEY is of yellow complexion, sixteen years old the 14th day of August last, five feet one and a half inches high in shoes, has white spots on her neck, some on her forehead & face, Some on her right hand and very gray, without any other apparent mark or scar on her face, head or hands- Given under my hand as Clerk of the said Court this 24th day of September 1852- L.Scruggs- order at Sept Court 1852 & copy furnished 24 Sept 1852

Number 467- **SALLY ANN WILEY** a free negro born free in Pittsylvania County is this day numbered and registered in the Clerks office of the County Court of said County according to law- The said SALLY ANN WILEY is of yellow complexion, eleven years old the 2nd day of February last, five feet half an inch high in shoes, has a small scar on the second joint of the [p 213] first finger of the left hand without any other apparent mark or scar on her face, head or hands- Given under my hand as Clerk of the said Court this 24th day of September 1852- L.Scruggs- order at Sept Court 1852 and copy furnished 24 Sept 1852

Number 468- **LUCINDY DODSON** a free negro born free in Pittsylvania County is this day numbered and registered in the Clerks office of the County Court of said County according to law- The said LUCINDY DODSON is of dark complexion, twenty one years old last August, five feet two and a half inches high in slippers, without any apparent mark or scar on her face, head or hands- Given under my hand as Clerk of the said Court this 24th day of September 1852- L.Scruggs- order at Sept Court 1852 and copy furnished 24 Sept 1852

Number 469- **QUINTINA GARNES** a free negro born free in Mechlenburg County is this day numbered and Registered in the Clerks office of the County Court of Pittsylvania County according to law- The said QUINTINA GARNES is of a tawny complexion, five feet four inches high in slippers, will be twenty three years old about Christmas next, has a small scar on the inner corner of the right eye, has a scar or speck in the left thumb nail, and is a little stiff in her right wrist, without any other apparent mark or scar on her face, head or hands- Given under my hand as Clerk of the said Court this 24th day of September 1852- L.Scruggs- order at Sept Court 1852 and copy furnished 24 Sept 1852

Number 470- **MARY ANN GARNES** a free negro born free in Mechlenburg County is this day numbered and Registered in the Clerks office of the County Court of Pittsylvania County according to law- The said MARY ANN GARNES is of a brown complexion, five feet five inches and three quarters of an inch high in slippers, nineteen years old, has two small scars near the left corner of the mouth, has a mole on the side of the left forefinger at the second joint, has a small scar on the back of the right forefinger at the second joint, without any other apparent mark or scar on her face, head or hands- Given under my hand as Clerk of the said Court this 24th day of September 1852- L.Scruggs- order at Sept Court 1852 and copy furnished 24 Sept 1852

[p 214] Number 471- **JESSE GARNES** a free negro born free in Mechlenburg County is this day numbered and registered in the Clerks office of the County Court of Pittsylvania County according to law- The said JESSE GARNES is of a black complexion, four feet nine and a half inches high in thin shoes, about thirteen years old, has black African hair, without any apparent mark or scar on his face, head or hands- Given under my hand as Clerk of the said Court this 24th day of September 1852- L.Scruggs- order at Sept Court 1852 and copy furnished 24 Sept 1852

Number 472- **SLAYTON VALENTINE** a free negro born free in Pittsa County is this day numbered and Registered in the Clerks office of the County Court of said Pittsylvania County according to law- The said SLAYTON VALENTINE is of dark complexion, about thirty years of age, five feet seven inches high in shoes, has a long scar on the right side of the face running back from the corner of the mouth, has a scar on the forehead above the left eye in the edge of the eye brow, without any other apparent mark or scar on his face, head or hands- Given under my hand as Clerk of the said Court this 24th day of September 1852- L.Scruggs- order at Sept Court 1852 and copy furnished 24 Sept 1852

Number 473- **ELIZABETH STEPHENS** a free negro born free in Pittsylvania County is this day numbered and registered in the Clerks office of the County Court of Pittsylvania County according to law- The said ELIZABETH STEPHENS is of dark complexion, about thirty five years old, five feet three inches high in thin shoes, has a small scar across the left temple near the corner of the eye, has a small one just above the inner corner of the left eye, has three moles about the end of her nose, without any other apparent mark or scar on her face, head or hands- Given under my hand as Clerk of the said Court this 24th day of September 1852- L.Scruggs- order at Septemr Court 1852 and copy furnished 24 Sept 1852

Number 474- **BETSY FRY** formerly **BETSY WILLIAMS** a free negro born free in the County of Amelia is this day numbered and registered in the Clerks office of the County Court of Pittsylvania County according to Law- The said BETSY FRY is of a brown complexion, about thirty eight years old, five feet five inches and a quarter of an inch high in shoes, has a mole on the corner of the right ear, another small mole on the lower side of the right cheek, without any other apparent mark or scar on her face, head or hands- Given under my hand as Clerk of the said Court this 29th day of September 1852- L.Scruggs- order at Sept Co '52 and copy furnished 29 Sept 1852

[p 215] Number 475- **ISRAEL WILEY** a free negro born free in Pittsylvania County is this day numbered and Registered in the Clerks office of the County Court of said County according to Law- The said ISRAEL WILEY is a yellow man, twenty two years old the 28th day of January next, five feet seven inches high in thin shoes, has a small scar on forehead above the right eye, without any other apparent mark or scar on his face, head or hands- Given under my hand as Clerk of the said Court this 20th day of October 1852- L.Scruggs- order at Octo Court 1852 & copy furnished 20 Oct 1852

Number 476- **JACKSON WILEY** a free negro born free in Pittsylvania County is this day numbered and Registered in the Clerks office of the County Court of said County according to Law- The said JACKSON WILEY is a yellow man, twenty two years old the 28th day of next January, five feet seven and a quarter inches high in thin shoes, has a small scar about an inch long on the side & near the second joint of the third finger of the left hand, without any other apparent mark or scar on his face, head or hands- Given under my hand as Clerk of the said Court this 20th day of October 1852- L.Scruggs- order at Octo Court 1852 & copy furnished 20th Oct 1852

Number 477- **POLLY HAZLEWOOD** a free negro born free in Lunenburg County is this day numbered and Registered in the Clerks office of the County Court afsaid Pittsylvania County according to Law- The said POLLY is a bright mulatto woman about thirty eight years old the 20th day of June next, five feet one inch high in shoes, straight black hair, freckles and blotches on her face and forehead with a slight crook in the little finger of the right hand, without any other apparent mark or scar on her face, head or hands- Given under my hand as Clerk of the said Court this 20th day of November 1852- L.Scruggs Clk- (order at Novemr Court 1852 & copy furnished 20 Nov 1852)

Number 478- **SAMUEL CARTER** a free negro born free in Pittsylvania County is this day numbered and Registered in the Clerks office of the County Court of said County according to Law- The said SAMUEL CARTER is a mulatto man Twenty one years old the 8th day of October 1852, five feet eight inches & a half high in thick boots, with a thick coat of hair on his head has a small scar on the first Joint of the little finger of the left hand [p 216] has another on the outside of the first finger of the left hand near the second Joint of the said finger, has another small scar on the right hand opposite the thumb, has another on the little finger of the right hand near the first Joint of said finger without any other apparent mark or scar on his face, head or hands- Given under my hand as Clerk of the said Court this 18th day of January 1853- L.Scruggs Clk

Number 479- **PARTHENIA COOPER** a free negro born free in the County of Pittsylvania in the State of Virginia is this day numbered and Registered in the Clerks office of the County Court of said County according to Law- The said PARTHENIA COOPER is about thirty eight years of age, of yellow complexion, five feet four inches high in shoes, has a small mole under her left ear has a scar on her forehead a few freckles on her face has a small scar on the 2nd joint of her right thumb without any other apparent mark or scar on her face, head or hands- Given under my hand this 16th day of May 1853- L.Scruggs Clk

Number 480- **SUSAN ANN GOOD** a free negro born free in the County of Pittsylvania in the State of Virginia is this Day numbered and Registered in the Clerks office of the County Court of said County according to Law- The said SUSAN ANN is about eighteen years of age of a light brown complexion five feet one inch and three quarters of an inch high in shoes, has a small scar about an inch in length on the inside of the left wrist nearly opposite the thumb another small scar on the back of the left hand near the wrist, without any other apparent mark or scar on her face, head or hands- Given under my hand this 16th day of May 1853- L.Scruggs Clk

[p 217] Number 481- **ISABELLA GOOD** a free negro born free in the County of Pittsylvania in the State of Virginia is this day numbered and Registered in the Clerks office of the County Court of said County according to Law- The said ISABELLA is about ten years of age of a light brown complexion four feet eight inches and a quarter of an inch high in thin shoes, has a small Knot near the outer corner of the left eye has a small scar on the first joint of the fore finger of the left hand another near the first joint of the forefinger of the right hand another near the second joint of said finger and both nearly on the outside of said finger without any other apparent mark or scar on her face, head or hands- Given under my hand this 16th day of May 1853- L.Scruggs Clk

Number 482- **EDDA BOWMAN** a free negro born free in the County of Halifax in the State of Virginia is this Day numbered and Registered in the Clerks office of the County Court of Pittsylvania County according to Law- The said EDDA BOWMAN is of a dark brown complexion about forty six years of age five feet seven inches and a half high in shoes, and crosseyed without any other apparent mark or scar on her face, head or hands- Given under my hand this 16th day of May 1853- L.Scruggs Clk

Number 483- **JOHN JACKSON** a free negro born free in the County of Halifax in the State of Virginia is this day numbered and Registered in the Clerks office of the County Court of Pittsylvania County according to Law- The said JOHN JACKSON is about twenty two years of age of a light brown complexion five feet ten inches and a half high in thin shoes, has a small scar on the left corner of the chin another scar (bract) [?] about an inch in Length on the right cheek running in a direction to the right corner of his mouth without any other apparent mark or scar on his face, head or hands- Given under my hand this 16th day of May 1853- L.Scruggs Clk

[p 218] Number 484- **HENRIETTA BOWMAN** a free negro born free in the County of Pittsylvania in the State of Virginia is this

Day numbered and Registered in the Clerks office of the County Court afsaid according to Law- The said HENRIETTA BOWMAN is about thirteen years of age of a dark complexion five feet three inches and a half high in shoes, without any apparent mark or scar- Given under my hand this 16th day of May 1853- L.Scruggs Clk

Number 485- **SALLY KEELING** a free negro born free in the County of Pittsylvania in the State of Virginia is this Day numbered and Registered in the Clerks office of the County Court of said County according to Law- The said SALLY KEELING is about twenty years of age of a yellow complexion five feet three inches high in shoes, has a scar on her right temple has a small Dimple on her right cheek a small mole near the right corner of her nose, has two small moles near each other below the left corner of her mouth, without any other apparent mark or scar on her face, head or hands- Given under my hand this 16th day of May 1853- L.Scruggs Clk

Number 486- **DUGGER COOPER** a free negro born free in the County of Mechlenburg in the State of Virginia is this day numbered and registered in the Clerks office of the County Court of Pittsylvania County according to Law- The said DUGGER COOPER is of a yellow complexion about eighteen years of age five feet three inches and three quarters of an inch high in shoes, has a small black mole on the left cheek opposite the nose a small one on the chin has a scar on the right hand another scar on the forefinger of the right hand near the second joint another scar on the first joint of the forefinger of the left hand without any other apparent mark or scar on his face, head or hands- Given under my hand this 16th day of May 1853 [p 219]   L.Scruggs Clk

Number 487- **NANCY COOPER** a free negro born free in the County of Mechlenburg in the State of Virginia is this day numbered and registered in the Clerks office of the County Court of Pittsylvania County according to Law- The said NANCY COOPER is about fourteen years of age of a yellow complexion five feet five inches and a half high in shoes, has a scar over the left eye has two small scars near the first joint of the third finger of the right hand another on the left thumb near the first joint another on the back of the left hand without any other apparent mark or scar on her face, head or hands- Given under my hand this 16th day of May 1853- L.Scruggs Clk

Number 488- **LATHY COOPER** a free negro born free in the County of Mechlenburg in the State of Virginia is this day numbered and registered in the Clerks office of the County Court of Pittsylvania County according to Law- The said LATHY COOPER is a mulatto boy about twelve years of age four feet nine inches and a half high in shoes, has a scar on his head near the right temple has another on the forefinger of the left hand by which the nail is disfigured & of an unnatural shape without any other apparent mark or scar on his face, head or hands- Given under my hand this 16th day of May 1853- L.Scruggs Clk

Number 489- **LETTY COOPER** a free negro born free in the County of Mechlenburg in the State of Virginia is this day numbered and registered in the Clerks office of the County Court of Pittsylvania County according to Law- The said LETTY COOPER is a girl of yellow complexion about ten years of age four feet half an inch high, has a small scar on her little finger of the right hand, without any other apparent mark or scar on her face, head or hands- Given under my hand this 16th day of May 1853- L.Scruggs Clk

[p 220] Number 490- **JAMES GARNES** a free negro born free in the County of Pittsylvania is this day numbered and registered in the Clerks office of the County Court of said County according to Law- The said JAMES GARNES is twenty three years old of a yellow complexion five feet five and a half inches high in thin shoes, has a small scar on his nose between the eyes a small scar on his right hand near the first joint of the forefinger two small scars on the front side of the forefinger of the left hand one of them opposite the first joint and the other opposite the second joint of said finger without any other apparent mark or scar on his face, head or hands- Given under my hand this 20th day of June 1853- L.Scruggs Clk

Number 491- **SUSAN GARNES** a free negro born free in the County of Pittsylvania is this day numbered and registered in the

Clerks office of the County Court of said County according to Law- The said SUSAN GARNES is twenty one years of age of a yellow complexion five feet two & three quarter inches high in thin slippers, has a small burn on the left hand near the first joints of the first and second fingers of said hand & a small scar on the right side of the neck without any other apparent mark or scar on her face, head or hands- Given under my hand this 20th day of June 1853- L.Scruggs

No 492- **JANE HOOD** a free negro born free in the County of Halifax as appears by her register made by the clerk of the County Court of said County on the 2nd day of June 1831 is this day Re-registered in the Clerks office of the County Court of Pittsylvania County according to Law- The said JANE HOOD is of a dark complexion, aged about forty one years the 19th day of July last five feet five Eight inches and a half high in thin shoes, has a small scar on the lower end of her left cheek another on the back of her left arm near the wrist three small ones on the back of her left hand near the knuckles, another small one on the outside [p 221] of said hand near the thumb another scar on the first finger of the right hand near the first joint without any other apparent mark or scar on her face, head or hands- Given under my hand this 17th day of October 1853- L.Scruggs Clk

No 493- **MILDRED JANE HOOD** a free negro born free in the County of Halifax is this day numbered and registered in the Clerks office of the County Court of Pittsylvania County according to Law- The said MILDRED JANE HOOD is of a dark complexion, nineteen years old the 30th day of this month five feet five inches and a quarter high in thin Shoes, has two small scars on the left side of her neck near the cheek has a small scar on the back of her right hand near the thumb another small one on the first joint of the little finger of said hand without any other apparent mark or scar on her face, head or hands- Given under my hand this 17th day of October 1853- L.Scruggs Clk

No 253- **ROBERT MASON** a free negro born free in the County of Pittsylvania & who has been heretofore numbered and registered in the said County is this day again registered in the Clerks office of the County Court of said County according to Law- The said

ROBERT MASON is of a dark complexion, about forty three years of age five feet Eight inches high has a small scar under and near the outer corner of the right Eye a very small one over the left Eye and a small scar on the forehead without any other apparent mark or scar on his face, head or hands- Given under my hand this 20th day of November 1853- L.Scruggs Clk **[Renewal]**

No 224- **LUCINDA VALENTINE** alias **LUCINDA MASON** wife of ROBERT MASON & who has been heretofore numbered & registered in the said County is this day again registered in the Clerks office of the County Court of Pittsylvania County according to Law- The said LUCINDA VALENTINE alias LUCINDA MASON is a mulatto [p 222] woman about forty five years of age five feet one & a half inches high in shoes has a small scar on her Forehead another on the right side of the Throat and another on the upper part of the right Hand near the wrist without any other apparent mark or scar on her face, head or hands- Given under my hand this 20th day of November 1853- L.Scruggs Clk **[This is a Renewal; however LUCINDA's correct number is 244.]**

Number 494- **GEORGE MASON** a free negro born free in the County of Pittsylvania Virginia is this day Numbered and registered in the Clerks office of the County Court of said County according to Law- The said GEORGE MASON is a man of dark complexion about twenty two years of age five feet eight inches and three quarters of an inch high in shoes has a very small scar on his right jaw bone not far from his chin, has another small scar near the outer corner of the left eye has another small wart on the back of the right hand & has another scar on the second joint of the right thumb without any other apparent mark or scar on his face, head or hands- Given under my hand this 22nd day of November 1853- L.Scruggs Clk

Number 495- **CHARLES DAVIS** a free negro born free in the County of Pittsylvania in the State of Virginia is this day numbered and registered in the Clerks office of the County Court of said County according to Law- The said CHARLES DAVIS is a man of yellow complexion about twenty four years of age in April next five feet six inches and a half high in boots, has two small scars on his forehead another near the outside corner of the right eye another scar on the back of the left hand another on the outside of the forefinger of said hand without any other apparent mark or scar on his face, head or hands- Given under my hand as Clerk of the said Court this 18th day of January 1854- L.Scruggs Clk

Number 496- **MOSES DAVIS** a free negro born free in the County of Pittsylvania in the State of Virginia is this day numbered and registered in the Clerks office of the County Court of Pittsylvania County in the State aforesaid according to Law- The said MOSES DAVIS is a bright mulatto man twenty one years of age this day five feet five inches and three quarters of an inch high in boots, has a small scar immediately in his forehead without any other apparent mark or scar on his face, head or hands- Given [p 223] under my hand as Clerk of the said Court this 16th day of January 1854- L.Scruggs Clk

Number 497- **PEYTON JACKSON** a free negro born free in the County of Mechlenburg in the State of Virginia is this day numbered and registered in the Clerks office of the County Court of Pittsylvania County in the State aforesaid according to Law- The said PEYTON JACKSON is a man of dark complexion about thirty four years of age, five feet six inches and a half high in thick shoes, has a scar about an inch in length on the back of the left hand a small scar on the back of the right wrist a scar on the right jaw just below the cheek bone, a small scar on the left cheek and a mole on the top of his nose about the centre [sic], without any other apparent mark or scar on his face, head or hands- Given under my hand as Clerk of said Court this 20th day of April 1854- L.Scruggs Clk

Number 498- **SALLY COLE** a free negro born free in the County of Pittsylvania in the State of Virginia is this day numbered and registered in the Clerks office of the County Court of said County according to Law- The said SALLY COLE is of a brown complexion about thirty one years old in December next, five feet four inches high in thin shoes, has a long scar on the left side of her neck & a scar on her left jaw without any other apparent mark or scar on her face, head or hands- Given under my hand this 16th day of January 1854- L.Scruggs Clk

No 427- **DICK MORGAN** a black man of colour who was emancipated by the last will and Testament of Robert Morgan decd is this day Registered again in the Clerks office of the County Court of Pittsylvania County according to Law- The said DICK MORGAN is about thirty seven years of age five feet six inches and a half high in boots has a small scar over the left eye, another near the outer corner of the right eye, another on the outside of the right wrist and several scars on the back of the left hand & another scar on the first joint of the forefinger of said hand without any other apparent mark or scar on his face, head or hands- Given under my hand as Clerk of the said Court this 19th day of September 1854- L.Scruggs Clk **[Renewal]**

[p 224] Number 499- **MILTON BOWMAN** a free negro born free in the County of Halifax in the State of Virginia is this day numbered and registered in the Clerks office of the County Court of Pittsylvania County according to Law- The said MILTON BOWMAN is about twenty two years of age of a tawny complexion five feet five and a half inches high, has a small scar on the first joint of the left thumb a small scar on the middle joint of the left forefinger & a small hole or scar near the centre [sic] of his forehead also a large scar between the first and second joints of the third finger of the right hand without any other apparent mark or scar on his face, head or hands- Given under my hand as Clerk of the said Court this 23rd day of September 1854- L.Scruggs Clk- (order at Decr Court 1853)

Number 500- **GEORGE STEPHENS** a free negro born free in the County of Pittsylvania is this day numbered and registered in the Clerks office of the County Court of Pittsylvania County according to Law- The said GEORGE STEPHENS is of a rather brown complexion about twenty four years old, five feet eight inches high has a long scar on the little finger of the left hand between the second and third joints, a large scar on the end of the middle finger of the left hand a scar between the second and third joints of the fore finger of the right hand and another on the end of the fore finger of the said right hand without any other apparent mark or scar on his face, head or hands- Given under my hand as Clerk of the said Court this 21st day of December 1854- L.Scruggs Clk

Number 501- **ALLIN GEE** a free negro born free in the County of Pittsylvania is this day numbered and Registered in the Clerks office of the County Court of said County according to Law- The said ALLIN GEE is of a yellow complexion twenty two years old, five feet eleven and a half inches high has a scar on the end of his thumb of the left hand one scar near the first joint of the middle finger of his right hand another scar on the third finger of the right hand near the end a large scar under the left eye a small scar [p 225] about and [sic] inch from the right corner of his right eye & a large scar on the top of his head without any other apparent mark or scar on his face, head or hands- Given under my hand as Clerk of the said Court this 21st day of December 1854- L.Scruggs Clk

Number 502- **WILLIAM DAVIS** a free negro born free in the County of Pittsylvania is this day numbered and registered in the Clerks office of the County Court of Pittsylvania County according to Law- The said WILLIAM DAVIS is of a yellow complexion twenty one years old, five feet eight inches high in shoes, has a very small scar on the back of his left hand without any other apparent mark or scar on his face, head or hands- Given under my hand as Clerk of the said Court this 21st day of December 1854- L.Scruggs Clk

Number 503- **ISAAC DAVIS** a free negro born free in the County of Pittsylvania is this day numbered and registered in the Clerks office of the County Court of Pittsylvania County according to Law- The said ISAAC DAVIS is of a brown complexion twenty four years old, five feet five inches and a quarter inch high in shoes, has a small scar on the forehead over the left eye has another on the back of his right hand near the wrist another on the back of the same hand very near the thumb, another on the back of the left hand and another on the forefinger of the same hand near the second joint without any other apparent mark or scar on his face, head or hands- Given under my hand as Clerk of the said Court this 21st day of December 1854- L.Scruggs Clk

[p 226] Number 504- **POLLY KEELING** a free negro born free in the County of Pittsylvania in the State of Virginia is this day numbered and registered in the Clerks office of the County Court of said County according to Law- The said POLLY KEELING is a

bright mulatto woman about twenty four years old, five feet five inches and a half high in shoes, has black straight hair without any apparent mark or scar on her face, head or hands- Given under my hand as Clerk of the said Court this 17th day of April 1855- L.Scruggs Clk

Virginia Pittsylvania County to Wit- At a Court held for the County of Pittsylvania the 18th day of August 1851- It appearing to the satisfaction of the Court that **ROBERT WASHINGTON VALENTINE** and **JAMES COLE** free persons of colour were born free in this County, it is ordered that the clerk of this court register the said ROBERT WASHINGTON VALENTINE and JAMES COLE according to law. Number 505- Pursuant to the above order the said JAMES COLE is this day numbered and registered in the clerks office of said County according to law- He is of dark complexion about twenty two years old five feet seven inches and a half high in thin slippers, has a scar above the nose nearly between his eyebrows, another on the right side of his neck and one on the back of his neck without any other apparent mark or scar on his face head or hands. Given under my hand this 12 day of June 1855. L. Scruggs Clk   [**This registration gives JAMES a number, which was omitted at the time Robert received number 454, and also describes JAMES.**]

State of Virginia Pittsylvania County Sc- At a County Court held for the County of Pittsylvania at the Court House thereof on Monday the 19th day of August 1850- It is ordered that the clerk of this court register the said **ROANN MAYO, LEANA REYNOLDS** wife of **JUBA REYNOLDS**, **LOUISA JANE MASON** wife of **STEPHEN MASON**, **PANTHEA REYNOLDS** and **TURNER ABERNATHY VALENTINE** free persons of colour according to law- Number 506- Pursuant to the above order [p 227] the said PANTHEA REYNOLDS is this day numbered and registered in the Clerks Office of the County Court of Pittsylvania County according to law; She is of a rather dark complexion, twenty years old in April last, five feet one and a half inches high in thin slippers, has a small scar on her forehead, another near the left temple above the eye, another on the left thumb near the second joint, another on the inside of the left hand near the little finger has a small mole on the inside of the said hand near the wrist has a small scar on the back of the right hand another near the little finger of said hand without any other apparent mark or scar on her face head or hands. Given under my hand as Clerk of the said Court this 18th day of August 1855. L. Scruggs Clk [Renewals for 5 persons under one number; Their previous numbers were 437, 438, 439, 440, and 441.]

State of Virginia to Wit- At a County Court held for the County of Pittsylvania at the Court House thereof on the 17th day of March 1856- The Court doth order the clerk to number and register **JACOB POUNDS** a free negro born free in this County- Number 507- Pursuant to the above order the said JACOB POUNDS is this day numbered and registered in the clerks office of the County Court of Pittsylvania County according to law- He is twenty five years old five feet six inches and a half high, of a yellow complexion, has a small scar near the first joint of the middle finger of the right hand a small scar about an inch above the left eye, without any other apparent mark or scar on his face head or hands. Given under my hand as Clerk of the said Court this 25th day of March 1856. L. Scruggs Clk

State of Virginia to Wit- At a County Court held for the County of Pittsylvania at the Courthouse thereof on the 19th day of May 1856- The Court doth order the clerk to register **PERMELIA BARKER** a free negro born free in this County- Number 508- Pursuant to the above order the said PERMELIA BARKER is this day numbered and registered in the Clerks office of the County Court of Pittsylvania County according to law- She is a white mulatto woman with straight hair, seventeen years old in February last five feet three and a half inches high in shoes, has a small scar on her forehead above the right eye, has a small scar in the middle of the inside of the left hand, without any other apparent mark or scar on her face head or hands. Given under my hand as Clerk of the said Court this 21st day of May 1856. L. Scruggs Clk

[p 228] State of Virginia to Wit- At a County Court held for the County of Pittsylvania at the Courthouse thereof on Monday the 19th day of May 1856- The Court doth order the clerk to register **ANNA S. BARKER** a free negro born free in this County- Number 509- Pursuant to the above order the said ANNA S. BARKER is

this day numbered and registered in the Clerks office of the County Court of Pittsylvania County according to law- She is a white mulatto woman with straight hair, sixteen years old in April last five feet five inches and a quarter high in thin shoes, without any apparent mark or scar on her face head or hands. Given under my hand as Clerk of the said Court this 21st day of May 1856. L. Scruggs Clk

State of Virginia to Wit- At a County Court held for the County of Pittsylvania at the Courthouse thereof on the 19th day of May 1856- The Court doth order the clerk to register **MARIAH BARKER** a free negro born free in this County- Number 510- Pursuant to the above order the said MARIAH BARKER is this day numbered and registered in the Clerks office of the County Court of Pittsylvania County according to law- She is a white mulatto woman with straight hair, about thirty nine years old five feet four and a quarter inches high in shoes, has two small moles on the right side of her face near the nose a scar on the chin a scar on her neck & another scar on the inside of her right wrist, without any other apparent mark or scar on her face head or hands. Given under my hand as Clerk of the said Court this 21st day of May 1856. L. Scruggs Clk

State of Virginia to Wit- At a County Court held for the County of Pittsylvania at the Courthouse thereof on Monday the 19th day of May 1856- The Court doth order the clerk to register **DICY DAVIS** a free negro born free in this County- Number 511- Pursuant to the above order the said DICY DAVIS is this day numbered and registered in the Clerks office of the County Court of Pittsylvania County according to law- She is a mulatto woman twenty two years old, five feet one and a half inches high in shoes, without any apparent mark or scar on her face head or hands. Given under my hand as Clerk of the said Court this 21st day of May 1856. L. Scruggs Clk

[p 229] State of Virginia to Wit- At a County Court held for the County of Pittsylvania at the Courthouse thereof on Monday the 19th day of May 1856- The Court doth order the clerk to register **DANIEL DAVIS** a free negro born free in this County- Number 512- Pursuant to the above order the said DANIEL DAVIS is this

day numbered and registered in the Clerks office of the County Court of Pittsylvania County according to law- he is a brown mulatto man about twenty one years old, five feet nine and three quarters inches high in shoes, has a small scar over the left eye another between his eyes, one under his throat, another on the left corner of his chin, has a small scar on the inside of the first finger of the left hand near the first joint, another on the back of the same hand near the first joints of the first and second front fingers, another scar on the back of the third finger of the right hand near the first joint without any other apparent mark or scar on his face head or hands. Given under my hand as Clerk of the said Court this 21st day of May 1856. L. Scruggs Clk

State of Virginia to Wit- At a County Court held for the County of Pittsylvania at the Courthouse thereof on Monday the 20th day of October 1856- The Court doth order the clerk to register **ELIZABETH RICHARDSON** a free negro born free in this County- Number 513- Pursuant to the above order the said ELIZABETH RICHARDSON is this day numbered and registered in the Clerks office of the County Court of Pittsylvania County according to law- She is of a brown complexion nineteen years old last May, five feet two inches high in thin shoes, has a scar on the left cheek about an inch below the eye, lower corners of ears disfigured without any other apparent mark or scar on her face head or hands. Given under my hand as Clerk of said Court this 24th day of October 1856. L. Scruggs Clk

[p 230] State of Virginia to Wit- At a County Court held for the County of Pittsylvania at the Courthouse thereof on Monday the 16th day of December 1856- The Court doth order the clerk to register **TOWNSEND GHEE** a free negro born free in this County- Number 514- Pursuant to the above order the said TOWNSEND GHEE is this day numbered and registered in the Clerks office of the County Court of Pittsylvania County according to law- he is of a light brown complexion twenty two years old next April, five feet seven and three quarter inches high in thin shoes, has a small scar on the first joint of the third finger of the right hand a small scar on the first joint of middle finger of right hand, a scar about an inch long on left thumb, several small scars on first joint of middle finger of left hand a scar about one & a half inches

long on forehead about one inch above right eye without any other apparent mark or scar on his face head or hands. Given under my hand as Clerk of the said Court this 20th day of Dec 1856. L. Scruggs Clk

State of Virginia to Wit- At a County Court continued and held for the County of Pittsylvania on the 19th day of March 1857- The Court doth order the clerk of this Court to register **JESSE HOOD** a free negro born free in this County- Number 515- Pursuant to the above order the said JESSE HOOD is this day numbered and Registered in the Clerks office of the County Court of said County according to law- He is a black man about twenty four years of age, has black kinky hair, a knot on the right wrist and is five feet nine and a half inches high- without any other apparent mark or scar on his face head or hands. Given under my hand this 30th day of March 1857. L. Scruggs Clk

State of Virginia to Wit- At a County Court continued and held for the County of Pittsylvania on the 19th day of March 1857- The Court doth order the [An unnumbered page between p 230 and p 231] Clerk of this Court to Register **THOMAS HOOD** a free negro born free in this County- Number 516- Pursuant to the above order the said THOMAS HOOD is this day numbered and Registered in the Clerks office of the County Court of said County according to law- He is about twenty one years of age of black complexion, black kinky hair, has a scar on the back of his right hand and is five feet seven inches high- without any other apparent mark or scar on his face head or hands. Given under my hand this 30th day of March 1857. L. Scruggs Clk

Virginia, Pittsylvania County Court, March Term 1857- It is ordered that the Clerk of this Court renew the Register of **CATHERINE ROBERTSON JANE STEPHENS** a free negro born free in this County according to Law- Number 448- The said CATHERINE ROBERTSON JANE STEPHENS is a bright mulatto woman twenty five years old in February last, five feet four inches high in shoes- has a scar on her right wrist caused by a burn, has light hair tolerably straight rather inclined to curl & hazel eyes- without any other apparent mark or scar on her face head or hands. Given under my hand as Clerk of County Court of Pittsylvania County this 13th day of April 1857. L. Scruggs Clk **[Renewal]**

State of Virginia to Wit- At a County Court held for the County of Pittsylvania on the 15th day of June 1857- The Court doth order the clerk of this Court to Register **WM NORRIS** a free negro born free in this County- Number 517- Pursuant to the above order the said WM NORRIS is this day numbered and Registered in the Clerks office of the County Court of said County according to law- He is about twenty two years old, yellow complexion- has a scar just above the right eyebrow, has two large scars on his right arm caused by a burn, five feet nine inches high, without any other apparent mark or scar on his face head or hands. Given under my hand as Clerk of the said Court this 10th day of July 1857. L. Scruggs Clk

[p 231] State of Virginia to Wit- At a Quarterly Court held for the County of Pittsylvania on the 17th day of August 1857- **WM ROSS** a free negro born free in this County desiring to be registered on his motion, it is ordered that the Clerk register him according to law- Number 518- Pursuant to the above order the said WM ROSS is this day numbered and registered in the Clerks office of the County Court of the said County according to law- The said WM ROSS is a black man five feet three and a half inches high in thin shoes, about thirty years old, has two small scars on his forehead immediately opposite his nose, another on his right temple near the jaw bone, has a small scar on the back of his right wrist near the right corner, another on the first joint of the little finger of the right hand, another on the back of said finger between the first and second joints, another small one on the back of said hand near the thumb, another on the first joint of the forefinger of said hand and another under the right eye, without any other apparent mark or scar on his face head or hands. Given under my hand this 22nd day of August 1857. L. Scruggs Clk **[This may renew No. 216, child of Mary MASON alias ROSS.]**

State of Virginia to Wit- At a Quarterly Court held for the County of Pittsylvania on the 17th day of August 1857- On the motion of **LUCINDA BURNETT** a free woman born free in this County the

Court doth order the Clerk to register her according to law- Number 519- Pursuant to the above order the said LUCINDA BURNETT is this day numbered and registered in the Clerks office of the County Court of the said County according to law- The said LUCINDA BURNETT is a black woman five feet three inches high in slippers, forty one years old the 8th day of June last, has a small scar on her forehead near the edge of her hair and opposite her left eye, another on the back of her left hand, several small scars on the front finger of said hand, two other scars on the second finger of said hand near the first joint [p 232] has another scar on the wrist of the right hand and another on the back of said hand nearly opposite the thumb, without any other apparent mark or scar on her face head or hands. Given under my hand this 22nd day of August 1857. L. Scruggs Clk

State of Virginia to Wit- At a Quarterly Court held for the County of Pittsylvania on the 17th day of August 1857- On the motion of **JULIA ANN DORCAS BURNETT** a free woman born free in this County the Court doth order the Clerk to register her according to law- Number 520- Pursuant to the above order the said JULIA ANN DORCAS BURNETT is this day numbered and registered in the Clerks office of the County Court of said County according to law- The said JULIA ANN DORCAS BURNETT is a yellow woman eighteen years old five feet three inches high in thin shoes, has a scar on the left corner of her chin, has a small scar on the back of her right wrist and another on the thumb of her left hand, several on the back of her right hand without any other apparent mark or scar on her face head or hands. Given under my hand this 22nd day of August 1857. L. Scruggs Clk

State of Virginia to Wit- At a Quarterly Court held for the County of Pittsylvania on the 17th day of August 1857- On the motion of **FRANCIS BOWMAN** a free woman born free in this County the Court doth order the Clerk to register her according to law- Number 521- Pursuant to the above order the said FRANCIS BOWMAN is this day numbered and registered in the Clerks office of the County Court of said County according to law- The said FRANCIS BOWMAN is a yellow woman five feet two inches high in slippers, about nineteen years old, has a small scar on the left arm near the wrist joint, another on the right arm near the wrist, and another on the right thumb near the first joint, without any other apparent mark or scar on her face head or hands. [p 233] Given under my hand this 22nd day of August 1857. L. Scruggs Clk

State of Virginia to Wit- At a County Court held for the County of Pittsylvania at the Courthouse thereof on Monday the 21st day of September 1857- The Court doth order the Clerk to register **GREENWOOD TURNER GOIN** a free Negro born free in this county, according to law- Number 522- Pursuant to the above order the said GREENWOOD TURNER GOIN is this day numbered and registered in the Clerks office of the County Court of said County according to law- He is a man of yellow complexion twenty two years old the 24th day of next April, Six feet and a half inch high in thin shoes, has a small scar on the forehead just above the right eye, a scar on the right hand about halfway between the wrist joint and the first joint of the third finger, another scar on the right hand near the first joint of the third finger, a small mole on the back of said hand, one scar between the first joints of the second and third fingers of said hand, a scar on the back of the left hand near the wrist joint, two scars on the forefinger of the left hand halfway between the first and second joints, three scars on the first joint of said finger, two scars on the first joint of the second finger, one other scar on said finger between the first & second joints, one small scar on the first joint of the third finger, one scar on the first joint of the Little finger & one other scar on the second joint of said finger, without any other apparent mark or scar on his face head or hands. Given under my hand this 25th day of September 1857. L. Scruggs Clk

[p 234] State of Virginia to Wit- At a County Court held for the County of Pittsylvania at the Courthouse thereof on Monday the 21st day of September 1857- The Court doth order the Clerk to register **ELIZA ANN GOIN** a free negro born free in this County according to law- Number 523- Pursuant to the above order the said ELIZA ANN GOIN is this day numbered and registered in the Clerks office of the County Court of said County according to law- She is a woman of bright yellow complexion twenty three years old the 3rd day of next March five feet seven and a quarter inches high in thin shoes, has two small scars on the back of the right hand

near the first joint of the little finger, two scars on the thumb of the left hand, one on the first joint and one between the first and second joints of the thumb, without any other apparent mark or scar on her face head or hands. Given under my hand this 25th day of September 1857. L. Scruggs Clk

State of Virginia to Wit- At a County Court held for the County of Pittsylvania at the Courthouse thereof on Monday the 21st day of September 1857- The Court doth order the Clerk to register **ANN DAVIS** a free woman of colour born free in this County- Number 524- Pursuant to the above order the said ANN DAVIS is this day numbered and registered in the Clerks office of the County Court of said County according to Law- She is of a yellow complexion about forty four years old, has a brown blister on both sides of her face caused by being scalded, a scar on the back of her right hand, one other on the back of said hand near the first joint of the forefinger, another on the first joint of the little finger of said hand, another on the inside of the wrist of the left hand, another on the inside of the second [p 235] joint of the second finger of said hand, without any other apparent mark or scar on her face head or hands. Given under my hand this 25th day of September 1857. L. Scruggs Clk

State of Virginia to Wit- At a County Court held for the County of Pittsylvania at the Courthouse thereof on Monday the 21st day of September 1857- The Court doth order the Clerk to register **ANDERSON DAY** a free negro born free in this County- Number 525- Pursuant to the above order the said ANDERSON DAY is this day numbered and registered in the Clerks office of the County Court of said County according to Law- He is of a dark brown complexion five feet seven inches high in thin shoes twenty one years old the 4th day of August last, has a small scar on the forehead above the left eye in the right temple a small scar on the first joint of the second finger one on the third joint of said finger, a scar on the left hand near the first joint of the thumb, one on the back of said hand near the first joint of the second finger of said hand, one other one on the back of said hand, near the first joint of the little finger, two scars on the back of said hand caused by a cut, without any other apparent mark or scar on his face head or hands. Given under my hand this 21st day of September 1857. L. Scruggs Clk [p 236] State of Virginia to Wit- At a County Court held for the County of Pittsylvania at the Courthouse thereof on Monday the 21st day of September 1857- The Court doth order the Clerk to renew the register of **BURWELL GOIN** a free negro born free in this County according to law- Number 209- BURWELL GOIN a free negro Pursuant to the above order is this day again registered in the Clerks office of the County Court of said County according to Law- He is of a Dark brown complexion fifty seven years old the 12th day of last April, Six feet one and a quarter inches high in heavy Shoes has a small black mole on the Right side of his face near his nose, has a scar on the wrist joint of the right hand, one on the left side of said hand near the wrist joint one on the first joint of the forefinger caused by a cut one other on the second joint of said finger, a small scar on the first joint of the thumb of said hand, a scar on the wrist of the left hand, one on the first joint of the forefinger of said hand, one between the first and second joints of said finger, one on the second joint of said finger, a scar on the second finger extending from the first joint halfway to the second joint of said finger, one between the second and third joints of said finger, one near the third joint of said finger, and one between the first joints of the second and third fingers of said hand, without any other apparent mark or scar on his face head or hands. Given under my hand this 25th day of September 1857. L. Scruggs Clk **[Renewal]**

[p 237] G Burnetts register- Virginia Pittsylvania County to Wit- At a County Court held for the County of Pittsylvania on the 19th day of October 1857- The Court doth order the Clerk of this Court to register **GEORGE BURNETT** a Free negro born free in this County- Number 526- Pursuant to the above order the said GEORGE BURNETT is this day numbered and registered in the Clerks office of the County Court of said County according to Law- He is of a dark brown complexion was fifty two years old the 13th day of September last- five feet ten inches high in heavy shoes has a large Wart on the forehead just above the right eye a scar on the left corner of the left eye a small Wart left side of the nose a scar between the first joint of the first and second finger of the right hand- a scar on the back of the wrist of the left hand without any other apparent mark or scar on his face head or hands. Given

under my hand as clerk of said Court this 11th day of November 1857. L. Scruggs Clk

Virginia Pittsylvania County to Wit- At a County Court held for the County of Pittsylvania on the 19th day of October 1857- The Court doth order the Clerk of this Court to register **NANCY BURNETT** a free negro born free in this County- Number 527- Pursuant to the above order the said NANCY BURNETT is this day numbered and registered in the clerks office of the county court of Pittsylvania court according to Law- She is of a bright yellow complexion about thirty three years old five feet six and one quarter inches high in heavy shoes has a small scar on the back of the right hand near the first joint of the forefinger and another scar on the first joint of the second finger of the left hand- without any other apparent mark or scar on her face head or hands. Given under my hand as clerk of said Court this 11th day of November 1857. L. Scruggs Clk

[p 238] Virginia Pittsylvania County to Wit- At a County Court held for the County of Pittsylvania on the 19th day of October 1857- The Court doth order the Clerk of this Court to renew the register of **JAMES GOIN** a free negro born free in this County- Number 211- Pursuant to the above order the said JAMES GOIN is this day again registered in the Clerks office of the County Court of said County according to Law- He is a Mulatto Man about fifty seven years old in May last- five feet seven and three quarter inches high in heavy shoes has a Wen in the left temple without any other apparent mark or scar on his face head or hands. Given under my hand as clerk of said Court this 11th day of November 1857. L. Scruggs Clk **[Renewal]**

Virginia Pittsylvania County to Wit- At a County Court held for the County of Pittsylvania on the 16th day of November 1857- The Court doth order the Clerk of this Court to register **GEORGE R. GOIN** a free negro born free in this County- Number 528- Pursuant to the above order the said GEORGE R. GOIN is this day numbered and registered in the Clerks office of the County Court of said County according to Law- He is of a bright yellow complexion was twenty one years the 30th day of November last- five feet six and one quarter inches high in thin shoes has a scar near the first joint of the thumb of the left hand, a small scar near the second joint of the first finger two other scars near the first joint of said finger- one other scar between the first and second joints of the second finger one other scar on the back of the said hand about halfway between the wrist joint and the first joint of the first finger two other scars on the back of said hand running down between the first joints of the first finger and thumb of said hand without any other apparent mark or scar on his face head or hands. Given under my hand as clerk of said Court this 16th day of November 1857. L. Scruggs Clk

[p 239] State of Virginia to Wit- At a County Court held for the County of Pittsylvania on the 16th day of November 1857- It is ordered that the Clerk register **MARY SUSAN COLE** a free negro born free in this County- Number 529- Pursuant to the above order the said MARY SUSAN COLE is this day numbered and registered in the Clerks office of the County Court of said County according to Law- She is a black woman was twenty one years old the 18th of December last- five feet four inches high in thin shoes without any other apparent mark or scar on her face head or hands. Given under my hand as clerk of said Court this 17th day of November 1857. L. Scruggs Clk

State of Virginia to wit- At a County Court held for the County of Pittsylvania on the 21st day of December 1857- It is ordered that the clerk register **WILLIAM DAY** a free negro born free in this County- No 530- Pursuant to the above order the said WILLIAM DAY is this day numbered and registered in the Clerks office of the County Court of said County according to law- He is of a dark brown complexion nearly black, was twenty one years the 28th day of November last- five feet eleven and a half inches high, in heavy shoes has a small scar on the left eyebrow one other on the first joint of the thumb of the right hand one on the right arm above the wrist joint one on the inside of the forefinger of the left hand near the third joint and one other on the second joint of said finger without any other apparent mark or scar on his face head or hands. Given under my hand as clerk of said Court this 23rd day of December 1857. L. Scruggs Clk

[p 240] State of Virginia to wit- At a County Court held for the County of Pittsylvania on the 21st day of December 1857- The

Court doth order the Clerk to renew the register of **REUBEN STEVENS** a free born man of color born free in this County- Number 408- Pursuant to the above order the said REUBEN STEVENS is this day again registered in the Clerks office of the County Court of said County according to the Law- He is a black man was thirty three years old the 3rd day of June last five feet five inches high in heavy shoes has a scar on his face near the right corner of his right eye a scar on the back of his right hand a scar extending from the first to the second joints of the first finger of the left hand, without any other apparent mark or scar on his face head or hands- Given under my hand as clerk of said Court this 23rd day of December 1857- L. Scruggs Clk **[Renewal]**

State of Virginia to wit- At a County court held for the County of Pittsylvania on the 21st day of December 1857- The Court doth order the Clerk to register **CATHERINE STEVENS** a free woman of color born free in this County- Number 530- Pursuant to the above order the said CATHERINE STEVENS is this day numbered and registered, in the Clerks office of the County Court of said County according to Law- she is a mulatto woman seventeen years old five feet seven and a half inches high in heavy shoes a scar on the back of the right hand a scar between this first joint of the second and third fingers of said hand five small scars between the first and second joints of the second finger of said hand three scars on the back of the left hand and one other between the first and second joints of the first finger of said hand without any other mark or scar on her face head or hands. Given under my hand as clerk of said Court this 23rd day of December 1857- L. Scruggs Clk **[This is a duplicate number. Number 530 has already been used for WILLIAM DAY above.]**

[p 241] State of Virginia to wit- At a County court held for the County of Pittsylvania on the 21st day of December 1857- The Court doth order the Clerk to register **ABNER STEVENS** a free born man of color born free in this County- Number 532- Pursuant to the above order the said ABNER STEVENS is this day numbered and registered, in the Clerks office of the County court of said County according to Law- he is a bright mulatto man was twenty two years old the 20th day of last August, five feet nine and three quarters inches high in thin shoes and a small scar on the

first finger of the left hand without any other mark or scar on his face- head or hands. Given under my hand as clerk of said Court this 23rd day of December 1857- L. Scruggs Clk **[This number is out of sequence.]**

State of Virginia to wit- At a County court held for the County of Pittsylvania on the 21st day of December 1857- The court doth order the clerk to renew the register of **AGGA STEVENS** a free woman of color born free in this county- Number 67- Pursuant to the above order the said AGGA STEVENS is this day again registered, in the clerks office of the county court of said county according to law- she is of dark brown complexion about fifty years of age five feet four and one quarter inches high in thin shoes has a small scar on the upper lip and a scar on the back of the right hand near the wrist joint without any other apparent mark or scar on her face- head or hands. Given under my hand as clerk of said court this 23rd day of December 1857- L. Scruggs Clk **[Renewal]**

[p 242] State of Virginia to Wit- At a County court held for the county of Pittsylvania on the 21st day of December 1857- The Court doth order the clerk to register **THOMAS STEVENS** a free man of color born free in this county- Number 531- Pursuant to the above order the said THOMAS STEVENS is this day numbered and registered, in the Clerks office of the County court of said County according to law- He is of a dark brown complexion was twenty six years old the 11th day of January last- five feet seven inches high in heavy shoes has a large scar on the left side of his neck a scar on the back of the right hand another scar on the back of the right hand between the first joint of the thumb and first finger of said hand a scar on the second joint of the first finger of the left hand without any other apparent mark or scar on his face head or hands. Given under my hand as clerk of said court this 23rd day of December 1857- L. Scruggs Clk **[Number is out of sequence.]**

State of Virginia to Wit- At a County court held for the county of Pittsylvania on the 21st day of December 1857- The Court doth order the clerk to register **JAMES STEVENS** a free born man of color born free in this county- Number 533- Pursuant to the above order the said JAMES STEVENS is this day numbered and registered, in the Clerks office of the County court of said County his face head or hands. Given under my hand as clerk of said court this 23rd day of December 1857- L. Scruggs Clk

[p 244] State of Virginia to wit- At a county court held for the county of Pittsylvania on the 21st day of December 1857- The court doth order the clerk to register **THOMAS TAYLOR STEVENS** a free boy of color born free in this county- Number 537- Pursuant to the above order the said THOMAS TAYLOR STEVENS is this day numbered and registered, in the clerks office of the county court of said county according to law- He is of dark brown complexion about seven years of age three feet ten inches high in heavy shoes without any apparent mark or scar on his face head or hands. Given under my hand as clerk of said court this 23rd day of December 1857- L. Scruggs Clk

State of Virginia to wit- At a County court held for the county of Pittsylvania on the 19th day of April 1858- The Court doth order the clerk to register **SARAH DAVIS** a free Woman of color born free in this county- Number 538- Pursuant to the above order the said SARAH DAVIS is this day numbered and registered in the clerks office of the county Court of said County according to law- she is a woman of [illegible] complexion about 22 years old five feet seven inches high in [left blank] shoes has a scar on her forehead between the eyes- & one on the left front finger on the inside of the middle joint without any other apparent mark or scar on her face head or hands. Given under my hand as clerk of said court this 19th day of April 1858- L. Scruggs Clk

[p 245] State of Virginia to Wit- At a County court held for the county of Pittsylvania on the 19th day of April 1858- The Court doth order the clerk to register **JAMES DAVIS** a free Negro born free in this county- Number 539- Pursuant to the above order the said JAMES DAVIS is this day numbered and registered, in the Clerks office of the County court of said County according to Law- He is a Mulatto Man five feet eleven inches high about twenty four years old last March in heavy shoes has a small scar over the right eye a scar on the back of the right hand- a scar on the first joint of the first finger of said hand and another on the second finger of said hand between the second and third joints of said finger two scars on the second joint of the thumb of the left hand- one small

according to Law- He is of a brown complexion about twenty six years of age five feet six and one half inches high in thin shoes has three scars on his forehead, one other scar on the nose between the eyes a small black mole on his chin a scar between first and second joints of the thumb of the right hand a scar on the second joint of the second finger of said hand, a small wart on the side of the second finger of the left hand and a black mark or scar under his right eye without any other apparent mark or scar on his face head or hands. Given under my hand as clerk of said court this 23rd day of December 1857- L. Scruggs Clk

[p 243] State of Virginia to wit- At a county court held for the county of Pittsylvania on the 21st day of December 1857- The court doth order the clerk to register **MARTHA ANN STEVENS** a free woman of color born free in this County- Number 534- Pursuant to the above order the said MARTHA ANN STEVENS is this day numbered and registered, in the clerks office of the County court of said County according to law- she is a black woman about twenty one years old, five feet four inches high in thin shoes- has a small protuberance on the right cheek caused by a cut a small mole on the right side of the right hand, one on the inside of the forefinger of said hand one below the first joints of the second and third finger of said hand, and a scar on the back of the left hand without any other apparent mark or scar on her face head or hands. Given under my hand as clerk of said Court this 23rd day of December 1857- L. Scruggs Clk

[Register Number 535 has been skipped.]

State of Virginia to wit- At a county court held for the county of Pittsylvania on the 21st day of December 1857- The Court doth order the clerk to register **ROBERT WILSON STEVENS** a free boy of color born free in this county- Number 536- Pursuant to the above order the said ROBERT WILSON STEVENS is this day numbered and registered, in the clerks office of the County court of said county according to law- He is a Mulatto Boy was nine years old the 4th day of august last, four feet four inches high in heavy shoes has a scar on the wrist of the right arm and two others on the back of the right hand, without any other apparent mark or scar on scar on the second joint of the first finger of the left hand and one other between the first and second joints of the middle finger of said hand without any other apparent mark or scar on his face head or hands. Given under my hand as clerk of said court this 22nd day of April 1858- L. Scruggs Clk

State of Virginia to Wit- At a county court held for the county of Pittsylvania on the 17th day of May 1858- It is ordered that the clerk register **BENJAMIN DAVIS** a free Negro born free in this county- Number 540- Pursuant to the above order the said BENJAMIN DAVIS is this day numbered and registered, in the Clerks office of the County court of said County according to Law- He is a Mulatto Man five feet nine inches high in thin shoes has two scars over the left eye and a small scar on the 2nd joint of the thumb of the left hand, without any other apparent mark or scar on his face head or hands. Given under my hand as clerk [p 246] of said court this 17th day of May 1858- L. Scruggs Clk

State of Virginia to Wit- At a quarterly court continued and held for the County of Pittsylvania at the Court House thereof on the 17th day of August 1858- The Court doth order the clerk to register **MARY PHILLIPS** a free negro born free in this county- Number 541- MARY PHILLIPS is this day numbered and registered in the Clerks office of the County Court of Pittsylvania County according to law- She is a woman of brown complexion twenty seven years old five feet four inches high has a natural mark on the right corner of her chin and a burn on her neck has two scars between the first & second joints of the forefinger of the right hand without any other apparent mark or scar on her face head or hands. Given under my hand as clerk of said court this 24th day of August 1858- L. Scruggs Clk

State of Virginia to Wit- At a quarterly court held for the County of Pittsylvania at the Court House thereof on the 16th day of August 1858- The Court doth order the clerk to renew the register of **MARTHA STEVENS** a free negro born free in this county it appearing to the Court that the said MARTHA STEVENS has never received her original papers- Number 449- MARTHA STEVENS is this day again registered according to law- She is a woman of black complexion five feet one & five eighths inches high in thin shoes has a scar on the forehead over the left eye another on the upper side of the right temple another on the largest joint of the left forefinger another on the end of the right forefinger & one on the back of the neck without any other apparent mark or scar on her face head or hands she is about thirty seven years of age Given under my hand as Clerk of the County Court of Pittsylvania County this 24th day of August 1858- L. Scruggs Clk **[Renewal]**

[p 247] State of Virginia to Wit- At a quarterly court [The words 'continued and' are crossed out.] held for the County of Pittsylvania at the Court House thereof on the 16th day of August 1858- The Court doth order the clerk to renew the register of **PARTHENIA STEVENS** a free negro born free in this county- Number 460- PARTHENIA STEVENS is this day again registered according to law- She is a woman of brown complexion twenty five years old the 19th day of June last five feet three inches and a quarter high in shoes has a small scar near the second joint of the middle finger of the right hand two small scars on the left thumb another small scar on the right thumb without any other apparent mark or scar on her face head or hands- Given under my hand as Clerk of the County Court of Pittsylvania County this 24th day of August 1858- L. Scruggs Clk **[Renewal]**

State of Virginia to Wit- At a quarterly court continued and held for the County of Pittsylvania on the 20th day of September 1858- The Court doth order the clerk to register **NANCY KEELING** a free negro born free in this county- Number 542- Pursuant to the above order the said NANCY KEELING is this day numbered and registered in the Clerks office of the county Court of said County according to law- She is a bright Mulatto Woman about thirty two years of age- Five feet two and one quarter inches high in thin shoes has a small black mole on the left side of her chin, two on her left cheek bone & one in the left temple without any other apparent mark or scar on her face head or hands. Given under my hand as Clerk of Said Court this 24th day of September 1858- L. Scruggs

[p 248] State of Virginia to Wit- At a County court held for the County of Pittsylvania on the 20th day of September 1858- The Court doth order the clerk to register **JOHN MITCHELL** a free Negro born free [the words 'Negro born free' have been duplicated

and crossed out] in this county- Number 543- Pursuant to the above order the said JOHN MITCHELL is this day numbered and registered in the Clerks office of the County Court of Said County according to law- He is of a dark brown complexion five feet five & a half inches high, about twenty two years of age in thin shoes has a small scar just below the right corner of his mouth five scars on the right side of his neck, a scar on the back of the right hand- a scar between the 1st & 2nd Joints of the 3rd finger of the right hand, a scar on the back of the left hand a scar on the inside of the thumb of the left & another scar between the 1st & 2nd Joints of the first finger of said hand without any other apparent mark or scar on his face head or hands- Given under my hand as Clerk of Said Court this 24th day of September 1858- L. Scruggs Clk

State of Virginia to Wit- At a quarterly court continued and held for the County of Pittsylvania the 20th day of September 1858- The Court doth order the clerk to renew the register of **PETER VALENTINE** a free Negro born free in this county- Number 345- Pursuant to the above order the said PETER VALENTINE is this day again registered in the Clerks office of the County Court of Said County according to law- He is a black Man about forty four years of age five feet two & one half inches high has a small scar about one inch immediately above the left eye a small scar about two inches above the left corner of the right eye- a scar about half inch long about half way between his left ear and his mouth a small scar near the lower end of the left ear a scar on the 2nd Joint of the forefinger of the right hand, a scar [p 249] about an inch in length on Joint of Wrist of right hand a small scar on 2nd joint of the 3rd finger of the left hand a small scar on 3rd Joint of forefinger of the left hand without any other apparent mark or scar on his face head or hands. Given under my hand as Clerk of Said Court this 24th day of September 1858- L. Scruggs Clk **[Renewal]**

State of Virginia to Wit- At a county court held for the County of Pittsylvania on the 20th day of September 1858- The Court doth order the clerk to register **RACHEL SHELTON** a free negro born free in this county- Number 544- Pursuant to the above order the said RACHEL SHELTON is this day numbered and registered in the Clerks office of the County Court of Said County according to law- She is a woman of black complexion about thirty two years of age five feet one and three fourth inches high in thin shoes has a small scar about an inch to the left of the lower corner of the left ear a small scar on the first joint of the middle finger on top & a small scar on the 3rd finger of the right hand half way between the first & second Joints on top, without any other apparent mark or scar on her face head or hands. Given under my hand as Clerk of Said Court this 24th day of September 1858- L. Scruggs Clk

[p 250] State of Virginia to Wit- At a county court held for the County of Pittsylvania on the 18th day of October 1858- The Court doth order the clerk to register **LIZZENIA KEELING** a free negro born free in this county- Number 545- Pursuant to the above order the said LIZZENIA KEELING is this day numbered and registered in the Clerks office of the County Court of said County according to law- She is a very bright mulatto Girl with strait [sic] dark hair- fourteen years old- five feet two and a half inches high in thin shoes- has two small black moles on her right cheek- another near the right side of her nose & another on the side of her left hand near the 1st joint of her forefinger- without any other apparent mark or scar on her face head or hands. Given under my hand as Clerk of Said Court this 22nd day of October 1858- L. Scruggs Clk

State of Virginia to Wit- At a county Court held for the County of Pittsylvania at the courthouse thereof on Monday the 18th day of October 1858- The Court doth order the clerk to renew the register of **JUBA REYNOLDS** a free Negro born free in this county- Number 28 Pursuant to the above order the said JUBA REYNOLDS is this day numbered & registered in the Clerks office of the County Court of Said County according to law- He is of a dark brown complexion five feet six and a half inches high in Shoes was sixty eight years old the 17th day of august last- has a small scar on the second joint of the middle finger of the right hand, & a small scar on the thumb of the left hand, without any other apparent mark or scar on his face head or hands. Given under my hand as Clerk of Said Court this 22nd day of October 1858- L. Scruggs Clk **[Renewal]**

[p 251] State of Virginia to Wit- At a county court held for the County of Pittsylvania on the 18th day of October 1858- The Court doth order the clerk to register **JANE RUMNEY** a free negro born

free in this county- Number 546- Pursuant to the above order the said JANE RUMNEY is this day numbered and registered in the Clerks office of the County Court of said County according to law She is a woman of light brown complexion about twenty one years of age- five feet three inches high in thin shoes- has a small scar under her right eye- a small mole on her forehead- a scar on the back of her right hand- two scars just below the first joint of the thumb- a long scar on the back of the left hand very near the middle two scars on the 2nd joint of the middle finger of said hand- a scar between the middle and third finger of said hand- one scar on the wrist joint & one just below the wrist joint & two scars just below the first joint of the thumb, of said hand. without any other apparent mark or scar on her face head or hands. Given under my hand as Clerk of said Court this 22nd day of October 1858- L. Scruggs Clk

State of Virginia to Wit- At a county court held for the County of Pittsylvania on the 18th day of October 1858- The Court doth order the clerk to renew the register of **SLAYTON VALENTINE** a free Negro born free in this county- Number 472- Pursuant to the above order the said SLAYTON VALENTINE is this day again registered in the Clerks office of the County Court of said County according to law- He is a black man about thirty six years of age- five feet seven and one half inches high in heavy shoes- has a long scar on the right side of his face running back from the corner of the mouth- has a scar on the forehead above the left eye in the edge of the eyebrow- a scar on the back of the right hand near the first joint of the thumb & a small protuberance between the first [p 252] joints of the first and second fingers of the left hand, without any other apparent mark or scar on his face head or hands- Given under my hand as Clerk of said Court this 22nd day of October 1858- L. Scruggs Clk **[Renewal]**

State of Virginia to Wit- At a county court held for the County of Pittsylvania on the 18th day of October 1858- The Court doth order the clerk to renew the register of **ELIZABETH STEVENS** alias **VALENTINE** a free Negro born free in this county- Number 473 Pursuant to the above the said ELIZABETH STEVENS alias VALENTINE is this [sic] again registered in the Clerks office of the County Court of said County according to law- She is a woman of a dark brown complexion about forty one years of age five feet two inches high in thin shoes- has a small scar across the left temple- near the corner of the eye- has a small scar just above the inner corner of the left eye. has three moles about the end of her nose- has a scar on the back of the right hand, has a scar on the first joint of the third finger of Said hand, has a long scar on the back of the left hand, near the first joint of the thumb and another scar on the back of said hand. without any other apparent mark or scar on her face head or hands. Given under my hand as Clerk of Said Court this 22nd day of October 1858- L. Scruggs Clk **[Renewal]**

State of Virginia to Wit- At a county court held for the County of Pittsylvania on the 15th day of November 1858- The Court doth order the clerk to renew the Register of **GEORGE DAVIS** a free Negro born free in this county- Number 542- GEORGE DAVIS a free negro is this day again registered in the Clerks office of the County Court of Pittsylvania County according to law. The said GEORGE DAVIS is a bright mulatto about twenty nine years old last August five feet seven inches high in thick shoes- has a small scar on the second joint of the left little finger- another on the left forefinger between the 1st and second joints, another on or near the first joint of the second finger of his left hand, has a Wart near the end of the right little finger, with [p 253] out any other apparent mark or scar on his face head or hands. Given under my hand as Clerk of Said Court this 3rd day of December 1858- L. Scruggs Clk **[Renewal, probably of No 452; This number belongs to NANCY KEELING.]**

State of Virginia to Wit- At a county Court held for the County of Pittsylvania on the 2nd day of December 1858- The Court doth order the clerk to register **MARIA REYNOLDS** a free negro born free in this county- Number 547- Pursuant to the above order the said MARIA REYNOLDS is this day numbered and registered in the Clerks office of the County Court of said County according to law She is a bright Mulatto Girl about twelve years of age- five feet three and three quarter inches high in heavy shoes- has a black mole just above the left corner of the right eyelash- another just below the right corner of the left eyelash- another on the right side of her face opposite the lower corner of the right ear- one in the right temple- a flesh mark or scar on the right side of her neck a black mole on the left side of her face just below the corner of her mouth another on her left Cheek another on the left side of her nose another just above the left corner of the left eyebrow and another on the left side of her neck- a scar on the back of her right hand near the wrist joint- a scar on the left hand between the second and third joints of the thumb a scar near the first joint of the thumb- a scar on the first joint of her forefinger & a mole on the back of the left hand- a small scar between the first and second joints of the second finger of said hand- without any other apparent mark or scar on her face head or hands. Given under my hand as Clerk of said Court this 23rd day of December 1858- L. Scruggs Clk

[p 254] State of Virginia to Wit- At a county Court held for the County of Pittsylvania on the 20th day of December 1858- The Court doth order the clerk to register **WILLIAM COLES** a free Negro born free in this county- Number 548- Pursuant to the above order the said WILLIAM COLES is this day numbered and registered in the Clerks office of the County Court of Said County according to law- He is a boy of dark complexion about sixteen years of age five feet two inches high in thin shoes- has a scar on the left wrist joint- without any other apparent mark or scar on his face head or hands. Given under my hand as Clerk of Said Court this 23rd day of December 1858- L. Scruggs Clk

State of Virginia to Wit- At a county Court held for the County of Pittsylvania on the 20th day of December 1858- The Court doth order the clerk to register **JULY ANN COLES** a free Negro born free in this county- Number 549- Pursuant to the above order the said JULY ANN COLES is this day numbered and registered in the Clerks office of the County Court of Said County according to law- She is a black Girl about fourteen years of age five feet two and one quarter inches high in thin shoes- a small scar on the right side of her face, a small scar on the left side of her face a scar on her right wrist and a black spot on her left wrist joint caused by a burn- without any other apparent mark or scar on her face head or hands. Given under my hand as Clerk of Said Court this 23rd day of December 1858- L. Scruggs Clk [p 255] State of Virginia to Wit- At a county Court held for the County of Pittsylvania on the 20th day of December 1858- The Court doth order the clerk to register **CALEB REYNOLDS** a free Negro born free in this county- Number 550- Pursuant to the above order the said CALEB REYNOLDS is this day numbered and registered in the Clerks office of the County Court of Said County according to law- He is a mulatto man about sixty four years of age- five feet five and three quarters inches high in heavy shoes- a black mole on the right side of his face- has a wart on the left side of his face just under the right corner of the right eye- a flesh mark on the back of the left hand- straight hair- is gray and Somewhat crippled in his feet- has no other apparent mark or scar on his face head or hands. Given under my hand as Clerk of Said Court this 23rd day of December 1858- L. Scruggs Clk

State of Virginia to Wit- At a county court held for the County of Pittsylvania on the 20th day of December 1858- The Court doth order the clerk to renew the register of **PLEASANT COLES** a free Negro born free in this county- Number 232- Pursuant to the above order the said PLEASANT COLES is this day again registered in the Clerks office of the County Court of Pittsylvania County according to law. He is of a dark complexion five feet eight and three quarter inches high in heavy shoes about forty nine years of age- has a scar on the nose between the eyes, the third finger of the right hand is stiff from the second joint to the end the same having been broken- without any other apparent mark or scar on his face head or hands. Given under my hand as Clerk of said Court this 23rd day of December 1858- L. Scruggs Clk **[Renewal]**

[p 256] State of Virginia to Wit- At a county court held for the County of Pittsylvania on the 20th day of December 1858- The Court doth order the clerk to renew the register of **ELIZA REYNOLDS** a free Negro born free in this county- Number 346- Pursuant to the above order the said ELIZA REYNOLDS is this day again registered in the Clerks office of the County Court of Pittsylvania County according to law. She is a bright Mulatto Woman Five feet two and one quarter inches high about forty one years of age- in thin shoes- has two moles under the left eye one on her left cheek bone and another on her chin one on the right side of her face near the lower corner of the left ear. Several pimples on

the left side of her face and a number of small moles on the left side of her neck and a small scar on the inside of the left wrist without any other apparent mark or scar on her face head or hands. Given under my hand as Clerk of Said Court this 23rd day of December 1858- L. Scruggs Clk **[Renewal]**

State of Virginia to Wit- At a county Court continued and held for the County of Pittsylvania on the 19th day of November 1858- The Court doth order the clerk to register **PARTHENIA GOINS** a free negro born free in this county- Number 551- Pursuant to the above order the said PARTHENIA GOINS is this day numbered and registered in the Clerks office of the County Court of Said County according to law- She is a bright mullatto [sic] girl about 16th [sic] years of age- five feet three and a half inches high in thin shoes- has a scar on the left corner of the left eyebrow a mole in the right corner of the left eyebrow a small mole on her forehead just in the edge of her hair a mole on the inside of the little [sic] of the right hand on the third joint a scar on the first joint of the thumb of the left hand a mole on the back of said hand near the first joint of the forefinger a mole on the inside of the middle finger of said hand on the second joint without any other apparent mark or scar on her face head or hands. Given under my hand as Clerk of the County [p 257] Court of said County this 9th day of January 1859- L. Scruggs Clk

State of Virginia to wit- At a county Court held for the County of Pittsylvania on the 17th day of January 1859- It is ordered that the clerk register **JOHN DAVIS** a free Negro born free in this county- Number 552- Pursuant to the above order the said JOHN DAVIS is this day numbered and registered in the Clerks office of the County Court of Said County according to law- He is a bright Mulatto Boy about twenty one years of age five feet five and one eighth inches high in heavy shoes- has a scar on the right cheek bone- a scar on the left side of his forehead near the edge of the hair- has a mole on the left side of his forehead just above the corner of the left eyebrow- a scar on the left cheek bone- a mole on the left side of his face near the last mentioned scar- & a scar on the inside of the ball of the little finger of the left hand- Without any other apparent mark or scar on his face head or hands. Given under my hand as Clerk of said court this 18th day of January 1859- L. Scruggs Clk

State of Virginia to wit- At a County Court held for the County of Pittsylvania on the 20th day of June 1859- The Court doth order the clerk to register **PERMELIA M GOIN** a free woman of color born free in this County- Number 553- Pursuant to the above order the said PERMELIA M GOIN is this day Numbered and Registered in the Clerks office of the County Court of said County according to Law- She is a bright mulatto woman [p 258] was 17 year [sic] old the 28th day of February 1859- Five feet three and a half inches high in thin shoes- has a small scar on her forehead- has a scar between the first and second joint of the forefinger of the left hand and one on the back of said hand just below the first joint of the forefinger- without any other apparent mark or scar on her face head or hands- Given under my hand as Clerk of said Court this 21st day of June 1859- L. Scruggs Clk

State of Virginia to wit- At a County Court continued and held for the County of Pittsylvania on the 21st day of June 1859- The Court doth order the Clerk to register **JOHN DODSON** a free negro born free in this County- Number 554- Pursuant to the above order the said JOHN DODSON is this day numbered and registered in the Clerks office of the County Court of said County according to Law- He is a black man- Twenty three years old. Five feet three and a quarter inches high in heavy shoes- has a small scar on his forehead just above the right eye- has another scar on the forehead just in the edge of the hair, has a long scar between the thumb and forefinger of the right hand- another scar just below the wrist joint running across the back of said hand, has a large scar on the back of the left hand, has a scar between the first and second joint of the middle finger of said hand, and has a mole on the second joint of the thumb of said hand- without any other apparent mark or scar on her [sic] face head or hands- Given under my hand as Clerk of said Court this 22nd day of June 1859- L. Scruggs Clk

[p 259] State of Virginia to wit- At a county court continued and held for the County of Pittsylvania on the 19th day of November 185[left blank] - The Court doth order the clerk to register **ELIZABETH GOING** a free Negro born free in this county- Number 555- Pursuant to the above order the said ELIZABETH GOING is this day numbered and registered in the Clerks office of the county court of Said County according to law- She is a bright

Mulatto Woman about forty three years old, five feet two & a half inches high in thin shoes- has a mole on the right side of her chin, has black strait [sic] hair, and very black eyes- without any [the word 'other' was written and stricken out] apparent mark or scar on her face head or hands- Given under my hand as Clerk of said Court this 20th day of November 1858- L. Scruggs Clk

State of Virginia to wit- At a county court held for the County of Pittsylvania on the 19th day of September 1859- The Court doth order the clerk to register **LUCINDA BOWMAN** a free Negro born free in this county- Number 556- Pursuant to the above order the said LUCINDA BOWMAN is this day numbered and registered in the Clerks office of the county court of said County according to law- She is of a dark brown colour nearly black- five feet two & three quarters inches high in thin shoes- has two small scars just above the right wrist joint- without any other apparent mark or scar on her face head or hands- Given under my hand as Clerk of said Court this 22nd day of September 1859- L. Scruggs Clk- Enclosed to Jno M Sutherlin Danville 22nd Septr 1859 [in margin].

[p 260] State of Virginia to Wit- At a county court continued and held for the County of Pittsylvania at the Courthouse thereof on the 21st day of June 1859- The Court doth order the clerk to Renew the Register of **MILLY ANN HAILEY** a free negro as appears from her Register made by the Clerk of Henry, the said MILLY ANN being now a resident of this County- Number 557- Pursuant to the above order the said MILLY ANN HAILEY is this day numbered and registered in the Clerks office of the County Court of said County according to law- She is of a dark brown colour, five feet and a half inches high in shoes twenty four years old- has a burn on the right cheek- a small scar on the right temple opposite the eye, without any other apparent mark or scar on her face head or hands. Given under my hand as Clerk of said Court this the [left blank] day of October 1859- L. Scruggs Clk

State of Virginia to wit- At a county court held for the County of Pittsylvania on the 17th day of October 1859- The Court doth order the clerk to register **DANIEL BARBER** a free Negro born free in this county- Number 558- Pursuant to the above order the said DANIEL BARBER is this day numbered and registered in the

Clerks office of the county court of said County according to law- He is a mulatto boy about twenty four years of age- five feet six and a half inches high in thin shoes- has straight black hair, a small scar on the left cheek & another small scar on the right wrist joint- without any other apparent mark or scar on his face head or hands- Given under my hand as Clerk of said Court this 17th day of October 1859- L. Scruggs Clk

[p 261] State of Virginia to wit- At a county court held for the County of Pittsylvania on the 21st day of November 1859- The Court doth order the clerk to register **LUCY WALLACE** a free Negro born free in Halifax county- Number 559- Pursuant to the above order the said LUCY WALLACE is this day numbered and registered in the Clerks office of the county court of said County according to law- She is a Mulatto Woman about forty five years of age five feet three inches high in thin shoes- has a small black mole under her chin & a scar on the underside of her wrist of the left hand without any other apparent mark or scar on her face head or hands- Given under my hand as Clerk of said Court this 30th day of November 1859- L. Scruggs Clk- Enclosed to Dr Jno H Estes Green Hills Campbell Cty Va Decr 5th 1859 **[Written in margin]**

State of Virginia to wit- At a county court held for the County of Pittsylvania on the 21st day of November 1859- The Court doth order the clerk to register **WILLIAM WALLACE** a free Negro born free in Halifax county- Number 560- Pursuant to the above order the said WILLIAM WALLACE is this day numbered and registered in the Clerks office of the county court of said County according to law- He is of a bright yellow complexion about twenty one years old five feet five and a quarter inches high in thin shoes- has a scar on the underlip and right corner of the mouth, a scar on the back of the right hand, a wart on the second joint of the third finger of said hand another on the second joint of the second finger, a scar on the back of the left hand near the wrist joint, a scar on the first joint of the forefinger, another on the second joint of said finger & a scar on the third joint of the third finger of said hand without any other apparent mark or scar on his face head or hands- Given under my hand as Clerk of said Court this 30th day of November 1859- L. Scruggs Clk- Do: **[In margin, regarding Register sent to Jno H Estes in Campbell county]** [p 262] State of Virginia to wit- At a county court held for the County of Pittsylvania on the 21st day of November 1859- The Court doth order the clerk to register **MARY WALLACE** a free Negro born free in Halifax county- Number 561- Pursuant to the above order the said MARY WALLACE is this day numbered and registered in the Clerks office of the county court of said County according to law- She is of a yellow complexion twenty years old four feet eleven inches high in shoes- has a scar on the wrist joint of the right hand has a scar between the forefinger and second finger of the left hand a scar on the third joint of the second finger of said hand, without any other apparent mark or scar on her face head or hands- Given under my hand as Clerk of said Court this 30th day of November 1859-   L. Scruggs Clk- Enclosed to Dr Jno H Estes Green Hills Campbell Cty Va Decr 5th /59 **[Written in margin]**

State of Virginia to wit- At a county court held for the County of Pittsylvania on the 21st day of November 1859- The Court doth order the clerk to register **ALEXANDER WALLACE** a free negro born free in this county- Number 562- Pursuant to the above order the said ALEXANDER WALLACE is this day numbered and registered in the Clerks office of the county court of said County according to law- He is a black boy 16 years of age three feet nine and a half inches high in thin shoes- has a scar on the back of his right hand- a scar between the first joints of the third & little finger of said hand, a scar about 1/2 of an inch in length on the back of the left hand, a scar on the inside of the wrist of the left hand, a scar on the thumb near the wrist joint- a scar on the inside of the first finger of the left hand, a scar between the first and second joints of said finger and a scar on the inside of the ball of the forefinger of said hand caused by a cut. Without any other apparent mark or scar on his face head or hands- Given under my hand as Clerk of said Court this 30th day of November 1859-   L. Scruggs Clk-   Do: **[In margin, regarding Register sent to Jno H Estes in Campbell county]**

[p 263] State of Virginia to wit- At a county court held for the County of Pittsylvania on the 21st day of November 1859- The Court doth order the clerk to register **JAMES DAVIS** a free negro born free in this county- Number 563- Pursuant to the above order the said JAMES DAVIS is this day numbered and registered in the

Clerks office of the county court of said County according to law- He is of a yellow complexion twenty two years old, five feet three and three quarters inches high in shoes- has a small wart on the second joint of the forefinger of the right hand, a small scar on the first joint of the thumb of said hand- a scar on the first joint of the thumb of the left hand. A wart on the first joint of the forefinger of said hand, two small warts just above the second joint of said finger- a scar on the wrist joint of said hand & two scars near the third joint of the third & fourth fingers without any other apparent mark or scar on his face head or hands- Given under my hand as Clerk of said Court this 30th day of November 1859- L. Scruggs Clk- Enclosed to [illegible] Dr Jno H Estes Green Hills Campbell County Va Decr 5th/59 **[Written in margin]**

State of Virginia to wit- At a county court continued & held for the County of Pittsylvania at the Courthouse thereof on Tuesday the 17th day of January 1860- The Court doth order the clerk to Register **BURTON GEE** a free negro born free in this county- Number 564- Pursuant to the above order the said BURTON GEE is this day registered in the Clerks office of the County Court of Pittsylvania County according to law- The said BURTON GEE is of a yellow complexion twenty years old five feet eight ['inches' crossed over] and a half inches high in shoes, has a fresh scar just above the corner of the left eye has two scars just below the second joint of the right thumb has a scar on the second joint of the left forefinger two small scars on the back of his left hand two small scars between the second & third joints of the third finger of said hand- without any other apparent mark or scar on his face head or hands- Given under my hand as Clerk of said Court this 15th day of February 1860- L. Scruggs Clk

[p 264] State of Virginia Pittsylvania County SC- At a county court held for the County of Pittsylvania at the Courthouse thereof on Monday the 20th day of February 1860- The Court doth order the clerk to Register **JAMES FRY** a free negro born free in this county- Number 565- Pursuant to the above order the said JAMES FRY is this day registered in the Clerks office of the County Court of Pittsylvania County according to law- The said JAMES FRY is a man of dark brown complexion twenty six years of age five feet four inches high in thin shoes, has a small scar over each eye & a small

one in the forehead, without any other apparent mark or scar on his face head or hands- Given under my hand as Clerk of said Court this 20th day of February 1860- L. Scruggs Clk

State of Virginia to wit- At a county court continued & held for the County of Pittsylvania at the Courthouse thereof on Tuesday the 19th day of March 1860- The Court doth order the clerk to Register **HENRY COLE** a free negro born free in this county- Number 566- Pursuant to the above order the said HENRY COLE is this day numbered and registered in the Clerks office of the County Court of Pittsylvania County according to law- The said HENRY COLE is a man of dark complexion five feet and a quarter of an inch high in shoes, twenty two years old the 1st day of January 1860 has a scar on the back of his left hand another on the upper part of the left temple a small scar and mole in his forehead, without any other apparent mark or scar on his face head or hands- Given under my hand as Clerk of said Court this 4th day of April 1860- L. Scruggs Clk

At a county court continued & held for the County of Pittsylvania on this 18th day of April 1859- The Court doth order the clerk to Register **MARIAH GOING** a free negro born free in this county- Number 567- Pursuant to the above order MARIAH GOING is this day numbered and registered in the Clerks office of the County Court of Pittsylvania County according to law- The said MARIAH GOING was twenty two years old the twenty eighth day of December last is a bright mulatto five feet one inch and a half high in thin shoes, has two small scars on her forehead, a small mol [sic] on her right cheek two small moles on her left cheek opposite her nose without any other apparent mark or scar on her face head or hands- Given under my hand 5th day of May 1860- L. Scruggs Clk

[p 265] State of Virginia to wit- At a County Court held for the County of Pittsylvania at the courthouse thereof on the 21st day of May 1860- The Court doth order the Clerk to renew the Register of **JOHN SOYARS** a free negro born free in this County. Number 376- JOHN SOYARS a free negro is this day again Registered in the Clerks office of the County Court of Pittsylvania County according to law. The said JOHN SOYARS is of a brown complexion, five feet six and a half inches high in shoes, thirty nine

years old the 25th day of March last. has a scar on the right side of the head, a scar on his nose, another near the joint of the wrist of the left arm on the outside. another on the back of the left hand. a small mole on the inside of the right hand. without any other apparent mark or scar on his face head or hands. Given under my hand this 21st day of May 1860- L. Scruggs Clk **[Renewal]**

State of Virginia to wit- At a County Court held for the County of Pittsylvania at the Courthouse thereof on the 21st day of May 1860- The Court doth order the Clerk to renew the Register of **MARY DAVIS** a free negro born free in this county. Number 369- MARY DAVIS a free negro is this day again registered in the Clerks office of the County Court of Pittsylvania County according to law. The said MARY DAVIS is a bright mulatto woman. thirty eight years old the 25th day of January 1860 five feet three inches high in thin shoes with heels. has a scar on the side of the right thumb near the end a small scar on the large joint of the left forefinger, and another on the left jaw. without any other [p 266] apparent mark or scar on her face head or hands. Given under my hand this 21st day of May 1860- L. Scruggs Clk **[Renewal]**

State of Virginia to Wit- At a County Court held for the County of Pittsylvania at the Court House thereof on the 21st day of May 1860- On the motion of **GREEN HAZLEWOOD** a free negro born free in the County of Lunenburg as appears by a copy of his Register the Court doth order the Clerk of this Court to renew the Register of the said HAZLEWOOD. Pursuant to the above order the said GREEN HAZLEWOOD is this day Numbered and Registered in the Clerks office of the County Court of Pittsylvania County according to law. Number 568. The said GREEN HAZLEWOOD is of a yellow complexion, five feet six and a quarter inches high in shoes, about fifty six years old, his left wrist a little disfigured by being out of place. without any apparent mark or scar on his face head or hands. Given under my hand this 21st day of May 1860- L. Scruggs Clk

State of Virginia to wit- At a County Court held for the County of Pittsylvania at the Courthouse thereof on the 15th day of July 1860- The Court doth order the clerk to register **WM ROE** a free negro born free in this county- Pursuant to the above order the

Said WM ROE is this day numbered and registered in the Clerks office of the County Court of Pittsylvania County according to law- Number 569- The Said WM ROE is of a dark complexion twenty three years old the 6th of April next five feet five and [p 267] a quarter inches high has a small scar near the inside corner of each eye brow, has three scars on his right hand one on the back the other two on & near the side just opposite the thumb, & a small scar on the back of his left hand near the wrist. without any other apparent mark or scar on his face head or hands- Given under my hand this 18th day of July 1860- L. Scruggs Clk

State of Virginia to wit- At a County Court held for the county of Pittsylvania at the Courthouse thereof on Monday the 20th day of August 1860- The Court doth order the clerk to register **JAMES ROE** a free negro born free in this county- Pursuant to the above order the said JAMES ROE is this day numbered and registered in the Clerks office of the county court of Pittsylvania County according to Law- Number 570. The said JAMES ROE is of a dark complexion, about twenty one years old, five feet six and a half inches high in shoes, has a scar in the brow over the left eye, another scar on the left side of his nose, and has two small scars on the back of his right hand, without any other apparent mark or scar on his face head or hands- Given under my hand as Clerk of said Court this 23rd day of August 1860- L. Scruggs Clk

State of Virginia to wit- At a County Court held for the County of Pittsylvania at the Courthouse thereof on monday the 20th day of August 1860- The Court doth order the Clerk to register **WILLIAM MITCHELL** a free negro born free in this county- Pursuant to the above order the said WILLIAM MITCHELL is this day numbered and registered in the Clerks [p 268] office of the County Court of Pittsylvania County according to Law. Number 571- The said WILLIAM MITCHELL is of a yellow complexion, about twenty two years old, five feet ten and a quarter inches high in shoes, has a scar on the back of his right hand just below the first joint of the little finger, another on the back of said hand, another on the first joint of the forefinger of said hand, has several small scars between the first and second joints of the middle finger of said hand, has a scar on the forefinger of the left hand on the the [sic] second joint, without any other apparent mark or scar on his face head or hands-

Given under my hand as Clerk of said Court this 23rd day of August 1860- L. Scruggs Clk

State of Virginia- At a County Court held for the County of Pittsylvania on Monday the 1st day of September 1860- **WILLIAM H REYNOLDS** a free negro born free in this county on his motion the court doth order the Clerk to register him according law [sic]. Pursuant to the above order the said WILLIAM HENRY REYNOLDS is this day numbered and registered in the Clerks office of said County Court according to Law. Number 572- The said REYNOLDS is of a very bright complexion, five feet nine and a quarter inches high in shoes, about 20 years old, has a scar on the second joint of the forefinger of the left hand has another on the middle finger of said hand between the first and second joints of said finger has another scar on the back of said hand- without any other apparent mark or scar on his face head or hands- Given under my hand as Clerk of said [p 269] Court this the 1st day of September 1860- L. Scruggs Clk

State of Virginia to Wit- At a County Court held for the County of Pittsylvania at the Courthouse thereof on Monday the 17th day of September 1860- **CHARLOTTE HOOD** a free negro born free in this county on her motion. the Court doth order the Clerk to register her according to Law. Number 572- Pursuant to the above order the said CHARLOTTE HOOD is this day numbered and registered in the Clerks office of said County Court according to Law. She is of a brown complexion, about 21 years old, five feet four inches high in thin shoes, has a scar on the right side of her neck just below the ear, another scar on the second joint of the thumb of the left hand without any other apparent mark or scar on her face head or hands- Given under my hand as Clerk of said Court this the 25th day of September 1860- L. Scruggs Clk **[Number 572 is a duplicate number; it was previously given to WILLIAM HENRY REYNOLDS just above.]**

State of Virginia to wit- At a Quarterly Court held for the County of Pittsylvania at the Courthouse thereof on Monday the 19th day of November 1860- The Court doth order the Clerk to renew the Register of **POLLY ROSS** a free negro born free in this county- Number 343- Pursuant to the above order the said POLLY ROSS is this day again registered in the Clerks office of Pittsylvania County Court according to law. The said POLLY ROSS is about forty one years old, of a brown complexion, five feet high in shoes, has a scar in the eyebrow over the left eye has three small scars on the back of the right hand. Another scar on the end of the little finger of the left hand, without any other apparent mark or scar on her face head or hands- Given under my hand as Clerk of said Court this the 28th day of November 1860- L. Scruggs Clk **[Renewal]**

[p 270] State of Virginia to wit- At a Quarterly Court held for the County of Pittsylvania at the Courthouse thereof on monday the 19th day of November 1860- The Court doth order the clerk to Register **MARY ANN ROSS** a free negro born free in this county- Number 573- Pursuant to the above order the said MARY ANN ROSS is this day Numbered and Registered in the clerks office of the County Court of Pittsylvania County according to law. The Said MARY ANN ROSS is about eighteen years old four feet eleven inches high in thin shoes is of tolerably bright complexion freckeled [sic] face has a mole on the left side of the face just below the eye has a Scar on the first joint of the forefinger of the right hand without any other apparent mark or scar on her face head or hands- Given under my hand as Clerk of the Said Court this 28th day of November 1860- L. Scruggs Clk

State of Virginia to wit- At a Quarterly Court held for the County of Pittsylvania at the Courthouse thereof on monday the 19th day of November 1860- The Court doth order the clerk to Register **AGNES TAYLOR ROSS** a free negro born free in this county- Number 574- Pursuant to the above order the Said AGNES TAYLOR ROSS is this day numbered and Registered in the clerks office of the County Court of Pittsylvania County according to law. The Said AGNES TAYLOR ROSS is about sixteen years old four feet eleven inches high in thin shoes of a bright complexion She is very lame in the right leg from Rheumatism & is without any other apparent mark or Scar on her face head or hands- Given under my hand as Clerk of the Said Court this 28th day of November 1860- L. Scruggs Clk

[p 271] State of Virginia to wit- At a [the word 'county' has been stricken] Quarterly Court held for the County of Pittsylvania at the

Courthouse thereof on Monday the 19th day of November 1860- The Court doth order the Clerk to Register **JAMES COOK** a free negro born free in the county of Spottsylvania in this State- Number 575- Pursuant to the above order the said JAMES COOK is this day numbered and registered in the Clerks office of Pittsylvania County Court according to Law. The said JAMES COOK is about thirty three years old of a brown complexion five feet nine and a half inches high in shoes, has a scar on the upper lip, another on the temple near the left eye, another scar on the second joint of the forefinger of the right hand, another on the third joint of the middle finger of said hand, another on the second joint of the forefinger of the left hand, has a stif [sic] joint on the middle finger of said hand, without any other apparent mark or scar on his face head or hands- Given under my hand as Clerk of said Court this 29th day of November 1860- L. Scruggs Clk

State of Virginia to Wit- At a County Court held for the County of Pittsylvania monday the 17th day of December 1860- The Court doth order the Clerk to renew the Register of **JOHN RICHARDSON** a free negro born free in Charlotte County Virginia- Number 262- JOHN RICHARDSON a free negro is this day again registered in the Clerks office of the County Court of Pittsylvania County according to Law. The said JOHN RICHARDSON is about fifty [the word 'four' has been stricken] five years old, five feet four and a half inches high, of a brown complexion, has a scar on the top of his head, another on his nose- without any other apparent mark or scar on his face head or hands- Given under my hand as Clerk of said Court this 21st day of December 1860- L. Scruggs Clk **[Renewal]**

[p 272] State of Virginia to Wit- At a County Court held for the County of Pittsylvania at the Courthouse thereof on the 21st day of January 1861- It is ordered that the Clerk register **LOUISA VAINWRIGHT** a free negro born free in this county. Number 576- Pursuant to the above order the said LOUISA VAINWRIGHT is this day numbered and registered in the Clerks office of the county court of said county according to Law- She is about 18 years old five feet three inches high in shoes, is of a bright yellow complexion, has a small scar on her forehead- has a mole near the right corner of her mouth, has a scar on the second joint of the thumb of the left

hand, has a fresh scar on the wrist of said hand, without any other apparent mark or scar on her face head or hands- Given under my hand as Clerk of said Court this 22nd day of January 1861- L. Scruggs Clk

State of Virginia to wit- At a County Court held for the county of Pittsylvania on the 17th day of June 1861- The court doth order the clerk to register **SAMUEL BURNETT** a free Negro born free in this county- Number 577- Pursuant to the above order the said SAMUEL BURNETT is this day Numbered and registered in the Clerks office of the county court of said county according to law- He is about twenty two years old five feet eight inches and three quarters high in thin shoes, of dark complexion, has a small scar on his forehead- the front finger of the left hand off at the second joint, a small scar near the first joint of the little finger of said hand, a small scar on the right thumb, another on the first joint of said thumb & another small scar on the 1st finger of the right hand, without any other apparent mark or scar on his face head or hands- Given under my hand as Clerk of said Court this 20th day of June 1861- L. Scruggs Clk

Virginia Pittsylvania County SCt- At a County Court held for the County of Pittsylvania on the 21st day of October 1861- It is ordered that the Clerk of this Court renew the register of **JAMES DAVIS** a free negro born free in this County- [Illegible] [p 273] to the above order the said JAMES DAVIS is this day again registered in the Clerks office of said County according to law. He is a mulatto man of rather a ginger cake colour thirty one years old the 30th day of August 1861 five feet eight inches and three quarters high in thin shoes has a slight scar on the right jaw has a scar on the side of the left-wrist-opposite the thumb a small scar on the left jaw and has lost the tooth on the left-of the two front ones, without any other apparent mark or scar on his face head or hands- Given under my hand this 22nd day of October 1861- L. Scruggs Clk **[Renewal]**

State of Virginia to Wit- At a County Court held for the County of Pittsylvania on the 18th day of November 1861- **DAVID SCOTT** a free negro born free in the county of Albermarle desiring to be Registered, it is ordered that the Clerk of this County register said negro according to law- Number 578- Pursuant to the above order the said DAVID SCOTT is this day numbered and registered in the Clerks office of the County Court of said County according to law- He is about fifty five years of age, five feet six inches and a half high, of dark complexion, has a scar over the left eye & one under the said eye, has another on the back of his neck & has had his right thumb sprained in the first joint; without any other apparent mark or scar on his face head or hands- Given under my hand as Clerk of said Court this 21st day of November 1861- L. Scruggs Clk

State of Virginia to wit- At a County Court held for the county of Pittsylvania on the 20th day of January 1862- It is ordered that the Clerk register **GEORGE STEPHENS** a free Negro born free in this county- Number 579- Pursuant to the above order the said GEORGE STEPHENS is this day Numbered and Registered in the Clerks office of the county court of said county according to law- He is about twenty two years old five feet one inch and three quarters high in shoes, of a yellow complexion, has a small scar near his right ear, another near the right eye, with an upper front tooth out, without any other apparent mark or scar on his face head or hands- Given under my hand as Clerk of said Court this 24th day of January 1862- L. Scruggs Clk

[p 274] State of Virginia SCt- At a County Court held for the county of Pittsylvania on the 17th day of March 1862- The court doth allow **NORMAN GOING** a free Negro born free in Patrick County to reside in this county & doth order the Clerk to Register the said negro- No. 580- Pursuant to the above order the said NORMAN GOING is this day Registered in the Clerks office of the county court of said county according to law- He is of dark complexion five feet nine inches high in shoes, has a small scar near the left eye, another over the right eye, another on the right wrist about four inches long, another on the arm near the left wrist & about twenty five years old, without any other apparent mark or scar on his face head or hands- Given under my hand this 26th day of March 1862- L. Scruggs Clk

State of Virginia Sct- At a County Court held for the County of Pittsylvania on the 18th day of August 1862- The court doth order the Clerk to register **MARTHA WALLS BIBY** a free Negro born free in this county- Number 581- Pursuant to the above order the said **MARTHA WALLS BIBY** is this day Registered in the Clerks office of the County Court of said County according to law- She is of yellow complexion five feet two inches high- Nineteen years old has a scar on the back of the right hand another nearly between the first joints of the first & second fingers another on the thumb of the left hand another on the first finger of said hand another on the left cheek & another on the top of the head without any other apparent mark or scar on her face head or hands- Given under my hand this 22nd day of August 1862- L. Scruggs Clk

State of Virginia Sct- At a County Court held for the county of Pittsylvania on the 18th day of August 1862- The court doth order the Clerk to register **POLLY THOMPSON** a free Negro born free in this county- Number 582- Pursuant to the above order the said POLLY THOMPSON is this day registered in the Clerks office of the county court of said county according to law- She is of yellow complexion five feet seven inches high twenty years old the 7th of June 1862 without any apparent mark or scar on her face head or [p 275] hands- Given under my hand as Clerk of said Court this 30th day of August 1862- L. Scruggs Clk

State of Virginia Sct- At a County Court held for the county of Pittsylvania on the 21st day of July 1862- The court doth order the Clerk to renew the Register of **MADOLA MARIAH STEPHENS** a free negro born free in this county- Number 462- Pursuant to the above order the said MADOLA MARIAH STEPHENS is this day again Registered in the Clerks office of the County Court of Pittsylvania County according to law- She is of dark complexion twenty four years old the 14th day of June last five feet three & a half inches high has a scar on the left cheek another on the left thumb another on the left fore finger without any other apparent mark or scar on her face head or hands- Given under my hand as Clerk of said Court this 2nd day of September 1862- L. Scruggs Clk
[Renewal]

State of Virginia Sct- At a County Court held for the county of Pittsylvania on the 21st day of July 1862- The court doth order the Clerk to renew the register of **CATHARINE STEPHENS** a free Negro born free in this county- Number 535- Pursuant to the above order the said CATHARINE STEPHENS is this day again Registered in the Clerks office of the County Court of Pittsylvania County according to law- She is of a brown complexion twenty one years old last December five feet seven and a quarter inches high has a scar on the back of her right hand another between the first joints of the second and third fingers of said hand another on said hand opposite the thumb without any other apparent mark or scar on her face head or hands- Given under my hand as Clerk of said Court this 2nd day of September 1862- L. Scruggs Clk **[Renewal]**

[Register Number 583 has been skipped.]

[p 276] State of Virginia Sct- At a County Court held for the county of Pittsylvania on the 20th day of October 1862- The court doth order the Clerk to Register **MARTHA DAVIS** a free Negro born free in this county- Number 584- Pursuant to the above order the said MARTHA DAVIS is this day registered in the Clerks office of the County Court of Pittsylvania county according to law- She is of yellow complexion five feet three & a half inches high twenty eight years old the 10th day of March last has a small mole on each side of her nose & one on her left cheek has a scar on the back of her right wrist without any apparent mark or scar on her face head or hands- Given under my hand as Clerk of said Court this 21st day of October 1862- L. Scruggs Clk

State of Virginia Sct- At a County Court held for the county of Pittsylvania on the 20th day of October 1862- The court doth order the Clerk to register **WILLIE SHACKLEFORD** a free Negro born free in this county- Number 585- Pursuant to the above order the said WILLIE SHACKLEFORD is this day registered in the Clerks office of the County Court of Pittsylvania according to law- She is of yellow complexion twenty four years old five feet three & a half inches high has a small scar on her right forefinger another between the thumb & finger of the left hand without any other apparent mark or scar on her face head or hands- Given under my hand as Clerk of said Court this 21st day of October 1862- L. Scruggs Clk

[p 277] State of Virginia Sct- At a County Court held for the county of Pittsylvania on the 20th day of October 1862- It appearing to the

Court that **MARTHA MAYHO** a free Negro born free in Halifax County was registered in the County court of said County & that her free papers have been destroyed it is ordered that the Clerk renew the Register of the said MARTHA MAYHO- Number 586- Pursuant to the above order the said MARTHA MAYHO is this day registered in the Clerks office of the County Court of Pittsylvania according to law- She is of dark complexion five feet high about forty years old has a small scar across the nose one on the left forefinger without any other apparent mark or scar on her face head or hands- Given under my hand as Clerk of said Court this 21st day of October 1862- L. Scruggs Clk

State of Virginia Sct- At a County Court held for the county of Pittsylvania on the 20th day of October 1862- It is ordered that the Clerk register **PARMELIA GOODE** a free Negro born free in Halifax County- Number 587- Pursuant to the above order the said PARMELIA GOODE is this day registered in the Clerks office of the County Court of Pittsylvania according to law- She is of dark complexion five feet two & a half inches high twenty three years old has a small scar over her right eye another on her right cheek & is near sighted Without any other apparent mark or scar on her face head or hands- Given under my hand as Clerk of said Court this 21st day of October 1862- L. Scruggs Clk

[p 278] State of Virginia Sct- At a County Court held for the county of Pittsylvania on the 20th day of October 1862- The court doth order the Clerk to Register **ELIZABETH BURNETT** a free Negro born free in this county- Number 583- Pursuant to the above order the said ELIZABETH BURNETT is this day registered in the Clerks office of the County Court of Pittsylvania according to law- She is of yellow complexion eighteen years old the 4th day of July last four feet nine inches high has a small scar under her left eye- two scars opposite the thumb of the left hand another scar on the right hand another on the third finger of the said hand another scar under her chin without any other apparent mark or scar on her face head or hands- Given under my hand as Clerk of said Court this 21st day of October 1862- L. Scruggs Clk **[This Register number has been added here, out of sequence.]**

State of Virginia Sct- At a County Court held for the county of Pittsylvania on the 20th day of October 1862- It is ordered that the Clerk Register **JAMES DAVIS** a free Negro born free in Halifax County- Number 588- Pursuant to the above order the said JAMES DAVIS is this day Registered in the Clerks office of Pittsylvania County Court according to law; he is of yellow complexion about twenty eight years old five feet eleven and a quarter inches high has several small scars above the left eye, has a scar on the back of the second finger of the left hand, another on the same hand not far from the first joint of the thumb, has a scar on the back of the right hand, another on the same hand near the 1st joint of the forefinger, another on the third finger of said hand- without any other apparent mark or scar on his face head or hands- Given under my hand as Clerk of said Court this 25th day of October 1862- L. Scruggs Clk

State of Virginia Sct- At a County Court held for the county of Pittsylvania on the 20th day of October 1862- The Court doth order the Clerk to Register **POLLY BURNETT** a free Negro born free in this County- Number 589- Pursuant to the above order the said POLLY BURNETT [p 279] is this day Registered in the Clerks office of Pittsylvania County Court according to law. She is of rather brown complexion about twenty five years old five feet two inches and a half high in shoes has two small scars on her forehead one in the first joint of the right thumb another on the left hand another on the little finger of said hand another on the left hand opposite the thumb without any other apparent mark or scar on her face head or hands- Given under my hand as Clerk of said Court this 6th day of December 1862- L. Scruggs Clk

State of Virginia Sct- At a County Court held for the county of Pittsylvania on the 21st day of July 186[left blank]- The Court doth order the Clerk to Register **ROBERT BOWMAN** a free Negro born free in this county- Number 590- Pursuant to the above order the said ROBERT BOWMAN is this day Registered in the Clerks office of Pittsylvania County Court according to law; He is of dark complexion twenty seven years old last March, has a small scar on the first joint of the third finger of the right hand, has a small scar mole [sic] near the left ear, has a scar [the word 'near' is stricken] on the left thumb and a large scar on his throat, without any other apparent mark or scar on his face head or hands- Given under my hand as Clerk of said Court this 13th day of January 1863- L. Scruggs Clk

State of Virginia Sct- At a County Court held for the county of Pittsylvania on the 19th day of January 1863- The Court doth order the Clerk to register **JANE CHATTIN** a free Negro born free in this County- Number 591- Pursuant to the above order the said JANE CHATTIN is this day Registered in the Clerks office of Pittsylvania County Court according to law- she is of yellow complexion about twenty three years old five feet, two & a half inches high has a joint felon on the second finger of the right hand- without any other apparent mark or scar on her face head or hands- Given under my hand as Clerk of said Court this 20th day of January 1863- L. Scruggs Clk

[p 280] State of Virginia Sct- At a County Court held for the county of Pittsylvania on the 19th day of January 1863- The Court doth order the Clerk to Register **PAULINA DAVIS** a free Negro born free in this County- Number 592- Pursuant to the above order the said PAULINA DAVIS is this day Registered in the Clerks office of the County Court of Pittsylvania County according to law- she is of yellow complexion about twenty two years old five feet seven inches high has a long mark on the left cheek has a scar on the back of the left hand another on the front finger of said hand without any other apparent mark or scar on her face head or hands- Given under my hand as Clerk of said Court this 20th day of January 1863- L. Scruggs Clk

State of Virginia Sct- At a County Court held for the county of Pittsylvania on the 19th day of January 1863- The Court doth order the Clerk to register **ELIZABETH DAVIS** a free Negro born free in this County- Number 593- Pursuant to the above order the said ELIZABETH DAVIS is this day Registered in the Clerks office of the County Court of Pittsylvania according to law- She is of brown complexion about twenty one years old five feet six inches high has a small scar on the left side of her neck- without any other apparent mark or scar on her face head or hands- Given under my hand as Clerk of said Court this 20th day of January 1863- L. Scruggs Clk [p 281] State of Virginia Sct- At a County Court held for the county of Pittsylvania on the 19th day of January 1863- The Court doth order the Clerk to Register **GEORGE W. BURNETT** a free Negro born free in this County- Number 594- Pursuant to the above order the said GEORGE W. BURNETT is this day Registered in the Clerks office of the County Court of Pittsylvania County according to law- He is of a ginger cake colour twenty one years old last October he is five feet & nine inches high in thick shoes has a scar on the back of his left hand has a small mole on his chin & a small scar on his forehead- without any other apparent mark or scar on his face head or hands- Given under my hand as Clerk of said Court this 20th day of January 1863- L. Scruggs Clk

State of Virginia Sct- At a County Court held for the county of Pittsylvania on the 19th day of January 1863- The Court doth order the Clerk to Register **DANIEL THOMPSON** a free Negro born free in this County- Number 595- Pursuant to the above order the said DANIEL THOMPSON is This day Numbered and Registered in the Clerks office of the County Court of said County according to law- He is of yellow complexion he was eighteen years old 19th of last March six feet two & one half inches high in thick shoes has a small scar on the back of his left hand another small scar on the second joint of the little finger of said hand has a small scar on his forehead without any other apparent mark or scar on his face head or hands- Given under my hand as Clerk of said Court this 31st day of January 1863- L. Scruggs Clk

[p 282] State of Virginia Sct- At a County Court held for the county of Pittsylvania on the 16th day of February 1863- The Court doth order the Clerk to Register **ADALINE DODSON** a free Negro born free in this County- Number 596- Pursuant to the above order the said ADALINE DODSON is this day Numbered and Registered in the Clerks office of the County Court of Pittsylvania County according to law- She is of a brown complexion twenty six years old Five feet three & a half inches high in thin shoes has a small scar immediately under her right eye, without any other apparent mark or scar on her face head or hands- Given under my hand as Clerk of said Court this 18th day of February 1863- L. Scruggs Clk

At a County Court held for the County of Pittsylvania on the 21st day of July 1862- The Court doth order the Clerk to renew the Register of **MARTHA JANE STEPHENS** a free Negro born free in this County- Number 384- Pursuant to the above order the said MARTHA JANE STEPHENS is this day Registered in the Clerks office of the Pittsylvania County Court- She is of a dark complexion thirty seven years old five feet four inches and a half high has a scar on the inside of the left wrist, a small scar on the left thumb has a scar on her under lip- without any other apparent mark or scar on her face head or hands- Given under my hand as Clerk of said Court this 7th day of April 1863- L. Scruggs Clk   **[Renewal]**

At a County Court held for the County of Pittsylvania on the 21st day of July 1862- The Court doth order the Clerk to renew the Register of **MARY ANN STEPHENS** a free Negro born free in this County- Number 385- Pursuant to the above order the said MARY ANN STEPHENS is this day Registered in Pittsylvania County Court Clerks Office; She is of a dark complexion five feet three inches high thirty seven years old has a small scar on the back of her right hand without any other apparent mark or scar on her face head or hands- Given under my hand this 7th day of April 1863- L. Scruggs Clk   **[Renewal]**

At a County Court held for the county of Pittsylvania on the 21st day of July 1862- The Court doth order the Clerk to register **SARAH VALENTINE** a free Negro born free in this County- Number 597- Pursuant to the above order the said SARAH VALENTINE is this day Registered in the Clerks office (according to law) of Pittsylvania County Court; She is of a dark complexion twenty five years old four feet ten inches high, has a small scar near the corner of the right eye, has a small scar on the forefinger of the left hand, another between the second & third fingers near the hand without any other apparent mark or scar on her face, head or hands- Given under my hand as Clerk of said Court this 7th day of April 1863- L. Scruggs

At a County Court held for the county of Pittsylvania on the 21st day of July 1862- The Court doth order the Clerk to Register **MARTHA JANE STEPHENS** a free Negro born free in this County- Number 598- Pursuant to the above order the said

MARTHA JANE STEPHENS is this day Registered in the Clerks office of the Pittsylvania County Court- She is of a dark complexion five feet three inches & a half high about fifteen years old; has a small scar over her right eye, has four small scars on the back of her right hand a small scar on the right thumb without any other apparent mark or scar on her face head or hands- Given under my hand as Clerk of said Court this 7th day of April 1863- L. Scruggs Clk

[p 283] At a County Court held for the county of Pittsylvania on the 21st day of July 1862- The Court doth order the Clerk to Register **PERMELIA STEPHENS** a free negro born free in this County- Number 599- Pursuant to the above order the said PERMELIA STEPHENS is this day Registered in the Clerks office of the Pittsylvania County Court- She is of a dark complexion twenty six years old five feet & three quarters of an inch high in shoes has a small scar near the left eye, another near the left corner of the nose, another on the little finger of the left hand, another on the third finger of the right hand, without any other apparent mark or scar on her face head or hands- Given under my hand as Clerk of said Court this 7th day of April 1863- L. Scruggs Clk

At a County Court held for the county of Pittsylvania on the 21 day [sic] of July 1862- The Court doth order the Clerk to Register **MARY ANN STEPHENS** a free negro born free in this County- Number 600- Pursuant to the above order the said MARY ANN STEPHENS is this day Registered in Pittsylvania County Court Clerks Office- She is of a brown complexion four feet seven inches & a half high, seventeen years old, has a small scar on her forehead, another near her chin, has a small scar on her right hand with three fingers on each hand crooked, without any other apparent mark or scar on her face, head or hands- Given under my hand as Clerk of said Court this 7th day of April 1863- L. Scruggs Clk

At a County Court held for the county of Pittsylvania on the 20th day of December [the word 'July' has been stricken] 1858- The Court doth order the Clerk to Register **JOHN REYNOLDS** a free negro born free in this County- Number 601- Pursuant to the above order the said JOHN REYNOLDS is this day Registered in the

Clerks office of the Pittsylvania County Court- He is of white complexion twenty four years old last March, five feet nine inches high in thin shoes, has a scar on his left forefinger, has straight hair rather Brown coloured, without any other apparent mark or scar on his face, head or hands- Given under my hand as Clerk of said Court this 7th day of April 1863- L. Scruggs Clk

State of Virginia- Pittsylvania County Court Sct- At a County Court held for the county of Pittsylvania on the 21st day of July 1862- The Court doth order the Clerk to Register **MARTHA DAVIS** a free Negro born free in this County- Number 602- Pursuant to the above order the said MARTHA DAVIS is this day Numbered and Registered in this Clerks office of the County Court of Pittsylvania County- She is of a brown complexion five feet three & a half inches high in thick shoes has a very small scar below the second joint of the thumb on her left hand 23 years old without any other apparent mark or scar on her face head or hands- Given under my hand as Clerk of said Court this 21st day of April 1863- L. Scruggs Clk

State of Virginia- Pittsylvania County Court Sct- At a County Court held for the county of Pittsylvania on the 21st day of July 1862- The Court doth order the Clerk to Register **SARAH ANN HENDRICK** a free Negro born free in this County- No. 603- Pursuant to the above order the said SARAH ANN HENDRICK is this day Numbered and Registered in the Clerks [p 284] office of the County Court of said County- She is of brown complexion Nineteen years old five feet one & a quarter inches high in thick shoes has two small scars on the forefinger of the left hand & a small scar on her little finger of said hand also two small scars on the back of said hand also a small scar on the first joint of the little finger of right hand & a small scar just above her left eye without any other apparent mark or scar on her face head or hands- Given under my hand as Clerk of said Court this 21st day of April 1863- L. Scruggs Clk

State of Virginia- Pittsylvania County Court Sct- At a County Court held for the county of Pittsylvania on the 21st day of April 1862- The Court doth order the Clerk to renew the Register of **JORDAN GREEN STEPHENS** a free Negro born free in this

County- No. 604- Pursuant to the above order the said JORDAN GREEN STEPHENS is this day again Numbered and Registered in the Clerks office of said County- He is about twenty seven years old of a brown complexion five feet eight & a half inches high has no apparent mark or scar at this time- Given under my hand as Clerk of said Court this 22nd day of April 1863- L. Scruggs Clk **[This Renewal should have been for Register No. 461.]**

State of Virginia- Pittsylvania County Court Sct- At a County Court held for the county of Pittsylvania on the 20th day of April 1863- The Court doth order the Clerk to renew the Register of **JAMES DAVIS** a free Negro born free in this County- Number 537- Pursuant to the above order the said JAMES DAVIS is this day again Numbered and Registered in the Clerks office of the County Court of said County according to law. He is a Mulatto Man five feet ten inches high about thirty- in heavy shoes- has a small scar over the right eye a scar on the second finger of his right hand between the first & second joints a scar on the third joint of the forefinger of said hand has two scars on the second finger of the left hand also a scar on the thumb of the left hand also two small scars on the middle finger of each hand- without any other apparent mark or scar on his face head or hands- Given under my hand as Clerk of said Court this 22nd day of April 1863- L. Scruggs Clk **[Renewal]**

[p 285] State of Virginia Sct- At a County Court held for the County of Pittsylvania on the 16th day of June 1863- The Court doth order the Clerk to Register **BOWLIN BURNETT** a free Negro born free in this County- No. 605 ["540" has been stricken] - Pursuant to the above order the said BOWLIN BURNETT is this day Numbered and Registered in the Clerks Office of the County Court of Pittsylvania County according to law- he is of a dark complexion five feet seven inches high- has a large scar on the back of his right hand, has a small scar on the second finger from the thumb of the left hand, has a scar just above the left eye- without any other apparent mark or scar on his face head or hands- Given under my hand as Clerk of said Court this 16th day of June 1863- L. Scruggs Clk **[Possibly a Renewal of No 282.]**

State of Virginia- Pittsylvania County Court- Sct- It appearing to the Court that the free papers of **HENRY COLE** have been destroyed-it is ordered that the Clerk renew the Register of said COLE- Number 566- Pursuant to said order the said HENRY COLE is this day Numbered and Registered in the Clerks office of said Court according to law- He is a man of dark complexion- twenty four years old, five feet six inches high- has a scar on the back of his left hand another on his fore head near the left temple- without any other apparent mark or scar on his face head or hands- Given under my hand as Clerk of said Court this 17th day of August 1863- L. Scruggs Clk **[Renewal]**

State of Virginia- Pittsylvania County Court- Sct- At a County Court held for the County of Pittsylvania on the 17th day of August 1863- The Court doth order the Clerk to Register **WM R. STEPHENS** a free Negro born free in this County. Number 606- Pursuant to the above order of Court the said Wm R. STEPHENS is this day Numbered and Registered in the Clerks office of Pittsylvania County Court according to law- he is a man twenty three years of age of a dark brown complexion [illegible] [p 286] scar on the back of his left hand, has a small scar between the two eyes- without any other apparent mark or scar on his face head or hands- Given under my hand as Clerk of said Court this 19th day of August 1863- L. Scruggs Clk

State of Virginia- Pittsylvania County Court- Sct- At a County Court held for the County of Pittsylvania on the 17th day of August 1863- The Court doth order the Clerk to Register **MARY GOING** a free Negro born free in this County- Number 607- Pursuant to the above order of Court the said MARY GOING is this day Numbered and Registered in the Clerks office of said Court according to law- She is a woman twenty one years of age of a yellow complexion she is five feet nine inches high has a scar on the top of her head- without any other apparent mark or scar on her face head or hands- Given under my hand as Clerk of said Court this 22nd day of August 1863- L. Scruggs Clk

State of Virginia Pittsylvania County Court Sct- At a County Court held for the County of Pittsylvania on the 17th day of August 1863- The Court doth order the Clerk to Register **LAVINA KEELING** a free Negro born free in this County- Number 608- Pursuant to the above order of Court- the said LAVINA KEELING is this day Numbered and Registered in the Clerks office of said Court according to law- She is a woman twenty five years of age five feet five & one half inches high has a mole on the left side of her left eye (She is of yellow complexion)- without any other apparent mark or scar on her face head or hands- Given under my hand as Clerk of said Court this 2nd day of September 1863- L. Scruggs Clk

[p 287] State of Virginia- Pittsylvania County Court- December Term 1863- The Court doth order the Clerk to Register **MARY COUSINS** a free Negro born free in Halifax County- Number 609- Pursuant to the above order the said MARY COUSINS is this day Numbered and Registered in the Clerks office of said Court according to law- She is a woman of brown complexion forty two years of age five feet & a half inch high in heavy shoes has a small scar near the end of the fore finger of the right hand has two large scars below the wrist of the same hand also a small scar over the right eye without any other apparent mark or scar on her face head or hands- Given under my hand as Clerk of said Court this 22nd day of December 1863- L. Scruggs Clk

State of Virginia- Pittsylvania County Court- Sct- At a County Court held for the County of Pittsylvania on the 18th day of January 1864- The Court doth order the Clerk to Register **WALKER GEE** a free Negro born free in this County- Number 610- Pursuant to the above order of Court the said WALKER GEE is this day Numbered and Registered in the Clerks office of said Court according to law- He is a man of dark brown complexion seventeen years old five feet nine inches & a quarter high in heavy shoes- has a small scar over the right eye three small scars near the first joint of the thumb & first finger of the left hand has a small scar on the second joint of the forefinger of the right hand- without any other apparent mark or scar on his face head or hands- Given under my hand as Clerk of said Court this 22nd day of January 1864- L. Scruggs Clk

[p 288] Virginia- to Wit- At a county Court held for the County of Pittsylvania on the 15th day of February 1864- The Court doth order the Clerk to renew the Register of **WM NORRIS** a free

Negro born free in this County- Number 517- Pursuant to the above order the said WM NORRIS is this day again Numbered and Registered in the Clerks office of Pittsylvania County Court according to law- he is a man of yellow complexion five feet nine and a quarter inches high, twenty nine years old has a scar just above the left eyebrow has two large scars on his right arm caused by a burn- without any other apparent mark or scar on his face head or hands- Given under my hand as Clerk of the said Court this 16th day of February 1864- L. Scruggs Clk [Renewal]

State of Virginia- to Wit- At a county Court held for the County of Pittsylvania on the 15th day of February 1864- The Court doth order the Clerk to renew the Register of **PARTHENIA GOINGS** a free Negro born free in this County- Number 551- Pursuant to the above order the said PARTHENIA GOINGS is this day again Numbered and Registered in the Clerks office of said County according to law- she is a bright mulatto girl about 22 years of age five feet four inches high has a scar on the left corner of the left eyebrow a mole in the right corner of the left eyebrow a small mole on her forehead just in the edge of her hair a mole in the inside of the little finger of the right hand on the third joint [an illegible line which has been stricken out] a mole on the back of each hand near the first joint of the forefinger a mole on the inside of the middle finger of said hand on the second joint- without any other apparent mark or scar on her face head or hands- Given under my hand as Clerk of the said Court this 16th day of February 1864- L. Scruggs Clk **[Renewal]**

At a county Court held for the County of Pittsylvania on the 1st day of March 1864- ['Number 552' has been stricken out.] The Court doth order the Clerk to Register **FREEMAN VALENTINE** a free Negro born free in this County- Number 552- Pursuant to the above order the said FREEMAN VALENTINE is this day Numbered and Registered in the Clerks office of the County Court of said county- he is a man twenty one years old five feet nine inches high he is of a dark brown complexion has a small scar on the back of his right hand another scar near the first joint of the third finger from the thumb of said hand has four small scars on the back of the left hand, his left arm and hand is deformed, he is unable to straiten [sic] the fingers of the left hand one tooth out in front without any other apparent mark or scar on his face head or hands- Given under my hand as Clerk of the said Court the 25 day of March 1864- L. Scruggs Clk [This Number already belongs to JOHN DAVIS.]

Virginia- to Wit- At a county Court held for the County of Pittsylvania on the 18th day of April 1864- The Court doth order the Clerk to Register **SARAH DAVIS** a free Negro born free in this County- Number 553- Pursuant to the above order the said SARAH DAVIS is this day Numbered and Registered in the Clerks office of said Court according to law- She is five feet four & one half inches high, Brown complexion thirty years old has a scar on her forehead a small scar on the inside of her of the first finger of the left hand- without any other apparent mark or scar on her hands- Given under my hand as Clerk of the said Court this 18th day of April 1864- L. Scruggs Clk [This Number already belongs to PERMELIA M. GOIN.]

Virginia- to Wit- At a County Court held for the County of Pittsylvania on the 18th day of April 1864- It is ordered that the Clerk Register **MARY DAVIS** [The name 'Mary' is written over the name 'Martha'.] a free Negro born free in this [p 289] County- Number 554- Pursuant to the above order of Court the said MARY DAVIS is this day Numbered and Registered in the Clerks office of said Court according to law- She is nineteen years old five feet one and a half inches high- she is of a brown complexion has a small mole & a small scar under the right eye has a small scar on the inside of the fore finger of the right hand- without any other apparent mark or scar on her face head or hands- Given under my hand as Clerk of the said Court this 18th day of April 1864- L. Scruggs Clk [This Number already belongs to JOHN DODSON.]

Virginia- to Wit- At a County Court held for the County of Pittsylvania on the 18th day of April 1864- It is ordered that the Clerk of this Court Register **POLLY GARNES** a free Negro born free in this County- Number 555- Pursuant to the above order of Court the said POLLY GARNES is this day Numbered and Registered in the Clerks office of said Court according to law- She is a woman twenty seven years of age- of dark complexion five feet four inches high- has a small scar on the back of her neck also a small scar on the back of her left hand near the thumb- without any other apparent mark or scar on her face head or hands- Given under my hand as Clerk of the said Court this 19th day of April 1864- L. Scruggs Clk   **[This Number already belongs to ELIZABETH GOING.]**

Virginia- to Wit- At a County Court held for the County of Pittsylvania on the 18th day of April 1864- It is ordered that the Clerk Register **AMY VALENTINE** a free Negro born free in this County- Number 556- Pursuant to the above order of Court the said AMY VALENTINE is this day Numbered and Registered in the Clerks office of said Court according to law- [p 290] She is a girl twenty two years old- of a yellow complexion- five feet one and a half inches high- has a small scar on her forehead has a scar on the right cheek near the ear has a small scar on the 2nd joint of the third finger of the left hand- also another small scar on the back of her right hand. Without any other apparent mark or scar on her face head or hands- Given under my hand as Clerk of the said Court this 19th day of April 1864- L. Scruggs Clk   **[This Number already belongs to LUCINDA BOWMAN.]**

Virginia- to Wit- At a County Court held for the County of Pittsylvania on the 18th day of April 1864- It is ordered that the Clerk of this Court register **WILLIAM GOING** a free negro born free in this County- Number 557- Pursuant to the above order of Court the said WILLIAM GOING is this day numbered and Registered in the Clerks office of the County Court of Pittsylvania County according to law- He is about twenty years old of black complexion five feet eight inches high- has a small scar near the outer corner of the left eye another on the left cheek, another on the left hand near the wrist and one on each of the 2nd and 3rd fingers of said hand without any other apparent mark or scar on his face head or hands- Given under my hand this 2nd day of May 1864- L. Scruggs Clk   **[This Number already belongs to MILLY ANN HAILEY.]**

State of Virginia- to Wit- At a County Court held for the County of Pittsylvania on the 20th day of April 1863- The Court doth order the Clerk to Register **WILLIE STEPHENS** a free Negro born free in this County- Number 558- Pursuant to the above order of Court the said WILLIE STEPHENS is this day Numbered and Registered in the Clerks office of said Court according to law- She is a woman twenty one years old four feet ten & a half inches high of a dark brown complexion- has a scar immediately over the left eye- without any other apparent mark or scar on her face head or hands-Given under my hand as Clerk of the said Court this 13th day of May 1864- L. Scruggs Clk [**This Number already belongs to DANIEL BARBER.**]

[p 291] State of Virginia- to Wit- At a County Court held for the County of Pittsylvania on the 16th day of May 1864- It is ordered that the Clerk Register **CHARLOTTE DAVIS** a free Negro born free in this County- Number 559- Pursuant to the above order of Court the said CHARLOTTE DAVIS is this day Numbered and Registered in the Clerks office of Pittsylvania County Court according to law- She is a girl about nineteen years old, five feet four inches high, of a brown complexion- has no apparent mark or scar on her face head or hands- Given under my hand as Clerk of said Court this 17th day of May 1864- L. Scruggs Clk [**This number already belongs to LUCY WALLACE.**]

Virginia- to Wit- At a County Court held for the County of Pittsylvania on the 16th day of May 1864- It is ordered that the Clerk Register **SARAH BOWMAN** a free negro born free in this County- Number 560- Pursuant to the above order of Court the said SARAH BOWMAN is this day Numbered and Registered in the Clerks office of Pittsylvania County Court according to law- She is a girl seventeen years of age five feet three and a quarter inches high of brown complexion- has no apparent mark or scar on her face head or hands- Given under my hand as Clerk of said Court this 17th day of May 1864- L. Scruggs Clk [**This number already belongs to WILLIAM WALLACE.**]

Virginia- to Wit- At a County Court held for the County of Pittsylvania on the 16th day of May 1864- It is ordered that the Clerk Renew the Register of **LUCINDA BOWMAN** a free negro born free in this County- Number 56[left blank]- Pursuant to the above order of Court the said LUCINDA BOWMAN is this day again Numbered and Registered in the Clerks office of said Court according to law- She is a woman twenty four years of age five feet three and a quarter inches high- of a dark brown complexion- has a scar on the left side of her [p 292] face near the nose also another scar on the same side of her face- without any other apparent mark or scar on her face head or hands- Given under my hand as Clk of said Court this 17th day of May 1864- L. Scruggs Clk. **[Renewal; however, her correct number is 556.]**

Virginia- to Wit- At a County Court held for the County of Pittsylvania on the 16th day of May 1864- It is ordered that the Clerk Register **PRISSIE BOWMAN** a free Negro born free in this County- Number 561- Pursuant to the above order of Court the said PRISSIE BOWMAN is this day Numbered and Registered in the Clerks office of said Court according to law- She is a girl fifteen years old four feet eleven & half inches high of a dark brown complexion- has no apparent mark or scar on her face head or hands- Given under my hand as Clerk of said Court this 17th day of May 1864- L. Scruggs Clk **[This number already belongs to MARY WALLACE.]**

Virginia- to Wit- At a County Court held for the County of Pittsylvania on the 21st day of December 1863- the court doth order the Clerk to renew the Register of **SAMUEL HENDRICK** a free Negro born free in this County. Number 37- Pursuant to the above order of Court the said SAMUEL HENDRICK is this day again Numbered and Registered in the Clerks office of Pittsylvania County Court according to law- he is a man of dark complexion about sixty two years of age five feet six and a half inches high- has a scar on the end of the thumb of the left hand- without any other apparent mark or scar on his face head or hands- Given under my hand as Clk of said Court this 10th day of October 1864- L. Scruggs Clk. **[Renewal.]**

[p 293] Virginia- to Wit- At a County Court held for the County of Pittsylvania on the 21st day of March 1864- the Court doth order the Clerk to Register **TRUMAN VALENTINE** a free Negro born free in this County- Number 562- Pursuant to the above order of Court the said TRUMAN VALENTINE is this day Numbered in the Clerks office of Pittsylvania County- He is a man twenty three years of age, of a dark brown complexion five feet seven inches

high- has a scar under the chin two small scars on the back of his right hand, without any other apparent mark or scar on his face head or hands- Given under my hand as Clk of the County Court of said County this 30th day of December 1864- L. Scruggs Clk. **[This number already belongs to ALEXANDER WALLACE.]**

Virginia- to Wit- At a County Court held for the County of Pittsylvania on the 16th day of January 1865. It is ordered that the Clerk of this Court Register **PRESTON GEE** a free Negro born free in this County. Number 563- Pursuant to the above order of Court the said PRESTON GEE is this day Numbered and Registered in the Clerks office of said Court according to law. He is twenty one years of age. Six feet one half inch high. He is of a yellow complexion. has two very small scars on the back of his right hand, without any other apparent mark or scar on his face head or hands- Given under my hand as Clk of said Court this 17th day of January 1865- L. Scruggs Clk. **[This number already belongs to JAMES DAVIS.]**

PERSONS FREED BY WILL AND DEED

The following are transcriptions of the Wills and Deeds by which former slaves found in the Register were emancipated.

It should be noted that many of the former slaves did not use the same surnames as the owners who freed them, and that a number of them were in fact already using different surnames than their masters prior to being freed. Others took surnames that were different after emancipation.

In several of these documents, additional slaves are named as being freed who did not register in Pittsylvania County, at least not under the expected name. There is a possibility that these may be relatives of the slaves who did register there, and for that reason are deserving of further study.

African-American researchers must use extra care in the study of the settlement and immigration patterns of former slaves during certain time periods. Changes in Virginia laws occurred which determined whether former slaves would or would not be allowed to remain in the State after their emancipation. Several slaveholders mentioned in this volume purchased land in other areas and arranged for their freed slaves to be re-settled. Data relative to their transportation may be found in the Accounts Current portion of the owners' probate papers as 'monies spent'.

For those freedmen whose former owners (or their estates) could not afford the expense of removal, arrangements were often made for the hiring of the slaves for a period of years to earn the money needed for their transportation and re-settling.

An asterisk beside the name of a slave in the following transcriptions indicates that he or she was later registered in Pittsylvania County.

FREED BY WILL:

I.   **John Mason**, **Greensville County**   In the Name of God Amen. I John Mason of Greensville County being of sound mind do ordain my last Will and Testament making void all other Wills heretofore made.

I leave my wife Mary Mason the parcel of Land held by Peter Wyche by purchase from William Harrison, but in case her pregnancy should prove abort_ or the child should not arrive to lawful age then I give and bequeath the abovementioned Land to my said Wife to her and her heirs forever. I give and bequeath to my expected Child all the Land I had of Edward Smith with the Land Peter Wyche had of William Walker (Waller?) and I had of Peter Wyche to the said Child and its heirs and assigns forever. I give and bequeath to my wife all my personal Estate of whatsoever kind after paying all my just Debts. I likewise give unto my said Wife all the rents arising from the abovementioned Land for to assist her in raising and Educating of my expected Child.

I give the land which I exchanged with my brother Edmund Mason to **ARTHUR**, **BOLING**, little **JAMES** and **JOHN** their heirs forever When ARTHUR is of age as I have directed in the Deed of emancipation and the rent untill [sic] then to be given to my said Wife to assist her in the raising and educating of my expected Child. I give and bequeath unto little **NANNY** and all the other slaves now claimed by me in whole or in part all that liberty and freedom which I might on the footing of Law lay claim to, with their offsprings forever.

It is my Will and desire that my abovementioned Lands should not be cleared nor cut to make any waste more than is necessary for the support of the same. It is my Will and desire that if my expected Child should arrive to a lawful age that it shall have the Land lent to my wife at her Death to that and its heirs and assigns forever.

I further desire that **NEGROE ANTHONY** should live where he has lately built him a House, uninterrupted, allowing him firewood, ground for a garden, cotton patch and potatoes rent free during life provided he behaves well and I believe he will. and likewise that **ANNE JEFFERSON** should enjoy the same privilege where she now lives if she chooses it upon the same terms.

It is my Will and desire that my uncle William Harrison my friends Ingram Blanks and Robert Rivers together with my Brother in Law Irwin Maclin when of age should act as my Executors and my Wife Executrix to this my last Will and testament. I desire to be buried in a plain manner without any spirits at all, by that person my Wife shall make choice of, I ordain this to be my last Will and Testament as Witness I have hereunto set my hand and seal this ninth day of April one thousand seven hundred and ninety three -- Signed, Seald & Acknowledged in the presence of Hubbard Hobbs, Frederick Hobbs, Nathaniel Mabry-   John Mason (Seal)

At Greensville August Court 1793, This Will was proved according to law by the Oath of Frederick Hobbs and the affirmation of Nathaniel Mabry witnesses thereto and ordered to be recorded, and on the Motion of Mary Mason the Executrix therein named who made oath thereto and together with William Harrison and Ingram Blanks her securities entered into and acknowledged their Bond in the penalty of two thousand Pounds conditioned as the Law directs. Certificate is granted her for obtaining a Probate thereof in due form. Liberty is reserved for the other Executors to join in the said Probate when they may think fit. Teste   P. Pelham CSC

(LDS Film #31,692) Will Book I, Page 229 -- Written 9 April 1793 Proved August Court 1793

[The Deed of Emancipation cited above has not yet been located.]

The Inventory and Appraisement of the Estate of John Mason dated November 5, 1793, was recorded in Greensville County Court April 1794. Found in Will Book I, Page 253, signed by Matthew Davis, Frederick Hobbs and Carril Gregg, it includes the following valuation of slaves:

ARTHUR L30	**BOLING** L40	**JOHN** L30
JAMES L30	**CHARLES** L20	* **MARY** L20

Registrations for ARTHUR and JOHN were seen in Wynne's Register of Free Negroes and also of Dower Slaves 1803-1850 for Brunswick county Virginia, on pages 62 and 90.

[Register No. 177 - ARTHUR a free man of black complexion - 5'9" high - scar on left side of face - Emancipated by John Mason of Greensville county- Dated, compared and found correct 25 August 1823.

Register No. 257 - JOHN a free man of dark complexion - 5'5" high - 43 yrs old - scars on right hand and one on right temple from cut of a machine, also scar on the lip - Emancipated by John Mason; from evidence of Phil Claiborne - ditcher - Dated and compared 29 May 1827.]

II. **William Ansley, Loudoun County** In the name of God Amen. I William Ansley of the County of Loudoun in the state of Virginey being weak of body but of sound Mind & Memory & calling to mind that it is appropriate for all men once to die do make & ordain this my Last will and Testament in manner and form following to wit.

I give and Recommend my soul into the Hands of Almighty God that gave it me and my body to the Earth to be buryed at the discretion of my Executors hereafter mentioned and named and as touching such worldly Goods as it hath pleased God to bless me with I give and bequeath in manner and form following Viz. Item. I give my negroes **DANIEL** and **JOSEPH** the negroe men both free at the end of Expiration of three years from the fifteenth Day of August which will be in the year of our Lord one thousand Eight hundred and one. **SARAH** likewise to be free at the same time as the fore mentioned and a negroe *****LEW** to be free at the age of twenty five negroe **MATILDA** to be free at the age of twenty one and **MIRIAH** to be free at the age of twenty one **JANE** to be free at the age of twenty one. Item. I give and bequeath to my Loving wife Ann Ansley all my Lands that I now have in possession and all the stock and all the house hold furniture & a bond against Christifur Grenup [?] of ninety Pound to her and to her heirs forever to dispose of as she may see proper she paying first my funeral charges and also my just Debts that shall be Lawfully Demanded and lastly I do hereby Constitute & appoint my Loving wife Ann Ansley Executor to this my Last will and Testament Ratifying and confirming this and this only [illegible] Disannulling all other and former wills heretofore by me made In Witness whereof I have herunto set my hand and affixed my seal this 14th day of June in the year of our Lord one thousand seven hundred and ninety Eight. Signed, sealed and pronounced in presents of us William Rhodes, John Milner (Seal), George Rhodes, Joseph Ashton   Ansleys mark   Wm Ans

    In a Court held for Loudoun County Sept the 11th 1798. This will was proved by the oath of William Rhodes & George Rhodes two of the Subscribing Witnesses thereto & ordered to be recorded and on the Motion of Ann Ansley the Executrix Herein named who made oath according to Law together with Robert Hereford & Francis Hereford her Securities entered into & acknowledged their bond in the penalty of two thousand Dollars with Condition as the law directs Certificate is granted her for obtaining a probate thereof in due form.

(LDS Film # 0032276)   Will Book F, Page 49 -- Written 14 June 1798 -- Proved 11 September 1798

[The surname Ansley in some documents was spelled as Insle.]

    III.   **Benjamin Webber, Cumberland County**   In the name of God Amen. I Benjamin Webber of Cumberland County, being very sick but in sound mind & memory do make & ordain this my last will & testament in manner as follows to wit:
    My desire is that my property (slaves excepted) shall be applyed in discharge of my debts, if this property is not sufficient to discharge my debts I desire my executors to treat with my Creditors or other persons for money to pay the balance of my debts on such moderate terms in the hire of negroes that may hinder the sale of any of them, I desire that after my debts is paid my negroes to be emancipated, if lawfull, if not I will three of my brothers (named) Richd Webber, Seth Webber & Simeon Webber to share equally in my estate. As my brother Phillip is infirm & in low

circumstances I will him fifty per cent more than one of my brothers, and as my sister Ann Ligon is in a state of more affluence, I will her one half as much as either of my first named brothers. I request that Mr. Thompson (a Methodist of Amelia) will preach my funeral & that generous compensations offerred in return, and lastly I appoint Messrs Andrew Nelson, John Dodson Sr & Edmund Eggleston, all of Cumberland County, Executors of this my last will & testament, and do hereby disannull & make void all other wills by me heretofore made. In witness whereof I have hereunto set my hand & seal this [left blank] one thousand eight hundred. [No signature, no witnesses and no date of writing.]

At a Court held for Cumberland County the 24th day of March 1800 -this writing purporting the last Will and Testament of Benjamin Webber decd was exhibited in Court by John Dodson and Andrew Nelson two of the executors therein named and proved by Seth Webber, Allen Chambers, Peter Kerrigan and Andrew Nelson to be the handwriting of the said Benjamin Webber decd and the same is ordered to be recorded - and on the motion of the said John Dodson & Andrew Nelson who made oath according to law certificate was granted them for obtaining probate thereof in due form they having entered into bond with security according to Law. Teste Jack Woodson

(LDS Film #0030739)- Will Book 3, page 145- Proved 24 March 1800

The Inventory and Appraisement of the Estate of Benjamin Webber, was Returned into Cumberland County Court on April 21, 1800, and ordered to be recorded. It is found in Will Book 3, Page 151, signed by Wm Walker, Warren Walker, and Allen Chambers, and includes the following valuation of slaves grouped as follows:

CHARLES L80	**JANE** L90	**AGGEY** L80	**POLLEY** L50
GEORGE L51.12.4	**CHARLES** L75	**BETTY** L60	**BILLY** L60
MOSES L55	**JOHN** L25	**PHEBE** L30	**SALLY** L25
* **SAM** L20	**PHILL** L20		

[**SAM** later used the name **SAMUEL SHORT** when he registered in Pittsylvania County.]

IV.   **Robert Morgan, Charlotte County**   I Robert Morgan of the County of Charlotte and State of Virginia, being of sound mind and disposing memory do make this my last will and testament in manner and form following (to wit):

    1st   I will and desire that all my Just debts be paid to my Creditors hereinafter named.

    2nd   It is my will and desire that the slaves which I own should enjoy their freedom after my decease and accordingly I do hereby emancipate and set free my following slaves (to wit) **BEN, LUCY, WILLIAM** and ***DICK** [added above the line] (and their future increase) to enjoy their freedom forever. But I cannot make any provisions for them to enable them to comply with the laws of the State in relation to emancipated slaves - by money arising from their hire. I do hereby will and desire that they all be hired out by my executors...for the term of three years after my decease and the money arising from such hire after paying all necessary expenses to be equally divided among them all share and share alike.

    3rd   After paying all my Just debts and expenses I give to my sister Mary Morgan of the County of Nottoway all the balance of money that shall remain and debts that may be due me, together with my riding horse and all other property of every kind not herebefore disposed of all of which I give to her and her heirs forever.

    4th   I hereby nominate and appoint my friends John H. Marshall and John H. Thomas executors of this my last will and Testament, hereby revoking all other wills and Testaments by me heretofore made.

    In witness whereof I have hereunto set may hand and affixed my seal this 7th day of February, one thousand eight hundred and twenty eight (1828). Signed Sealed and Acknowledged in Presence of us   Elijah W. Roach, John Armistead, Daniel W. Williamson, W.A. Fuqua   Robert Morgan   (Seal)

    At a Court held for Charlotte County the 5th day of May 1828 This last Will and Testament of Robert Morgan decd was presented in Court and the same was proved by the oaths of Daniel W. Williamson and William A. Fuqua subscribing witnesses thereto and ordered to be Recorded. And on the Motion of John H. Thomas one of the Executors therein named who made an oath according to law probate thereof is granted him in due form on entering into bond with security: Whenceforth he with Elijah W. Roach and John Thomas has secured and entered into and acknowledged bond according to Law for that purpose.   Teste- Winston Robinson Cl

(LDS Film # 30,778) Will Book 6, page 133 -- Written 7 February 1828, Proved 5 May 1828

The Inventory and Appraisement of the Estate of Robert Morgan, dated May 24, 1828, was returned into Charlotte County Court on October 6, 1828, and ordered to be recorded. It is found in Will Book 6, Page 155, signed by John H. Marshall, Chs A. Raine, and Daniel W. Williamson, and gives the following valuation of slaves:

1 Negro man **BEN** $300.00   * 1 Negro Boy **DICK** $200.00
1 Negro Girl **LUCY** $175.00   1 Negro ditto **WILLIAM** $200.00

[Since the law prescribed that these ex-slaves register in Charlotte County as free persons, they did so and were listed in the Book of Registers of Free Negroes and Mulattoes. Reportedly, this Register may no longer exist; researchers are fortunate that the list was copied and published as part of a compilation of their county records in Charlotte County, Rich Indeed in 1979, pages 485-516.

#135 BEN, emancipated by will of Robert Morgan, dark, age 21, born a slave, registered 2 January 1832
#149 LUCY ANN MORGAN, emancipated by will of Robert Morgan, black, age 18, born a slave, Registered 4 March 1834
#171 Dick,at times called *DICK MORGAN, emancipated by will of Robert Morgan, black, age 21, born a slave, registered 5 February 1838
#174 WILLIAM MORGAN, emancipated by will of Robert Morgan, black, age 21, born a slave, registered 22 February 1839

If their ages are given correctly in the Charlotte Register, their approximate birth years would be as follows: BEN-1811, LUCY-1816, DICK-1817, and WILLIAM-1818.]

V.	**George Harroway, Charlotte County**	In the name of God Amen. I George Harroway of the county of Charlotte & State of Virginia being of sound mind and knowing that it is appointed unto man and to me to make & ordain this Instrument of writing to be my last will & testament. First it is my will and desire that all my just debts be paid out of my estate. Secondly it is my will & desire that all my slaves to wit: *__JAMES__ and *__MOLLEY__ his wife, __SAM, EDMUND,__ *__CLEM__ and __DAFNEY__ be free at my decease. Thirdly it is my will & desire that each of them have one hundred dollars in Money and be moved out of the state at the enforce of my estate. Fourthly it is my will & desire that all my land be sold on a credit of one two and three years also all my stock of every description household and kitchen furniture and plantation tools upon a credit of one year and all the money coming from such sale or sales I give to be equally divided between my brothers and sisters hereinafter named to wit: Samuel Harraway, Eppaphroditus Harraway, Susannah Swan wife of John Swan and Polley Alen widow of William Alen and to them and their heirs forever and lastly I do hereby my friend [illegible] McKinney and [illegible] McKinney Jr Executors of this my last will and Testament [illegible].

At a Court held for Charlotte County the 3rd day of July 1820. The last Will and Testament of George Harroway Decd was presented in Court and there being no witnesses to the said Will Samuel [illegible], John P. Richardson and John D. Sprogins being [illegible] and say they are well acquainted with the Testator's hand writing and verily believed this [illegible] of the Testator's proper hand writing [illegible] on the motion of William and [illegible] who made oath according to law probate [illegible] and security whereupon they with John Marshall [illegible] entered into and acknowledged their land record [illegible] purpose. Teste- Winston Robinson Cl- Duly Recorded- Winston Robinson Cl

(LDS Film #30,777)   Will Book 5, Page 51   Proved 3 July 1820

[This film was extremely dark; the bottom of the page could not be read, although the signature of the testator could be made out.]

The Inventory and Appraisement of the Estate of George Harroway, was returned into Charlotte County Court on February

4, 1822, and ordered to be recorded. It is found in Will Book 5, Page 119, and includes the following valuation of slaves:

    * **JAMES** a man slave $450   * **MOLLEY** a woman $250
    SAM $460   **DAFNEY** $350
    EDMUNT $600   ***CLEM** $350

[None of the Harroway ex-slaves were seen in the published Charlotte county Register in <u>Charlotte County, Rich Indeed</u>.]

VI.   **Caleb Ellis, Sussex County**   I, Caleb Ellis of Sussex County experiencing the decay of nature and being weak in body but of sound mind do make an ordain this my last Will and Testament.

    Item - to son Ira Ellis the sum of 12 pounds cash to be raised out of my estate & pd to him by my executor

    Item - to son Bolin the Tract of Land whereon I now live including the land I purchased of Wm Jordan on condition he pays to my son Ira seventy eight pounds current money of Virginia in 2 annual payments, the first to be the Christmas 12 months after my decease.

    It is my will and desire that my 3 negro men **JOE**, **JACOB** and **LEWIS** be hired out 2 years after my decease at the direction of my executors & that the money arising from the hire for to my son Bolin & be applied by him to the discharge of the 78 pounds mentioned above & if there be any surplus after the raising of 78L arising from their hire, it is my will & desire that such surplus be equally divided between the said negroes JOE, JACOB & LEWIS. If my son Bolin refuses to pay to my son Ira the sum of 78L as mentioned above In that case it is my will that the land abovementioned be equally divided between these my oldest and youngest sons & that the above named negro men be free the Christmas after my death. After the expiration of the time above mentioned for the above negroes to be hired out, It is my will & desire that they be free & at perfect liberty from my heirs, executors, etc in as full and ample a manner as if they had been born free.

    If my decease should be at any period after the 10th day of March in any year of our Lord, it is my desire that all the negroes

& the rest of my property be kept together til the crops is finished & a division of my Estate take place as shall hereafter be directed and that the above JOE, JACOB & LEWIS have all the time after my decease counted in the 2 years they are to serve & that they be allowed out of my estate for their labour from the time of my death till the end of the year whatever three persons shall judge their services to be worth and that the same go to my son Bolin to enable him to comply with the above condition of his holding the land herein mentioned.

It is my will & desire that all the rest of my negroes except **BEN** that shall have arrived at the age of 25 years shall be free at my death, provided it happen in any year previous to the 10th of March otherwise that they be free at the end of the year of my decease.

It is my will & desire that all my negroes that shall be under the age of 25 years at the time of my decease shall be free as soon as they shall respectively arrive at the age of 25 years and also that all the children that may be born of any of them before their freedom shall be free from my heirs etc as soon as they shall be 21 years old.

It is my will & desire that all my negroes under the age of 25 years be equally divided among my own children Ira, Micajah, Wyatt, Bolin, Patty & Anna Cheatham provided they return to my estate the negroes they now have or may hereafter have in their possession as lent from me - But if any of my children shall claim and hold in slavery my negro or negroes that I may have lent them: In that case I desire that they shall have no other part of my estate whatsoever, and further

It is my will that if any of my negroes that shall be under the age of 25 years be removed or sold out of the state of Virginia unless the person removing or selling them first give a bond with a sufficient penalty to my executors or the Court of Sussex County to see them for the coming of the time of their freedom herein mentioned & in case of failing to give such Bond when required & then removing them they shall forfeit the services of the negro or negroes & the rest of my children shall be entitled.

As 2 of my negroes **RALPH** and **BECK** are growing old & as they will enjoy their liberty as so late a person in life it is possible that they may become chargeable to my estate. I therefore authorize & assign my executors to take a Bond of each legatee to my Estate Binding them each to pay 1/6th part of such expenses should any arise previous to the paying to them their final proportions of my estate.

It is my will & desire that if any of my children should die before me that their children should receive whatever their parents would have been entitled to. It is my will & desire that all the rest of my estate not having already been disposed of after the payment of my just debts be equally divided among my children.

It is my will & desire that my negro man **BEN** should be sold and that the moneys arising from his sale [illegible]. I will that my Niece [illegible] Ellis shall have L12 & son Bolin L20 and the balance equally among children.

(LDS Film # 0034158) - Will Book F, page 159 - Written 4 January 1799-Proved 5 September 1799 - Additional Proof 7 November 1799

The Accounting of the Estate of Caleb Ellis is recorded in Will Book G, and includes the following information regarding his slaves:

As of December 1799:   Monies spent for negroes:
        2.18.7 1/2   for negroes clothes
        6   for 4 cert of emancipation of negroes
        9   for making negroes clothes
pd negroes (for hire of negroes May until Christmas):
        8   [pd **JOE** ?]
        6   Pd **JACOB**
        7   Pd **LEWIS**
        1.5   Four Free negroes
As of December 1806:   Other Negroes listed
        Income: **Negro AMY** 23 yrs old   3
                        PATIENCE 19   "   10.6
                        *****DAVY**   15   "   30
                        *****FAITHY**   14   "   13.16
                        ESTHER   14   "   13.10
                        ELITHA   4   "   --
                        MATILDA   2   "   --
                        *****JESSE**   7 months   1.5.3

[When they registered, JESSE used the name **JESSE BOOKER**, while FAITHY used the name **FAITHY ROBINSON**. In Vol 21, page 237 of Aug Court Orders 1820, FAITHY used the name **FAITHY CHARLES** when her children **DILPHA, SALLY, DIANNA** and **THOMAS** were bound out to Ira Ellis. It is not known at this time what surname FAITHY was using, if any, when emancipated. Researchers should also note the exchange of ROBERTSON for ROBINSON as a surname. It is not beyond the realm of possibility that **DELPHA COOK** of the 1830 Census and *****DELPHIA ROBERTSON,** who registered in 1852, may be the above child DILPHA; *****THOMAS ROBERTSON,** who registered in 1839 and reregistered in 1843, could be the above child THOMAS.]

VII. **James Richardson**, **Pittsylvania County** In the Name of God Amen. I James Richardson Senr of Pittsylvania County and State of Virginia being sick in body but of perfect mind and memory and calling to mind the mortallity [sic] of my body and knowing it is appointed for all Men once to die do my Last Will and Testament in manner and form following Viz

I give my slave Woman *****MOLLEY** her freedom at the beginning of the year one thousand eight hundred and seven and all her children that she now has or may have with their increase to have their freedom as they arrive to the age of twenty one years -

Item. I give unto my loving Wife Mary Richardson the use of my Land and Plantation where I now live with all my Personal Estate after paying my just Debts during her Widowhood and in case she should Marry my Will and desire is that she should have one third of the Estate before mentioned during her natural life and then return and be equally divided between my children namely William, James, Lucy, Henry, Benjamin, and Robert as such of them should be then living or having Heirs lawfully begotten of their bodies -

Item. I desire that my lands purchased of Robert Scott and Joseph Goldston be rented out during my Wife's natural life, but not planted [?] in Corn every year and so much Money paid to my four oldest Children out of the Rents as was left them from Vaiden's and Morris's Estate and then my two youngest Children to be made equal and of the sd Rents and then the rest of the rents with the two thirds of my other Estate to be equally divided all my Children in case my Wife should marry again, and at my Wife's death my desire is that all my Lands be valued and divided between all my Sons, namely William, James, Henry, Benjamin and Robert and my Personal Estate Sold and as much Money paid to my Daughter Lucy as will make her equal with my Sons and if anything remains to be equally divided among them all and if there is not a sufficiency to make her equal according to the Valuation of the Lands, each Son must pay his proportion.

I further desire my Children may have Schooling out of my Estate and after they have a sufficiency of Learning my desire is that they may be bound out to some Trade that may be thought most proper by my Exr Luccaflor [?] named.

Lastly I do appoint my Brother William Richardson, Joseph Dodson and [left blank] my Execrs to this my last Will and Testament and further I do make null and void any other Will or Wills by me before made in Witness whereof I have hereunto set my hand and affixed my Seal this Twenty first day of Sep 1797 - Signed, Seald and delivered in presence of - Peter x Smith, Thomas x Turbish   James Richardson   (Seal)

At a Court held for Pittsylvania County December the 16th 1799. This Will was presented in Court and it appearing that the same is of a later date than a Will of the within named James Richardson heretofore proven and Recorded in this Court, it is Ordered that the Probate of the said former Will and all proceedings concerning the same be rescinded and this Will being proven by the Oath of Thomas Turbish a witness thereto and by the oaths of William Richardson and Henry Cook to be in the handwriting of the said Testator Ordered that the same to be Recorded and on the Motion of Joseph Dodson one of the Executors therein named who took the Oath required by law and together with the said Henry Cook and William Richardson his securities entered into and acknowledged their bond in the penalty of one thousand pounds Conditioned as the Law directs Certificate is granted him for obtaining a probate of the said Will in due form- Teste Will Tunstall

(LDS Film # 0033290)　　　　　　Deeds & Wills, Vol II, Page 225
Written 21 September 1797　　　　Proved 16 December 1799

[**MOLLY**'s surname has not yet been ascertained. Her daughter, ***PEGGY**, also used an unknown surname, and was registered upon reaching the age of twenty one, as specified in the Will.]

VIII. **John Worsham, Pittsylvania**   I John Worsham of the County of Pittsylvania & State of Virginia being of sound mind but knowing the uncertainty of the mortal life do make and publish my last Will & Testament in manner & form following hereby revoking all others by me heretofore made, First. I wish all my Just debts to be paid by my Executors herein after named.

 2nd I will and bequeath unto my beloved wife Mary Worsham all my lands, negroes, houses & kitchen furniture & plantation tools & utensils, five head of horses, half in Value of my stock of sheep & hogs & one third in Value of my cattle during her natural life with the exception of so much and such party thereof as may be herein after otherwise disposed of She to have choice of the horses after taking out my stud colt & Jim Crack mare, my Executors (other than my wife) to divide my sheep into two parts as near equal in Value as may be, & my wife then to have choice, my cattle & hogs to be also divided by them in the same manner & she to take choice of the proportions herein before bequeathed to her. I allow my wife the privilege of disposing of one hundred pounds in money to any person or persons she may appoint in uniting under her hand to be raised out of my estate and paid by my Excutors after her death.

 3rd I devise unto my friend Thomas Stewart of Danville, one hundred acres of Land to be laid off adjoining the Lands of James D. Patton in Pittsylvania County to be put into his possession immediately after my Death and to be held by him and his heirs forever.

 4th I bequeath unto my brother Thomas Worsham my stud colt & Jim Crack mare & my two negro boys **EDWARD & JACOB**, the horse and mare to be delivered to him immediately after my death, the two boys immediately upon the death or marriage of my wife.

 5th   I bequeath unto my brother Daniel Worsham fifty pounds to be raised out of my estate after the death of my wife & paid by my Executors.

6th It is my will and desire that my three old Negroes *JAMES, *PHILLIS & *JINNEY be set free & I do hereby emancipate them to take effect at the death of my wife & for support of them I will & bequeath to them (after the death of my wife) Jointly & to the survivor or survivors of them during their Joint living & the lives of the survivor or survivors the following property real & personal, To Wit a Tract of Land lying in Caswell County N Carolina adjoining the Lands of Greenberry Vass [?] & Henry McClasney Containing between one and two hundred acres, be the same more or less, a horse of about the Value of Ten pounds, a Cow & Calf, one Cotton wheel, a pair of Cotton cards, one Loom & Gin & my Carpenters Tools & Coopers tools, but after the death of the three negroes above mentioned the property herein devised & bequeathed to them to revert back to my Executors herein after named (other than my wife) or to such of them as may take it upon themselves the burthen of the Executors of this my last Will & Testament & in Case of the death of any of my acting Executors (other than my wife) before the sd property reverts then their legal representatives to take the part which he or they if alive would have been entitled to under the devise & bequest-

7th I wish my Executors as soon as convenient after my death to sell and dispose of such of my horses, cattle sheep & hogs as have not been herein before disposed of, the proceeds of which together with any monies on hand at my death & such as may be due me, will be a fund in their hands to the payment of my debts & if after payment of my debts funeral expenses and other necessary expenditures there should of this fund remain a surplus, then the Legacy to Daniel Worsham may be paid without waiting till the death of my wife if such surplus will be sufficient for that purpose-

8th It is my will and desire after the death of my wife that all the land Negroes & other property herein before Lent to my wife except such parts thereof as may have been herein before otherwise disposed of, together with all the rest & residue of my estate not herein before otherwise disposed of shall be sold by my Executors in such manner as they may think advisable & the proceeds of such sale together with the proceeds of such of my personal property as is directed to be sold immediately ater my death, money on hand at my death & outstanding debts Collected, or such surplus therefrom may then remain in their hands undisposed of I bequeath to be equally divided among Thomas Stewart herein before named,

Ludwell Worsham & the Legitimate Children of my brothers Robert Worsham & Joshua Worsham (who is now decd) and Thomas Worsham & of my Sisters Michael Ferguson, Phoebe Wynne (which last is also dead) share and share alike but if any of the legatees whosoever have a right to any part of my estate under the Eighth section of my last Will & Testament should die before my Wife leaving children Who may be alive at the time of the death of my Wife, then such children to take the parts which its parents would have taken had he or she been alive.

    9th   Lastly I do hereby appoint my beloved wife Mary Worsham, my brother Thomas Worsham and my friends Thomas Stewart and James D. Patton Executors of this my last Will & Testament Given under my hand this 20th day of July 1813 - The words life "in the first page" & "other than my wife" in the second mentioned before signed.   John Worsham

    John Worsham whose name is subscribed to the foregoing instrument Acknowledged to us the day of the date thereof, that he subscribed his name thereto with his own hand He Acknowledged & published the same as his last Will & Testament & requested us to Witness the same which we now do in his presence-Fr. Dabney, William Dodson, Daniel L. Coleman

    At a Court held for Pittsylvania County the 21st of March 1814. This last Will and Testament of John Worsham Decd was presented in Court and proved by the Oaths of two Witnesses hereto subscribed and Ordered to be Recorded - and on the motion of James D. Patton one of the Executors herein named who made Oath according to law - Certificate is granted him for obtaining probate of the said Will in due form he giving security - Whereupon he together with Nathaniel Wilson, Francis Dabney, Thomas Stewart, William Dodson, John Ross & Selby Benson his Security entered into and Acknowledged their bond in the penalty of Thirty Thousand Dollars - Conditioned as the law directs - Thomas Stewart and Thomas Worsham the other Executors in the said Will named refusing to qualify -   Teste   Will Tunstall Clc

(LDS Film # 0033290)   Deeds & Wills, Vol II, Page
384 Written 20 July 1813   Proved 21 March 1814

[**JAMES**, **JINNEY**, and probably **PHILLIS** did move to Caswell County NC using the surname **WORSHAM** (sometimes spelled WASHAM), where they were found on the 1830 Federal Census, all aged 55-100.]

IX. **Sarah Herndon**, Pittsylvania County   In the name of God. Amen. I Sarah Herndon of Pittsylvania County being in a low state of health but sound mind and memory calling to mind the uncertainty of human life do make and ordain this my last Will and Testament & as to such worldly Estate whereof it has pleased God to help me with in this life I give and devise and dispose of in the following manner. To wit.   I give to Mary Witsher wife of William Witsher Sen after my death my Negro girl *****MALINDAY** & one feather bed of furniture till she becomes of age of twenty one years. Should I die before she arrives to that age then my will and disire is that my Executor when she arrives at that age to see that she is freed.   I give to Polly Witsher one large cherry chest after my death. My Will and desire is that my Negroes to wit **AMANDAY** a girl **TANDAY** [?] a boy **SAFORONIA** a girl **CANDICE** a girl **LANDY LANKSFORD** a boy together with the residue of my other Estate shall be sold and my just debts paid. After the payment thereof my will and desire is that the balance left should be equally divided between Abel Hutson, Drury Hutson, Sarah Whiat & Elizabeth Razor's children wife of George Razor all of which I give to them & their heirs forever. My desire is that my Negro woman **MARY** should not be sold but have the liberty of going with her children. Lastly I do appoint and ordain John Witsher Sen & William Graves my Executors of this my last Will and Testament. In witness whereof I have hereunto set my hand & seal this 17th day of July 1818. Signed Sealed and delivered in presence of Vincent Witcher, John Keen, William Witcher Jr- Sarah Herndon   Seal

    At a Court held for Pittsylvania County this 15 Day of February 1819 This Last will and Testament of Sarah Herndon Decd was presented in Court and proved by the Oaths of three of the Subscribing Witnesses thereto. Ordered that the Same be recorded. And on the Motion of John Witcher and William Graves the Executors named in Said will who made Oath thereto according to law and together with William Witcher Sen and Charles W. Bobbitt the Executors entered into and acknowledged their bond in the penalty of Five thousand dollars Conditioned according to Said Certificate as granted them for obtaining a probate of Said Will in due form- Teste- Will Tunstall

(LDS Film # 0033290)   Deeds & Wills, Vol II, Page 504
Written 17 July 1818   Proved 15 February 1819

[It is not known at this time what surname **MALINDAY** used when emancipated. A family relationship between the slave children and **MARY** is stated in the Will; she is said to be their mother. The woman, MARY, "with her increase", had been left by George Herndon to his "well beloved wife Sarah", in his Will of 16 May 1806, proved 16 June 1806, Deed & Wills Vol II, page 292. No relationship is stated for MARY and MALINDAY in either document. It is possible that MALINDAY may have been Sarah's separate property during the marriage, and unrelated to MARY.]

FREED BY DEED:

I.   **Charles Kennon, Halifax County**   Know all men by these presents that I Charles Kennon of Halifax County and State of Virginia do fully liberate and set free according to an act of Assembly for that case made and provided the folowing negroes (viz) **BRISTER, FANNY, LEWIS, VALENTINE, ROBIN, RACHEL, MURYEAR, HANAH, INDIA, JOHN, *JONAH, MOSES, ABRAHAM, SUCKEY, TOM, MILDRED, BILLY, PATIENCE, AMEY, TOM, AMEY, HARRY** and **PETER** - in witness whereof I do hereunto set my hand & seal this 9th day of February 1785. Teste Thos Walkins, Will P Martin
                                                     Charles Kennon

     At a Court held for Halifax the 17th day of February 1785 the above instrument of writing of Emancipation from Charles Kennon to sundry negroes was proved by the oath of the witnesses hereto and Ordered to be Certified & at another Court held for the sd County the 17th day of March following the same was further proved by other witnesses hereto subscribed & Ordered to be recorded.

(LDS Film # 31885); Deed Book 13, page 161; Dated 9 February 1785; Certified 17 February 1785; Recorded 17 March 1785

[**JONAH**, mentioned above, used the surname **FISHNECK** for registration in Pittsylvania County, as well as in the 1830 census enumeration for Pittsylvania County. His relationship to the other freedmen listed above is unknown, as there are no other freedmen of that surname registered or enumerated on the censuses for Pittsylvania county.]

II. **John Terry, Pittsylvania County** Know all Men by these presents that I John Terry of Pittsylvania County for divers causes me thereunto moving and in Obedience to the Will of my Father do hereby Emancipate the following Slaves, to wit, *****CATHERINE STEVENS** a Negro woman aged 21 years *****LUCRETIA STEVENS** a Negro girl aged one year. And it is my Will and my desire that the abovementioned Negroes and all their progeny shall be a free people and enjoy all the liberties now providing as that the laws of this County allows them. In Witness whereof I have hereunto set my hand and affixed my seal this 17th day of June 1799. Teste. Thos B. McRobert, William C[illegible]
           John Terry Seal

At a Court held for Pittsylvania County July the 15th 1799 - this Writing purporting the Emancipation of CATHERINE STEVENS and her Child LUCRETIA [STEVENS] was produced in Court and acknowledged by the within named John Terry to be his and said Law Ordered that the same be Recorded. Teste. Will Tunstall CPC

(LDS Film # 33290); Deed & Will Book Vol II, page 495; Dated 17 June 1799; Recorded 15 July 1799

[John Terry's father appears to have been Stephen Terry, who lived for some time in Orange county North Carolina, according to Clement's <u>History of Pittsylvania</u>, page 172. Stephen's

Will, recorded in October 1797 is found in Pittsylvania Deed and Will Book 11, page 196. In this Will, there is no mention of CATHERINE or LUCRETIA; in fact, several other slaves belonging to Stephen Terry are bequeathed to his wife and children. Perhaps John had a verbal agreement with his father regarding this matter.

February Court Orders of 1819 show that the Overseers of the Poor for Pittsylvania County bound **AGNESS**, ***SILVEY**, **NANCY**, and ***WILLIAM STEPHENS**, children of KATIE STEPHENS a free Woman of Colour to Jno Terry in Volume 19, Page 246. By 1826, CATHERINE's other daughters, ***WILMOTH**, ***PHILLIS** and ***AGGY** had also registered as free, and other free children of these women are named in Court Orders, all due to John Terry's emancipation of CATHERINE and LUCRETIA.]

III.   **Moses Hodges, Pittsylvania County**

[October 1812 Court Orders, found in LDS film 33,313 at page 395, shows ***NANCY DAY** petitioning for and being granted the right to sue Moses Hodges. George Tucker Gentleman was assigned as her counsel. This request was based on her assertion that she was a freeborn woman being illegally held in slavery by Hodges.

In the November Court Orders 1812 found at page 414, NANCY's Register, stating that she is a freeborn mulatto woman, is certified as correct; however, a Deed of Emancipation for NANCY DAY granted by Moses Hodges has not yet been found.]

IV.   **Joseph Fowler, Pittsylvania County**

[No Will, Deed or information on his heirs which identifies Joseph Fowler has as yet been located by this author in Pittsylvania county records. Fowler's heirs freed ***ROBERT FOWLER** by Deed in 1825, according to ROBERT's Register. One would expect to find court records of an application for ROBERT requesting permission to remain in Virginia, since his Register states that such permission was granted; however, this record has not yet been located.

It would seem that Fowler family members were either not long-time residents of the county, or were not involved in many business transactions leaving a paper trail. One lawsuit (Fowler v

Dixon, February Court 1825, LDS film 33,316, page 83) grants Fowler judgment to recover money he paid to Daniel Edwards for Dixon. Fowler's death apparently took place later that same year, since ROBERT was free by September. Perhaps Joseph's heirs were daughters who married Pittsylvania county men.

Two early Bills of Sale were found for land transactions in Pittsylvania county for a possible relative, John Fowler of Bedford County, who may have been an absentee landlord. Both were recorded 28 March 1771, in Volume 2 of Pittsylvania Land & Property Deeds, and involve the purchase and sale of the same land. In both cases, the other parties also lived outside the county.]

V. **James, Fanny and Patsy Arthur, Pittsylvania County**

Whereas *MILLY CHAVIS and her Child NANCY [CHAVIS] who have been held in bondage by me and who claims their freedom and has sit now defending for the recovery thereof in the County Court of Pittsylvania and whereas I believe that the said MILLY CHAVIS and her child NANCY are entitled to their freedom. now therefore these present writings that I James Arthur do Emancipate and set free the said MILLY CHAVIS and her Child NANCY so that from this day forward neither I or any person or persons Claiming by through or under me shall have any authority or power or right or Interest in & to or over the aid MILLY CHAVIS & her child NANCY, that the said MILLEY CHAVIS & her Child NANCY shal be from this day forward clearly & absolutely to all intent and purposes free and moreover I the said James Arthur having a ful belief that the said MILLEY CHAVIS & her Child NANCY have a ful right to their freedom have executed these presents for the purpose of assuring it to them and do further declare that it is my desire that Judgment shall be entered in the suits defending aforesaid in favor of the said MILLEY CHAVIS and NANCY her Child hereby renouncing and disclaiming any right of property in me to the said MILLEY CHAVIS or NANCY her Child.
In witness whereof I have hereunto set my hand and affixed my seal this 16th day of January 1829, Signed, sealed, acknowledged & delivered in the presence of Edward Dalton, Nancy Dalton, Francis [Pales?], Francis Aston   James Arthur

At a Court held for Pittsylvania County the 16th day of March 1829 The within Deed of emancipation was presented in Court and proved by two of the subscribing Witnesses to be the act and deed of the within named James Arthur and by the Court Ordered to be recorded.

Orders,Vols.28-30, 1829-1833   (LDS Film # 33317)
Vol. 30, Page 561, [date of Court not given]

        Whereas **HANNAH [CHAVIS]** and her child **WINNEY [CHAVIS]**, **MILLEY [CHAVIS]** and her child **MARY JANE [CHAVIS]** who had been held in bondage by us and have been defending for their freedom therefrom these presents witness that we Fanny Arthur and Patsey Arthur do by these presents Emancipate and set free the said HANNAH and her child WINNEY, MILLEY and her child MARY JANE, and from this time renounce and disdain any right of ownership over them and having a ful belief that they are justly Entitled to their freedom have executed this deed in order to secure it to them and it is our desire that Judgments shall be entered in and in favor of the said HANNAH and her child WINNEY, MILLEY and her child MARY JANE. In Witness whereof we have hereunto set our hands and affixed our seals this 31st day of May 1829. Witness James Echols, Anna X Arthur   Fanny X Arthur (Seal)   Patsey X Arthur (Seal)

In the Clerks Office of the County Court of Pittsylvania the 31st day of September 1829 This Deed of Emancipation from Fanny Arthur and Patsy Arthur to **HANNAH [CHAVIS]** & others was proved by the subscribing witness to be the act and deed of the sd Fanny & Patsey as above attested.   Teste. Will Tunstall ClC

Orders,Vols.28-30, 1829-1833   (LDS Film # 33317)
Vol. 31, Page 309, [date of Court not given]

[Another CHAVIS female, ***UNA CHAVIS**, registered under the same circumstances of freedom, but is not named in either of these documents. Perhaps she is one of those included above in the phrase "& others".]

THE FEDERAL CENSUSES OF
1820, 1830 AND 1840

The following extractions pinpoint households where Free Negroes were enumerated as residing in the federal censuses of Pittsylvania County for 1820, 1830 and 1840. Prior to 1850, the names of many Free Negroes are missing, since only the name of the head of household was given. As time passed, however, the number of Free Black families who were enumerated as living in their own households increased. Beginning with the 1850 census, all free persons are listed by name. For that reason, no extractions for 1850 or later dates are included in this volume.

Researchers will note that numerous Free Negro children were enumerated as living in white households of Pittsylvania County with no Free Negro adult in the same household. It is probable that a number of apprenticeship indentures will be found in the Court Orders, which will account for the presence of these children in white homes. Children were often bound out by the Overseers of the Poor and by the Church Wardens.

It should prove helpful and interesting, not only to African-American researchers, to learn which white families had Free Negroes residing on their property. Researchers who wish to further investigate the white families with whom these unnamed Free Negroes lived may well be able to determine their names from private papers and other sources. It should be possible to reconstitute at least some of these Free Black families through a comparison of records, family papers and other documents of Pittsylvania County.

Free Negroes living in white households are enumerated as "FN" below. The names of white heads of household are in listed in lower case. The names of the Free Negro heads of household are capitalized. All names are shown in bold, as is all data (sex and gender) regarding persons residing in households headed by Free Negroes.

1820 FEDERAL CENSUS, LDS Film No. 0193699

The 1820 census for Pittsylvania county Virginia shows 33 white families on whose property Free Negroes were living, and 3 Free Black heads of household.

Page 47
- Wilson Vaden, family + 3 slaves, and 1 FN male age 14-26
- Abram Pistole Sr., family, 0 slaves, 1 FN female age 26-45
- Armstead Aline, family + 1 slave, and 1 FN male age <14

Page 48
- Jesse Smith, family + 6 slaves, and 1 FN female age <14
- William Beavers, family, 39 slaves, 5 FN females, 1 age 45+, 1 age 26-45, and 3 age <14
- William Linn, family + 7 slaves, and 1 FN male <14

Page 49
- John B. Roy & Co., (a business), 1 white male + 3 slaves, and 7 FNs: 1 male 45+, 1 female 45+, 1 female 26-45, 1 male 14-26, and 4 females <14
- **LETHY FLAG, female age 14-26, living alone**
- Obadiah Hamm, family + 5 slaves, and 3 FNs, 1 male age 14-26, and 2 males age <14
- John Nichols, family, 0 slaves, and 1 FN male <14
- John Trayhorn, family + 17 slaves, and 1 FN male <14
- Robert Hairston, family + 45 slaves, and 1 FN male <14

Page 50
- **CLEM BURNETT, male age 14-26, living alone**
- Obadiah Reynolds, family + 13 slaves, and 1 FN male 14-26
- Nelson Tucker, family + 12 slaves, and 1 FN male age <14
- James Robertson, family + 6 slaves, 1FN male age 14-26
- James Hodges, family + 6 slaves, 2 FN males both age 26-45
- Jonathon Dawson, family + 20 slaves, and 8 FNs 1 female 26-45, 1 female 14-26, 1 male <14, and 5 females <14

Page 52
- Charles Williams, family + 1 slave, and 1 FN male <14
- Ira Ellis, family + 19 slaves, 6 FNs: 1 male 26-45, 2 males 14-26, 2 males <14, and 1 female <14
- Chloe Coleman, family + 13 slaves, 2 FN females: 1 at age 14-26, and 1 <14

Page 53
-ROBERT BIRD, 1 male age 45+, 1 female 45+, 1 male 26-45, 1 female 14-26, 1 male 14-26, and 1 female age <14
-Isham Lansford, family + 1 slave, and 1 FN male age 45+
Page 54
-William Dixon, family + 7 slaves, and 3 FNs: 2 males and 1 female, all age <14
-Jesse Walton, family + 8 slaves, 2 FNs: 1 male age 14-26 and 1 female <14
Page 56
-James Blair, family + 2 slaves, and 1 FN male age <14
-Edwd Copejoy, family, 0 slaves, and 1 FN male age 14-26
Page 57
-William Newton, family + 1 slave, and 5 FNs 1 female 45+, 1 male age 26-45, 1 female age 14-26, 2 males <14
Page 58
-Major Soyers, family with no slaves, and 1 FN male age <14
-Wm Atkinson, family with 1 slave, and 1 FN male age <14
-Samuel Lovill, family with 16 slaves, and 1 FN male age <14
-Mj Richd Johnson, family, 21 slaves, 3 FN males age 45+
-Thos Davis, family with 9 slaves, and 1 FN male age 15-26
-John Williams, family + 10 slaves, and 1 FN male age 14-26
Page 60
-Doc C. Williams, family + 17 slaves, and 1 FN male age 45+
-Joseph Ferguson, family + 0 slaves, 3 FNs: 1 female age 26-45, 1 male age <14, and 1 female age <14

1830 FEDERAL CENSUS, LDS Film No. 0029680

The 1830 census for Pittsylvania County indicates that there were 93 white families on whose property Free Negroes were living. Households headed by Free Negroes increased to 43. Several white families listed below as 'with slaves' held between 7 and 45 slaves each, but most slave owners held 5 slaves or less.

Noteworthy about several Black households, and deserving of much more study, were several facts which emerged relative to what might be considered "lifestyle" by today's standards. It was found that in five households headed by Free Negro men, there were white women living. In one instance, an adolescent white male also resided in the household. Residing in another household with a Free Negro man, was a female slave of his age category. In each of two other households headed by Free Negroes, a slave was enumerated. One wonders about the relationships between the individuals in each of these households. The pertinent sections have been underlined in the transcriptions.

Page 312
-Briant Nowlin, family + slaves, 1 FN, a female age 10-24
Page 313
-David Irby, family + slaves, 2 FN females: 1 age 10-24 and
    1 age <10
Page 314
-Robert M. Smith, family + slaves, 1 FN, a female age 10-24
Page 315
-Anthony Lipford, family + slaves, 1 FN, a female age 10-24
Page 316
-Sexton W. Smith, family + slaves, 1 FN, a female age 10-24
-Francis Callaway, family + slaves, 1 FN, a male age 10-24
-Jacob Shelhouse, family + 1 slave, 2 FN males age 10-24
-Friend S. Terry, family + 4 slaves, 1 FN, a male age 24-36
-John Robertson, family + 0 slaves, 2 FN males age 10-24
-Frances McClanahan, family + 1 slave, 2 FNs, 1 male age
    10-24, and 1 female age 10-24
**-ELISHA REYNOLDS, 7 FNs and 1 white female, age
    20-30; a FN male 24-36, 1 female 24-36, 1 female
    10-24, 3 males age <10, 1 female <10**
-Ethldred Carrol, family + 0 slaves, 1 FN, a female age <10
Page 319
**-UNIS CHAPIN, 1 female 24-36, 2 females <10, and 2
    males <10**
-Caley Ramsey, family + 1 slave, and 1 FN male 24-36
Page 322
-Cornelius Lawhorn , family, 0 slaves, 1 FN female age <10

Page 323
-FAITH ROBERTSON, 1 female 36-55, 1 female age 10-24, 1 male 10-24, 2 males <10, and <u>1 male slave age 55-100</u>
Page 332
-George Parker, family, 0 slaves, 2 FNs, 1 female 10-24 and 1 male <10
-Thomas Newton, family, 0 slaves, 1 FN, a male age 10-24
Page 334
-James Burton, family + slaves, 1 FN, a male age 10-24
-Harrison Douglas, family + 2 slaves, 1 FN: a male age 10-24
-John Giles, Jr., family, 0 slaves, and 1 FN, a male age 10-24
-Samuel Love, family + 1 slave, 1 FN: a male age 36-55
Page 335
-Robert Adams, family + slaves, 1 FN, a male age 24-36
Page 336
-Wm Blair, family, 0 slaves, and 1 FN female age <10
-Wm Ferguson, family + 1 slave, and 1 FN, a male age 10-24
-William Riddle, family, 0 slaves, and 1 FN, a male age 10-24
Page 337
-KESAH REYNOLDS, 1 female 36-55, 2 females age 10-24, and 2 females age <10
Page 340
-LETITIA HENDRICK, 1 female 36-55 lives alone
-Archd Haley, family + 7 slaves, and 1 FN, a male age 10-24
Page 342
-Mourning Lawhorn, family, 0 slaves, 1 FN female age 10-24
Page 343
-ROBERT TOLER, 5 FNs <u>and 1 white female age 30-40 & 1 white female 15-20;</u> 2 FN males 24-36, 1 female 24-36, 2 males <10
Page 344
-Lynch Dillard, family, 0 slaves, and 1 FN, a male age 36-55
Page 345
-JOHN GOINGS, 5 FNs <u>and 1 white female 30-40 & 1 white female 10-15;</u> 1 FN male 36-55, 1 female 10-24, 1 male 10-24, 1 female <10, 1 male <10
Page 346
-JAMES GOING, 2 males 24-36, 2 females age 24-36

251

-George DiJennett, family + slaves, and 2 FNs, 1 female 24-36; 1 female age <10

Page 350
-John Hunt, family + slaves, and 1 FN, a male age 36-55
-Nelson Tucker, family + slaves, and 1 FN, a male age 10-24

Page 351
-John Penwell, family, 0 slaves, 1 FN, a female age 55-100
-Samuel Lovell, family + slaves, 2 FNs both males age 10-24
-Wm A Anthony, family + 3 slaves, and 1 FN male age 10-24
-Hugh Weir, family + 3 slaves, and 1 FN male age 36-55
-**BURTON REYNOLDS, 1 male 24-36, 1 female age 10-24; 1 female age <10**
-**DELPHA COOK, 1 female 10-24, and 1 male age <10**

Page 352
-Ann Dorson, family + 1 slave, and 5 FNs: 4 females 10-24 and 1 male <10

Page 353
-George Vaughn, family, 0 slaves, and 1 FN male age 24-36
-Stephen Dove, family, 0 slaves, and 1 FN, a male age 36-55
-Francis Haley, family + slaves, and 9 FNs, 1 female 36-55, 2 females 10-24, 3 females <10, and 3 males age <10
-**HENRY CARTER, 1 male 24-36, 1 female 10-24, 2 males 10-24, 2 females age <10**
-**JUDITH SHELTON, 1 female 36-55, 2 females <10, and 1 male age <10**
-**PEGGY DAY, 1 female 24-36, living alone**

Page 356
-Betsey Keeling, 2 white females, 0 slaves, 4 FNs, 1 male age <10, 3 females of age <10

Page 357
-James Bolling, family, 0 slaves, and 1 FN, a male age 36-55
-Young Shelton, family + 1 slave, and 2 FNs, 1 female 10-24, and 1 female <10

Page 359
-**HUBBARD BOWMAN, 2 males 36-55, and 1 female age 36-55**
-Abram Shelton, family + 2 slaves, and 1 FN male age 24-36
-Wm Rohr, family, 0 slaves, and 1 FN, a female age <10

Page 365
-**GEORGE BARKER, 3 FNs and 1 white female 20-30 &**

1 white female 15-20; 1 FN male age 10-24 and 2
females age <10
-JESSE BOOKER, 1 male 36-55, 1 male age 10-25, and 1
female slave age 10-24
-GREEN BARKER, 6 FNs, with 1 white male age 10-15
& 1 white female age 20-30; 1 FN male 24-36, 4
females <10, and 1 male age <10
-Elizabeth Still, family + slaves, and 1 FN female age 36-55
-Thos Crane, family, 0 slaves, and 1 FN, a male age 36-55
Page 368
-Mary Butcher, family, 0 slaves, and 1 FN, a male age 24-36
-DICK REDMOND, 1 male 36-55, 1 female 24-36,
1 female 10-24, 2 males 10-24, 1 male <10, and 4
females age <10
-HEZEKIAH COUSINS, 1 male 10-24, 1 female age 10-
24, and 2 males <10
-Samuel Meador, family + 2 slaves, and 1 FN, a male age <10
-John Calhoun, family, 0 slaves, and 1 FN, a male age 10-24
-Anthony Oaks, family, 0 slaves, and 1 FN, a male age <10
Page 371
-Reuben Hall, family, 0 slaves, 3 FNs, 1 female age 24-36,
2 males <10
-MAN VALENTINE, 1 male 24-36, lives alone
-Wm Travish Sen, family, 0 slaves, 2 FNs, 2 females age <10
-James Jeffreys, family, 0 slaves, and 1 FN, a male age 10-24
-JANE COLE, 1 female 24-36 and 1 male age <10
-Charles West, family, 0 slaves, and 2 FNs, 1 female 10-24
and 1 male 10-24
-Elijah Lewis, family, 0 slaves, and 1 FN, a female age 10-24
-Wm Holley, family, 0 slaves, and 2 FNs, 1 female age 24-36,
and 1 male age <10
-Benj Walker, family, 0 slaves, and 1 FN, a male age <10
Page 375
-Peyton Talley, family + 5 slaves, and 1 FN, a male age 24-36
-Washington Shelton, family, 0 slaves, 1 FN male age 10-24
-Frederick Payne, family, 0 slaves, and 1 FN male age 24-36
-CALEB REYNOLDS, 1 male 24-36, 1 female age 24-36,
1 male 10-24, and 3 females <10
-NANCY VALENTINE, 1 female 24-36, 1 female age 10-
24, 2 females <10, and 3 males <10

Page 377
-Julius Allen, family + slaves, and 1 FN, a male age 55-100
-SAMUEL HENDRICK, 1 male 24-36, 1 female age 24-
  36, 3 males 10-24, 2 males <10, 2 females age <10
Page 378
-BAKER FREEPORT, 1 male 55-100, 1 female age 10-24,
  1 female <10, and 1 male <10
-THOMAS STEWART & BROTHER, 2 males age 36-55,
  1 female 36-55, 1 female 24-36, a female 10-24, 3
  males <10, 1 female <10
-JOHN FREEMAN, 1 male 36-55, 2 females 10-24, and 1
  male age <10
-Pendleton Walker, family, 0 slaves, 1 FN a female age 24-36
Page 381
-LETHY FLAG, 1 female 36-55, 1 female age 10-24, and
  3 males age <10
-GRIEF HARRIS, 1 male 24-36, 1 female 24-36, and 1
  female age <10
Page 382
-Wm R Chaplin, family + 2 slaves, 2 FN females age 10-24
-Edwin Webb, family, 0 slaves, and 5 FNs, 1 female 10-24, 2
  males <10, and 2 females <10
Page 387
-Thomas Rawlins, family + slaves, and 1 FN male age 36-55
-J.M. Williamson, family + slaves, and 2 FNs, 1 female 10-24,
  and 1 male 10-24
Page 390
-Tunstall Shelton, family, 0 slaves, 1 FN, a male age 10-24
Page 391
-Wm Compton, family with no slaves, 1 FN male <10
-SALLY DUPUEY, 1 female 55-100, lives alone
-Dance Pearman, family, 0 slaves, 3 FNs 1 male 36-55,
  1 female 10-24, and 1 female <10
Page 393
-CHARLES WINBUSH, 1 male 55-100, 1 female age 36-
  55, and 1 female age 10-24
-John Walrond, family + 4 slaves, and 1 FN female age 24-36
Page 394
-John Terry Jr., family + slaves, and 1 FN, a male age 10-24
-Wm W Farmer, family + 2 slaves, and 1 FN, a male age <10

-Wm Mottley, family + slaves, and 5 FNs, 1 female 24-36, 3males <10, 1 female age <10
-Obadiah P Terry, family + slaves, and 2 FNs, 1 female 10-24, and 1 male <10
-Stokely Turner, family, 0 slaves, 2 FN males, age 10-24

Page 396
-David Fitzgerald, family, 0 slaves, 2 FNs, 1 female age 24-36; and 1 male age <10

Page 397
-Walter B Huse, family, 0 slaves, and 1 FN female age 10-24
-Lucy Holt, family + slaves, 6 FNs: 1 female 24-36, and 5 females age <10

Page 399
-John Williams (Cole), family + slaves, 3 FNs, 1 female 36-55, 2 females 10-24, 1 female <10

Page 400
-LEWIS REYNOLDS, 1 male 10-24, and 1 female 10-24

Page 402
-BENJ SHAVERS, 1 male 55-100, 1 female 55-100, and 1 male age 10-24

Page 403
-SAMUEL BEACH, 1 male 55-100, 1 female age 55-100, 1 female 10-24, 1 female <10, and 1 male age <10

Page 404
-CHARLES SOYARS, 1 male 55-100, 1 female age 55-100, and 1 male <10
-JOHN SOYARS, 1 male 24-36, 1 female age 10-24, 1 male age <10 and 1 female age <10

Page 405
-MASON (MOSES?) FREEMAN, 1 male age 36-55, 1 female age 24-36, 1 male age 10-24, 3 males age <10, and 3 females age <10
-BOB LOGAN, 1 male 55-100, and 1 female age 55-100
-Elizabeth Parsons, family, 0 slaves, 1 FN female age 24-36

Page 406
-Robert Findley, family + 1 slave, and 3 FNs, 1 female 24-36, 1 male <10, and 1 female age <10
-George Harper, family + slaves, and 1 FN female age 10-24

Page 407
-Wm Newton, family + 4 slaves, 3 FNs, 1 female 36-55, 1

male 24-36, and 1 male age 10-24
- Wm Payne, family + slaves, and 1 FN, a male age 10-24
- Jarald Patterson, family, 0 slaves, and 2 FNs, 1 female age 24-36, and 1 male age <10
- A.B. Edwards, family, 0 slaves, and 1 FN, a male age 10-24
- Peter Griggs, family + 1 slave, and 1 FN, a female age 10-24

Page 408
- George Gardner, family, 0 slaves, and 1 FN, a male age <10
- Wm Dixon, family + slaves, and 1 FN, a female age 24-36
- Silvany Gardner, family, 0 slaves, 1 FN female age 10-24

Page 409
- **LUCY COLE**, 1 female 36-55, 1 female age 10-24, 1 male age <10, and 1 female age <10
- **CUFF MAYHU**, 1 male 24-36, 2 females 10-24, and 3 females age <10
- Charles Thomas, family, 0 slaves, and 1 FN male age 10-24
- **JONAS FISHNECK**, 1 male 24-36, lives alone

Page 410
- Wm Shackleford, family, 0 slaves, and 1 FN male age 24-36

Page 411
- John Roe, family, 0 slaves, and 1 FN female age <10
- Sally Taylor, family, 0 slaves, and 1 FN female <10
- Betty Logan, family + 1 slave, and 2 FN males age <10
- **GEORGE WISDOM**, 1 FN male 55-100, and <u>1 female slave age 55-100</u>

Page 412
- **DEBORAH WILEY**, 4 females 24-36, and 1 male 10-24, 1 male age <10, and 1 female age <10
- **NANCY COLE**, 1 male 24-36, 2 males age 10-24, and 2 males age <10
- Pleasant Coles, family, 0 slaves, and 2 FN males age 10-24

1840 FEDERAL CENSUS, LDS Film No. 0029691

The 1840 census for Pittsylvania County shows 101 white families on whose property there were Free Negroes living, and 78 Free Negro heads of household. Only one Free Negro who had been head of a racially diverse household in

1830 was still living in Pittsylvania County, and the composition of his household had changed. A different, but equally interesting item found in this census was a household headed by a white female with no slaves, in which a Free Negro male, aged 100+, was residing. Research in various records may uncover the reason for this rather unusual arrangement. The pertinent section has been underlined in the following transcription.

101st REGT

Page 66
-Robert S. Burt, family + slaves, and 1 FN male age 10-24
-John Giles, family + 1 slave, and 3 FNs 1 female age
    24-36, 1 male 10-24, and 1 female age <10
Page 68
-Polley Austin, family, 0 slaves, and 2 FNs a female age 24-
    36 and a male <10
Page 69
-Henry Arno, family + slaves, and 1 FN female age <10
Page 70
-Jamison Adkins, family + slaves, and 1 FN male age 10-24
Page 72
-Vincent Witcher, family + slaves, and 2 FNs 1 female age
    24-36 and 1 female age <10
Page 73
-Corns Layhorn, family, 0 slaves,and 1 FN male age 10-24
-Samuel Cryder, family + slaves, and 1 FN male age <10
Page 76
-John Barber, family, 0 slaves, and 3 FN males, all age <10
-Christr Wright, family + slaves, and 1 FN male age <10
Page 80
-Sally Pemberton, family, 0 slaves, and 1 FN female age <10
Page 82
-Geo Parker, family + slaves, and 5 FNs: 1 female 24-36, 1
    male 10-24, 2 females age <10 and 1 male age <10
Page 83
-Joseph Barber, family, 0 slaves, and 1 male FN age 24-36
Page 84
-Charles Hailey, family + slaves, and 1 female FN age 10-24

Page 86
- Charles Lovelace, family + slaves, and 3 FNs: 1 female 24-36, 1 female 10-24, and 1 male age 10-24
- Robert Findley, family, 0 slaves, and 2 FNs, 1 male 10-24, 1 female age <10
- Wm Ferguson, family, 0 slaves, and 3 FNs: 1 female 24-36, 1 female <10, 1 male <10
- Wm A Anthony, family + slaves, and 1 male FN age 36-55

Page 87
- Betsey Keeling, 1 white female, 0 slaves, 4 FNs: 1 female age 24-36, 1 female age 10-24, 2 females age <10
- James Walton, family, 0 slaves, and 1 male FN age <10

Page 89
- **JAMES GOING 1 male age 36-55, & 1 female age 36-55**
- **BURWELL GOING 1 male 36-55, 1 female 24-36, 1 male age <10, and 2 females age <10**

Page 91
- Bynum Lacy, family, 0 slaves, and 2 male FNs <10

Page 92
- John Wilson, family + slaves, and 1 male FN age 36-55

Page 93
- Wm McHainey, family with slaves, and 1 male FN 10-24

Page 94
- Ezekeil Dews (?), family + slaves, and 2 FNs: 1 male age 10-24, and 1 male <10
- **SALLEY DAVIS 1 female 24-36, 1 female age <10, and 2 males <10**
- Samuel Worsham, family, 0 slaves, 1 FN female age 10-24

Page 96
- John Hailey, family + slaves, and 7 FNs: 1 male 10-24, 2 females 10-24, and 4 males age <10
- **REBECCA DAVIS 1 female 36-55 and 1 female 10-24**
- John Miller, 1 white male, slaves, and 2 FNs: 1 female age 24-36, and 1 male age <10
- Edw Elsmith, family, 0 slaves, and 2 FNS: 1 female age 24-36 and 1 male age <10

Page 97
- Edw Atkinson, family, no slaves, and 1 female FN age 10-24
- Young Shelton, living on same property, 0 slaves, and 1 male FN age 10-24

-John Butcher, living on same property, 0 slaves, and 1 female FN 10-24

Page 98

-JUDY STAR 1 female 36-55, 1 female age 10-24, 1 female age <10 and 1 male age <10

-Joseph Mays, family, 0 slaves, and 2 FNs: 1female age 24-36, 1female <10

-Polley Wilson, 2 white females, slaves, and 6 FNs: 1 male 36-55, 1 female 10-24, 2 females <10 and 2 males <10

-Samuel Shelton, family + slaves, and 1 male FN age 24-36

Page 99

-Joseph Meador, family, 0 slaves, and 3 FNs: 1 female 24-36, 1 female <10, and 1 male <10

-Lynch Dillard, family + slaves, and 1 male FN age 55-100

Page 101

-John L White, 1 white male, slaves, and 3 FNs: 1 male 10-24, 1 female 10-24, and 1 male <10

-WILLIAM FRY 1 male 36-55, 1 male 24-36, 1 male <10

-George Fackley (?), family, 0 slaves, 1 FN male age 10-24

Page 102

-Wm Payne, family + slaves, and 1 male FN 10-24

Page 103

-POLLY REYNOLDS, 1 female 36-55, 2 females 24-36, 1 male 24-36, 3 females 10-24, 5 males <10, and 2 females age <10

-BURTON REYNOLDS 1 male 55-100, 1 female 55-100, 1 male 36-55, 1 female age 36-55, and 1 female age 10-24

-KIPSEY REYNOLDS 1 female 55-100, 2 females age 10-24, and 2 males <10

-David Clark, family + slaves, and 1 male FN 24-36

Page 106

-John Coles, family + slaves, and 1 male FN 36-55

-Jacob Coles, family + slaves, and 1 male FN 24-36

Page 112

-LUCINDA GEE 1 female age 24-36, 1 female <10, and 3 males age <10

Page 114
-RAMSEY BURNETT, 1 male 10-24, 1 female age 10-24,
    1 male <10, and 1 female 55-100
-JESSE BARKER, living on the same property, 1 male
    55-100, 1 female 24-36, and 1 female age <10
-DORCAS BURNETT, living on same property, 1 female
    age 24-36 and 2 males <10

Page 120
-Charles Keen, family + slaves, and 1 male FN age <10
-Walter Fitzgerald, family + slaves, and 1 male FN age 10-24
-John Keen, family + slaves, and 1 male FN age 24-36

Page 121
-John Blair, family + slaves, and 2 FNs: 1male 24-36 and 1
    female 10-24
-Nancy Terry, family, 0 slaves, and 1 male FN age 10-24
-SALLY JONES 1 female age 10-24, 2 males age <10 and
    1 female age <10
-Wm Newton, family + slaves, and 1 male FN age 10-24

Page 122
-GEORGE BARKER, 1 male 24-36, 1 female 24-36, 1
    female 10-24, 2 females <10, 3 males <10
-JAMES JENKINS, 1 male 24-36, 1 female 36-55, 1 male
    10-24, 2 females 10-24, 3 males <10, and 4 females
    age <10
-Matthew Deason, family, 0 slaves, and 1 FN male age <10

Page 123
-AMY VALENTINE, 1 female 55-100, 2 females 24-36, 2
    males 10-24, 2 females <10 and 1 male age <10
-Reuben Hall, family + 1 slave, and 1 FN male age 10-24

Page 124
-Aaron Herndon, family + slaves, and 4 FNs: 1 female 24-36,
    2 females <10 and 1 male age <10
-Edwin Beavers, family + slaves, and 1 FN male age 10-24

Page 125
-JIM TOOMS, 1 male 36-55, 1 female 36-55, 1 fem 10-24
-JOHN JACKSON, 1 male 36-55, 1 female 24-36, 1 male
    10-24, 2 females <10, and 1 male age <10
-CLEM BOWMAN, 1 male 24-36, 1 female 10-24, and 3
    females age <10
-Thomas Wilson, family, 0 slaves, and 1male FN age 10-24

Page 126
-Residents of the County Poorhouse: 5 slaves and 3 female
    FNs age <10
Page 127
-Arthur Baugh, family + slaves, and 1 male FN age 10-24
Page 128
-William Davis, family, 0 slaves, and 1 male FN age 36-55
-Betsy Logan, family, 0 slaves, 2 female FNs both age 10-24
-John Bennett Jr, family + slaves, and 1 male FN age 24-36
Page 129
-BOOKER HENDRICK, 1 male 24-36, 1 female 24-36, 1
    male age 10-24, and 3 males <10
-JOHN MASON, 1 male 36-55 and 1 female age 55-100
Page 130
-Nathl P. Thomas,Plantation, 22 slaves; 1 FN male age 36-55
-John Roe, 1 white male, 0 slaves, and 1 FN male age 55-100
Page 131
-ISAAC JACKSON, 1 male 10-24, 1 female 10-24, 1
    female 24-36, 2 males <10 and 1 female age<10
-SAM BOWMAN, 1 male 36-55, 1 female age 24-36, 2
    females 10-24, 1 male <10 and 2 females age <10
Page 132
-CHARLES ROBINSON, 1 male 36-55, 1 female 24-36, 2
    females 10-24, 1 male 10-24, and 3 females <10
-Aron Blair, family, 0 slaves, and 1 FN female 10-24
-Washington Pass, family + slaves and 1 FN male age <10
Page 133
-John Travis, family, 0 slaves, and 1 FN female age 10-24

TOWN OF DANVILLE

Page 134
-Robert Johnson, family + slaves and 2 FNs, 1 female 24-36
    and 1 male 10-24
-Thomas D. Neal, family + slaves and 1 FN female age 36-55
-John Watson, family, 0 slaves, 4 FNs: 1 female 36-55, 1
    female 24-36, and 2 males age <10
-John Pennell, family + slaves, and 1 FN male age 24-36
-RICHARD JUMPER, 2 males 24-36, 2 females 10-24

Page 135
- Robert Linn, family, 0 slaves, and 2 FNs: 1 female 55-100 and 1 female age 10-24
- DAVID LEWIS, 1 male 36-55, 1 female age 24-36, 2 females 10-24, and 2 males age <10
- HALL REYNOLDS, 1 male 24-36, 1 female 24-36, 1 female 10-24, 1 male <10, and 2 females <10
- Thompson Coleman, family + slaves, 1 FN a female age <10

Page 136
- JANE REYNOLS, 1 female 24-36, 1 female age 10-24, and 3 females <10
- DAVID REYNOLS, 1 male 24-36, 1 female age 24-36
- JEFF EDWARDS, 1 male 24-36, 1 female 24-36, 1 male age <10, and 1 female <10
- PATSY PARR, 1 male 24-36, 1 female age 24-36, 1 male age <10 and 1 female <10
- SAM JONES, 1 male 24-36, 1 female 24-36, 1 female <10
- SUSAN GARNES, 1 female 24-36, 1 male 10-24, and 2 females age <10
- RICKY REYNOLS, 1 male 24-36, 1 female 36-55, 1 female 10-24, and 1 female age <10
- POLLY DAVIS, 1 female 24-36, 2 females age <10, and 1 male age <10
- SAM RICHARDSON, 1 male 24-36, 1 female age 24-36, and 2 females age <10
- BOB COUSINS, 1 male 36-55, 1 female age 36-55, 1 female 24-36, and 1 female age 10-24
- LETHA FLAGG, 1 female 36-55, 1 male 24-36, 1 female 24-36, 1 female 10-24
- MADISON REYNOLS, 1 male 24-36, 1 female 24-36, 1 female 10-24, and 1 female age <10

Page 137
- GRIEF HARRIS, 1 male 24-36, 1 female 24-36, 1 male 10-24, 1 female 10-24, 3 males age <10, and 2 females <10
- GODFREY RICHARDSON, 2 males 24-36, 2 females 24-36, and 3 females <10
- BRANTON REYNOLS, 1 male 24-36, 1 female 24-36, 1 female 10-24, 1 male <10 and 1 female age<10

-WILEY MITCHELL, 1 male 24-36, 1 female 24-36, 1 female 10-24, and 1 female <10
-WILLIAM GARNES, 2 males 10-24, and 2 females age 24-36
-STEPHEN WOODSON, 1 male 36-55, 1 female 36-55
-JOHN GARNES, 1 male 36-55, 1 female 36-55, 4 females 10-24, and 1 male age <10
-DAVID ELLIS, 1 male 25-36, and 1 female age 10-24
-LINDSAY WILLIAMS, 2 males 24-36, 1 female age 10-24, and 1 male <10
-GILBERT DICKINSON, 1 male 36-55, 1 male age 24-36
-JOHN PATTERSON, 1 male 24-36, 1 male age 10-24
-GEORGE HEWLET, 1 male 24-36, and 1 female 24-36
-James M Williams, family + slaves, and 4 FNs, 2 females 10-24 and 2 males <10
-Ellick McKnight, family + slaves, and 3 FNs, 1 male 10-24, 1 female 10-24, and 1 female 55-100

Page 138
-Byrd Smith, family + slaves, and 4 FNs, 2 males 36-55, 1 female 10-24, 1 male age <10
-Wiley Williams, family + slaves, and 1 FN female age 10-24
-ROBERT MASON, 1 male 24-36, 1 female 24-36, and 1 male <10

END OF DANVILLE

Page 138
-WILLY STEPHENS, 1 female 36-55, 4 females 10-24, and 1 male <10
Page 139
-Samuel Meadors, family + slaves, and 1 FN a male age <10
-John M Atkinson, family + slaves, and 1 FN male age 10-24
Page 140
-JACK HENDRICK, 1 male 24-36, 3 females age 24-36, 1 female 10-24, 5 females <10, and 2 males <10
-SAM HENDRICK, 1 male 24-36, 1 female 36-55, 1 female 10-24, 4 females <10, 1 male <10
-BOB COLES, 2 males 24-36, 1 female age 10-24, and 1 female <10
-Alexander Walters, family + slaves, 3 FN males age 10-24

-NANCY VALENTINE, 1 female 55-100, 1 male 10-24, 1 female 10-24, 2 females <10, and 1 male age <10

Page 141
-Charles Dodson, family + slaves, and 1 FN male age 36-55
-Daniel Sladen, family, 0 slaves, and 2 FNs 1 female 10-24 and 1 male <10
-JANE COLE, 1 female 10-24, 1 female <10, and 1 male age <10
-John Wills, family + slaves, and 3 FNs: 1 male 10-24 and 2 males age <10

Page 142
-NED GOINS, 1 male 55-100, 1 female age 36-55, and 3 males age 10-24
-William Hardy, family + slaves, and 1 FN, a male 10-24
-Elizabeth Bryant, white females, 0 slaves, and 1 FN female age 10-24
-John C Cabiness ?, family + slaves, and 1 FN male age <10
-DAVID STAMP, 1 male 55-100, 1 female 36-55, and 1 female age 24-36
-RICE DANIEL, 1 male 36-55, and 1 female age 24-36
-BOB LOGAN, 1 male 55-100, and 1 female 55-100
-AFFY MAHO, 1 male 24-36, 1 female 24-36, and 1 female age <10
-DEBBY WILEY, 1 female 36-55, 5 males 10-24, and 2 females 10-24, 3 males <10, and 1 female <10

Page 143
-John Arnett, family, 0 slaves, and 2 FNs, 1 male 24-36 and 1 female age 10-24
-DICK DURAITH, 1 male 55-100 living alone
-WILL LIGANS, 1 male 36-55, 1 female age 24-36, 1 female 10-24, and 1 male age <10
-William Norman, family + slaves, and 2 FNs 1 male 10-24 and 1 female 10-24

Page 144
-SAM BEACH, 1 male 55-100, and 1 female age 24-36, 1 female 10-24, 1 male <10, and 1 female <10
-JOSHUA BANKS, 1 male 36-55, 1 female 24-36, 1 female 10-24, 1 male <10, and 1 female <10

-Polly Tate, family with no slaves, **1 FN male age 100+**

-JOE BEACH, 1 male 24-36, 1 female 36-55, 2 males 10-24, 1 female <10, and 1 male <10
Page 145
-Spencer Vaughan, family, 0 slaves, 1 FN a female age <10
-Wm Jackson, family + slaves, and 1 FN, a male age 10-24
-John Carmichael, family, 0 slaves, 1 FN a female age 10-24
-Sutherland Booth, family + 1 slave, and 1 FN male age <10
-JESSE MASON, 1 male 36-55, and 1 female 36-55
-CUFFE MAYO, 1 male 36-55, 1 female 24-36, 3 females age 10-24, and 1 female age <10
Page 146
-JAMES SCANTLISH, 1 male 55-100, 1 female age 36-55, 1 male 24-36, 1 female 24-36, 1 female 10-24, and 3 females age <10
Page 147
-Humphrey Dodson, family, 0 slaves, 1 FN female age 10-24
-Giles Ford, family, 0 slaves, and 2 FNs: 1 female age 10-24 and 1 female <10
-Stephen Dodson, family + slaves, and 1 FN male age 10-24
Page 148
-PHILLIS STEVENS, 1 female 24-36, 1 male <10 and 2 females age <10
-SILVY CRANE, 1 female 24-36, 1 male age 10-24 and 2 females age <10
-Charles McLaughlin, family + slaves, 1 FN male age 10-24
-George Dodson, family, 0 slaves, and 1 FN, a male age <10
-James Mays, family, 0 slaves, and 1 FN, a male age 36-55
Page 149
-SAMUEL DANIEL, 1 male 24-36, 1 female 24-36, 1 male 10-24, and 4 females age <10
-Larkin Ingram, family, 0 slaves, and 2 FNs, 1male 10-24 and 1 female 10-24
-CHARITY STEPHENS, 1 female 24-36, 1 male age 10-24, 2 females <10, and 1 male <10
Page 150
-Martha Terry, family + slaves, and 1 FN, a male age 10-24
-Henry Sikes, family, 0 slaves, and 1 FN a female age 24-36
Page 152
-John Power, family + slaves, and 2 FNs, a male <10 and a female age <10

Page 153
- Wm Plunket, family + slaves, and 6 FNs, 1 female 24-36, 1 male 10-24, 1 female 10-24, 2 males age <10 and 1 female age <10
- Wm Farmer, family + slaves, and 1 FN, a male age 10-24
- Henry Coleman, family, 0 slaves, and 1 FN a female age <10
- **ESTER DAY, 1 female 24-36, 1 female age 10-24 and 2 females age <10**

APPENDIX A

Slaves of John Ward, Sr.

John Ward, Sr., is known for having emancipated the largest number of slaves at any one time in Pittsylvania county. Known as John Ward "of Sulphur Springs", and "John Ward Senior" to distinguish him from other family members named John, he was the son of Major John Ward and his wife Anne Chiles of Campbell county. The Ward family owned much property in several counties, and was well connected through intermarriage and business dealings with other important families throughout the area. Their holdings included Ward's Road and Ward's Ferry, and interests in a Toll Bridge. John Ward, Sr. does not appear to have married or had children, and left his considerable estate primarily to his nephews and other relatives.

The names and descriptions of Ward's 136 former slaves are given in the Register, and are numbered as Registers No. 70 through No. 204. Researchers are fortunate that this is the case, since few of Ward's slaves were mentioned by name in his Will.

As listed in the Register, only 38 of Ward's slaves were using the surname Ward at the time of their emancipation. It will be seen in the transcription below that slaves over age 15 were bequeathed a sum of money ($20). Ward's favorite slaves were given larger sums of money ($150), certain slaves were bequeathed property, and a request was made that they be allowed to remain in the state of Virginia.

Will of John Ward, Sr., Pittsylvania County
Probated 20 Nov 1826   WB1, pages 109-112

I John Ward, Sr., of the county of Pittsylvania and state of Virginia, being in a low state of health but of sound mind and disposing memory do make this my last will and testament, in manner & form following: to wit-

I give to John Smith, Ralph Smith, Sallie Leftwich and Paulina Clayton each the sum of three hundred dollars. I give to the children of Elizabeth Leftwich, deceased, formerly Elizabeth Smith, three hundred dollars to be equally divided between them.

Item, I give to the children of Mildred Jones, deceased, formerly Mildred Smith, three hundred dollars to be equally divided between them.

I give to Matilda, Sally and Dosha Callaway the sum of three hundred dollars each.

I give to Seth Barber the tract of land of mine called Mayhew's old tract and the tract I bought of Shadrach Mustain and the tract I bought of Thomas Hutson adjoining thereto.

I give to Carter Barber my tract of land on Beech Tree Creek whereon James Lester now lives.

I give to John Dillard the sum of twelve hundred dollars out of my estate to be paid to him by his brother Lynch Dillard at such times and in such sums s the said Lynch Dillard in his judgment may think best, having regard to his necessities. The said $1200 to be paid out of my estate & not to be a charge upon the said Lynch Dillard separately.

I give to my nephew Robert A. Ward the full amount of what he is now due me, and it is my will and desire that he have no more of my estate of any sort. But should the said Robert A. Ward make any demand of my executors as a creditor of mine, then in that event I give him no part of my estate.

I give to Matilda Adams, Lucinda Rutledge, Julian Barber, Henrietta Barber, John Barber, William Barber, Robert Barber, and Jeremiah Edwin Barber, children of Patsy Barber, all my interest or estate in the Toll Bridge across Staunton River.

It is my will and desire that all my slaves now living or which may be living at the time of my death be free, and I do hereby bequeath to each and every one of them their freedom immediately upon my death in as full and unlimited a manner as the laws of Virginia will admit of. But should any of my slaves choose not to avail themselves of this bequest of their freedom with the conditions which the law may annex, then it is my will and desire that they have the privilege of choosing their master, who may take them at the valuation of two good men to be chosen by my executors, and should the females thus electing choose to keep any of their children with; it is my will that said children be at liberty to obtain their freedom at the age of 21 in the same manner.

It is my wish and particular desire that in consideration of the general good conduct of my slaves **DAVY** and his sister **NANCY** (of which I hereby [left blank] testimony) that they should be permitted, together with the children of said NANCY to remain in the state of Virginia, hereby meaning DAVY & NANCY, the children of old **MOLLEY**. I give to the said DAVY & NANCY the sum of one hundred and fifty dollars. I also give them, equally to be divided, my tract of land I first bought of Henry Pickral containing about three hundred acres.

I give to four old slaves, **WILL, SAM, NED & BEN**, the land I bought of Cook's estate.

I give to all my slaves over 15 years of age at the time of my death, the sum of twenty dollars (excepting Davy and Nancy, having already given them $150 each).

I give to my above named favorite servants Davy & Nancy each a horse worth $40 and each two cows.

I give to my nephew, John Ward, Jr., all my tract of land lying in Campbell County and Staunton River at Cherleses (?) ford, supposed to be between twelve and sixteen hundred acres. I also give to my said nephew, John Ward, all my tract of land lying on the James River in the county of Amherst just above Lynchburg, supposed to be between seven hundred fifty and eight hundred acres. I also give to my said nephew, John Ward, all my tract of land lying in the county of Pittsylvania on Pigg River and Frying Pan Creek which I bought of Walter Coles, supposed to be between six and seven hundred acres.

I give to my nephew, Lynch Dillard, all my tract or tracts of land lying in Campbell County on Staunton River at the Pockett, supposed to be fourteen hundred twenty-four acres. I also give my said nephew, Lynch Dillard, all my tract or tracts of land lyng in Pittsylvania on Straightstone Creek, whereon I formerly lived, supposed to contain between fifteen hundred and two thousand acres.I also give to my said nephew, Lynch Dillard, my tract of land lying in the lower end of Pittsylvania, lying near to or adjoining the lands of George West and others, supposed to be between three and five hundred acres. I also give to my said nephew, Lynch Dillard, my tract of land called Frank Smith's place & all my lands adjoining that tract on Sycamore Creek, supposed to be between five hundred and one thousand acres.

After the payment of all my just debts and the pecuniary bequests herein mentioned & devised, I give all the rest and residue of my estate and property both real and personal of every sort and description whatever nor herein disposed of to my two nephews, John Ward, Jr., & Lynch Dillard.

Not meaning to die intestate as to any part of my estate whatever, I appoint my nephews, John Ward, Jr., & Lynch Dillard, my executors to this my last will and testament, hereby revoking all wills by me heretofore made.

In witness whereof, I have hereunto set my hand and seal this 30th day of July in the year of Christ 1826.

Witness: Abraham Chilton, Crispen Dickenson and Peter H. Clark
Presented for probate, securities bond of $50,000 by George Townes, Abraham Chilton and Edward Franklin

[In Clement's book, History of Pittsylvania County Virginia (page 227), it is stated that 70 of Ward's freed slaves were resettled in Lawrence county, Ohio. One wonders not only how they were transported, but when they left, which of them went, and which may have elected to go elsewhere. What happened in their lives as a result?

Pittsylvania Court Records 1823-1827, LDS film no. 33,316, tells us that **NANCY, DAVID, GEORGE** and **JOSEPH WARD** were not allowed to stay in Virginia. In November 1826, a motion was made by the newly emancipated slaves for permission to be allowed to remain. Despite being summoned to hear the motion in January 1827, a majority of the Justices did not appear, and the hearing was continued. At the March 1827 hearing, several members of the Court opposed the application, and the necessary permission was not granted. Where did NANCY, DAVID, GEORGE and JOSEPH WARD go, and what happened to the land that John Ward, Sr. wanted them to have?

No attempt was made to trace **WILL, SAM, NED** or **BEN**, or the land that John Ward, Sr. bequeathed to them.]

APPENDIX B

Sample Court Orders

Court records hold a vast amount of information about the quality of life in Pittsylvania County, and make wonderful reading! The information varies from year to year, and the language is stilted, dry and to the point. Handwriting varies from tiny and cramped, to open and looping, often with many curlicues making it hard to decipher. The ink may have bled through from the reverse side of the page, or may have faded. The page may have suffered a spill onto it. This author highly recommends that students of history look for their ancestors in Court Orders and Minutes.

A cursory pass through the Pittsylvania County Court Orders indicated several items of importance regarding Free Negroes. Occasionally children of different surnames were mentioned in the same Order, but were not all listed in the Index. Family relationships were occasionally given in Orders that identified the siblings or children of those Free Negroes who had registered. A large number of Free Negro children were found to have been bound out whose later Registers gave no indication of them ever being apprenticed to anyone. There were also Orders rescinding their apprenticeships from certain masters, and binding them out anew. Orders relating to Free Negroes who had never registered were seen. A few registrations were certified correct in Orders but were not found in the Register.

Apparently the Registration number was to be given and the data entered into the Register book shortly after a Court hearing. In some cases, it will be seen that the entry was not made in the Register until several years later. In other cases, there does not seem to have been a Court hearing at all. Whatever may have been the procedure, it was not carried out in a consistent manner.

In addition to the potpourri of day-to-day living and conflicts that resulted in Court actions against free persons, there were also lawsuits which involved slaves and named their owners. There were trials of slaves accused of crimes; actions to exempt owners from paying taxes on certain slaves; suits against whites for attempting to steal slaves; and actions against whites for holding as slaves Free Negroes who had been born free.

It is sometimes difficult to determine the ethnicity of an individual in the Court Orders as race was not consistently noted, particularly in the early records. It would be highly inaccurate to assume that any child bound out by the Overseers of the Poor was African American unless the Order specifically states this to be a fact. Often the designation "person of colour" is used. It would be well to note that there were many white "orphans" and "bastards" who were bound out to prevent their becoming a public burden. Some may have had the same surnames as Free Negroes. Obviously such data need very careful study.

The following examples from the Court Orders are intended to whet the appetites of researchers of African-American history in Pittsylvania County.

Orders, Vols. 19-23 1818-1823   LDS Film No. 33315

Vol. 19, page 141, August Court 1818   It is Ord to be Certo that the registers of **JAMES, PHILLIS & JENNY** Negroes emancipated by the Will of Jno Worsham Decd are correctly taken-

Vol. 20, page 58, May Court 1819   It is Ord That the overseers of the Poor of this County do bind out **JENNEY REYNOLDS** a bastard Child of **KEZIAH REYNOLDS** a free woman of Colour to George Robinson Sen according to Law.

Vol. 21, page 97,   Court 1820,   It appearing to the satisfaction of the Court that Burgess Riddle to whom were bound by the overseer of the Poor of this County 2 bastard Children **ESTHER [DAY]** and **MARIA DAY** hath removed from this County and that previous to his removal he had sold the term of the sd Children's apprenticeships to John Tompkins and Wm Riddle. It is and that the Indentures of apprenticeship by which the sd Children were bound be Cancelled.

Vol. 21, page 200, June Court 1820   It is Certified by the Court that the Register of **ALEXANDER CHAVERS (& DANIEL**

SCOTT [added above the line]) was Correctly taken by the Clerk of this Court. DANIEL SCOTT who was Committed to the Jail of this County for want of a copy of his Register when called upon, and being brought into Court and fully heard by Counsil. It is Considered by the Court that the said DANIEL SCOTT be discharged on paying of his prison fees and on failing to pay said fees, that he was bind and by the Sheriff forthwith for so long a time as shall be necessary to pay the said fees -

Vol. 22, page 159, May Court 1821   It is Ordered that the Overseer of the Poor of this County do bind out to Jesse Walton - **SAMUEL VALENTINE** and **LUCY VALENTINE** (free persons of Colour [added above the line in a different handwriting]) according to Law.

Vol. 23, page 234, January Court 1823   William Beach and Samuel Hunt came into Court and made Oath that **SAMUEL HENDRICK** a black man who served his time with Obadiah Ham is free born.

Orders, Vols. 24-27 1823-1824   LDS Film No. 33316

Vol. 25, page 147, November Court 1824   Obadiah Ham to whom two free boys of Colour to wit: **BOOKER HENDRICK** and **JOHN HENDRICK** were apprenticed, being decd, It is Ordered that the said BOOKER & JOHN be bound by the Overseer of the Poor of this County to William Fontaine.

Vol. 25, page 170, June Court 1825   It is Ordered that the Overseers of the Poor of this County do bind out **RANDOLPH SHELTON** a boy of Colour to Matthew Fitzgerald & **SANDY POUNDS** a boy of Colour to Samuel Beach & also bind out William Carver Son of Hyraim Carver accg to Law.

Vol. 26, page 41, June Court 1826 4th Day   It is Ordered that the Indenture of apprenticeship binding **RANDOLPH SMITH DAY** [the surname DAY was added above the line] a boy of Colour to Sion Hodges be recinded [sic].

Vol. 27, page 286, December Court 1828   For reasons appearing to the Court it is and that the Indenture for binding **PATRICK** a free bornd [sic] boy of Colour to Charles Bailey be transfered to Washington Shelton. [No surname was given, but this is probably PATRICK STAR.]

Orders, Vols. 28-30 1829-1833   LDS Film No. 33317

Vol. 31, Page 552, [date of Court not given]   This is to certify that I hereby renounce the idea of Standing any further Contest in the [illegible] suitz [sic] of **MILLEY CHAVIS** against me and also of the Suit of **HANNAH CHAVIS** and others against me and hereby request the Clerk of Pittsylvania to Enter Judgments in their favor and I also declare that I never did directly or indirectly put or place the two paupers viz **ENOCK [CHAVIS]** and **RHODA [CHAVIS]** in the possession of James Riggins of Lynchburg as [illegible]. I have hereunto set my hand this fifth day of March 1830. Teste James Arthur (Seal) Edward Carter, J.H. Echols, James Echols

At a Court continued and held for Pittsylvania County the 16th day of March 1830 This writing from James Arthur to MILLEY CHAVIS & others was proved by two of the subscribing witnesses to be the act and deed of the said Arthur and Ordered to be recorded.   Teste   Will Tunstall ClC

APPENDIX C

Volume of Registrations/Renewals By Year

As previously stated, there has been no Register yet located which covers the period between 1 January 1794, when such law took effect, until 16 March 1807, when the first registration in the extant Register was recorded.

The following chart, showing the year and number of registrations, points out the many gaps in time when few, if any, Free Negroes were registered. In other years, there is a substantial increase in the number of registrations. The best example of this is 1827, when John Ward Senior's slaves were emancipated, adding 136 registrations to the total for that year. It should also be noted that the registrations for 1865 cover only the month of January. On average, there were approximately five registrations and/or renewals during a usual year.

A study of Pittsylvania County history during those periods when registration was particularly sparse may prove quite helpful in understanding these annual fluctuations.

1807 - 1	1825 - 8	1839 - 9	1853 - 19
1810 - 3	1826 - 8	1840 - 8	1854 - 10
1812 - 2	1827 - 144	1841 - 9	1855 - 3
1813 - 1	1828 - 14	1842 - 5	1856 - 7
1815 - 1	1829 - 3	1843 - 6	1857 - 28
1816 - 7	1830 - 6	1844 - 7	1858 - 23
1817 - 6	1831 - 38	1845 - 14	1859 - 12
1818 - 4	1832 - 13	1846 - 3	1860 - 17
1819 - 4	1833 - 15	1847 - 9	1861 - 4
1820 - 3	1834 - 5	1848 - 5	1862 - 13
1821 - 2	1835 - 9	1849 - 20	1863 - 23
1822 - 4	1836 - 9	1850 - 19	1864 - 16
1823 - 1	1837 - 14	1851 - 4	1865 - 1
1824 - 18	1838 - 54	1852 - 25	

APPENDIX D

Free Negroes, Originally Registered Elsewhere

Place	Person	Reg. in Pittsylv	Age
Albermarle	SCOTT, David	1861	55
Amelia	FLOOD, Alexander	1816	51
	FRY, Betsy (WILLIAMS)	1852	38
Brunswick	FLOOD, Levina	1816	48
Campbell	DAVIS, Charles	1851	24
	HARRAWAY, Jane	1838	29
Charlotte	HARRAWAY, Jim	1825	44
	HARRAWAY, Molley	1825	37
	HARRAWAY, Clem	1838	31
	JACKSON, Samuel B.	1833	23
	LAURENCE, Berry	1817	50
	MORGAN, Dick	1849	32
	RICHARDSON, John	1832	25
	YOUNG, Chesley	1825	23
Chesterfield	SMITH, Robert	1839	19
	SMITH, Thomas	1839	24
Cumberland	SHORT, Samuel	1832/5	34
Franklin	CHAVERS, Benjamin	1826	50
Halifax	BOWMAN, Edda	1853	46
	BOWMAN, Milton	1854	22
	COUSINS, Mary	1863	42
	DAVIS, James	1862	28
	FISHNECK, Jonah	1831	52
	FREEMAN, Daniel	1847	35
	GOOD, Parmelia	1862	23
	HOOD, Mildred Jane	1853	19

Halifax (Cont.)	HOOD, Jane	1853	41
	JACKSON, John	1853	22
	MAYHO, Martha	1862	40
	REDMON, Richard	1829	42
	VALENTINE, Angeline Green	1850	25
	WALLACE, Lucy	1859	45
	WALLACE, Mary	1859	20
	WALLACE, William	1859	21
Henrico	WILLIAMS, Lindsey W.	1839	25
Henry	HAILEY, Milly Ann	1859	24
Loudoun	(FREE NEGRO), Lue	1813	28
Lunenburg	COOPER, Claiborne	1852	14
	HAZLEWOOD, Green	1860	56
	HAZLEWOOD, Polly	1852	38
	VALENTINE, Nancy	1831	54
Lynchburg	COUSINS, Frank	1851	39
Mechlenburg	COOPER, Dugger	1853	18
	COOPER, Lathy	1853	12
	COOPER, Letty	1853	10
	COOPER, Nancy	1853	14
	DAVIS, Rebecca (MACKLIN)	1840	NG
	GARNES, Jane	1852	42
	GARNES, Jesse	1852	13
	GARNES, Mary Ann	1852	19
	GARNES, Quintina	1852	23
	JACKSON, Peyton	1854	34
Middlesex	ROBERTS, Henry	1832	25/35
Patrick	GOING, Norman	1862	25
Rockbridge	WALLS, Samuel	1840	37
Southampton	DENSON, James	1822	39

Spottsylvania	**COOK, James**	1860	33
Sussex	**BOOKER, Jesse**	1824	25
	OWEN, William	1820	38
	ROBINSON, Faithy	1831	50

APPENDIX E

Renewed Registrations

The following is a list of those persons who renewed their registrations, along with the dates renewed and Register Numbers used. Most Free Negroes did not renew, and for those who did, more than three years often elapsed between renewals.

In one case, designated by a question mark [?], there was difficulty in determining that the same person was involved. In a second such case, the registration states that it is a renewal; however, neither the previous date, county nor original registration number was given in the Register. In one case designated by an asterisk [*], either two parties have been confused by the Clerk, or their documents have been exchanged.

The following headings should be used in reading the list: Name, Original Register Number, Date of First Registration, New Number (if given at Renewal), Renewal Date(s), Number of Years Between Registrations.

BOOKER, Jesse - 38 - 17 May 1824 - same - 25 June 1831 - 7 yrs
? BOWMAN, Lucinda - 556 - 22 Sept 1859 - 56_ - May 1864 - 5 yrs
BURNETT, Reamy - 287- 19 Jan 1835 - same - 18 July 1842 - 7 yrs
CHAVERS, Alexander - 27 - 2 March 1819 - 31 - 20 June 1820 - 1 yr
COLE, Panthea - 235 - 26 May 1831 - same - 18 June 1838 - 7 yrs
COLE(S), Pleasant - 232 - 26 May 1831- same - 23 Dec 1858 - 27 yrs
COLE, Henry - 566 - 4 Apr 1860 - same - 17 Aug 1863 - 3 1/2 yrs
COLE, James - none given - 20 Aug 1851 - 505 - 12 June 1855 - 4 yrs
COUSINS, Jacob - 273 - 18 Mar 1833 - same - 10 June 1840 - 7 yrs
DAVIS, George (#2) - 452 - 24 Apr 1851 - 542/452 - 3 Dec 1858 - 7 yrs
DAVIS, James (#1) - 29- 17 Nov 1819- 39 - 5 June 1824 - 5 yrs
DAVIS, James (#2) - 456 - 16 Feb 1852 - same - 22 Oct 1861 - 9 yrs
DAVIS, James (#3) - 539 - 22 Apr 1858 - same - 22 Apr 1863 - 5 yrs
DAVIS, Mary - 369- 20 Sept 1841- same - 16 Oct 1848 - 7 yrs; and
    21 May 1860 - 12 yrs
DAVIS, Patty - 41- 7 June 1824 - same - 21 June 1831 - 7 yrs
DAVIS, Rebecca - 22 - 18 Nov 1817 - same - 17 Apr 1848 - 31 yrs
DOBSON, Dotia- 2 - 18 May 1810 - same - undated 1821/2 - 11/12 yrs
DENSON, James - 34 - 11 Sept 1822 - 59 - 19 Sept 1825 - 3 yrs;
    17 Nov 1828- 3 yrs; 7 Dec 1832 - 4 yrs; 15 Aug 1835 - 3 yrs

ELLIS, David - 323 - 18 June 1838 - same - 24 Aug 1843 - 5 yrs
GOING/GOIN, Burwell- 52 - 16 Nov 1824 - 209 - 17 Dec 1827- 3 yrs - 20 Dec 1830 - 3 yrs; 20 Jan 1834 - 4 yrs; 25 Sept 1857- 23 yrs
GOING/GOIN, James - 49 - 16 Nov 1824 - 211 - 20 Dec 1830 - 6 yrs; 20 Jan 1834 - 4 yrs; 11 Nov 1857- 23 yrs
GOING, John (#2) - 50 - 16 Nov 1824 - same - 21 Nov 1831 - 7 yrs
GOING, Polly - 51- 16 Nov 1824 - 208 - 17 Dec 1827 - 3 yrs
GOING, Thomas - 205 - 16 July 1827 - same - 1 Dec 1832 - 5 yrs; and 19 Sept 1836 - 4 yrs
GOING/GOIN, William- none given - 21 June 1830 - 285 - 20 Oct 1834- 4 yrs
GOINGS/GOINS, Parthenia - 551 - 9 Jan 1858 - same - 16 Feb 1864 - 5 yrs
HENDRICK, Booker - 69 - 18 Sept 1826 - same - 18 June 1849 - 23 yrs
HENDRICK, Letitia - 43- 8 June 1824- same- 18 June 1827- 3 yrs; and 18 June 1832 - 5 yrs
HENDRICK, Susannah - 47- 22 June 1824- same - 21 June 1831 - 7 yrs
HENDRICK(S), Samuel - 37- 23 Feb 1823 - same - May 1831 - 8 yrs; and 10 Oct 1864 - 33 yrs
JENKINS, James - 334 - 19 June 1838 - same - 20 Sept 1841 - 3 yrs
JENKINS, Susan - 335 - 19 June 1838 - same - 15 Nov 1841 - 3 yrs
MASON, George - 218 - 21 Jan 1828 - 494 - 22 Nov 1853 - 25 yrs
MASON, Louisa Jane - (formerly Louisa Jane REYNOLDS, now wife of Stephen MASON) 439 - 22 Aug 1850 - 506, included in a group - 18 Aug 1855 - 5 yrs
MASON, Lucinda - 244 as Lucy VALENTINE, unmarried- 20 May 1831- 224 - 16 July 1838 - 7 yrs; same - 24 Sept 1852- 14 yrs; and same - 20 Nov 1853 - 1 yr
MASON, Robert - 253 - 1 Oct 1831 - same - 16 July 1838 - 7 yrs; and 20 Nov 1853 - 15 yrs
MASON, Stephen - 217- 21 June 1828 - same - 15 Oct 1849 - 21 yrs
MAYO, Roann - 437- 22 Aug 1850 - 506, included in a group- 18 Aug 1855 - 5 yrs
MORGAN, Dick - 427- 18 Jun 1849 - same - 19 Sept 1854 - 6 yrs
NORRIS, Wm - 517- 10 July 1857 - same - 16 Feb 1864 - 7 yrs
REYNOLDS, Coleman - 331- 19 June 1838- same - 19 Nov 1849- 11 yrs
REYNOLDS, David - 329 - 19 June 1838 - same - 21 Dec 1840 - 2 yrs
REYNOLDS, Doctor - 274 - 18 Mar 1833 - 332 - 19 June 1838 - 5 yrs
? REYNOLDS, Elisha Sr.-19 Nov 1836- renewed at 291- no prior# given
REYNOLDS, Eliza - 346 - 22 Aug 1838 - same - 23 Dec 1858 - 20 yrs
REYNOLDS, Henry - 207 - 26 Oct 1827 - 315- 18 June 1838 - 10 1/2 yrs- same - 21 Dec 1840 - 2 1/2 yrs
REYNOLDS, Jubia (Juba)- 28- 17 Aug 1819- same - 22 Oct 1858 - 39 yrs

REYNOLDS, Leanna (Leana)- 438 - 22 Aug 1850 - 506, included in a group- 18 Aug 1855 - 5 yrs
REYNOLDS, Martha - 266 - 29 Aug 1832 - same - 21 June 1838 - 6 yrs
REYNOLDS, Panthea - 440 - 22 Aug 1850 - 506, included in a group - 18 Aug 1855 - 5 yrs
REYNOLDS, Winifred (Winny) - 220 - 10 Mar 1828 - 336 - 19 June 1838 - 10 yrs - same - 30 June 1852 - 14 yrs
RICHARDSON, John - 262 - 16 Apr 1832 - same - 16 Aug 1842 - 10 yrs; and 21 Dec 1860 - 18 yrs
RIVERS, George - 4 - 20 Dec 1810 - 44 - 21 June 1824 - 14 yrs; and 22 Nov 1831 - 7 yrs
RIVERS, Wyat - 8 - 19 June 1815 - 26 - 19 Oct 1818 - 3 yrs; and 18 June 1821 - 3 yrs; and 21 June 1824 - 3 yrs
ROBERTS, Henry - 266 - 17 Dec 1832 - same - 15 Nov 1835 - 3 yrs
ROBERTSON, Thomas- 362 -16 Sept 1839- same- 15 Sept 1843- 4 yrs
ROSS, Fanny (probably Fanny MASON, child of Mary MASON alias Mary ROSS) - 215 - 21 Jan 1828 - 394 - 18 Oct 1845 - 17 yrs - same - 17 July 1848 - 3 yrs
ROSS, Polly (probably Polly MASON, child of Mary MASON alias Mary ROSS) 214 - 21 Jan 1828 - 343 - 16 July 1838 - 10 1/2 yrs - same - 28 Nov 1860 - 22 yrs
ROSS, Wm (probably Wm MASON, child of Mary MASON alias Mary ROSS) - 216 - 21 Jan 1828 - 518 - 22 Aug 1857 - 29 yrs
SHORT, Samuel - 260 vacated - 21 Feb 1832 - 290 new - 19 Oct 1835- 3 yrs; and 16 Sept 1839 - 4 yrs
SOYARS, John - 376 - 21 June 1842 - same - 21 May 1860 - 18 yrs
STEPHENS, Agga - 67 - 20 June 1826 - same - 17 Feb 1845 - 19 yrs; and 23 Dec 1857 - 12 yrs
STEPHENS, Catherine - 530 - 23 Dec 1857 - 535 - 2 Sept 1862 - 5 yrs
STEPHENS, Catherine Robertson Jane - 448 - 30 Nov 1850 - 13 Apr 1857 - 7 yrs
STEPHENS, Henry - 387- 16 Sep 1844 - same - 19 March 1850 - 6 yrs
STEPHENS, Jordan Green - 461 - 21 July 1852 - 604 - 22 Apr 1863- 11 yrs
STEPHENS, Madola Mariah - 462 - 21 July 1852 - same - 2 Sept 1862- 10 yrs
STEPHENS, Martha Jane - 384 - 16 Sept 1844 - same - 7 Apr 1863 - 19 yrs
STEPHENS, Mary Ann - 385 - 16 Sept 1844 - same - 7 Apr 1863- 19 yrs
STEPHENS, Phillis - 66 - 20 June 1826 - same - 17 Feb 1845 - 19 yrs; and 30 June 1852 - 7 yrs
STEPHENS, Wilmoth - 65- 20 June 1826- same - 13 March 1834 - 8 yrs and 16 Sept 1844 - 10 yrs
STEVENS, Catherine - 530 dupl - 23 Dec 1857 - renumbered as 535 - 2 Sept 1862 - 5 yrs

STEVENS Elizabeth - (later married a **VALENTINE**) - 473 - 24 Sept 1852 - same - 22 Oct 1858 - 6 yrs - (also as **STEPHENS**)
STEVENS, Martha - 449 - 30 Nov 1850 - same - 24 Aug 1858 - 8 yrs
STEVENS, Parthenia - 460 - 21 July 1852 - same - 24 Aug 1858 - 6 yrs (also as **STEPHENS**)
STEVENS, Reuben -408 - 10 Aug 1847- same - 23 Dec 1857 - 10 yrs (also as **STEPHENS**)
VALENTINE, Peter - 345 - 22 Aug 1838 - same - 17 Dec 1849 - 11 yrs; and 24 Sept 1858 - 9 yrs
* **VALENTINE, Polly/Amy** - 240/241 - 26/30 May 1831 - same - then 22 Aug 1838 - 7 yrs
VALENTINE, Royal - 246 - 30 May 1831 - same - 22 Aug 1838 - 7 yrs
VALENTINE, Samuel - 243 - 30 May 1831 - same - 22 Aug 1838 - 7 yrs
VALENTINE, Slayton - 472 - 24 Sept 1852 - same - 22 Oct 1858 - 6 yrs
VALENTINE, Turner Abernathy - 441 - 22 Aug 1850 - 506, included in a group - 18 Aug 1855 - 5 yrs
WILEY, Debora - 9 - 18 March 1816 - same - 24 Sept 1852 - 36 yrs

INDEX

ADAMS, David, 53-5
[ADAMS], James, 54
ADAMS, Mary, 55
Adams, Matilda, 268
ADAMS, Milly, 54-6
Adams, Robert, 251
ADAMS, Sally, 55
Adkins, Jamison, 257
Alen, Polley, 232
Alen, William, 232
Aline, Armstead, 248
ALLEN, Caezar, 41
Allen, Julius, 254
Ansley, Ann, 227
Ansley, William, 2, 227
Ansley, Wm, 3
Anthony, Wm A., 252, 258
Armistead, John, 230
Arnett, John, 264
Arno, Henry, 257
Arthur, Anna, 246
Arthur, Fanny, 245-6
Arthur, James, 8, 245, 274
Arthur, John, 17
Arthur, Patsey, 245-6
Ashton, Joseph, 228
Aston, Francis, 245
Atkinson, Edw, 258
Atkinson, John M., 263
Atkinson, Wm, 249
Austin, Polley, 257

Bailey, Charles, 274
BANKS, Joshua, 264
Barber, Carter, 268
BARBER, Daniel, 194, 221
Barber, Henrietta, 268
Barber, Jeremiah Edwin, 268
Barber, John, 257, 268
Barber, Joseph, 257
Barber, Julian, 268
Barber, Patsy, 268
Barber, Robert, 268
Barber, Seth, 268
Barber, William, 268
BARKER, Anna S., 169

BARKER, George, 252, 260
BARKER, Green, 253
BARKER, Jesse, 260
BARKER, Mariah, 170
BARKER, Permelia, 169
Baugh, Arthur, 261
BEACH, Joe, 265
BEACH, Sam, 264
Beach, Samuel, 273
BEACH, Samuel, 255
Beach, William, 273
Beal, William, 10
Beavers, Edwin, 260
Beavers, William, 248
Bennett, John Jr., 261
Bennett, William, 8, 17
Benson, Selby, 240
BIBY, Martha Walls, 205
Blair, Aron, 261
Blair, James, 249
Blair, John, 260
Blair, Wm, 251
Blanks, Ingram, 226
Bobbitt, Charles W., 242
BOBBITT, George, 60
BOLLING, Eliza, 101
Bolling, James, 252
BOLLING, Royal, 100
BOOKER, Jesse, 10, 93, 235, 253, 278-9
Booth, Sutherland, 265
BOWMAN, Clem, 260
BOWMAN, Edda, 160, 276
BOWMAN, Francis, 174
BOWMAN, Henrietta, 160
BOWMAN, Hubbard, 252
BOWMAN, Lucinda, 194, 220-1, 279
BOWMAN, Milton, 166, 276
BOWMAN, Prissie, 222
BOWMAN, Robert, 209
BOWMAN, Sam, 261
BOWMAN, Sarah, 221
BROOKS, Holliday, 33
Bryant, Elizabeth, 264
BURNETT, Boling, 88

BURNETT, Bowlin, 215
BURNETT, Clem, 248
BURNETT, Clement, 138
BURNETT, Dorcas, 260
BURNETT,Elizabeth, 208
BURNETT, George, 177
BURNETT, George W., 211
BURNETT, James, 71
BURNETT, Julia Ann Dorcas, 174
BURNETT, Lucinda, 173
BURNETT, Nancy, 178
BURNETT, Polly, 209
BURNETT, Ramsey, 260
BURNETT, Reamy, 90, 122, 279
BURNETT, Samuel, 123, 204
BURNETT, Theny, 89
Burt, Robert S., 257
Burton, James, 251
Butcher, John, 259
Butcher, Mary, 253
BYBEE, Joseph, 99
BYRD, Robert, 9, 249

C[illegible], William, 243
Cabiness ?, John C., 264
Calhoun, John, 253
Callaway, Dosha, 268
Callaway, Francis, 65, 250
CALLAWAY, Jack, 40-1
[CALLAWAY], Letty, 40
[Callaway], Matilda, 268
CALLAWAY, Polly, 41
[Callaway], Sally, 268
Carmichael, John, 265
Carrol, Ethldred, 250
Carter, Edward, 2, 274
CARTER, Henry, 252
CARTER, Samuel, 159
Carver, Hyraim, 273
Carver, William, 273
Chambers, Allen, 229
CHAPIN, Unis, 250
Chaplin, Wm R., 70, 254
CHARLES, Faithy, 236
CHATTIN, Jane, 210

CHAVERS, Alexander, 6-7, 272, 279
CHAVERS, Benjamin, 18, 276
CHAVIS, Anna, 117
[CHAVIS], Enock, 274
[CHAVIS], Hannah, 246, 274
[CHAVIS], Mary Jane, 246
CHAVIS, Milley, 246, 274
CHAVIS, Milly, 8, 245
CHAVIS, Nancy, 245
[CHAVIS], Rhoda, 274
CHAVIS, Una, 17, 246
CHAVIS, William, 89
[CHAVIS], Winney, 246
Cheatham, Anna, 234
Chiles, Anne, 267
Chilton, Abraham, 270
Claiborne, Phil, 227
Clark, David, 259
Clark, Peter H., 270
Clayton, Paulina, 268
COLE, Elender, 74
COLE, Henderson, 131
COLE, Henry, 198, 216, 279
COLE, James, 150, 168, 279
COLE, Jane, 253, 264
COLE, Jincey, 75
COLE, Lucy, 74, 256
COLE, Mary Susan, 179
COLE, Nancy,73,131, 256
COLE, Narcissa Adaline, 102
COLE, Nathan, 139
COLE, Panthea, 74, 103, 279
COLE(S), Pleasant, 73, 191, 279
COLE, Polly, 97
COLE, Ritter, 72
COLE, Robin, 73
COLE, Sally, 165
COLE, William, 83
Coleman, Chloe, 248
Coleman, Daniel L., 240
Coleman, Henry, 266

Coleman, Thompson, 262
COLES, Bob, 263
Coles, Jacob, 259
Coles, John, 259
COLES, July Ann, 190
Coles, Pleasant, 256
Coles, Walter, 269
COLES, William, 190
Compton, Wm, 254
COOK, Delpha, 236, 252
Cook, Henry, 237
COOK, James, 203, 278
COOPER, Claiborne, 151, 277
COOPER, Dugger, 161, 277
COOPER, Lathy,162, 277
COOPER, Letty, 151, 162, 277
COOPER, Nancy,161,277
COOPER, Parthenia,159
COPAGE, Mary Ann, 107
Copejoy, Edwd, 249
County Poorhouse, 261
COUSINS, Bob, 262
COUSINS, Frank,150,277
COUSINS, Hezekiah, 253
COUSINS, Jacob, 86, 117, 279
COUSINS, Mary, 217,276
COUSINS, Milley, 78
COUSINS, Robert, 110
CRADDOCK, CoryAnn,30
CRADDOCK,Jefferson,29
CRADDOCK, John, 30
CRADDOCK, Lewis, 28-31
CRADDOCK, Lucy, 29
CRADDOCK, Martha, 29
CRADDOCK, Mary, 31
CRADDOCK, Mourning, 31
CRADDOCK, Permelia, 30
CRADDOCK,Winney, 28-31
CRANE, Benjamin O., 71
CRANE, Silvy, 265
Crane, Thos, 253
Cryder, Samuel, 257

DABNEY, Cato, 64
Dabney, Francis, 240
Dalton, Edward, 245
Dalton, Nancy, 245
DANIEL, Rice, 264
DANIEL, Samuel, 265
DAVIS, Albert, 130
DAVIS, Alfred, 130
DAVIS, Ann, 176
DAVIS, Rebecca (Becky), 5, 136
DAVIS, Benjamin, 184
[DAVIS], Catherine, 128, 144
DAVIS, Charles, 149, 164, 276
DAVIS, Charlotte, 221
DAVIS, Daniel, 170
DAVIS, Dice, 170
DAVIS, Elijah, 121
DAVIS, Eliza, 130
DAVIS, Elizabeth, 210
DAVIS, George, 138, 149, 189, 279
DAVIS, Giles, 20
DAVIS, Isaac, 167
DAVIS, James, 209, 223
DAVIS, James (#1), 7, 11, 279
DAVIS, James (#2), 151, 204, 279
DAVIS, James (#3), 183, 215, 279
DAVIS, James (#4), 196
DAVIS, James (#5), 276
DAVIS, James W., 154
DAVIS, Jane, 99, 137
DAVIS, Jeffrey, 11
DAVIS, John,118,192,219
DAVIS, Lucinda, 129
[DAVIS], Mariah, 144
DAVIS, Martha, 144, 207, 214
DAVIS, Mary, 120, 136, 199, 219, 279
Davis, Matthew, 226
DAVIS, Milly, 11, 128
DAVIS, Moses, 165
DAVIS, Nancy, 129
DAVIS, Patty, 11, 93, 279

DAVIS, Paulina, 210
[DAVIS], Philip, 144
DAVIS, Polly, 102, 262
DAVIS, Rebecca, 118,
  136, 258, 277, 279
DAVIS, Richard, 138
DAVIS, Salley, 258
DAVIS, Sarah, 183, 219
DAVIS, Susannah, 12
Davis, Thos., 249
Davis, William, 261
DAVIS, William, 129, 167
Dawson, Jonathon B., 7, 11,
  20, 248
DAY, Anderson, 72, 176
[DAY], Esther, 266, 272
DAY, Josiah, 132
DAY, Maria, 272
DAY, Nancy, 2, 244
DAY, Peggy, 97, 252
DAY, Randolph Smith,
  273
DAY, William, 179-80
Deason, Matthew, 260
DENSON, James (Jim),
  9, 17, 69, 84, 91, 277, 279
Dews ?, Ezekeil, 258
Dickenson, Crispen, 270
DICKINSON, Gilbert, 263
DiJennett, George, 252
Dillard, John, 268
Dillard, Lynch, 20-64, 251,
  259, 268-70
Dixon, William, 249, 256
Dixon, (Unknown), 245
DOBSON, Lucy Ann, 98
DODSON, Adaline, 211
Dodson, Charles, 264
DODSON /DOBSON,
  Dotia, 1, 9, 279
DODSON, Eliza, 79
DODSON, Emily, 125
Dodson, George, 265
Dodson, Humphrey, 265
Dodson, John, 229
DODSON, John, 193, 219
Dodson, Joseph, 237
DODSON, Lucindy, 156
Dodson, Stephen, 265
Dodson, William, 240

Dorson, Ann, 252
Douglas, Harrison, 251
Dove, Stephen, 252
DUDLEY, Aaron, 57
DUDLEY, Annica, 56
DUDLEY, George, 57
DUDLEY, Henry, 53-4,
  56-9
DUDLEY, Henry (Jr), 59
DUDLEY, Hundley, 58
DUDLEY, John, 58
DUDLEY, Lucy, 59
DUDLEY, Lusey, 56
DUDLEY, Mary, 57
DUDLEY, Sally, 54, 56-9
DUDLEY, Sam, 58
DUDLEY, Wm Green, 59
DUPUEY, Sally, 254
DURAITH, Dick, 264
DURHAM, Samuel, 87
Dyer, James, 69

Echols, J.H., 274
Echols, James, 246, 274
Echols, Moses, 8
Edwards, A.B., 256
Edwards, Daniel, 245
EDWARDS, Jeff, 262
Eggleston, Edmund, 229
Ellis, [illegible], 235
[Ellis], Bolin, 233-5
Ellis, Caleb, 10, 81, 233, 235
ELLIS, David, 103, 124,
  235, 263, 280
Ellis, Ira, 10, 66-7, 81, 233-
  4, 236, 248
[Ellis], Micajah, 234
[Ellis], Patty, 234
[Ellis], Wyatt, 234
Elsmith, Edw, 258
Estes, Dr. Jno H., 195-7

Fackley ?, George, 259
Fadely, Jacob, 2
FARMER, James, 33
Farmer, Wm, 266
Farmer, Wm W., 254
FELLS, James, 104
Fentross, William L., 15
Ferguson, Joseph, 249

Ferguson, Michael, 240
Ferguson, Wm, 251, 258
Findley, Robert, 255, 258
FISHNECK, Jonah(s), 79, 242-3, 256, 276
Fitzgerald, David, 255
Fitzgerald, Matthew, 273
Fitzgerald, Walter, 260
FLAG, Alexander, 104, 276
FLAG, Lethe, 248, 254
FLAGG, Lethe, 87, 262
FLOOD, Alexander, 3-4, 276
FLOOD, Charity, 4
FLOOD, Coleman, 3
FLOOD, Levina, 3-4, 276
FLOOD, Phura, 4
FLOOD, Sithe, 4
Fontaine, William, 273
Ford, Giles, 265
Fowler, John, 245
Fowler, Joseph, 18, 244
FOWLER, Robert, 17, 244
Franklin, Edward, 270
FREEMAN, Daniel, 134, 276
FREEMAN, John, 254
FREEMAN, Mason (Moses?), 255
FREEPORT, Baker, 254
FRIEND, Sarah, 81
FRY, Betsy, 158, 276
FRY, James, 197
FRY, William, 259
Fuqua, William A., 230

GAINES, Susan, 102
Gardner, George, 256
Gardner, Silvany, 256
GARNES, James, 162
GARNES, Jane, 153, 277
GARNES, Jesse, 157, 277
GARNES, John, 263
GARNES, Mary Ann, 156, 277
GARNES, Polly, 219
GARNES, Quintina, 156, 277
GARNES, Susan, 162, 262

GARNES, William, 263
GEE, Allin, 167
GEE, Burton, 197
GEE, Lucinda, 69, 259
GEE, Preston, 223
GEE, Walker, 217
GHEE, Townsend, 171
Giles, John, 257
Giles, John Jr., 251
GOIN, Eliza Ann, 175
GOIN, George R., 178
GOIN, Greenwood Turner, 175
GOIN, Permelia M., 193, 219
GOING, Betsy, 15
GOING/GOIN, Burwell, 14, 66, 72, 88, 177, 258 280
GOING, Elizabeth, 193, 220
GOING/GOIN, James, 13, 89, 92, 178, 251, 258,280
GOING, Jesse, 80
GOING/GOIN, John, 13, 65, 71, 89, 94, 251, 280
GOING, John (#2), 14
GOING, Mariah, 198
GOING, Mary, 216
GOING, Norman,205, 277
GOING, Polly, 14, 66, 280
GOING, Thomas, 65, 84, 95, 280
GOING/GOIN, William, 71, 89, 220, 280
GOINGS, Marshall, 137
GOINGS/GOINS, Parthenia, 192, 218, 280
GOINS, Ned, 264
Goldston, Joseph, 236
GOOD, Isabella, 160
GOOD, Susan Ann, 159
GOODE, Parmelia, 208
Grammer, J., 7
Graves, William, 241
GRAY, Elizabeth, 5
GREENHILL, John,31-2
GREENHILL, Sylva, 32
Gregg, Carril, 226
Grenup, Christifur, 227

Griggs, Peter, 256

Hailey, Charles, 257
Hailey, John, 258
HAILEY, Milly Ann, 194, 220, 277
Hairston, Robert, 248
Haley, Archd, 251
Haley, Francis, 252
Hall, Reuben, 253, 260
Ham, Obadiah, 20, 248, 273
Hammat, Geo, 2
Hardy, William, 264
Harper, George, 255
HARRAWAY, Clem, 112, 232-3, 276
Harraway, Eppaphroditus, 232
Harraway, George, 16, 112, 232
HARRAWAY, Jane, 112, 276
[HARRAWAY], Jim, 16, 232-3, 276
[HARRAWAY], Molley, 16, 232-3, 276
Harraway, Samuel, 232
HARRIS, Fanny, 152
HARRIS, Green, 132
HARRIS, Grief, 254, 262
HARRIS, James, 142
Harrison, William, 225-6
HAZLEWOOD, Green, 199, 277
HAZLEWOOD, Polly, 158, 277
HENDRICK, Betsey, 124
HENDRICK, Booker, 20, 140, 261, 273, 280
HENDRICK, Creacy, 12
HENDRICK, Jack, 263
HENDRICK, John, 97, 273
HENDRICK, Letitia, 11, 92, 94, 251, 280
HENDRICK, Sally, 124
HENDRICK, Sarah Ann, 214
HENDRICK, Susanna(h), 13, 93, 280

HENDRICK, Temperance, 98
HENDRICK, William, 97
HENDRICK(S), Samuel, 10, 77, 222, 254, 263, 273, 280
HENRY, Patsey, 52
Hereford, Francis, 228
Hereford, Robert, 228
Herndon, Aaron, 260
Herndon, George, 242
Herndon, Sarah, 18, 241
HEWLET, George, 263
Hobbs, Frederick, 226
Hobbs, Hubbard, 226
Hodges, James, 248
Hodges, Moses, 2, 244
HODGES, Ned, 60, 269-70
Hodges, Sion, 273
Holley, Wm, 253
Holt, Lucy, 255
HOOD, Charlotte, 201
HOOD, Jane, 163, 277
HOOD, Jesse, 172
HOOD, Mildred Jane, 163, 276
HOOD, Thomas, 172
Hunt, John, 252
Hunt, Samuel, 10, 273
Huse, Walter B., 255
Hutcherson, Nathan, 72
Hutson, Abel, 241
Hutson, Drury, 241
Hutson, Thomas, 268

Ingram, Larkin, 265
Insle, William, 228
Irby, David, 250

JACKSON, Isaac, 261
JACKSON, John, 160, 260, 277
JACKSON, Peyton, 165, 277
JACKSON, Samuel B., 88, 276
JACKSON, Vervain, 107
Jackson, Wm, 265
JEFFERSON, Anne, 225
Jeffreys, James, 253

JENKINS, Clement, 135
JENKINS, Elizabeth, 135
JENKINS, James, 106, 121, 260, 280
JENKINS, Martha, 134
JENKINS, Mary Jane, 121
JENKINS, Nancy, 135
JENKINS, Robert, 120
JENKINS, Sally Ann, 121
JENKINS, Susan, 106, 122, 280
JENKINS, William, 120
JENKINS, Wyatt, 120
Johns, Robert, 7-8
JOHNSON, Annaca, 50
JOHNSON, Benjamin, 25-6, 61-3, 269-70
JOHNSON, Benjamin[Jr], 26
JOHNSON, Charles, 52
JOHNSON, Charlotte, 62
JOHNSON, Dorcas, 62
JOHNSON, George, 50
JOHNSON, Gib, 63
JOHNSON, Jerry, 25
JOHNSON, Letitia, 99
JOHNSON, Matilda, 61-3
JOHNSON, Moses, 63
Johnson, Mrs. Lattice, 70
[JOHNSON], Nancy, 62
JOHNSON, Rachel, 49-50
JOHNSON, Randol, 108
Johnson, Richd (Mj.), 249
Johnson, Robert, 261
[JOHNSON], Sophia, 49
JOHNSON, Sucky, 63
Jones, Mildred, 268
JONES, Nancy, 102
JONES, Sally, 260
JONES, Sam, 262
JONES, Susan Ann, 154
JORDAN, Thomas, 56
Jordan, Wm, 233
JUMPER, Richard, 106, 261

Keeling, Betsey, 252, 258
KEELING, Lavina, 216
KEELING, Lizzenia, 187

KEELING, Nancy, 185, 189
KEELING, Polly, 167
KEELING, Sally, 161
Keen, Charles, 260
Keen, John, 241, 260
Kennon, Charles, 79, 242
Kerrigan, Peter, 229
KIRKS, Susan, 107

Lacy, Bynum, 258
LANKSFORD, Landy, 241
Lansford, Isham, 249
LAURENCE, Berry, 4-5, 276
LAURENCE, Hannah, 5
[LAURENCE], Louisa, 5
LAURENCE, Mary Ann, 5
LAURENCE, Sally Ann, 5
Lawhorn, Cornelius, 250, 257
Lawhorn, Mourning, 251
Leftwich, Elizabeth, 268
Leftwich, Jesse, 2
Leftwich, Sallie, 268
Lester, James, 268
LEWIS, David, 104, 262
Lewis, Elijah, 253
LEWIS, Mildred, 118
LIGANS, Will, 264
Ligon, Ann, 229
Linn, Robert, 262
Linn, William, 248
Lipford, Anthony, 250
Localities
    Africa, x, xiii, xvi
    Albermarle Co., 204, 276
    Amelia Co., 3, 158, 229, 276
    Amherst Co., 269
    Bedford Co., 245
    Brunswick Co., 4, 227, 276
    Campbell Co., 112, 149, 195-7, 267, 269, 276
    Caswell Co., NC, 239, 241

Charlotte Co., 4, 15-6, 88, 112, 140, 203, 230-2, 276
Charlottesville, v
Chatham, vii
Chesterfield Co., 116, 276
Cumberland Co., 82, 91, 117, 228-9, 276
Danville, v, vii, 153, 194, 238, 261, 263
England, xii
Franklin Co.,18, 276
Greensville Co., 66, 225-7
Haiti, xiii
Halifax Co., 70, 79, 134, 146, 160, 163, 166, 195-6, 208-9, 217, 242, 276-7
Henrico Co., 116
Henry Co., 194, 277
Jamestown, ix
Lawrence Co OH, 270
Liberia, Africa, xiv
Loudoun Co., 2, 227, 277
Lunenburg Co., 78, 151, 158, 199, 277
Lynchburg, 150, 269, 274, 277
Mechlenburg Co, 118, 153, 156-7, 161-2, 165, 277
Michigan, xiv
Middlesex Co., 84, 92, 277
North Carolina, xiv
Nottoway Co., 230
Ohio, xiv
Orange Co., NC, 243
Patrick Co., 205, 277
Pennsylvania, xiv
Petersburg, 7
Pittsylvania Co.,most
Rockbridge Co., 118, 277
Southampton Co., 9, 17, 69, 84, 91, 277

Spottsylvania Co., 203, 278
St Domingue, xiii
Sussex Co., 7, 10, 81, 233-4, 278
Virginia, many
Washington D.C., xv
West Indies, x, xiii
Logan, Betsy, 261
Logan, Betty, 256
LOGAN, Bob, 255, 264
Love, Samuel, 251
Lovelace, Charles, 258
Lovell, Saml M., 2
Lovell, Samuel, 249, 252
LYNCH, Chany, 44
[LYNCH], Dorcas, 21
LYNCH, Peter, 24
LYNCH, Phil, 43
LYNCH, Rhoda, 21
LYNCH, Richard, 20-1

Mabry, Nathaniel, 226
MACKLIN, Rebecca, 118, 277
Maclin, Irwin, 226
MAHO, Affy, 264
MANN, James, 115-6
Marshall, John, 230, 232
MARSHALL,Martha, 112
Martin,Will P., 242
Mason, Edmund, 225
MASON, Fanny, 67, 281
MASON, George, 68, 164, 280
MASON, Harry, 67
MASON, Jefferson, 86
MASON, Jesse, 265
Mason, John, 66, 225-7
MASON, John, 225-7, 261
MASON, Louisa Jane, 145, 168, 280
MASON, Lucinda, 109, 164, 280
Mason, Mary, 225-6
MASON, Mary, 66-7, 89, 109, 129, 136, 173, 226, 281
MASON, Polly, 67, 281

MASON, Robert, 80, 109,
    163-4, 263, 280
MASON, Silvia, 66, 68
MASON, Stephen, 68, 141,
    145, 168, 280
MASON, Ted, 10
MASON, William, 67
MASON, Wm, 281
May, George, 89
[May], James, 89
Mayhew (Estate), 268
MAYHO, Martha, 208,
    277
MAYHU, Cuff, 256
MAYO, Cuffe, 265
MAYO, Roann, 145, 168,
    280
Mays, James, 265
Mays, Joseph, 259
McClanahan, Frances, 250
McClasney, Henry, 239
McCormick, John, 3
McHainey, Wm, 258
McKinney, [illegible], 232
McKinney, Charles, 16
McKinney, Jr., [illeg.], 232
[McKinney], William, 16
McKnight, Ellick, 263
McLaughlin, Charles, 265
McRobert, Thos B., 243
Meador, Joseph, 259
Meador, Samuel, 253, 263
Miller, John, 258
Milner, John, 228
MITCHELL, John, 185
MITCHELL, Wiley, 263
MITCHELL, William, 200
MORGAN, Dick, 140, 166,
    230-1, 276, 280
MORGAN, Lucy Ann,
    230-1
Morgan, Mary, 230
Morgan, Robert, 140, 166,
    230-1
MORGAN, William, 230-1
Morris (Estate), 236
Mottley, Wm, 255
MUNDAL, Betsy, 45
MUNDAL, Critty, 44-7
MUNDAL, Doctor, 47

MUNDAL, Eliza, 45
MUNDAL, Joseph, 44, 47
MUNDAL, Laurenzo, 46
MUNDAL, Peter, 44
MUNDAL, Thomas, 45
MUNDAL, William, 46
MUNDAL, Woodson, 46
Murvey, Alexr, 3
Mustain, Shadrach, 268

Neal, Thomas D., 261
NEGRO, Abraham, 242
NEGRO, Aggey, 229
NEGRO, Amanday, 241
NEGRO, Amey, 242
NEGRO, Amy, 235
NEGRO, Anthony, 225
NEGRO, Arthur, 225-7
NEGRO, Beck, 234
NEGRO, Ben, 230-1, 234-5
NEGRO, Betty, 229
NEGRO, Billy, 229, 242
NEGRO, Boling, 225-6
NEGRO, Brister, 242
NEGRO, Candice, 241
NEGRO, Charles, 226,
    229
NEGRO, Dafney, 232-3
NEGRO, Daniel, 227
NEGRO, Dianna, 236
NEGRO, Dilpha, 236
NEGRO, Edmund, 232-3
NEGRO, Edward, 238
NEGRO, Elitha, 235
NEGRO, Esther, 235
NEGRO, Fanny, 242
NEGRO, George, 229
NEGRO, Hanah, 242
NEGRO, Harry, 242
NEGRO, India, 242
NEGRO, Jacob, 233, 235,
    238
NEGRO, James, 225-6
NEGRO, Jane, 227, 229
NEGRO, Joe, 233, 235
NEGRO, John, 229, 242
NEGRO, Joseph, 227
NEGRO, Lewis, 233, 235,
    242

NEGRO, Lue (Lew), 2, 227, 277
NEGRO, Malinda, 18
NEGRO, Malinday, 241
NEGRO, Mary, 241
NEGRO, Matilda, 227, 235
NEGRO, Mildred, 242
NEGRO, Miriah, 227
NEGRO, Molley, 236
NEGRO, Molly, 1, 238
NEGRO, Moses, 229, 242
NEGRO, Muryear, 242
NEGRO, Nanny, 225
NEGRO, Patience, 235, 242
NEGRO, Patrick, 274
NEGRO, Peggy, 1, 238
NEGRO, Peter, 242
NEGRO, Phebe, 229
NEGRO, Phill, 229
NEGRO, Polley, 229
NEGRO, Rachel, 242
NEGRO, Ralph, 234
NEGRO, Robin, 242
NEGRO, Safronia, 241
NEGRO, Sally, 229, 236
NEGRO, Sam, 232-3
NEGRO, Sarah, 227
NEGRO, Suckey, 242
NEGRO, Tanday, 241
NEGRO, Thomas, 236
NEGRO, Tom, 242
NEGRO, Valentine, 242
Nelson, Andrew, 229
Newton, Thomas, 251
Newton, William, 249
Newton, Wm, 255, 260
Nichols, John, 248
Norman, William, 264
NORRIS, Wm, 173, 217, 280
Nowlin, Briant, 250

Oaks, Anthony, 253
OWEN, William, 7, 278

Pales?, Francis, 245
Parker, Geo, 257
Parker, George, 251

PARR, Patsy, 262
Parsons, Elizabeth, 255
Pass, Washington, 261
Patterson, Jarald, 256
PATTERSON, John, 263
Patton, James D., 238, 240
Payne, Frederick, 253
Payne, Wm, 88, 256, 259
Pearman, Dance, 71, 254
Pelham, P., 226
Pemberton, Sally, 257
Pennell, John, 261
Penwell, John, 252
PHILLIPS, Mary, 184
PHILLIPS, Nancy, 115-6
Pickral, Henry, 269
Pistole, Abram Sr., 248
Plunket, Wm, 266
POUNDS, Alexander, 119
POUNDS, Jacob, 169
POUNDS, Priscilla, 72
POUNDS, Sandy, 273
POWELL, William, 59, 269-70
Power, John, 265

Raine, Chs A., 231
Ramsey, Caleb, 250
RANDOLPH, Biddy, 32
RANDOLPH, Gilbert, 32
Rawlins, Thomas, 254
Razor, Elizabeth, 241
Razor, George, 241
REDMON, Richard, 70, 277
REDMOND, Betsy, 78
REDMOND, Dick, 253
REYNOLDS, America, 96
REYNOLDS, Ann Caroline, 97
REYNOLDS, Anthony, 96
REYNOLDS, Branton, 262
REYNOLDS, Burton, 113, 252, 259
REYNOLDS, Caleb, 191, 253
REYNOLDS, Cinda, 91
REYNOLDS, Coleman, 105, 142, 280

REYNOLDS, David, 105, 119, 262, 280
REYNOLDS, Doctor, 86, 105, 280
REYNOLDS, Elisha Sr., 95, 250, 280
REYNOLDS, Elisha Jr., 96
REYNOLDS, Eliza, 111, 191, 280
REYNOLDS, Esther, 69
REYNOLDS, Hall, 262
REYNOLDS, Hannah, 90, 97
REYNOLDS, Henry, 65, 101, 119, 280
REYNOLDS, Jane, 262
REYNOLDS, Jane Harriett, 100
REYNOLDS, Jenney, 83, 272
REYNOLDS, Joanna, 85
REYNOLDS, Joel, 85
REYNOLDS, John, 213
REYNOLDS,Jubia /Juba, 7, 145, 168, 187, 280
REYNOLDS, Julia Ann, 99
REYNOLDS, Kesah, 251
REYNOLDS, Keziah, 272
REYNOLDS, Kipsey, 259
REYNOLDS, Leanna (Leana), 145, 168, 281
REYNOLDS, Lewis, 68, 255
REYNOLDS, Louisa Jane, 280
REYNOLDS, Madison, 262
REYNOLDS,Maria, 189
REYNOLDS,Mariah, 95, 149
REYNOLDS, Martha, 83, 109, 113, 281
REYNOLDS, Mary,74, 95
REYNOLDS, Mary Ann, 82
REYNOLDS, Milly, 96
REYNOLDS, Milton, 108
Reynolds, Obadiah, 248
REYNOLDS, Panthea, 145, 168, 281
REYNOLDS, Patsey, 101
REYNOLDS, Polly, 113, 139, 259
REYNOLDS, Rebecca, 84
REYNOLDS, Richard, 86
REYNOLDS, Ricky, 262
REYNOLDS, Sally, 105
REYNOLDS, Sarah Winn, 100
REYNOLDS, Sophia, 70
REYNOLDS,William, 108
REYNOLDS, William Henry, 201
REYNOLDS, Winifred (Winny), 68, 107, 153, 281
Rhodes, George, 228
Rhodes, William, 228
[Richardson], Benjamin, 236-7
RICHARDSON, Betsy, 83
RICHARDSON, Elizabeth, 171
RICHARDSON, Godfrey, 262
[Richardson], Henry, 236-7
[Richardson], James, 236-7
Richardson, James (Sen.), 1, 236-7
RICHARDSON, Jane, 144
RICHARDSON, John, 82, 123, 203, 276, 281
Richardson, John P., 232
RICHARDSON, Liza, 87
[Richardson], Lucy, 236-7
Richardson, Mary, 236
[Richardson], Robert, 236-7
RICHARDSON, Sam, 262
[Richardson],William,236-7
Richardson, William (Sr.), 237
RICHARDSON, Wm, 136
Riddle, Burgess, 272
Riddle, William, 251
Riddle, Wm, 272
Riggins, James, 274

RIVERS, George, 1-2, 12, 94, 281
Rivers, Robert, 226
RIVERS, Wyat(t), 3, 6, 8, 12, 281
Roach, Elijah W., 230-1
ROBERTS, Betsy, 21
ROBERTS, Charles, 23
ROBERTS, Elvy, 22
[ROBERTS], Hannah, 21-4
ROBERTS, Henry, 84, 92, 277, 281
ROBERTS, John, 23
ROBERTS, Laura, 22
ROBERTS, Molly, 64
ROBERTS, Paulina, 22
ROBERTS, Penelope, 23
ROBERTS, Pleasant, 21-4
ROBERTSON, Delphia, 151, 236
ROBERTSON, Faith, 251
Robertson, James, 248
Robertson, John, 250
ROBERTSON, Stephen, 123
ROBERTSON, Thomas, 117, 124, 236, 281
ROBERTSON, William, 131
ROBINSON, Charles, 261
ROBINSON, Faithy, 81, 235, 278
Robinson, George Sen., 272
Robinson, Winslow, 16
Robinson, Winston, 231-2
ROE, Abram, 4
ROE, James, 200
ROE, Jane, 139
Roe, John, 256, 261
ROE, Nancy, 139
ROE, Rhoda, 80
ROE, Wm, 199
Rohr, Wm, 252
ROSS, Agnes Taylor, 202
[ROSS], Amy, 136
ROSS, Fanny, 129, 136, 281
Ross, John, 240

ROSS, Mary, 66-7, 89, 109, 129, 136, 173, 281
ROSS, Mary Ann, 202
ROSS, Polly, 108, 201, 281
ROSS, Wm, 173, 281
Roy, John B. & Co., 248
RUMLEY, Rhody, 69
RUMNEY, Jane, 187
Rutledge, Lucinda, 268

Sadler, Benja, 70
SCANTLISH, James, 265
SCOTT, Daniel, 15, 272
SCOTT, David, 204, 276
Scott, Robert, 236
Scruggs, Langhorne, viii, 152-223
SHACKLEFORD, Willie, 207
Shackleford, Wm, 256
SHAVERS, Benjamin, 255
Shelhouse, Jacob, 250
Shelton, Abram, 252
SHELTON, Buck, 61
SHELTON, Judith, 252
SHELTON, Rachel, 186
SHELTON, Randal, 81
SHELTON, Randolph, 273
Shelton, Samuel, 259
Shelton, Tunstall, 254
Shelton, Washington, 90, 253, 274
Shelton, Young, 252, 258
SHORT, Samuel, 82, 91, 117, 229, 276, 281
Sikes, Henry, 265
Sladen, Daniel, 264
SLONE, William, 103
SMITH, Berry, 143
Smith, Byrd, 263
Smith, Edward, 225
Smith, Elizabeth, 268
SMITH, Fanny, 87, 152
Smith, Frank, 269
SMITH, James, 79
Smith, Jesse, 248

Smith, John, 268
SMITH, Lethe, 87
SMITH, Maria, 85
Smith, Mildred, 268
Smith, Peter, 237
Smith, Ralph, 268
SMITH, Robert, 116, 276
Smith, Robert M., 250
Smith, Sexton W., 250
SMITH, Silva, 85
SMITH, Thomas, 116, 276
Smith, William, 1-3, 6, 8, 12
SOYARS, Bryant, 101
SOYARS, Charles, 255
SOYARS, John, 122, 198, 255, 281
Soyers, Major, 249
Sprogins, John D., 232
STAMP, David, 264
STAR, Caty, 98
STAR, Judy, 123, 259
STAR, Patrick, 90, 274
STAR, Polly, 131
STAR, Winny, 98
STARR, Isaac, 132
STEPHENS, Agga(y), 19 127, 181, 244, 281
STEPHENS, Caroline, 143
STEPHENS (STEVENS), Catherine, 18-9, 94, 125, 127-8, 184, 206, 243-4, 281
STEPHENS, Catherine Robertson Jane, 148, 172, 281
STEPHENS, Chaney, 125
STEPHENS, Charity, 127, 265
STEPHENS, Disse/Dice, 65
STEPHENS, Elizabeth, 157
STEPHENS, George, 166, 205
STEPHENS, Henry, 126-7, 143, 281
STEPHENS, Jordan Green, 154, 214, 281
STEPHENS, Lucretia, 19

STEPHENS, Madola Maria(h), 154, 206, 281
STEPHENS, Martha Jane, 126, 212, 281
STEPHENS, Mary Ann, 126, 212, 281
STEPHENS, Mary Ann, (#2), 213
STEPHENS, Nancy, 244
STEPHENS (STEVENS), Parthenia, 153, 185, 282
STEPHENS, Permelia, 213
STEPHENS, Phillis, 19, 127, 152, 244, 265, 281
STEPHENS (STEVENS), Reuben, 133, 180, 282
STEPHENS, Sally, 128
STEPHENS, Sally Elizabeth, 148
STEPHENS, Scott, 140
STEPHENS, Silva, 126, 244
STEPHENS, Washington, 137
STEPHENS, Willie, 220
STEPHENS, Willy, 263
STEPHENS, Wilmoth, 19, 94, 125, 281
STEPHENS, Wm, 128, 141, 244
STEPHENS, Wm R., 216
STEVENS, Abner, 180
STEVENS, Elizabeth, 188, 282
STEVENS, James, 181
STEVENS, Lucretia, 243
STEVENS, Martha, 148, 184, 282
STEVENS, Martha Ann, 182
STEVENS, Robert Wilson, 182
STEVENS, Thomas, 181
STEVENS, Thomas Taylor, 183
STEWART, James, 80
Stewart, Thomas, 238-40
STEWART, Thomas, 254

Still, Elizabeth, 253
Sutherlin, Jno M., 194
Swan, John, 232
Swan, Susannah, 232

Talley, Peyton, 253
TANTAROBOGUS, William, 34
Tate, Polly, 264
Taylor, Sally, 256
Terry, Friend S., 250
Terry, John, 18-9, 94, 125, 127-8, 243-4
Terry, John Jr., 254
Terry, Martha, 265
Terry, Nancy, 260
Terry, Obadiah, 255
Terry, Stephen, 243-4
Thomas, Charles, 256
Thomas, John H., 230-1
Thomas, Nathl P., 261
THOMPSON, Daniel, 211
[THOMPSON], Daniel Thomas, 134
[THOMPSON], Eliza Jane, 134
[THOMPSON], Mary Elizabeth, 134
Thompson, Mr., 229
THOMPSON, Polly, 134, 206
TOLBERT, Christopher, 33
TOLER, Robert, 251
Tompkins, John, 272
TOOMS, Jim, 260
Townes, George, 270
Travis, John, 261
Travish, Wm Sr., 253
Trayhorn, John, 248
Tucker, George, 244
TUCKER, Milly, 64
Tucker, Nelson, 248, 252
Tunstall, William, vii
Tunstall, William H., vii, 95-153
Tunstall, William Jr., vii, 1-95
Turbish, Thomas, 237

Turner, Stokely, 255

Vaden, Wilson, 248
Vaiden (Estate), 236
VAINWRIGHT, Louisa, 203
VALENTINE, Amy, 76, 111, 220, 260
VALENTINE, Angeline Green, 146, 277
VALENTINE, Charles Carrington, 146
VALENTINE, Eliza Ann, 75
VALENTINE, Elizabeth, 188, 282
VALENTINE, Freeman, 218
VALENTINE, James Edwin, 147
VALENTINE, John, 138
VALENTINE, Jordan M., 147
VALENTINE, Judy, 111
VALENTINE, Lucinda (Lucy), 77, 109, 164, 273, 280
VALENTINE, Manuel (Man), 77, 253
VALENTINE, Nancy, 78, 253, 264, 277
VALENTINE, Nancy Margaret, 147
VALENTINE, Peter, 110, 143, 186, 282
VALENTINE, Polly, 75, 111
VALENTINE, Polly #2, 76, 282
VALENTINE, Robert Washington, 150, 168
VALENTINE, Royal, 77, 110, 282
VALENTINE, Samuel, 76, 111, 273, 282
VALENTINE, Sarah, 212
VALENTINE, Slayton, 157, 188, 282
VALENTINE, Truman, 222

VALENTINE, Turner
   Abernathy, 146, 168,
   282
Vass, Greenberry, 239
Vaughn, George, 252
Vaughn, Spencer, 265

Walker, Benj, 253
Walker, Pendleton, 254
Walker, Warren, 229
Walker, William, 225
Walker, Wm, 229
Walkins, Thos, 242
WALLACE, Alexander,
   196, 223
WALLACE, Lucy, 195,
   221, 277
WALLACE, Mary, 196,
   222, 277
WALLACE, William, 195,
   221, 277
Waller?, William, 225
WALLS, Samuel, 118, 277
Walrond, John, 254
Walters, Alexander, 263
Walters, John, 79
Walton, James, 258
Walton, Jesee (Sen.), 4
Walton, Jesse, 249, 273
WARD, Aaron, 35
WARD, Amanda, 43
WARD, Anderson, 27
WARD, Bob, 27
[WARD], Charles, 35, 37
[WARD], Christian, 39
WARD, Daniel, 25
WARD, David, 41, 269-70
WARD, George, 42, 270
WARD, Handy, 35
WARD, Hannah, 37-9
WARD, Harrison, 38
WARD, Harry, 26, 28
WARD, Isbel, 50-1
WARD, Jack, 39
WARD, James, 40
WARD, John, 37
Ward, John Jr., 20-64,
   269-70
Ward, John Sen., 20-65,
   267, 270, 275

WARD, Joseph, 42, 270
WARD, Judith, 28
WARD, Lindy, 38
WARD, Lucy, 34-7
WARD, Lydia, 26-8
WARD, Lynch, 39
Ward, Major John, 267
WARD, Mary, 36
WARD, Molley (Molly),
   43, 269
WARD, Nancy, 42, 269-70
WARD, Patsy, 36
WARD, Peggy, 51
WARD, Peter, 51
WARD, Rachel, 36
Ward, Robert A., 268
WARD, Samuel, 34-7, 39-
   40, 269-70
WARD, Samuel Jr, 53
WARD, Sary, 27
WARD, Saul, 60
WARD, Simon, 38, 52
WARD, Viney, 51
Watson, John, 261
WATTS, Jarvis, 104
Webb, Edwin, 254
Webber, Benjamin, 82, 91,
   117, 228-9
Webber, Phillip, 228
Webber, Richd, 228
Webber, Seth, 228-9
Webber, Simeon, 228
Weir, Hugh, 252
West, Charles, 253
WEST, Clary, 48-9
West, George, 269
WEST, Jincey, 49
WEST, Nancy, 48
[WEST], Otey, 48
WEST, Rowland, 47
WEST, Walker, 49
Whiat, Sarah, 241
White, John L., 259
WHITTICER, John, 103
WILEY, Deborah, 3, 155,
   256, 264, 282
WILEY, Evans, 142
WILEY, George, 133
WILEY, Israel, 158
WILEY, Jackson, 158

WILEY, Martha Jane, 155
WILEY, Nathaniel, 155
WILEY, Richard, 141
WILEY, Sally Ann, 156
WILEY, Woody, 133
Williams (Cole), John, 255
WILLIAMS, Betsy, 158, 276
Williams, Charles, 248
Williams, Doc C., 249
WILLIAMS, Jackson, 33
Williams, James M., 263
Williams, John, 64, 249
WILLIAMS, Lindsay, 263
WILLIAMS, Lindsey Washington, 116
Williams, Wiley, 263
Williamson, Daniel W., 230
Williamson, J.M., 254
Wills, John, 264
Wilson, John, 258
Wilson, Nathaniel, 240
WILSON, Peter, 81
Wilson, Polley, 259
Wilson, Thomas, 260
WINBUSH, Charles, 254
WISDOM, George, 256
Witcher, Jr., William, 241
Witcher, Vincent, 241, 257
Witsher, Mary (Polly), 241
Witsher, Sr., John, 241
Witsher, Sr., William, 241-2
Woodson, Jack, 229
WOODSON, Stephen, 263
Woody, William, 2
WOOTEN, Milly, 8
Worsham, Daniel, 238-9
[WORSHAM], James, 6, 239, 241, 272
[WORSHAM], Jenny (Jinney), 6, 239, 241, 272
Worsham, John, 6, 238, 240, 272
Worsham, Joshua, 240
Worsham, Ludwell, 240
Worsham, Mary, 238, 240

[WORSHAM], Phillis, 6, 239, 241, 272
Worsham, Robert, 240
Worsham, Samuel, 258
Worsham, Thomas, 238, 240
Wright, Christr, 257
Wyche, Peter, 225
Wynne, Phoebe, 240

YOUNG, Anthony, 15, 114
YOUNG, Chesley, 15, 276
YOUNG, Martha, 114
[YOUNG], Mary, 15, 113
YOUNG, Parthenia, 114
YOUNG, Sally Ann, 115

www.ingramcontent.com/pod-product-compliance
Lightning Source LLC
Chambersburg PA
CBHW070722160426
43192CB00009B/1276